STATE OF THE
WORLD
1988

Other Norton/Worldwatch Books

Lester R. Brown et al.
State of the World 1984
State of the World 1985
State of the World 1986
State of the World 1987

STATE OF THE WORLD

1988

A Worldwatch Institute Report on Progress Toward a Sustainable Society

PROJECT DIRECTOR
Lester R. Brown

ASSOCIATE PROJECT DIRECTOR
Edward C. Wolf

EDITOR
Linda Starke

SENIOR RESEARCHERS
Lester R. Brown
William U. Chandler
Christopher Flavin
Jodi Jacobson
Sandra Postel
Cynthia Pollock Shea
Edward C. Wolf

RESEARCHERS
Alan Durning
Lori Heise

W·W·NORTON & COMPANY

NEW YORK   LONDON

First Edition

ISBN 0-393-02515-2

ISBN 0-393-30440-X {PBK}

W. W. Norton & Company, Inc., 500 Fifth Avenue, New York, N.Y. 10110
W. W. Norton & Company Ltd., 37 Great Russell Street, London WC1B 3NU

1 2 3 4 5 6 7 8 9 0

341407

Acknowledgments

Nineteen eighty-eight marks the fifth anniversary of *State of the World.* As we review the last five years, two heartening themes stand out: first, the extraordinary surge in public concern about global issues that has occurred since our first annual assessment appeared in early 1984 and, second, the dedication of a staff that has grown with the project and shows no signs of letting up.

We owe special thanks to William Dietel, President of the Rockefeller Brothers Fund (RBF). Although Bill has stepped down as the Fund's President this year to devote more time to breeding sheep in Virginia's Blue Ridge Mountains, we hope he always looks on the *State of the World* series with a certain paternal pride. RBF, the Winthrop Rockefeller Trust, and the George Gund Foundation provide the core of financial support that makes production of *State of the World* possible.

In addition, we are grateful for general support provided by the Geraldine R. Dodge, William and Flora Hewlett, W. Alton Jones, Andrew W. Mellon, Edward John Noble, and Jessie Smith Noyes Foundations, and for project support provided by the United Nations Fund for Population Activities.

We also mark five years of an uncommon partnership with W.W. Norton & Company, and in particular with Iva Ashner and Andy Marasia. Their tolerance of our idiosyncracies and their flawless coordination of the book's production is an author's dream.

Credit for the strengths of *State of the World* reaches far from our Washington offices to all who shared their expertise and insights as the work progressed. This year the reviewers of various chapters include Walter Truett Anderson, Mary Barberis, Deborah Bleviss, Sandra Brown, Ashton B. Carter, Kim Christiansen, Terry Clausen, Gary Davis, Dan Deely, Willem Floor, Howard Geller, Paul Gipe, Robert Goodland, Holly L. Gwin, Reginald Gwin, Michael Hanson, Carl Haub, Judy Hinds, Maureen Hinkle, Richard Houghton, Judith Jacobsen, Daniel Janzen, Thomas Jaras, Mike Jones, William R. Jordan III, Dunbar Lockwood, Donald Marier, Thomas Merrick, Evan Mills, Norman Myers, Bampot Napompeth, Jørgen Nørgaard, Kevin Porter, Peter Raven, Katherine Reichelderfer, Walter Rosen, Art Rosenfeld, Marc Ross, Roger Schecter, Graham Searle, Mark Shaffer, John Spears, Joseph Speidel, Steven Stanley, Christopher Uhl, and Edward O. Wilson. We are grateful to all who sharpened our thinking; the authors alone bear responsibility for any errors that remain.

Linda Starke, editor of all five editions of *State of the World,* has more than anyone given the book its identity and voice. Gently sardonic and unfailingly meticulous, Linda sets a standard few authors would achieve by themselves. In between editing *State of the World 1987* and *State of the World 1988,* Linda spent several months in Geneva editing *Our Common Future,* the landmark report of the

World Commission on Environment and Development. Bart Brown's index, a creative contribution in its own right, adds to *State of the World*'s versatility as a reference tool.

Angela Coyle (Chapter 7), Gretchen Daily (Chapter 7), Alan Durning (Chapters 2, 3, and 6), Hilary French (Chapters 4 and 8), Bruce Goldstein (Chapter 1), and Lori Heise (Chapters 1 and 7) provided the authors with imaginative and resourceful assistance. Alan and Lori, coauthors of Chapters 3 and 5 respectively, shouldered an uncommon load and made an uncommon contribution to the book.

The Worldwatch Institute support staff is the catalyst that makes production of *State of the World* possible. Linda Doherty, Reah Janise Kauffman, and Susan Norris handled the typing of countless chapter drafts and assembled the 4-pound, 5-ounce manuscript in record time. Cynthia Bainton handled orders and sales, with much-needed assistance from Chas Chiodo and, in the summer, Claver Bickman. Robin Bell orchestrated outreach for the book and edited Worldwatch Papers, and we all shared in the excitement when Robin and Dick Bell celebrated the birth of their daughter Cleo in early June. Brian Brown kept the office information flow functioning smoothly and made trips to Costa Rica and Europe to keep his spot near the top in international kayaking competition.

Worldwatch Vice President Blondeen Gravely, and the Institute's Board of Directors and Chairman Orville Freeman, can mark the first five years of *State of the World* with special satisfaction.

Lester R. Brown and Edward C. Wolf

Contents

Tables and Figures

LIST OF TABLES

LIST OF FIGURES

Foreword

In this foreword to our fifth annual assessment of the state of the world, we reflect on the events of the past five years. As always, we are concerned with the relationship between ourselves and the natural systems and resources on which we depend. Both that relationship and people's perception of it are changing.

Changes in atmospheric chemistry—air pollution, acid rain, ozone depletion, and the buildup of greenhouse gases—have attracted the attention of scientists and aroused concern among the general public. Ozone depletion due to the discharge of chlorofluorocarbons into the atmosphere seemed to stir little more than academic interest when we were launching this series. Today, it is a concern of national governments everywhere.

Evidence accumulating over the last five years indicates that the earth's temperature has begun an upward climb. Within governments, a vague awareness of the environmental consequences of climate change is giving way to a deepening concern. This is perhaps most pronounced in some low-lying countries, where rising sea level could be at best extraordinarily costly—at worst, catastrophic.

Public perceptions of the links between human activity and environmental degradation are also changing. Five years ago, famine in Africa was attributed exclusively to drought. Today, the spectre of famine that again threatens Africa is seen as the result of a complex mix of politics, economic pressures, and the deteriorating relationship between a population expanding at 17 million per year and the natural systems on which those people depend. Simple prescriptions are yielding to more challenging yet more realistic appraisals.

The last few years have witnessed an extraordinary burst of international concern over the future of the earth's tropical rain forests. People are starting to realize that if this irreplaceable resource is lost, much of the earth's diversity of plant and animal life would also disappear. They have come to share a sense of foreboding, a sense that the human prospect may be tied more closely to the future of these forests than is generally realized.

On a broader level, threats to human security are now seen much more in environmental and economic terms and less in political ones. In both the United States and the Soviet Union, there is a growing awareness that the arms race has sapped economic strength and eroded rather than reinforced political influence. The notion advanced in *State of the World 1986* that Japan was the only winner of the U.S.-Soviet arms race is now widely accepted.

Major leadership changes have occurred in some key countries. Nowhere has this been more dramatic than in the Soviet Union. Attention has focused on Mikhail Gorbachev's economic and political reforms, but his environmental vision seems equally far-reaching. Several years before he became General Secretary of the Communist Party, Gorbachev urged a much greater soil conservation effort to protect the Soviet Union's rapidly eroding soils. Scarcely a year after Gorbachev took office, the Soviet Union appears to have abandoned the long-standing dream of diverting southward the rivers that empty into the Arctic Ocean. Attention has turned to the more modest but sustainable path of irrigating more efficiently with existing water supplies. Gorbachev's avowed vision of restructuring Soviet society seems based on acceptance of environmental as well as economic realities.

China, home for over a fifth of humanity, is leading the way in redefining security. It has reduced the military share of its gross national product by half; greatly increased the share devoted to reforestation, family planning, and food production; and introduced extensive reforms designed to raise economic efficiency. As a result, food production per person has risen by half over the last decade and living standards have improved dramatically. China's reappraisal has already paid handsome economic dividends.

At the international level, the report of the U.N.-established World Commission on Environment and Development marks a milestone in recognition of the common challenges that face nations today. Led by Norwegian Prime Minister Gro Harlem Brundtland, Commissioners from 21 countries with differing cultures, economic systems, and political ideologies reached an unprecedented consensus on a global agenda for change—change among nations and between human institutions and the environment that sustains them.

The World Bank, faced with failed development policies in a number of countries, initiated a reorganization that includes elevating environmental concerns to a central position in the formulation and execution of development policy. The Bank's directors now acknowledge that economic development strategies that are not environmentally sustainable are doomed to failure. Indeed, the concept of sustainable development has gained widespread acceptance. Although the criteria for judging sustainability are still being developed, the need to incorporate environmental considerations into planning is now an article of faith among planners in some quarters.

One small indication of the rising public concern about these issues is the growing interest in the *State of the World*. As public awareness of the population arithmetic, energy policies, and environmental trends threatening to undermine the human prospect has become more widespread, sales of the annual report have climbed. Print runs have increased from 27,000 for *State of the World 1984* to 88,000 copies for *State of the World 1987*. Sales of this volume are expected to top 100,000.

Translation into other languages also continues to expand. In addition to English, *State of the World* now appears in Spanish, Arabic, Chinese, Japanese, German, Italian, Polish, and several less widely spoken languages. Discussions are under way on a Russian language edition. With a worldwide market estimated at nearly a quarter of a million copies, *State of the World* may be the most widely read work of public policy research in the world today.

The adoption of *State of the World* for course use in U.S. colleges and universities has grown dramatically too. *State of the World 1984* was ordered by 102 U.S. colleges and universities; *State of the World 1987* has been adopted for course use in over 400 such centers of learning. Advance orders for *State of the World 1988* indicate that this trend is continuing. Although not designed as a textbook, *State of the World* has become one of the most popular college texts in the United States.

Course adoptions account for nearly one fifth of U.S. sales of *State of the World*, but no single category of buyers dominates. Perhaps the largest single group consists of concerned citizens—people who are worried about toxic wastes, mounting population pressures, or the loss of biological diversity. Government officials, national and local, generate a steady stream of orders for the English edition from all over the world. Some foundations distribute *State of the World* to their trustees. At Cable News Network, it is required reading for some 200 senior producers and reporters.

The challenge to scientific and political leaders everywhere, and indeed to this institute, is to raise public awareness past the threshold needed to mount effective political responses to a new generation of problems. The past five years have been punctuated by the emergence of unexpected environmental threats, new evidence of environmental deterio-

ration, and, on occasion, dramatically successful responses to these threats. There can be little doubt, however, that the pace of environmental deterioration continues to accelerate.

We are left with the sobering realization that our generation is the first whose decisions will determine whether the earth will remain habitable. Unless ripples of public awareness build to a groundswell of support for far-reaching change, we may not be able to reverse the trends that are undermining our children's future.

Lester R. Brown
Project Director

Edward C. Wolf
Associate Director

Worldwatch Institute
1776 Massachusetts Ave., N.W.
Washington, D.C. 20036

December 1987

STATE OF THE
WORLD
1988

1

The Earth's Vital Signs

Lester R. Brown and Christopher Flavin

In preparing this annual assessment during each of the last five years, we have in effect given the earth a physical examination, checking its vital signs. The readings are not reassuring: The earth's forests are shrinking, its deserts expanding, and its soils eroding—all at record rates.

Each year thousands of plant and animal species disappear, many before they are named or catalogued. The ozone layer in the upper atmosphere that protects us from ultraviolet radiation is thinning. The very temperature of the earth appears to be rising, posing a threat of unknown dimensions to virtually all the life-support systems on which humanity depends.

Assessing these threats to the future can easily lead to apathy or despair, particularly given policymakers' preoccupation with the East-West political conflict and global economic issues. Yet we can do something about the planet's deteriorating physical condition. Some of the steps needed to restore its health, including investment in energy efficiency, reforestation, and population stabilization, are sketched out in the chapters that follow.

Time is short, since the deterioration of some life-support systems appears to be accelerating. As we worked on the first of these annual assessments in 1983, we debated whether to report that a West German forest survey had found some 8 percent of that nation's forests showing signs of damage, possibly from air pollution and acid rain. That discovery, though disturbing, seemed little cause for international alarm. Today, over half of West Germany's forests are damaged, and the link to air pollutants is all but conclusive. The most recent tally for Europe, excluding the Soviet Union, shows some 31 million hectares of damaged forests, an area the size of West Germany.[1]

Four years ago the so-called greenhouse effect expected to result from rising atmospheric concentrations of carbon dioxide (CO_2) was a widely accepted hypothesis, but an actual warming seemed remote. Since then new evidence indicates that the long-projected warming of the earth is already under way. And in the last few years, scientists have concluded that emissions of several other gases—including chlorofluorocarbons (CFCs), nitrous oxide, and methane—are contributing to the warming.[2]

Units of measurement are metric unless common usage dictates otherwise.

The depletion of the ozone layer due to CFC production was also seen as a remote threat just four years ago, one not expected to materialize until sometime well into the next century, if ever. Since then, puzzling new findings have lent urgency to this issue. A dramatic depletion of ozone occurs over Antarctica each September, scientists have discovered, and each year since 1979 it has grown worse. By 1987, what had become known as the ozone "hole" was twice the size of the continental United States. Though the hole involves a series of as yet poorly understood chemical reactions, it could portend an unexpectedly rapid ozone depletion globally and translate into lowered crop output and rising skin cancer and eye damage as more ultraviolet radiation reaches the earth.[3]

All human activities affect the earth's physical condition, but two are disproportionately important: energy use and population growth. Heavy dependence on fossil fuels has caused a buildup of carbon dioxide in the atmosphere that threatens to warm the earth. Pollutants from fossil fuel burning have also led to acidification and the death of lakes and forests. Advances in human health have led to unprecedented reproductive success and a growth of population that in many countries is overwhelming local life-support systems.

Although efforts to deal with these threats are lagging badly for the world as a whole, some important national steps have already been taken. With China's substantial reduction in its birth rate, nearly half the world's people now live in countries where fertility is either below replacement level or approaching it. Energy efficiency gains in the Western industrial countries and Japan have slowed the depletion of world oil reserves and the rise in carbon emissions that cause the greenhouse effect. A five-year U.S. soil conservation program could cut excessive soil erosion from the nation's croplands by four fifths when fully implemented. Other national commitments are badly needed in areas ranging from deficit reduction to forest planting.[4]

Many of the world's problems, including ozone depletion and climate protection, cannot be solved without international action. In these areas, any one country's efforts to change would be overwhelmed without global cooperation. This sense of international responsibility marked the September 1987 signing in Montreal of international accords to limit the production of chlorofluorocarbons to protect the earth's ozone layer. These accords, although modest in scope, were a signal achievement and could become a model for future agreements.[5]

Another example of renewed international cooperation was the unanimous agreement by the United Nations Security Council in September 1987 to call for a cease-fire in the Iran-Iraq war, based on a detailed peace proposal fashioned by the United States and the Soviet Union. Whether the effort succeeds or not, this willingness by the superpowers to give the Security Council the active peacekeeping role its creators intended augurs well for the increased effectiveness of this long-neglected instrument of international cooperation.[6]

These developments suggest a new era, one in which attention shifts away from East-West ideological conflicts and toward the reestablishment of an earth with stable, healthy vital signs. The world has come a long way from the mid-seventies, when environmental concerns were considered something that only the rich could afford to worry about. Today, they are concerns no one can afford to ignore.

THE EARTH'S ANNUAL PHYSICAL

Tree cover is one of the most visible indicators of the earth's health and, because trees are an integral part of basic life-support systems, one of the most vital. On sloping land, the loss of trees can accelerate rainfall runoff and increase soil erosion, diminishing land productivity and aggravating local flooding. Where tree cutting exceeds regrowth, deforestation releases carbon that contributes to the buildup of atmospheric carbon dioxide and a warming of the earth. (See Chapter 5.)

Despite the essential ecological and economic contribution of trees, data on changes in the earth's tree cover are not regularly gathered. The most recent assessment of tropical forests was published in 1982 by the U.N. Food and Agriculture Organization (FAO), and even this was based largely on extrapolations from incomplete data rather than comprehensive surveys. Yet, when India turned to satellite photography, scientists there discovered a far more rapid forest loss than had been previously estimated. Between 1972–75 and 1980–82, the country lost 9 million hectares of tree cover, roughly 1.3 million hectares per year. At this rate, India will lose most of its remaining 31 million hectares of forest by the end of the century.[7]

The best available estimates on forest cover in 76 tropical countries indicate that 11 million hectares of forests are being cleared each year. (See Table 1–1.) Land clearing for agriculture is the principal claimant, followed by commercial logging, firewood gathering, and, in Latin America, conversion to pasture for cattle ranching.[8]

In addition to the loss of forests in the Third World, woodlands in the northern tier of industrial countries are being degraded by air pollution and acid rain. By 1986 half the forests in the Netherlands, Switzerland, and West Germany showed signs of damage. As noted earlier, forests throughout Europe are now affected to some degree. As chemical stresses mount, this resource is not only losing productivity, but changes in soil chemistry on some types of soils make replanting impossible.[9]

One consequence of declining tree cover and expanding agriculture is accelerated soil erosion. Over long stretches of geological time, soil formation exceeded erosion, leading to the accumulation of a rich layer of topsoil, typically 6–10 inches deep, over much of the earth's surface. In recent times, deforestation, overgrazing, and the spread of agriculture onto erodible lands have reversed this long-term trend, leading to a gradual depletion of this life-sustaining layer.

A 1982 survey of soil erosion in the United States, based on at least a million readings, showed that farmers are annually losing more than 2 billion tons of topsoil in excess of new soil formation. Worldwide, an estimated 26 billion tons are being washed or blown off cropland each year. Despite topsoil's essential economic role, only a few countries regularly monitor these losses.[10]

As erosion continues, land gradually loses its inherent productivity, threatening the livelihood of those who depend on it. A study commissioned by the Society for Promotion of Wastelands Development in India found that 39 percent of that nation's land is now degraded. (See Table 1–2.) In a 1985 radio address to the nation, Prime Minister Rajiv Gandhi reflected the plight of many Third World countries: "Continuing deforestation has brought us face to face with a major ecological and economic crisis. The trend must be halted." Gandhi went on to commission a National Wastelands Development Board charged with turning 5 million hectares of degraded land

Table 1-1. Changes in the Earth's Physical Condition

Indicator	Reading
Forest Cover	Tropical forests shrinking by 11 million hectares per year; 31 million hectares in industrial countries damaged, apparently by air pollution or acid rain.
Topsoil on Cropland	An estimated 26 billion tons lost annually in excess of new soil formation.
Desert Area	Some 6 million hectares of new desert formed annually by land mismanagement.
Lakes	Thousands of lakes in the industrial north now biologically dead; thousands more dying.
Fresh Water	Underground water tables falling in parts of Africa, China, India, and North America as demand for water rises above aquifer recharge rates.
Species Diversity	Extinctions of plant and animal species together now estimated at several thousand per year; one fifth of all species may disappear over next 20 years.
Groundwater Quality	Some 50 pesticides contaminate groundwater in 32 American states; some 2,500 U.S. toxic waste sites need cleanup; extent of toxic contamination worldwide unknown.
Climate	Mean temperature projected to rise between 1.5 and 4.5 degrees Celsius between now and 2050.
Sea Level	Projected to rise between 1.4 meters (4.7 feet) and 2.2 meters (7.1 feet) by 2100.
Ozone Layer in Upper Atmosphere	Growing "hole" in the earth's ozone layer over Antarctica each spring suggests a gradual global depletion could be starting.

SOURCE: Compiled by Worldwatch Institute from various sources.

every year into fuelwood and fodder plantations.[11]

One of the most difficult things to measure is the contamination of soil and water. With hundreds of millions of tons of chemicals produced each year, and some 70,000 different ones now in everyday use, keeping tabs on their whereabouts and monitoring their effects on people and the environment are impos-

sible. Many manufactured chemicals are toxic to human beings, yet millions of people are inadvertently exposed through the use of pesticides in agriculture and the disposal of industrial chemical waste. (See Chapter 7.)[12]

The health of the earth's inhabitants cannot be separated from that of the planet itself. Contaminations by industrial chemicals in communities such as

Table 1-2. India: Extent of Land Degradation, Circa 1980

Land Type	Area
	(million hectares)
Degraded Nonforested Land	94
Saline and Alkaline Land	7
Wind-eroded Land	13
Water-eroded Land	74
Degraded Forested Land	35
Total Degraded Land	129
National Land Area	329

SOURCE: D.R. Bhumba and Arvind Khare, "Estimate of Wastelands in India," Society for Promotion of Wastelands Development, New Delhi, undated.

Love Canal in the United States and Seveso in Italy have led to permanent evacuations, creating a new class of environmental refugees. In Brazil, where concentrations of industrial wastes along the southern coast have reached life-threatening levels, the industrial city of Cubatão is locally referred to as the "Valley of Death."[13]

Eastern Europe suffers from some of the highest concentrations of industrial waste found anywhere. In Poland, where chemical contamination has rendered one fourth of the soil unfit for food production and left only 1 percent of the water safe for drinking, life expectancy for men between 40 and 60 years old has fallen back to the level of 1952. Thirteen million of the country's 40 million residents are expected to acquire at least one environmentally induced illness—respiratory disease, cancer, skin disease, or afflictions of the central nervous system. In Poland, "environmental devastation has become a feature of everyday life," observes French scientist Jean Pierre Lasota.[14]

Similar horror stories are reported for East Germany and Czechoslovakia, which like Poland have spent little on pollution control and are shifting from reliance on oil to low-grade brown coal. In Czechoslovakia's heavily industrialized northern Bohemia, the incidence of skin disease, stomach cancer, and mental illness is at least double that in the rest of the country. And life expectancy there is up to 10 years shorter than elsewhere in Czechoslovakia.[15]

At the global level, the ink on the Montreal accord to reduce chlorofluorocarbon use was scarcely dry when research teams reported another dramatic drop in the earth's protective shield of ozone during the Antarctic spring months of September and October. In congressional testimony on their findings, Peter E. Wilkniss, director of polar programs at the National Science Foundation, expressed concern over the health of the scientists stationed in Antarctica. Expedition leaders were particularly concerned about eye damage. Wilkniss said the foundation was discussing team findings with the governments of Argentina and Chile, two of the countries whose residents would be affected most immediately by increased ultraviolet radiation if the ozone "hole" over Antarctica continues to expand.[16]

The health of the earth's inhabitants cannot be separated from that of the planet itself.

Other witnesses before the congressional panel addressed the question of ozone depletion elsewhere. F. Sherwood Rowland, atmospheric chemist from the University of California, who initially postulated the link between chlorofluorocarbons and ozone during the early seventies, reported that monitoring stations in North Dakota, Maine, and Switzerland had recorded wintertime drops in the ozone layer of up to 9 percent. As a result of these findings, several prominent atmospheric scientists, such as Rowland and Michael McElroy of Harvard, are already urging much more stringent reductions of chlorofluorocarbons than the Montreal accord calls for.[17]

Another of the earth's vital indicators, the amount of carbon dioxide and other greenhouse gases in the atmosphere, can be measured rather precisely. Since 1958, careful recordings have shown that the atmospheric CO_2 concentration is rising each year. This increase, combined with that of trace gases, may be warming the earth more rapidly than had been anticipated.[18]

As forests disappear, as soils erode, and as lakes and soils acidify and become polluted, the number of plant and animal species diminishes. This reduction in the diversity of life on earth may well have unforeseen long-term consequences. (See Chapter 6.) One thing is certain: Without a dramatic reordering of priorities, our grandchildren will inherit a less healthy, biologically impoverished planet, one lacking in aesthetic pleasure as well as economic opportunities.

POPULATION GROWTH AND LAND DEGRADATION

When the rate of world population growth began to slow after reaching an all-time high of around 2 percent in 1970, many saw this as a healthy sign. Since then the rate of growth has gradually declined, falling below 1.7 percent per year during the eighties. Unfortunately, it has not declined fast enough.

The annual increment of births over deaths has climbed from 74 million in 1970 to 83 million in 1987. During the nineties, it is projected to surpass 90 million before moderating as the next century begins. (See Table 1–3.)

As the global population increment passed 80 million per year and as the addition in the industrial countries approached zero, more of the annual increment has been concentrated in the Third World, where human demands often overtax local life-support systems already. As a result of this record population addition, the relationship between people and life-support systems is also changing at an unprecedented speed, and in ways that are poorly understood.

When annual population additions are coupled with heightened stress on local life-support systems, shortages of food, fodder, and fuel can emerge almost overnight. Development economists

Table 1-3. World Population, 1950–85, With Projections to 2000

Year	Population	Annual Growth Rate	Annual Increase
	(million)	(percent)	(million)
1950	2,516	1.6	40
1960	3,019	1.8	54
1970	3,693	2.0	74
1980	4,450	1.8	80
1985	4,837	1.7	82
1990	5,246	1.6	84
1995	5,678	1.6	91
2000	6,122	1.5	92

SOURCE: Derived from United Nations, *World Population Prospects, Estimations, and Projections as Assessed in 1984* (New York: 1986).

typically focus on changes in the rate of population growth, but a more vital sign is the relationship between population size and the sustainable yield of local forests, grasslands, and croplands. If the demands of a local population surpass these sustainable yields, the systems will continue to deteriorate even if population growth stops.

Most often, the demands of rapidly expanding Third World populations first exceed the sustainable yield of local forests. An FAO study estimated that in 1980 some 1.2 billion people were meeting their firewood needs only by cutting wood faster than nature could replace it. The result of this obviously unsustainable trend is deforestation.[19]

Current demand for firewood is satisfied by sacrificing the longer term supply. As nearby forests dwindle and disappear, women and children travel further and work harder to meet minimal firewood needs. Eventually, as in some villages in the Andes and the African Sahel, firewood scarcity reduces people to one hot meal per day.[20]

Population growth and skewed land distribution drive farmers onto marginal land that is highly erodible.

In 1982, India's remaining forestland could sustain an annual harvest of only 39 million tons of wood, far below the estimated fuelwood demand of 133 million tons. The gap of 94 million tons was closed either by overcutting, thus compromising future forest production, or by burning cow dung and crop residues, which compromises future soil fertility. By the end of the century, the gap will be far larger if India's population continues to grow and if its forests continue to shrink.[21]

Although no comprehensive global survey has been done of pressure on grasslands, available data indicate that excessive demands closely parallel those for firewood. As human numbers multiply, so do the livestock populations that supply draft power, food, and, increasingly, fuel in the form of cow dung. The fodder needs of livestock populations in most Third World countries now exceed the sustainable yield of grasslands and other forage resources. A study on grassland conditions in nine countries of southern Africa reports that cattle numbers exceed carrying capacity in each by 50 to 100 percent.[22]

In India, demand for livestock fodder by the year 2000 is expected to reach 700 million tons, while the supply will total just 540 million tons. The National Land Use and Wastelands Development Council has observed that in states with the most serious land degradation, such as Rajasthan and Karnataka, fodder supplies satisfy only 50–80 percent of need, leaving large numbers of emaciated cattle. When drought occurs, hundreds of thousands of cattle die.[23]

A similar situation exists with cropland. Continuous population growth and skewed land distribution drive land-hungry farmers onto marginal land that is highly erodible, incapable of sustaining cultivation over the long term. In other situations, traditional rotations of cultivation and fallow that were ecologically stable have become unstable as the fallow cycle is shortened.

The end result of deforestation, overgrazing, and overplowing is often desertification, a process that begins as the finer particles of soil are washed or blown away, eventually leaving only the coarser particles of sand and gravel. Land misuse and mismanagement drives the process of desertification, but it is often brought into focus by drought. The West African drought of the early seventies marked not only the beginning of wholesale land degradation and desertification of the continent, but also the downturn in per capita food production and the onset of periodic famine.

In recent years, drought and desertification have often been confused. Drought is a meteorological phenomenon, a below-normal amount of rainfall. Desertification is a product of land misuse and of mismanagement that degrades the land. Low rainfall does not necessarily lead to desertification. By the same token, high rainfall does not insure against it.

Efforts to monitor trends in Africa over the last decade show that desertification is now an ongoing process in some 22 countries for which data are available. In the seven Sahelian zone countries of West Africa where the rate of deforestation is seven times the Third World average, desertification is rampant. The World Bank reports that "desertification in just one country, Mali, has drawn the Sahara 350 kilometers farther south in the last 20 years."[24]

One of the better measurements of the onset of Africa's environmental decline comes from an atmospheric monitoring station thousands of miles away. Robert Mann, with nearly three decades of experience in African agriculture, writes that "dust fallout across the Atlantic from the African continent, measured at Barbados in the West Indies, increased from 8 micrograms per cubic meter in 1967/68 to 15 micrograms in 1972 and 24 micrograms in the summer of 1973. Here is the Sahel catastrophe: a 3-fold increase in measured fallout at a distance of 4,700 kilometers west of the Sahel, and that dust is not sand but topsoil."[25]

Concern with a similar situation in India led to a May 1986 seminar in New Delhi entitled "Control of Drought, Desertification, and Famine," attended by nearly 100 professionals. The organizers were concerned that the "temporary phenomenon of meteorological drought in India is tending to be converted into the permanent and pervasive phenomenon of desertification, undermining biological productivity of soil over large parts of the country."[26]

Participants pointed out that studies in India reveal that "scarcity of water, food, and fodder are occurring systematically over a longer time span and even during years of normal rainfall." The official response to water shortages often is simply to drill deeper wells, but this treats the symptoms, not the cause. Echoing Prime Minister Gandhi's concerns about a major ecological and economic crisis, those at the seminar concluded that "the threat of desertification and its most acute expression through famine may become a real and massive one in the years to come."[27]

In developing countries, the bottom line in the relationship between rapid population growth and land degradation is its effect on per capita food production. As recently as 1970, Africa, China, and India each produced between 160 and 200 kilograms of grain per person a year. Since then Africa's grain output per person has fallen by one fifth. (See Figure 1–1.) Eroded soils and poorly nourished crops inevitably lead to poorly nourished people. Without a massive effort to restore the health of the land in Africa, recurring famine will give way to chronic famine.[28]

In contrast to Africa, food output per person in China has been rising, and doing so dramatically over the past decade. China has instituted fundamental agricultural reforms, steadily reduced the military share of its budget, and simultaneously shifted resources into family planning, reforestation, and soil conservation. Per capita grain production has risen by a third, with most of the increase coming over the last decade. With per capita grain production at close to 300 kilograms, animal protein intake

Kilograms

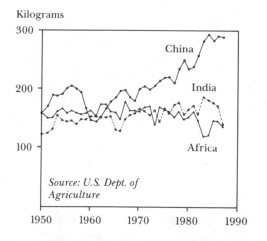

Figure 1-1. Annual Grain Production Per Person in Africa, China, and India, 1950-87

has risen, malnutrition has largely disappeared, and the threat of famine in China may now belong to history.[29]

India, a Green Revolution success story, has boosted output enough to eliminate grain imports, but not enough to raise per capita food consumption markedly. Faced with eroding soils and falling water tables, its per capita food production could turn downward. Although India's massive grain reserves should permit it to weather the poor monsoon of 1987, it will be in serious trouble if there is a second. If it fails to check population growth and reorder priorities by shifting resources into the battle to restore its soil and water base, it is more likely to follow Africa than China.

A DESTRUCTIVE ENERGY PATH

Energy trends are an important indicator of the world's economic and ecological health. One major affliction—overdependence on Middle Eastern oil—was greatly alleviated in the late seventies, as energy efficiency and structural adjustments in the world economy sharply reduced the need to import oil and led to the dramatic price collapse of 1986. But world energy trends are not yet on a sustainable course. World oil consumption is again on the rise, and trends in energy use now appear to be at the root of some of the world's most intractable environmental problems.

Between 1950 and 1979, fossil fuel use worldwide quadrupled. Oil, the most versatile and easily transported fossil fuel, led this phenomenal growth, overtaking coal as the world's leading energy source. This period was one of remarkable economic expansion, with a fourfold growth in the world economy roughly paralleling the growth in fossil fuel use. Food production more than doubled as farmers increased petroleum use at least fivefold. World auto production climbed from 8 million cars in 1950 to 31 million in 1979. Electrical generation multiplied eightfold.[30]

World energy growth slowed dramatically between 1979 and 1985, to an average rate of just 1.5 percent per year, well under the rate of economic growth. This slowdown was led by an actual decline in oil use during a period of unprecedentedly high prices, but it was partially offset by an increase in coal consumption, as many countries switched to more economical but dirtier solid fuels. World coal use is now growing at a rate of 2.5 percent per year, led by the world's three energy superpowers—China, the Soviet Union, and the United States.[31]

Trends since early 1986 point to a partial resurgence of growth in world oil consumption and continued growth in coal use. Although Persian Gulf oil ministers and Wyoming coal operators are undoubtedly cheered by this turn of events, it is in fact an ominous one. Any additional energy growth will add to the dangerous chemistry experiment we are conducting on the earth's atmosphere. Lakes, estuaries, forests, human health, and the climate itself are now at risk.[32]

In the aftermath of the 1986 accident at Chernobyl, many policymakers have turned to coal as an alternative to their moribund nuclear plans. The International Energy Agency, for example, projects a 32-percent increase in coal-fired generating capacity in its member countries by the year 2000. Meanwhile, China, which has the world's largest coal reserves and which recently passed the Soviet Union as the world's largest producer, has plans to almost double coal consumption by the year 2000. Due to its limited oil resources and a population of over 1 billion, growth in China's coal use could well rank as the largest added source of sulfur dioxide and carbon emissions.[33]

By the early eighties, activities such as generating electricity, driving automobiles, and producing steel were each year releasing into the atmosphere over 5 billion tons of carbon, close to 100 million tons of sulfur, and lesser quantities of nitrogen oxides. Carbon emissions closely track world energy trends, but because coal releases more carbon than does either oil or natural gas, the shift to coal accelerates the rise in carbon emissions. Having paused at 5.0–5.2 billion tons per year in the early eighties, carbon emissions are again moving up, adding over 100 million additional tons each year. (See Figure 1–2.) At a time when climatological evidence points to a need to reduce carbon emissions, they are actually rising.[34]

Sulfur, nitrogen, and hydrocarbons are some of the dangerous pollutants produced when fossil fuels are burned. Although no reliable global figures exist on these pollutants, emissions are on the rise, except in those countries that have enacted strict pollution controls. Even

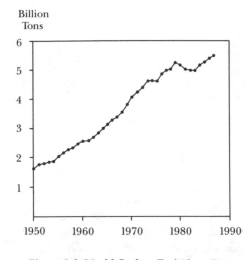

Billion Tons

Figure 1-2. World Carbon Emissions From Fossil Fuels, 1950-87

the United States has only managed a modest reduction of these emissions. The cities of most developing countries are meanwhile becoming increasingly choked with pollution, taking an unknown toll on buildings, human health, and nearby cropland.[35]

The first signs of long-range ecological damage from these pollutants appeared in Scandinavia during the sixties, with reports of dwindling fish populations in lakes. Soon thereafter it was found that in some bodies of water all aquatic life was disappearing. Sweden was the first country to report lifeless lakes, but other Scandinavian countries soon followed. (See Table 1–4.) Today, dying lakes can be found across northeastern North America, Western Europe, and Eastern Europe.[36]

Nearly two decades were to pass before evidence surfaced that the pollutants leading to acid precipitation and chemical changes in watersheds were also damaging and destroying trees. The first solid warning came in the summer of 1982 from West Germany. Since then, evidence of damage has come from

Table 1-4. Acid Rain Damage to Lakes in Selected Areas

Area	Damage
Canada	Some 140 acidified lakes devoid of fish in Ontario in 1980; thousands experiencing biological damage.
Denmark	Soils naturally high in buffering capacities; evidence of lake acidification in some poorly buffered areas.
Finland	Of 107 lakes surveyed near Helsinki in 1984, half either severely acidified or projected to lose all fish.
Norway	Extensive acid deposition damage found in south; of 5,000 lakes studied, fish population losses in 1,750 and serious acidification projected in 900 others.
Sweden	All bodies of fresh water now acidic; roughly 15,000 too acidified by airborne pollutants to support sensitive aquatic life; 6,500 lakes acidic for reasons other than air pollution; 1,800 lakes nearly lifeless.
United Kingdom	Declining fish catches in Scotland, Wales, and Lake District of England; losses by fish farmers in Scotland and Cumbria in England.
Eastern United States	Some 9,000 lakes threatened; 3,000 lakes east of Mississippi River acid-altered as of 1980; 212 lakes in Adirondack Mountains devoid of fish.
Western United States	No aquatic ecosystems completely acidified as yet; most sensitive lakes in Sierra-Cascade system, Rockies, Coast Range.

SOURCE: Compiled by Worldwatch Institute from John McCormick, *Acid Earth* (Washington, D.C.: International Institute for Environment and Development, 1985) and from various other sources.

every corner of Europe. Data from a 1986 survey released in September 1987 reported that 30.7 million hectares of forests in Europe were damaged. This increase over earlier surveys reflected in part the inclusion of Bulgaria and Spain for the first time. But it also reflected an increase in the damaged area in the reporting countries. (See Table 1-5.)[37]

As more data are gathered, certain patterns of damage are beginning to emerge. Coniferous species are slightly more vulnerable than broad-leaved ones, with damage to coniferous stands usually showing up two years or so before that of adjacent, broad-leaved species. And mountain forests are more vulnerable than lowland ones: Forest damage in the Alps is reportedly reaching catastrophic proportions. One observer reports that "the Erzgebirge mountains along the Czech-East German border are rapidly becoming a huge tree cemetery, the world's best showcase of the effects of acid rain."[38] As of mid-1986, some 19 countries in Europe reported damage to their woodlands, ranging from roughly 5–15 percent of the forested area in Yugoslavia and Swe-

Table 1-5. Estimated Forest Damage in Europe, 1986

Country	Total Forest Area	Estimated Area Damaged	Portion of Total Area Damaged
	(thousand hectares)		(percent)
Netherlands	311	171	55
West Germany	7,360	3,952	54
Switzerland	1,186	593	50
United Kingdom	2,018	979	49
Czechoslovakia	4,578	1,886	41
Austria	3,754	1,397	37
Bulgaria	3,300	1,112	34
France	14,440	4,043	28
Spain	11,789	3,313	28
Luxembourg	88	23	26
Norway[1]	6,660	1,712	26
Finland[1]	20,059	5,083	25
Hungary	1,637	409	25
Belgium	680	111	16
Poland	8,654	1,264	15
Sweden[1]	23,700	3,434	15
East Germany	2,955	350	12
Yugoslavia[1]	9,125	470	5
Italy	8,328	416	5
Other	12,282	n.a.	n.a.
Total	142,904	30,718	22

[1]Data on forest damage gathered for coniferous forests only; all entries in first column include both coniferous and broad-leaved forests.

SOURCE: Belgium and East Germany from *Allegemeine Forst Zeitschrift*, Munich, West Germany, No. 46, 1985 and No. 41, 1986; all others from International Co-operative Programme on Assessment and Monitoring of Air Pollution Effects on Forests, "Forest Damage and Air Pollution: Report on the 1986 Forest Damage Survey in Europe," Global Environment Monitoring System, United Nations Environment Programme, Nairobi, mimeographed, 1987.

den to 50 percent or more in the Netherlands, Switzerland, and West Germany. All told, more than one fifth of Europe's forests are now damaged.

For Canada, a heavy importer of air pollutants and acid rain from the United States, the threat has many dimensions. Canadian Minister of the Environment Tom McMillan says that acid rain "is destroying our lakes, killing our fish, undermining our tourism, retarding our forests, harming our agriculture, devastating our built heritage, and threaten-

ing our health." Fully half the fossil fuel emissions that affect Canada come from U.S. power plants and automobiles.[39]

Although few good studies have been done so far, it seems likely that developing countries are among the victims of environmental damage from the use of fossil fuels. Evidence is now beginning to emerge, for example, that China is suffering from its massive use of coal. A study in the southern Chinese province of Guizhou, which uses high-sulfur coal, found precipitation considerably more acidic than that measured in areas of eastern North America that suffer acid rain damage. In a forested section of Sichuan province, 90 percent of one local area that was once covered with pines is now bare, apparently as a result of air pollution.[40]

Since China generally lacks both tall smokestacks and pollution control equipment, city dwellers and surrounding farmland are likely to be suffering severe damage from coal-fired air pollution. And as the use of tall stacks grows, rural areas of China that are already under stress could be hit hard by acid rain. The Third World as a whole will have to exert enormous effort in order to avoid the apparent environmental fate of Eastern Europe.

It was not until the beginning of this century that Swedish scientist Svante Arrhenius pointed out that burning fossil fuels could transform the earth's climate by upsetting the natural balance between the amount of carbon dioxide released into the atmosphere from the decomposition of organic material and that being absorbed through photosynthesis. And it was not until 1958 that scientists began taking monthly air samples to measure systematically the changing atmospheric concentration of carbon dioxide.[41]

Fossil fuel use now adds some 5.4 billion tons of carbon to the atmosphere annually, and deforestation adds between 1 billion and 2.6 billion tons. Using the midpoint of this range and combining these two sources yields a total discharge of roughly 7 billion tons. Together, fossil fuel combustion and deforestation have raised atmospheric carbon dioxide levels from 280 parts per million in the immediate preindustrial period to 348 parts per million in 1987, a rise of 24 percent.[42]

According to climate models as well as preliminary scientific measurements, these changes in the composition of the atmosphere have already raised the earth's average temperature by about a half-degree Celsius. Even without any additional carbon dioxide buildup, scientists believe that these changes ensure another 1 degree increase during the next few decades—enough to make the earth far warmer than at any time since civilization began.[43]

More than one fifth of Europe's forests are now damaged.

If current energy trends continue, the temperature rise by the middle of the next century could cause unpredictable but potentially catastrophic shifts in the earth's climate.[44]

The principal contributors to rising CO_2 levels from fossil fuels are the United States and the Soviet Union, each accounting for roughly a fifth of worldwide carbon emissions from fossil fuel use. (See Table 1–6.) Next in order are China, Japan, and West Germany. In per capita terms, the United States and East Germany lead the list, each emitting nearly five tons of carbon per person a year, compared with a global average of just over one ton. Japan, the leading industrial exporter, uses less than half as much energy per capita as the United States and East Germany. Of course, when carbon emissions from all sources, not just fossil fuel use, are considered, several other countries join the list of top contributors: Brazil, Indonesia, Colombia, and Côte d'Ivoire.

In developing energy strategies, the benefits of reducing acidification and carbon dioxide emissions should be considered together. The combined societal cost of acidification and climate warming of the sort projected may justify a more fundamental redirection of the world's

Table 1-6. Carbon Emissions from Fossil Fuel Use in Selected Countries, 1985

Country	Carbon Emissions	Carbon Per Capita
	(million tons)	(tons)
United States	1,186	5.0
Soviet Union	958	3.5
China	508	0.5
Japan	244	2.0
West Germany	181	3.0
United Kingdom	148	2.6
Poland	120	3.2
France	107	1.9
Italy	101	1.8
East Germany	89	5.2

SOURCES: Carbon data from Ralph Rotty, University of New Orleans, private communication, November 4, 1987; population from Population Reference Bureau, *1985 World Population Data Sheet* (Washington, D.C.: 1985).

energy systems than any seriously considered to date. (See Chapter 2.)

THE CLIMATIC CONSEQUENCES

Recent years have brought three new developments regarding human-induced climate change. First, carbon dioxide turns out not to be the only gas contributing to the earth's warming. As noted, scientists now estimate that rising atmospheric levels of methane, nitrous oxides, ozone, and chlorofluorocarbons may together contribute as much to the "greenhouse effect" as does CO_2 alone. Second, recent U.S. and U.K. studies show that the projected warming appears to have begun. And third, many scientists now believe that important climate shifts could occur abruptly, causing

losses in agricultural production that could not be readily adjusted for.

The most advanced global climatic models indicate that a doubling of the preindustrial level of carbon dioxide, or the equivalent when the effect of trace gases is taken into account, would raise the global temperature by between 1.5 and 4.5 degrees Celsius (2.7 to 8.1 degrees Fahrenheit). If the world continues on a business-as-usual path, the most recent projections show this occurring between 2030 and 2050. This global warming could occur when children born this year are in their early forties.[45]

Scientists now agree that the increase in temperature would not be spread evenly, but would be far greater in the higher latitudes. Temperatures near the equator are projected to go up very little as the earth warms, while rises in the upper latitudes could easily be twice the average projected for the globe as a whole. Curiously, a global warming could cause shifts in ocean currents that might make some areas, including northern Europe, colder.[46]

The impact of this becomes more meaningful at the local level. In Washington, D.C., for example, a doubling of preindustrial levels of atmospheric CO_2 appears likely to cause far hotter summers. Instead of one day each year with temperatures of at least 100 degrees Fahrenheit (38 degrees Celsius), Washingtonians could expect 12 such days. And instead of 36 days when the thermometer reached 90 degrees Fahrenheit (32 degrees Celsius), the city would swelter through 87 such days.[47]

Some consequences of a global warming, such as agricultural changes, have already received considerable attention. But others, such as the effect on patterns of hydroelectric generation, water supply systems, and settlement patterns, are more difficult to anticipate. A warming is likely to change rainfall patterns, prevailing winds, and ocean currents, which might lead to more severe storms as the temperature differential between the equatorial region and higher latitudes widens. Higher temperatures in some areas would also bring an overall increase in evaporation and rainfall, but the changes would not be evenly distributed. Some regions would become wetter; others, drier.[48]

Two of the most serious effects of the projected warming would be the impact on agriculture and sea level. Today's agriculture evolved in response to a global climatic regime that has changed little since farming began, so any changes may well carry a price. Meteorological models, though they remain sketchy, suggest that two of the world's major food-producing regions—the North American heartland and the grain-growing regions of the Soviet Union—are likely to experience a decline in soil moisture during the summer growing season as a result of moisture loss from cropland due to increased evaporation.[49]

If so, land in the western U.S. Great Plains that now produces wheat would revert to grassland. The western U.S. Corn Belt would become semiarid, with wheat or other drought-tolerant grains that yield 40 bushels per acre replacing corn that yields 100 bushels. Land values would drop in anticipation of the shift to less productive crops. On the plus side, as temperatures increased the winter wheat belt would shift northward, with 40-bushel-per-acre winter wheat replacing 30-bushel-per-acre spring wheat. A longer growing season would also permit a northward expansion of spring wheat production in areas such as Canada's Alberta province, thus increasing its cultivated area.[50]

Perhaps the most costly price tag facing world agriculture would be the adjustment of irrigation and drainage systems. As the warming proceeds and rainfall patterns change, both these systems would become redundant in some

situations and inadequate in others. According to an analysis in *State of the World 1987*, adjusting irrigation systems alone might require an investment of some $200 billion.[51]

A somewhat more predictable result of a hotter earth is a rise in sea level. As the water in the ocean warms, it will expand accordingly. In addition, the warming will reduce the amount of water trapped in glaciers and ice caps. Projections by the U.S. Environmental Protection Agency (EPA) show a rise in sea level by 2100 of between 1.4 and 2.2 meters (4.7 to more than 7 feet). This would hurt most in Asia, where rice is produced on low-lying river deltas and floodplains. Without heavy investments in dikes and sea walls to protect the rice fields from saltwater intrusion, even a relatively modest one-meter rise (about three feet) would markedly reduce harvests.[52]

Temperature rises in the upper latitudes could easily be twice the average projected for the globe as a whole.

A rise in sea level would also affect many of the world's coastal cities. A one-meter rise would threaten New Orleans, Cairo, and Shanghai, to cite a few. At some point political leaders would have to decide whether to invest massive amounts of capital into dikes and other structures to prevent inundation, or to abandon low-lying cities. The Netherlands already spends nearly 6 percent of its gross national product to save itself from the sea—more than it spends for military defense from external aggression.[53]

In an address to the U.N. General Assembly in October 1987, Maumoon Abdul Gayoom, President of the Maldives, described the threat to his country posed by the rising sea level. With most of its 1,196 islands barely two meters above sea level, the Maldives' survival would be in jeopardy with even a one-meter rise in sea level in the event of a storm surge. In an impassioned speech, he referred to his country as "an endangered nation," pointing out that it lacks the economic and technological capability to deal with a rise in sea level of the sort projected. He observed that "we did not contribute to the impending catastrophe to our nation and alone we cannot save ourselves."[54]

A team at the Woods Hole Oceanographic Institute in Massachusetts has calculated the state's loss of land to the rising sea as the warming progresses. Using EPA projections of sea level rise by 2025, they calculate that Massachusetts would lose from 7,500 to 10,000 acres of land to the sea. Assuming the lower estimate and using their nominal land value of $1 million per acre for ocean front property, this would amount to a loss of at least $7.5 billion of particularly expensive property by then. Some of the 72 coastal communities included in the study would lose far more land than others: Nantucket could lose over 6 acres per year and Falmouth, 3.8 acres, while Winthrop would lose only 0.1 acres. Making reasonable cost estimates of the rising sea level component of climate change requires thousands of such detailed studies for coastal communities around the world.[55]

The earth's biological diversity is also bound to be affected by a global warming. The abruptness of the change would probably surpass the capacity of many species to adjust to higher temperatures or altered seasons. Both plant and animal species typically adapt to changing conditions by migrating as temperatures go up or down. Unfortunately, the extent of deforestation and other human disruptions of the environment make this natural migration much more difficult and, in some cases, impossible. As a result, many species would likely disappear.

The detailed effects of climate change cannot be predicted with great accuracy. We do know, however, that human civilization has evolved within a narrow range of climate conditions. Any major departure from those conditions will cause enormous hardship and require incalculable investments during the adjustment. Because some of the most important changes could occur abruptly, with little warning, most of the costs would simply have to be borne by an unwitting society. Ways to avoid massive climate change now deserve serious consideration. (See Chapters 2 and 10.)

FROM ONE EARTH TO ONE WORLD

Our Common Future, the landmark report of the World Commission on Environment and Development released in April 1987, opened its first chapter with the words: "The Earth is one but the world is not. We all depend on one biosphere for sustaining our lives. Yet each community, each country, strives for survival and prosperity with little regard for its impact on others." The mounting, interrelated threats that the world now faces can be overcome only with a new commitment to international cooperation. As the Commission put it, we need to move from one earth to one world. Rich and poor alike have a great deal to gain from cooperation—and everything to lose if we continue down separate, destructive paths.[56]

The past year was marked by a series of important initiatives to address shared problems cooperatively. These range from largely political developments like the Central America Peace Plan to environmental ones, such as the Montreal accord on ozone protection. In addition, existing international organizations are being reinvigorated and redirected to focus on emerging problems. Although the world remains split by deep economic, cultural, and ideological divisions, these sometimes can be bridged when circumstances call for it.

The deepest split of all—between East and West—is being reduced by a new emphasis on pragmatism over ideology. The Congress and the Politburo now seem to agree that the perilous economic condition of the superpowers can only be reversed if tensions are eased and defense budgets cut.

The Soviets have embarked on a fundamentally new course of openness and economic reform, in apparent recognition that previous policies had failed. In the past year, Soviet authorities have invited foreign technical experts to visit highly sensitive defense installations, and have allowed domestic environmental groups to criticize government policies publicly. Top Soviet officials traveling abroad now openly discuss the country's serious environmental problems and the need to address them. The emergence of the Soviet Union as a full participant in studying and resolving global problems might well help spark action worldwide.

The 1987 agreement in principle between the United States and the Soviet Union to limit medium- and short-range missiles is an encouraging sign. It will not in itself lead to a meaningful reduction in military expenditures, but if the current dialogue between the superpowers leads to a mutual reduction of conventional military forces in Europe and to a strategic arms agreement, the impact would be substantial. The leadership time and financial resources saved could be an effective down payment in the effort to reverse the deterioration in the earth's health.

The Montreal protocol to restrict the use of chlorofluorocarbons is a broader example of international cooperation in that 24 nations were involved. The agreement calls for a 50-percent cut in ozone-damaging CFC production by 1999. The largest reductions must come in industrial countries, which contribute most heavily to the problem, while developing countries can use additional chlorofluorocarbons but are committed to never becoming major users. The accord—a major achievement for the United Nations Environment Programme, which crafted it and shepherded it through many months of international negotiations—is notable for drawing together countries with very different economic systems, environmental policies, and political philosophies.[57]

The emergence of the Soviet Union as a full participant in studying and resolving global problems might well help spark action worldwide.

By publicly recognizing the threat posed by ozone depletion, the Montreal agreement stimulates decision makers in both the public and the private sector to take further steps. Belgium and the Nordic countries have already banned CFC production altogether. In the United States, Vermont has banned the use in state institutions of all polystyrene cups and plates containing chlorofluorocarbons. And McDonald's, the worldwide fast-food chain, announced in August 1987 that it will phase out the use of food containers manufactured with CFCs.[58]

The accord on chlorofluorocarbons is in essence a double victory. In addition to helping preserve the ozone layer, the reduction in emissions of CFCs—one of the four trace gases contributing to the greenhouse effect—will help reduce the global warming. The Montreal protocol is also an important psychological victory. Coming at a time when all the earth's vital signs show a continuing deterioration, it provides an important boost to public confidence and morale. It indicates that the international community is capable of cooperating when faced with a common threat.

Rising concern over the projected warming makes it the logical candidate for the next round of international environmental deliberations. Two international scientific meetings have been held on global warming, but it remains an issue around which it has been difficult to mobilize national action, let alone actual investment in climate protection. Although the prospective warming of the planet and the forces driving it are now broadly understood, the precise regional climatic and human effects are not. And it is difficult to prepare for an unknown threat, particularly one that will affect various countries differently.

Climate change is a Tragedy of the Commons writ large. Although industrial countries are responsible for a disproportionate share of the problem, carbon emissions are increasing worldwide, most rapidly in Eastern Europe and the Soviet Union. Unless all act together, there is little reason to act separately. Because climate change is driven by fossil fuel combustion and is not amenable to quick technical fixes, slowing its progress will inevitably require new initiatives—ones that will be infinitely more demanding than the one signed in Montreal.

Several chapters of this report attempt to sketch the broad dimensions of a program of increased energy efficiency, renewable energy development, and reforestation that could protect the global climate. (See Chapters 3, 4, and

5.) It is not too late to act, but the scale of the needed action will increase each year that we delay. The worldwide tide of deforestation can be stopped only if remaining forests are protected, tree planting is accelerated, and the devastating poverty that drives forest clearing in so many countries is relieved. Increased energy efficiency can actually reduce energy use in the rich countries, and hold it in check in poorer ones.

Large economic outlays are justified by the unprecedented costs of unchecked climate change, but they can also be justified on more parochial grounds. In many cases the funds will be raised privately in order to boost corporate profits or by local governments wishing to reduce air pollution. However, the critical goal of climate protection should be used as incentive to step up all these investments. A broad international agreement that the climate must be protected would encourage increased commitments to energy efficiency and reforestation—with one eye on national self-interest and the other on the common global interest.

Climate change is a Tragedy of the Commons writ large.

The difficulty in mobilizing joint action to address the global problems we face cannot be denied. Third World debt, trade disputes, and growing military arsenals are all deeply divisive forces. The worldwide improvement of living conditions that characterized the third quarter of this century can no longer be taken for granted. Africa has demonstrated that. The deterioration in living conditions there is not irreversible, but the steps needed to reverse the decline have not yet been taken. And now living standards are falling in Latin

America, undermined by some of the same pressures that have forced Africa to the wall. As drought accelerates the desertification of the Indian subcontinent, the nineties may witness a downturn in this region as well.[59]

Not since the depression decade of the thirties and the war decade of the forties have so many dark clouds gathered on the horizon. Perhaps this new generation of challenges will spawn its own set of new attitudes and new cooperative initiatives. Indeed, the World Bank—in recognition of the failure of development strategies that have not taken basic ecological principles into account, and in response to pressure from private environmental groups and several governments—has adopted a new attitude. Environmental protection has become a priority. In a speech in May 1987, new Bank President Barber Conable said, "We must reshape not just the Bank's outlook and activities but also the customs and ingrained attitudes of hundreds of millions of individuals and of their leaders."[60]

A strengthened environment department with perhaps 50 professionals has been promised, with a charge to identify environmentally damaging projects and ways to improve them. This is an important step, but most Bank loans are still based on conventional economic criteria. The institution has not yet made the broader commitment to an ecologically sustainable development strategy that would redirect its entire lending program, and it is not yet clear whether it will be able to carry out this broader mission.

In October 1987, Prime Minister Gro Harlem Brundtland of Norway presented the report of the World Commission on Environment and Development to the U.N. General Assembly. It calls for redirection of international institutions and a new focus on sustainable development. As Prime Minister Brundtland stated in her Chairman's foreword to the report, "If we do not succeed in putting our message of urgency through to today's parents and decision makers, we risk undermining our children's fundamental right to a healthy, life-enhancing environment. . . . We call for a common endeavour and for new norms of behaviour at all levels and in the interests of all."[61]

It remains to be seen how sovereign nations respond to the recommendations of the World Commission report. But its presentation to and discussion in the General Assembly marks a major step forward. It has forged a strong link between the inseparable goals of reducing poverty and protecting the world's life-support systems.

2

Creating a Sustainable Energy Future

Christopher Flavin

The importance of the world's energy path can scarcely be overstated: It is central to many of our most critical problems. Our economies are powered by fuels that are not only nonrenewable, but that damage lakes, forests, and human health. In addition, our energy systems are irrevocably altering the climate by adding 5.4 billion tons of carbon to the atmosphere each year, more than a ton for each person on the planet. Simply put, an environmentally sound energy strategy is a prerequisite to a sustainable society. In few other areas is change so essential if we wish to create a healthy and prosperous world.[1]

Increasingly, it seems neither oil, nor coal, nor nuclear power can be counted on to meet future energy needs. A decade ago, the mandate was relatively simple: reduce oil dependence. That goal has been partly achieved, though not by the grandiose schemes to replace oil that were trumpeted by politicians at that time. Rather, greater energy efficiency has been the key to success. Meanwhile, programs to produce millions of barrels of synthetic fuels from coal have never made it off the drawing board. Nuclear power now supplies just 5 percent of world energy, and plans for expansion are being scaled back in the face of cost overruns and safety concerns raised by the 1986 accident at Chernobyl.[2]

The question that comes up among policymakers again and again is: If not coal, and if not nuclear, then what? It is the central energy question today, and it *does* have an answer. The key to resolving the coal-nuclear conundrum is simple but potentially revolutionary: greatly improved energy efficiency in the short run, complemented by renewable energy in the long run.

Energy efficiency has a demonstrated economic capability to substitute for 25 percent of projected energy supply by the year 2000—at less than the cost of new supplies. (See Chapter 3.) Indeed, improved energy efficiency should be a centerpiece of all government energy policies during the next two decades. It can be used to begin immediately limiting the economic and environmental damage caused by today's energy systems—and to buy time for the development of other sources.

Renewable energy technologies are for the most part not as economical as improved efficiency, but their costs are falling and reliability is improving. During the nineties and beyond, renewables could make a substantial contribution, fitting well with the much more efficient energy systems then in place. (See Chapter 4.) With a revived commitment to research and development, by the end of the century we could have available a host of new renewable-energy-based technologies, most of them small and decentralized.

Developing a viable energy system while limiting fossil fuel use is feasible, but there is no guarantee that it will take place. Energy policy is often a morass of contradictory incentives that are not easily reformed. Many governments, for example, subsidize coal mining while paying large sums to clean up the air pollution from coal burning. Yet change is possible. The deregulation of oil and natural gas prices in the United States led to substantial efficiency gains. Government-sponsored home weatherization programs in Canada and Sweden helped reduce energy losses. Programs to spur the development of technologies, such as solar photovoltaics and efficient light bulbs, have met with success.

The question that comes up among policymakers again and again is: If not coal, and if not nuclear, then what?

Many of these lessons were learned the hard way, but as a result, it is now possible to put together the outlines of an energy policy that makes sense. Governments must create the conditions needed for continued innovation and the commercialization of new energy technologies. They must ensure that energy markets work far more effectively, and that the broad environmental implications of our energy choices be explicitly taken into account. But millions of private companies and individual consumers have the responsibility of actually carrying out the needed changes. Given the dangers of continuing on the current path, the cost of inaction is likely to be far greater.

PROTECTING AIR QUALITY AND CLIMATE

The annual report of the International Energy Agency (IEA) published in 1987 is the first by that organization to include a reference to the greenhouse effect. But the sometimes alarmist IEA is sanguine about the global climate, concluding that the "situation does not justify hasty measures aimed at rapid reductions in fossil fuel use but . . . a well co-ordinated international effort aimed at gathering further information is certainly indicated."[3]

The IEA's indifference to the possibility of severe climate change reflects the attitude taken by top energy officials in most countries—that this is still a scientific issue of little practical relevance. Governments throughout the world have not only been slow to respond to new environmental threats, they are actively pursuing energy policies that aggravate them. Ignoring the greenhouse problem reflects a deeper failing of energy policy: fixation on the short-run concerns of energy prices and supply at the expense of the planet's future economy and ecology.

Fossil fuels are the main source of the

air pollution now choking rural areas and cities. Even in the United States, which has relatively stringent air pollution standards, sulfur dioxide and carbon monoxide emissions are down less than 20 percent since 1975. Nitrogen oxide emissions are actually up 5 percent. Many American cities still do not comply with air quality standards laid down more than a decade ago. In the U.S. Congress, acid rain bills have languished for several years, due in large part to opposition from those representing coal-producing states.[4]

In most other countries, air pollution continues to increase, particularly in the coal-rich regions of Eastern Europe and China. As documented in Chapter 1, the incidence of respiratory and cardiac disease is growing rapidly in these areas, as is damage to lakes and forests. Despite strong evidence that air pollution is killing the forests of central Europe, the European Community has been able to agree only on relatively weak standards for emissions reduction, and most East European governments have yet to act at all.

Energy efficiency can be a new weapon in the air pollution wars, complementing flue-gas scrubbers and catalytic converters. Czechoslovakia, East Germany, Poland, and others could limit the damage now occurring to their forests by adopting a program to improve industrial energy efficiency. Rome could attack the cause of much of the city's respiratory disease and slow damage to its ancient ruins by doubling the fuel efficiency of its cars. A 1987 study by the American Council for an Energy-Efficient Economy concluded that increased efficiency could help widen the scope and improve the cost-effectiveness of proposed acid rain control programs.[5]

The most intractable atmospheric problem is global warming caused by the buildup of "greenhouse" gases, the most important of which is the carbon

dioxide being formed as some 6–8 billion tons of carbon are added to the atmosphere annually by deforestation and fossil fuel combustion. (See Chapter 1.) Slowing these trends will require increasing energy efficiency, stemming deforestation, and developing technologies based on renewable energy sources. (For further discussion of this combined strategy, see Chapter 10.)

Energy efficiency can be a new weapon in the air pollution wars.

Tree planting on a scale that will satisfy future demands for fuelwood, lumber, and paper and that will stabilize soils and the hydrological regime would also help restore balance to the carbon cycle by transferring carbon from the atmosphere to terrestrial systems. Planting fast-growing trees on 110 million hectares of land by the year 2000 to provide fuelwood and ecological stability (as suggested in Chapter 5) could reduce the carbon emissions of the world's forests by 41 percent, helping slow the global warming.

Checking carbon emissions to ameliorate the warming will require both a considerable increase in energy efficiency and a change in the mix of energy sources. In the next two decades, efficiency will have to play the largest role, since enormous investments can already be justified by conventional economic criteria alone. Later, as the technologies mature, the transition to renewable energy must begin in earnest.

Most official energy projections assume that worldwide energy efficiency will increase by between 0.5 and 1.0 percent per year. But carbon dioxide buildup is ongoing and cumulative. Even a 1-percent rate of efficiency improvement would allow an increase in atmospheric carbon dioxide from 348 parts per million in 1987 to about 600 parts per million in 2075, causing unprecedented changes in climate.[6]

An alternative energy scenario based on the global energy model of the Institute for Energy Analysis in the United States found that a successful effort to improve worldwide efficiency by 2 percent annually would keep carbon dioxide concentrations to 463 parts per million in 2075. The world's climate would still be at least 1 degree Celsius warmer than today, but the most catastrophic climatic effects would probably be avoided. Irving Mintzer of the World Resources Institute in Washington, D.C., using another model, calculates that a 1.5-percent annual rate of improvement—together with deliberate policies to limit coal use, to restrict the production of other greenhouse gases, and to halt deforestation—would reduce the warming projected by 2075 by half.[7]

Renewable energy and nuclear power also contribute to carbon reduction by substituting for fossil fuels. For example, fossil-fuel-fired power plants alone now produce one quarter of the world's fossil-fuel-related carbon emissions. Hydropower effectively displaces 578 million tons of carbon emissions from coal-fired power plants each year, equivalent to over 10 percent of the 1987 total. Nuclear power displaces somewhat less carbon—about 414 million tons annually.[8]

In recent years, nuclear power has grown rapidly, making a significant contribution to climate protection, but its growth will slow in the next few years as nuclear plant completions dwindle. While nuclear power advocates at the International Atomic Energy Agency and elsewhere have argued that this energy source can help protect the climate, its technical, economic, and political problems now appear severe enough to rule out substantial expansion.[9]

The use of renewable energy sources, on the other hand, could grow rapidly for many years. As indicated in Chapter 4, a large number of hydropower projects are in the pipeline, and within the next decade, major increases in geothermal, wind, and solar electricity are likely. Nonetheless, some important countries, including China, India, and the Soviet Union, are still planning on large increases in coal-fired generating capacity. Greater reliance on renewable energy is essential in the long term if a global greenhouse is to be averted.

Most of the progress so far in slowing the rate of carbon dioxide buildup was stimulated by market forces. However, energy markets will have to be greatly improved in order to deal with the problem. Indeed, any significant delay in improving energy efficiency will make it far more difficult to avoid a damaging increase in the earth's temperature. Avoiding the costs and disruption associated with the warming may well justify expenditures in energy efficiency several times greater than those currently being made.

One question for policymakers is where to find tens of billions of dollars for climate protection at a time when public treasuries are being called on to meet a host of pressing needs, from debt repayment to education. Fortunately, most of the funds for energy efficiency and renewables could be diverted from the billions of dollars spent annually on conventional energy supply projects. The new path would actually be less expensive than the old one.

The investments in climate protection can be made by governments interested in economic competitiveness, by grassroots organizations wishing to create sustainable fuelwood supplies, by state governments concerned about air pollution, and by corporations worried about the bottom line. In most cases the funds can be raised privately and justified economically, but the end result would be an important step toward climate protection. New policy initiatives can play an important role in encouraging governments and individuals at all levels to increase commitments to energy efficiency, renewable energy, and reforestation.

ENERGY PRICES AND TAXES

Energy prices are the key to a rational energy system. Prices determine the overall economic efficiency of the energy system and the value that is placed on climate protection and other environmental considerations. Unfortunately, energy prices in most countries reflect neither the true replacement cost of nonrenewable resources nor the environmental damage that their use can cause.

Price provides the incentive to develop new energy sources and determines the efficiency with which energy is used. In centrally planned economies, low or nonexistent prices have encouraged wasteful practices and quite low levels of energy efficiency. An effective energy pricing system is a necessary but not a sufficient condition of a well-designed energy policy.

The most important energy price is that of oil. Indeed, world oil prices have become one of the most closely watched economic indicators. The impact of major price shifts is felt by everyone from Brazilian charcoal vendors to Tokyo stock traders. Prior to 1973, regional crude oil prices varied substantially, but today a shift in the price of Saudi Light is quickly matched in the price of West Texas Intermediate. Obviously, the prices of gasoline and diesel fuel are influenced by that of crude oil. But other energy sources are also affected: When the price of oil fell in 1986,

average U.S. wholesale natural gas prices declined almost 40 percent in 15 months; coal prices fell 8 percent.[10]

One of the most difficult challenges to energy policymakers today is the instability and unpredictability of the price of oil. After increasing more than eightfold during a seven-year period in the seventies, real oil prices fell 75 percent between 1981 and 1986, hitting a low of about $12 per barrel before rebounding to $18 in 1987. (See Figure 2–1.) These shifts directly affect the viability of billions of dollars in investments and help shape the world economy.[11]

Many energy economists are asking what the true price of oil is. The concept of marginal cost pricing is used to indicate the price that reflects the cost of the next unit to be produced of a particular good. Ideally, this should encourage the development of alternatives while a resource such as oil is gradually depleted. Organizations such as the IEA and the World Bank have been laudably active in promoting marginal cost pricing in recent years. But in heavily manipulated and complex energy markets, marginal

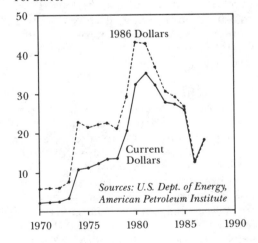

Figure 2-1. World Price of Oil, 1970-87

cost pricing becomes almost a black art.[12]

The marginal cost of oil production in the Middle East, where there is substantial unused production capacity, is reportedly still under $2 per barrel. However, a significant share of the world's oil is being extracted in places like the Alaska North Slope and the North Sea at costs of between $10 and $20 per barrel. A truly competitive market, free of cartels, could cause prices to fall considerably, but would wreak havoc on the petroleum industry of the United States and some other countries.[13]

Since the early eighties the world oil market has been dominated by excess production capacity, caused in large measure by conservation. This is likely to last for some years, given the large excess production capacity in the Middle East. Among the imponderables are the rate at which world consumption will increase, the rate of production declines outside the Organization of Petroleum-Exporting Countries, and the political situation in the Middle East. Although pressures on oil prices during the next few years are likely to be mainly on the downward side, sudden and catastrophic increases are possible, and even likely later.[14]

For oil-importing countries, the fact that the true marginal cost of oil is below even today's depressed prices is a concern. Market forces are now pointing to much higher levels of dependence on Middle Eastern oil—a region with 22 percent of the world's 1986 production, but 57 percent of the world's proven reserves. Low oil prices will make it more difficult for governments to maintain momentum in energy efficiency and renewable energy programs.[15]

Relying on imported oil entails a national security cost that is not included in market prices. In recognition of this, industrial countries have wisely spent billions of dollars building up "strategic petroleum reserves." The United States has filled salt caverns in Louisiana with stockpiled oil, while Japan has a fully loaded tanker fleet in Tokyo Bay. Perhaps less wisely, $47 billion was spent by the United States alone to "protect" the Persian Gulf in 1987. This comes to $26 per barrel of oil shipped through the Strait of Hormuz.[16]

One means of ensuring that cheap imported oil does not undermine alternative energy investments is to tax oil or oil products. The impact of varying tax systems is seen in the differing prices paid for gasoline and diesel fuel around the world. (See Table 2–1.) Gasoline prices in 1987 ranged from 71¢ per gallon in Mexico to $2.89 per gallon in Japan and $3.71 in Italy. Costs of kerosene ranged from 30¢ to $1.82 per gallon.[17]

The impact of major oil price shifts is felt by everyone from Brazilian charcoal vendors to Tokyo stock traders.

In Europe, heavy taxes are commonly used to raise government revenues and discourage gasoline consumption; in many countries, these levies account for over half the retail price of gasoline. In the United States, however, efforts to raise gasoline taxes have been beaten back by the oil industry, consumer groups, and wary politicians. U.S. retail gasoline prices plummeted in 1986, encouraging more driving; in Europe prices declined moderately, and the conservation incentive remains strong.[18]

In many Third World countries, kerosene and diesel fuel are subsidized, a practice that places a heavy burden on government treasuries but that is highly popular among consumers. An August 1987 attempt by the beleaguered Aquino government in the Philippines to

Table 2-1. Prices of Petroleum Products in Selected Countries, 1987

Country	Gasoline	Diesel	Kerosene
		(dollars per gallon[1])	
Italy	3.71	1.55	1.56
Denmark	3.58	2.29	1.82
France	2.95	1.91	n.a.
Brazil	2.94	1.92	1.07
Japan	2.89	1.80	1.08
Ethiopia	2.40	1.44	1.20
United Kingdom	2.24	1.77	n.a.
India	2.17	1.01	0.65
West Germany	2.09	1.67	n.a.
Thailand	1.30	0.92	0.89
United States	0.82	0.87	0.83
Mexico	0.71	0.61	0.30

[1]Figures are for average consumer prices as of January 1, 1987. They include taxes, which account for the largest differences in price.
SOURCE: U.S. Department of Energy, *International Energy Annual 1986* (Washington, D.C.: 1987).

raise fuel prices caused street demonstrations led by drivers of jeepneys, a primary mode of transport for Manila's poor. Such reactions are common and create a dilemma in countries where most of the population cannot afford fuel at the world price. In order to ensure that fuel taxes do not exacerbate equity problems, they should be offset by eliminating income taxes for low-income people or even providing government loans for the purchase of vehicles and appliances that are more fuel-efficient.[19]

A few countries have deliberate policies to use fuel taxes to encourage conservation. In 1983, Sweden passed a law requiring the government to use fuel taxes to dampen fluctuations in world oil prices, a provision that was activated by the 1986 price collapse. Also in 1986, Denmark and Portugal took steps to raise taxes, keep retail gasoline prices high, and promote conservation. As of late 1987, Austria's Energy Efficiency Agency had proposed a new energy conservation and environmental protection tax. Although such policies are generally not popular, they encourage needed investments and will benefit consumers in the long run.[20]

Energy prices should also reflect the environmental effects of using particular energy sources. Burning coal in a power plant creates air and water pollution, and often entails land-damaging strip mining. Yet without government intervention, consumers use large quantities of cheap electricity without regard to the wider costs. A pollution tax can put a price tag on these wider costs and so discourage pollution. No country has yet enacted such a tax, but the time may be ripe.

Most governments have chosen to deal with conventional pollutants by enacting regulatory standards or requiring the use of emission control devices, but the carbon dioxide problem is not amenable to technical fixes. So far, the only practical means of limiting carbon output seems to be to increase energy efficiency levels or to switch away from fossil fuels.

One way to encourage this would be to place a carbon tax on all fossil fuel use—in effect, a climate protection tax. Such a tax would ensure that the cost of burning any fuel would reflect the risk of damage to the world climate. If it were tied to the fuel's carbon content, coal would be taxed most heavily, oil somewhat less, and natural gas the least. A tax of $1 per million Btu. on coal and 80¢ per million on crude oil would boost average electricity prices by 10 percent and increase gasoline prices by 11¢ per gallon, while raising $53 billion in revenues in the United States alone.[21]

One advantage of a climate protection tax is that it could provide steady revenues to help pay for the substantial investments needed in energy efficiency, renewable energy, tree planting, and the other elements of a sustainable society. Enactment of such a tax would present enormous challenges, including the desirability of doing it on an international basis so industries in some countries are not put at a competitive disadvantage. As with taxes on gasoline and other fuels, steps must be taken to ensure that the climate protection tax does not harm the poor.

SETTING STANDARDS

Market incentives are generally more efficient than legislated standards in encouraging change. Even the most omniscient legislators cannot foresee all the perverse effects that new laws might have, or the ingenious efforts to get around those laws. It is also difficult to anticipate future changes in technology, and so legislated standards can lock society into a less than ideal solution to a particular problem. One example is acid rain legislation that would mandate expensive flue gas desulfurization but not

allow utilities to achieve the same sulfur dioxide reductions via investments in improved energy efficiency.

Despite these drawbacks, mandatory efficiency standards do have a role to play. Often the impact of standards is easier to predict than is the impact of financial incentives. They can ensure that the least efficient or most wasteful practices are eliminated, so that even the least responsive parts of society get the benefit of needed improvements. Dozens of countries have enacted minimum energy efficiency standards since the early seventies. Overall, the United States has shown the most fondness for such legislation, perhaps as a way of counteracting the country's low energy prices, which traditionally encouraged inefficiency. However, support for this approach has fluctuated over the years.[22]

Most industrial market economies have automobile efficiency standards, but only in the United States are they mandatory. Between 1976 and 1985, U.S. auto manufacturers were required to gradually increase the average fuel efficiency of new cars from 14 to 27.5 miles per gallon. These standards were crucial in encouraging the carmakers to invest in a new generation of lighter, front-wheel-drive cars in the years between the two oil price increases. The mandated levels were easily met until 1985, when in the face of falling oil prices and auto company pressure, the Reagan administration relaxed them. This misguided move sent manufacturers a signal to go back to the bad old days at the very time that continued long-term improvement in fuel efficiency was most needed. A new set of tough but achievable standards is needed to take average new-car fuel efficiency up to at least 40 miles per gallon by the year 2000. (See Chapter 3.)

The most common standards are for new residential buildings, now found throughout the industrial world as well as in many developing countries. Some are mandatory and others just provide general guidance to builders. The toughest building efficiency standards are found in California, South Korea, and Sweden, each of which has been quite successful in reducing energy requirements. Sweden's manufactured buildings industry makes it far easier to set efficiency standards than in countries where the construction industry is more fragmented. Studies in Europe indicate that in most countries further tightening of standards could be economically justified.[23]

By the turn of the century the new U.S. appliance efficiency standards will keep 342 million tons of carbon out of the atmosphere.

Energy efficiency standards for household appliances have been hotly debated in the United States. In November 1978, Congress directed the Department of Energy to issue minimum standards for common appliances. In the face of fierce opposition from appliance manufacturers and its own distaste for government regulation, the incoming Reagan administration stalled on implementation. Finally, it claimed in 1982 that the best way to regulate appliance efficiency is to not regulate it at all, and then went to court to fight the ensuing lawsuits.[24]

Meanwhile, California instituted its own tough appliance efficiency standards in December 1984, and New York followed suit, after calculating that consumers would save billions of dollars' worth of electricity. As such legislation proliferated, manufacturers' worst nightmares seemed to be coming true: Even a relatively tough national appliance efficiency law would be less onerous than a plethora of varying state laws.

Manufacturers, utilities, consumer advocates, and environmentalists began negotiating in 1986 to develop a new appliance efficiency bill. After several months of tough bargaining, a historic agreement was reached; the resulting bill sailed through Congress and was finally signed by a reluctant president.[25]

The ultimately successful saga of the appliance efficiency standards can be viewed as a strategic model. Efficiency standards have an important role to play in complementing the use of improved market signals. Manufacturers themselves can benefit when future requirements are clear to everyone and all competitors face the same standards. The potential savings are enormous. It is estimated that by the turn of the century the new U.S. appliance efficiency standards will have saved $28 billion worth of electricity and gas and will keep 342 million tons of carbon out of the atmosphere.[26]

OPENING UP THE POWER MARKET

The electric power industry is probably the single most important energy institution, and also the one most in need of reform. In most countries, the industry is composed of either government-owned or government-regulated monopolies. These institutions decide what kind of power plants to build and when to build them. Electricity prices are determined by fiat or by regulation, and often bear little relation to the cost of building new power sources, as they would in a market-based system.

Electric power systems generally have their roots in the early part of the century, when electricity seemed like a naturally monopolistic industry and ever-larger power plants were believed necessary to reduce costs. Over the years, most countries lost perspective on the inefficient behemoths they had created. Commissioner Charles Stalon of the U.S. Federal Energy Regulatory Commission (FERC) says that the current electricity system and regulation "exist by grace of inertia. They lack an intellectual economic defense."[27]

These systems have nonetheless proved resilient, and it is only in the United States that fundamental change has begun. The Public Utility Regulatory Policies Act (PURPA), passed by Congress in 1978, made it possible for a wide range of newcomers to compete in the power industry. It created a new category of nonregulated "qualifying facilities," consisting of small cogeneration and renewable energy projects that are free to sell power to utilities at the "avoided cost" of planned utility power generation.[28]

By late 1987, projects that would generate more than 63,000 megawatts had been granted licenses by FERC, equivalent to 63 nuclear plants or over two thirds of the current nuclear industry. (See Table 2–2.) In fiscal year 1987 alone, 15,000 megawatts' worth of projects, with an estimated value of about $15 billion, were registered. So far, 74 percent of the planned capacity is fossil-fuel-based cogeneration and 26 percent is based on renewable energy.

A 1987 Edison Electric Institute study found that the great majority of these projects are being built and going into operation. As of the end of 1985, some 9,500 megawatts had been installed, a figure that may well have surpassed 20,000 megawatts by the end of 1987. The independent power industry is now doing $4–5 billion in business annually. Since 1980, orders for utility coal plants have slowed to one or two per year, and nuclear orders have stopped entirely. A transition, it seems, has occurred.[29]

The competitive power industry has already sped innovation. For both cogeneration and renewable-energy-based generating plants, independent production of electricity is providing the first commercial market and therefore encouraging private investment. Costs are

Table 2-2. United States: Planned Cogeneration and Renewable Power Projects, 1980–87

Fiscal Year	Cogeneration[1]	Renewables	Total
		(megawatts)	
1980	282	422	704
1981	795	524	1,319
1982	3,121	1,123	4,244
1983	3,758	1,929	5,687
1984	3,743	2,145	5,888
1985	8,430	2,779	11,209
1986	13,742	5,617	19,359
1987	13,311	1,796	15,107
Total	47,182	16,335	63,517

[1]Cogeneration using biomass is included under renewables. Small power producers burning fossil fuel wastes are listed under cogeneration.
SOURCE: Federal Energy Regulatory Commission, "Qualifying Facilities Report," Washington, D.C., January 1, 1987 and private communication, November 4, 1987; *Cogeneration and Small Power Monthly*, July, August, and September 1987.

falling and reliability is improving in plants that are on average 50 times smaller than before. A 1987 study by the California Energy Commission found that many of these technologies are already more economical than conventional nuclear and coal plants. They are also environmentally preferable.[30]

Although PURPA is a federal law, its implementation is largely at the discretion of state regulators. Some have encouraged the development of independent power; others have set rules that essentially preclude it. The result, not surprisingly, is wide variation in the pace of independent power development in different parts of the country.[31]

Like any industry with monopoly power, the utilities have little interest in competition.

California aggressively opened the market to independent power in 1981 by requiring that utilities offer long-term power contracts at "avoided cost" or competitive prices. California now has more than one fourth of the country's independent power. Also out in front are New Hampshire, which has projects planned equal to 73 percent of its total installed capacity, Maine at 33 percent, and Texas at 12 percent. The nationwide average has reached 6 percent. The trend is toward relaxing regulatory requirements and offering long-term power sales contracts that reflect the market price of power.[32]

Much of the utility industry has fought vigorously against PURPA and the independent power industry. Like any industry with monopoly power, the utilities have little interest in competition. But in recent years the industry has been losing key regulatory and legislative battles at both the state and federal levels. After

listening to extended testimony by all parties at hearings in the spring of 1987, FERC ignored utility calls for the emasculation of PURPA, and is now considering even more fundamental reforms.[33]

The logical next step being considered by FERC and several states is opening the generation market to competitive bidding for all new power plants, gradually eliminating the practice of administratively determined prices. The regulated utilities would control only the transmission and distribution of electricity, as is the case with local telephone companies since American Telephone and Telegraph was broken up in the United States. This would give the utilities a much clearer and less conflict-ridden mission. Regulators would allow them to earn the revenues needed to carry out the role of providing consistent service to customers. Utilities would become honest brokers between producers and consumers. Existing generating plants might eventually be sold to private companies. A small but growing number of utilities have embraced this new role, happy to let others handle the risky business of plant construction.[34]

Such a system would have many advantages. It would be more economically efficient, according to economic theory, and it should in the long run lead to lower prices for consumers, in part because it would encourage innovation across a wider array of technologies. Logically, this competitive market should be extended to efficiency, so that a company that can provide "saved energy" in an office building or a factory for less than the cost of building a new power plant would win the bid. (See next section of this chapter.)

The U.S. electric power industry is moving toward a new, competitive structure, but thorny issues remain to be resolved. So far, only cogeneration and renewable energy projects have been able to qualify as independent power producers. Renewable energy's share of this market is now falling steeply, and changes are being considered that would widen the competition to all manner of large and small power plants and probably further reduce the role of renewables. Some incentives will be needed to ensure that the industry does not come to rely entirely on conventional fossil-fuel-burning plants with the lowest initial costs. Innovation itself has a special value, as do technologies such as wind and geothermal power that do not use fuel, do not pollute, and are invulnerable to oil price increases.[35]

Another question is whether utilities themselves should be able to compete in this new market through unregulated subsidiaries, a concept that some regulators refer to as self-dealing. Given the inevitable conflict of interest, it should probably be ruled out, though utilities could be allowed to supply power in other utility districts. In addition, many independent producers would like freer access to "wheeling" of power, allowing them to rent utility lines as common carriers for selling power to distant customers. Although this would enhance competition, it raises difficult problems regarding how to guarantee service, how to allocate access to the transmission grid, and how to protect small consumers, who are not in a good position to compete for the lowest priced power.

Competitive power has begun to attract international interest, but change is slow. Denmark and Greece now allow certain categories of renewable power producers to sell electricity to the utilities, but they are far from creating a competitive market. The United Kingdom allows limited independent cogeneration and is considering "privatizing" the power industry. However, the Thatcher government seems to view this as a means of substituting private monopolies for a public one. New Zealand passed a new law in 1986 that should in theory open the power market to full competition, but the ultimate impact of this change is not yet clear. The U.S. experience is providing an important example as structural reform in the power industry becomes a live issue in many countries for the first time.[36]

INSTITUTIONALIZING EFFICIENCY

If energy efficiency is to realize its full potential to revitalize economies and protect the environment, major institutional reforms will be needed, as indicated in Chapter 3. The most serious current obstacle is what energy conservation professionals call the "payback gap." Energy consumers—from homeowners to factory managers—rarely invest in efficiency measures with payback periods longer than two years, while energy producers look to new supply options with payback periods of up to 20 years. If institutional changes can bridge this simple but critical gap, energy efficiency might largely take care of itself.

The key is developing markets for saved energy. Consumers do not want energy; they want the services energy provides. Improved efficiency cuts the energy needed to provide these services. With generating capacity already in place to produce additional power, the energy saved can then be used for other purposes. Firms that find the cheapest ways to conserve energy, while still meeting standards of quality and reliability, should be rewarded. And as more utility systems are opened to competitive bidding, saved energy can compete with independent power.

A large and growing energy conservation industry has developed for commercial buildings and factories in the United

States, Canada, and some European countries. The industry will only come into its own, however, when electric and gas utilities are prepared to buy *saved energy*. If properly rewarded, private energy conservation firms could keep societies on the crest of technical efficiency advances without unduly straining public coffers.

Energy conservation companies provide one-stop shopping. They inspect the building or factory; select, buy, and install retrofit measures and new equipment; and often operate and maintain the equipment. Currently they recoup their investment either by taking a share of the owner's savings for a set period or by receiving prearranged monthly payments. More than 100 firms now hold contracts on some 2,000 U.S. buildings. Because of economies of scale, most contracts to date have been for buildings or factories with potential savings over $50,000; at least one small company in Minnesota, however, offers home retrofits on a shared savings basis.[37]

In energy supply, technology is the central concern, but in energy conservation, contract negotiations and financing are the key to success. The reason is simple: Energy conservation companies sell saved energy, something that cannot be metered. Its quantity can only be estimated based on past experience and current conditions. Detailed, computer-based methodologies must be developed to measure saved energy, and standardized legal and financial practices must be used to streamline the process.

State and local governments have become a major market for energy conservation. One successful example is the city-owned utility in Osage, Iowa, which since 1974 has invested heavily in energy efficiency by funding extensive energy audits of almost half the town's residences. These audits, combined with peer pressure to encourage participation, led to weatherization of hundreds of homes. As a result, Osage managed to cut electric demand growth to zero through 1985, defer planned construction programs, and cut electric rates three times in two years. The lower electricity bills have also helped Osage to attract new industry.[38]

Electric and gas utilities have a central role to play in institutionalizing energy efficiency. Since the late seventies, many have been pushed by regulators and legislators to adopt conservation programs, often based on the concept of least-cost planning. (See Chapter 3.) Using this approach, utilities invest in improving customers' efficiency as long as greater efficiency costs less than new supply. This is essentially an attempt to mimic the effects of a market: The cheapest options sell first in a market, and they are chosen first in least-cost planning.

Central Maine Power may be the first utility to take the next logical step: putting energy savings and supply on an equal footing.

According to a survey of U.S. electric utilities by the Investor Responsibility Research Center of Washington, D.C., 75 utilities spent $582 million on conservation programs in 1985. Aggressive conservation programs at six of the largest utilities have offset the need for 7,240 megawatts of generating capacity—at less than a fifth the price of new plant construction. The more comprehensive programs include building inspections, free energy-saving showerheads and water tank insulation, rebates for efficient appliances, and loans for home weatherization. Unfortunately, many programs are little more than public relations campaigns, and others are being reduced in the face of power gluts. (See *State of the World 1986* for a more thorough discussion.)[39]

At least two utilities are now buying saved energy. General Public Utilities Company of Pennsylvania (owner of the infamous Three Mile Island plant) pays for conservation by offering companies a fixed return on every kilowatt-hour saved. Conservation companies take out contracts for blocks of houses, inspect them, choose the most cost-effective investments, and make the improvements. The companies are chosen by competitive bidding, and they take all of the risk of cost overruns or faulty installations. The utility helps with low-cost financing, and monitors the resulting improvements to measure the saved energy. A similar program instituted by the Oregon-based Bonneville Power Administration in 1983 was put on temporary hold, a short-sighted response to the region's excess electricity supply.[40]

Central Maine Power may be the first utility to take the next logical step: putting energy savings and supply on an equal footing. Regulators are now examining a plan to accept energy conservation proposals in the next round of power contract bidding. Energy conservation firms representing blocks of consumers or individual large consumers could make proposals to provide the utility with "negawatts" of power. The proposals would be weighed against independent power options on the basis of price, reliability, and other factors.[41]

This competitive bidding formula may be the key to boosting efficiency to its maximum cost-effective level and giving the energy conservation industry a solid long-term footing. Unprecedented amounts of engineering and business ingenuity would be brought to bear. If the economic potential of efficiency is as large as experts believe (see Chapter 3), efficiency could become a sizable industry.

Competitive bidding that included conservation would be particularly effective in rental housing, where waste is perpetuated by the diverging interests of tenants and owners. Conservation companies would identify potential improvements and provide the capital, removing the need for either the landlord or tenant to raise large sums of money. In addition, competitive bidding would counteract the tendency of many conservation improvements to be superficial or unreliable. A full-fledged conservation industry would have the necessary skills, equipment, and professional standards to perform effective, high-quality retrofits.

Even with competitive bidding, utilities—because of their links to energy users—will remain the linchpin of the energy system, providing the centralized billing and metering services. Most important, utilities, regulators, and government bodies will have to vigorously police the market. Precautions should be taken against counterproductive "cream skimming" (making improvements with high return rates while bypassing worthwhile but less profitable improvements). Energy conservation firms will have to be licensed by the government, and projects will have to be inspected to verify savings. If efficiency programs are to be treated like new power plants, they must be planned, designed, and implemented with the highest of standards.

RESEARCH AND DEVELOPMENT NEEDS

Technological advances are central to the shaping of energy futures, and in recent years technology development has accelerated drastically. Governments have led the way in commercializing a number of large technologies, most notably nuclear power plants, while private industry, particularly since the mid-seventies, has focused on much smaller systems.

The fruits of these efforts are everywhere. Oil drilling is being extended to depths unimaginable two decades ago. Coal can be burned with much lower sulfur emissions. Nine-watt desk lamps are available that use just 10¢ of electricity per month. And some villagers are now generating their power directly from sunlight. Research and development is by nature a hit-and-miss process, and there have been as many failures as successes. The key is to design the R&D process in a way that maximizes the success rate while still pursuing technological options with potentially high payoffs.

The late seventies witnessed a dramatic increase in government spending on energy R&D. The industrial market countries doubled their energy research, development, and demonstration expenditures from $5.1 billion in 1975 to $10.2 billion in 1980. (See Table 2–3.) Most have leveled off since then, though

budgets have declined precipitously in the United States and West Germany. Today, Italy and Japan lead the members of the Organisation for Economic Co-operation and Development (OECD) in energy R&D expenditures as a proportion of gross national product, while the United States has fallen to last place.[42]

The most important legacy of the mid-seventies is the creation of new programs to develop renewable energy and efficiency technologies. These grew rapidly until 1981, when they began to level off or fall in most countries. In 1986, the OECD member countries spent $484 million on renewable energy R&D and $622 million on improved energy efficiency R&D. (See Table 2–4.) This is 6.8 and 8.4 percent, respectively, of total energy R&D expenditures, still a small sum compared to the $4.5 billion spent on nuclear technologies, including breeder reactors and fusion. Spending on renewables and efficiency has been uneven since the early eighties, with greater than 50-percent cuts in the U.S. and some other programs, and increases

Table 2-3. Government Energy R&D Budgets in OECD Member Countries, 1975–86

Country	1975	1980	1983	1986	1986 R&D Expenditures per $1,000 GNP
	(million 1986 dollars)				(dollars)
Italy	278[1]	398	610	761	1.99
Japan	821	1,987	2,128	2,311	1.73
Canada	222	282	394	336	0.98
West Germany	818	1,050	848	566	0.91
United Kingdom	458	475	492	378	0.85
Sweden	71	128	127	79	0.79
United States	2,317	5,229	2,916	2,261	0.59
Other OECD[2]	95	663	641	441	—
Total OECD[2]	5,080	10,212	8,156	7,133	—

[1]1977.   [2]Excludes France.
SOURCE: International Energy Agency, *Energy Policies and Programmes in IEA Countries, 1986 Review* (Paris: Organisation for Economic Co-operation and Development, 1987).

in Greece, Italy, and the United Kingdom.[43]

No simple measures of the overall success of these programs are available, but substantial evidence exists of individual projects that have already led or will soon lead to important new commercial technologies. Some of the clearest successes involve small programs with minimal expenditures. The common ingredients seem to be a well-thought-out development process and successful collaboration between the public and private sectors.

The tiny country of Denmark has led the world in developing intermediate scale, grid-connected wind turbines, an industry that did not exist before the eighties but reached sales of over $500 million in 1985. (See Chapter 4.) Starting in the mid-seventies, Denmark began a program to build on its historical experience with wind power technology. Less than $10 million of annual government funding was used to develop improved blades, rotors, and braking systems. In addition, the government established a national wind turbine test center to support the development of private commercial machines. Turbines had to pass a stringent certification test for tax credit eligibility.[44]

The Danish wind power industry grew slowly until 1982, when wind farming took off in California. Although the Danish machines were generally heavier and less aerodynamically efficient than the American ones, years of painstaking progress made them much more reliable, a key factor in any new technology. Since 1982, the Danish share of California's wind power market has grown steadily, reaching 65 percent in 1986. As of 1987, Denmark not only dominates the worldwide wind power industry but has helped make wind a reliable, economically competitive energy source.[45]

U.S. government-supported energy efficiency programs have also spawned some small but important success stories. In 1976, the Department of Energy and the Lawrence Berkeley Laboratory began a program to develop solid-state ballasts that would make fluorescent lamps 15–30 percent more efficient. (See Chapter 3.) By 1980, prototype lamps

Table 2-4. Government Energy R&D Budgets in OECD Member Countries, by Energy Source, 1986

Country	Fossil Fuels	Nuclear	Renewables	Efficiency	Total[1]
		(million dollars)			
Japan	310	1,801	99	78	2,311
United States	294	1,134	177	275	2,261
Italy	4	658	30	48	761
West Germany	122	352	66	21	566
United Kingdom	20	271	16	43	378
Canada	138	144	11	34	336
Sweden	9	12	17	29	79
Greece	3	2	10	0	15
Denmark	5	0	3	5	14
Total OECD[1]	990	4,503	484	622	7,133

[1]Total includes minor additional expenditures. Excludes France.
SOURCE: International Energy Agency, *Energy Policies and Programmes in IEA Countries, 1986 Review* (Paris: Organisation for Economic Co-operation and Development, 1987).

installed at a federal office building met both reliability and performance standards.[46]

Several small U.S. manufacturers began producing the new models, taking just 1.4 percent of the ballast market by 1984. Large electronics companies in Europe and Japan developed a similar technology. In 1984, General Electric, GTE, and all the other major lamp manufacturers entered the market for solid-state ballasts, which are now expected to take half of the U.S. market by 1990. The American Council for an Energy-Efficient Economy found that the 2 million ballasts in use in 1987 were already saving $15 million worth of electricity each year. Over the next 30 years, the new ballasts are expected to save $25 billion worth of electricity—not bad, considering that the government seed money amounted to only $2.7 million.[47]

The Department of Energy began another program in 1976 to develop special window coatings that allow light to pass unimpeded but retain heat within a building. Federal contractors developed several early generations of the new coatings, and after a few years some were able to raise venture capital to continue the process privately. The technology did not really catch on until 1983, however, when a large window manufacturer adopted it. Just $2 million was spent on the initial federal program to spur the development of the new windows, and private industry later spent over $150 million on facilities to manufacture them. The windows are projected to save $120 million worth of heating fuel annually in the mid-nineties, with cumulative savings reaching $3 billion in the year 2000.[48]

It is hard to know just how common such success stories are, but anecdotal evidence indicates that they are widespread. Researchers in dozens of fields report that the state of technology has advanced by huge strides since the late seventies. (See Chapters 3 and 4.) However, most of these advances have not yet reached a stage of commercialization that commands public attention. One example is thin-film photovoltaic cells, which are now used mainly for consumer electronic devices. But the costs are falling so rapidly that household solar power may become practical in little more than a decade.

Government energy research programs should be seen as selective seeding efforts. Not all of the seeds need to sprout in order for the program to be a success. Unfortunately, such programs are put to a yearly political test in many countries, and budgets rise and fall depending on the fashion of the moment and whether a particular project can benefit a powerful constituency. Such uncertainty makes long-term planning difficult and makes investment in renewables less attractive for private investors.

Japan, in contrast to other countries, has maintained a steady commitment to energy research and development programs—from nuclear power to coal gasification and photovoltaics. Government policy states that "it is necessary to offer the appropriate guidance to the private sector's energy conservation efforts, and to prevent the consciousness toward energy conservation or the incentive toward investment in energy conservation from being affected and weakened by short-term trends in the oil markets."[49]

Japanese energy R&D spending reflects this commitment. It rose 140 percent between 1975 and 1980 and then increased another 17 percent between 1980 and 1986, reaching $2.3 billion. For the first time, Japan leads the world in government energy R&D spending. The Sunshine Program for renewable energy and Moonlight Program for energy efficiency are yielding excellent results, with effective links to the private sector.[50]

By contrast, U.S. spending peaked in 1980 at $5.2 billion, then declined sharply to about $2.3 billion in 1986. U.S. budgets were affected by the Reagan administration's desire to cut all programs with imminent commercial prospects (except some big-ticket nuclear demonstration projects). The administration has also sought to virtually eliminate government support of renewable energy and energy efficiency technologies. Congress has continued to provide funds for these programs, but at less than half the levels of 1980–81. As a result of growth in military expenditures, the Department of Energy has become mainly a nuclear weapons agency.[51]

U.S. energy programs have been skewed toward long-term nuclear projects with dubious prospects, notwithstanding the small successes mentioned earlier. A 1987 General Accounting Office study found that in most cases where federal support of technologies has been limited to basic research, private industry has not gone forward with commercialization efforts. Overall, U.S. energy R&D programs are marked by an extraordinary degree of confusion and bureaucratic infighting. The Department of Energy's own Inspector General has stated that there is no coherent long-term plan guiding the Department's programs.[52]

Recognition is growing in the United States and throughout the world that effective coordination between the public and private sectors is an essential ingredient of success in R&D. Only by working with the thousands of companies that make equipment for producing and consuming energy can the world's vast scientific and engineering expertise be effectively harnessed to develop commercial equipment that will have a meaningful impact.

An effective process must be set up to choose among myriad proposals for research and development. In many countries a built-in bias favors the proposals of large, well-established companies. The better programs, however, are usually those where new projects are chosen on their merits. Independent engineering panels can be set up to ensure that this occurs, something that has been successful with some of the U.S. energy efficiency programs. Large increases in spending on renewable energy and efficiency will be required in order to right the current imbalance in spending, but these increases will have to proceed gradually, with close technical guidance, if the funds are to be used effectively.

U.S. energy R&D programs are marked by an extraordinary degree of confusion and bureaucratic infighting.

International collaboration in energy R&D should also be made a high priority. The recent mushrooming of energy technology development means that even wealthy nations can no longer afford to have independent research programs in every promising field. So far, the European Economic Community has the largest such joint effort, and many European countries channel most of their energy R&D funds through the program. Total funding is now about $60 million per year for non-nuclear energy R&D, split almost evenly between renewables and efficiency. In addition, the International Energy Agency maintains a cooperative program among OECD member countries that has spent about $600 million during the past decade.[53]

It is unfortunate that for the most part such programs have not been broadened to include centrally planned and developing nations. The Third World has been able to fund only small projects on its own and needs to share in the latest energy technology developments, particularly those involving decentralized technologies. The United Nations Conference on New and Renewable Sources of Energy in 1981 was supposed to lead to such an effort, but it became bogged down in political infighting and bureaucratic inertia. Although some foreign aid programs have effectively promoted the development of indigenous energy resources, these are neither as strong nor as numerous as they could be.

In all nations, the creation of an effective energy policy involves the successful blending of many different elements, any one of which taken in isolation is likely to be inadequate. Perhaps the most important principle is reliance on market forces. Their role is shown by what has happened through their absence in the Soviet Union and Eastern Europe. Inefficient use of energy, lagging technology development, and choking air pollution have become synonymous with the centrally planned world. The Soviet Union, for example, has pioneered the development of some sophisticated efficiency technologies, but its buildings waste heat due to a lack of simple things like fiberglass insulation and caulking. Many developing countries that rely on state-run enterprises and heavily subsidized energy prices now face similar problems.

The market-based economies have done better, but still not well enough. Even the most capitalistic countries have a long history of inappropriate government intervention, reliance on monopolistic enterprises, and deeply entrenched obstacles to more-efficient buildings and transportation. Large energy supply projects are generally favored over smaller, renewable energy technologies. In short, a real market approach to energy has yet to be given a fair chance.

Governments can unleash the vigor of markets by reforming institutions and reorienting enery subsidies and taxes so that prices reflect marginal costs, including environmental costs. So long as energy is priced as if it were almost free, and so long as consumers have neither the means nor the information to make cost-effective investments in energy efficiency, we will continue to squander our remaining fossil fuels. Reasoned, graduated efficiency standards, though seemingly in contradiction to an emphasis on markets, can play a crucial and consistent role by encouraging manufacturers to develop the technologies that market forces point toward.

The many goals of energy policy—lowered oil dependence, economic competitiveness, environmental protection, and climate preservation—make the formulation of a comprehensive, consistent policy difficult. Any proposed quick solutions to the complex of problems are almost certainly unworkable. The key is to unleash the power of private innovation and individual action, without attempting to force broad government mandates on society.

A goal of reducing national energy expenditures, if pursued rigorously, can lead to a strong emhasis on energy efficiency, improve economic competitiveness, and limit growth of oil dependence. However, specific disincentives will be required to ensure that countries do not become too heavily dependent on fossil fuels that threaten life-support systems. If all governments work toward this goal, we can immediately embark on a path that will replace creeping disaster with gradual improvement.

3

Raising Energy Efficiency

Christopher Flavin and Alan Durning

A 1987 report of the International Energy Agency contains a simple but remarkable statement: "Investment in energy conservation at the margin provides a better return than investment in energy supply." Environmentalists and advocates of "soft path" energy have been saying the same thing for a decade. But today the evidence is unequivocal, even to government officials and industrialists who have devoted their careers to expanding energy supply: Energy efficiency is one of the best buys in town, for consumers and companies, as well as nations.[1]

Enormous strides have already been made, outstripping most national efficiency targets and representing the single largest step in reducing dependence on imported oil. Most market-oriented industrial economies have improved their energy efficiency by between 20 and 30 percent since 1973. During a time when there was almost no net increase in supplies, efficiency developed to a point where it now displaces $250 billion worth of oil, gas, coal, and nuclear power annu-

ally in industrial market countries.[2]

Technologies now mature could hold energy use in industrial countries level or even reduce it for the foreseeable future. In developing countries, efficiency can slow energy growth while actually accelerating the improvement of living standards.

Energy efficiency can save more than fossil fuels. It is a powerful response to some of the most troublesome problems facing the modern world. The Persian Gulf now has one of the largest concentrations of naval forces amassed since World War II, and dependence on Middle East oil is growing. Acid rain is wreaking destruction on the forests of central Europe. Rising carbon dioxide levels may be the harbingers of catastrophic climate change. And economic predicaments from Third World debt to falling international competitiveness threaten to mire the world economy in stagnation or worse.

These seemingly unrelated threats to the health of the world's economy and ecology are, on closer scrutiny, all potent arguments for a global effort to increase energy efficiency. As will be argued in the final section of this chapter, energy efficiency is not only the most

An expanded version of this chapter appeared as Worldwatch Paper 82, *Building on Success: The Age of Energy Efficiency.*

cost-effective response to these problems, it may offer the only viable solution.

EXTENDING THE EFFICIENCY REVOLUTION

When the Ford Foundation completed a landmark study of the U.S. energy future in 1974, it presented three scenarios. One curve was identified as the "historical growth scenario" and envisioned national energy use doubling between 1970 and 1987. The lowest consumption forecast, termed the "zero growth scenario," still involved an almost 20-percent increase in energy use. Since that report was published the U.S. economy has expanded by over 35 percent, but U.S. energy use has fallen.[3]

While most analysts underestimated the potential for greater efficiency, they overestimated the world's ability to live with the side effects of high levels of energy consumption. It was assumed, for example, that world energy consumption could more than double by the year 2000 without debilitating price increases. The Organization of Petroleum-Exporting Countries (OPEC) was expected to be pumping at least three times as much oil as it now does, unhindered by tanker wars or a revolutionary regime in Teheran. Nuclear power was believed capable of supplying at least five times as much energy as it does today, untouched by billion-dollar cost overruns or accidents in Pennsylvania or the Ukraine.[4]

As circumstances changed, energy use patterns changed with them. Between 1973 and 1985, the energy intensities of all industrial market countries fell. (See Table 3–1.) However, the improvement varied widely—from about 6 percent in Australia and Canada, to 18 percent in West Germany, and 23 percent in the United States. Japan improved by 31 percent, remarkable since the nation started with one of the world's most efficient economies. It continues to widen its lead during the eighties.[5]

Table 3-1. Energy Intensity of Selected National Economies, 1973–85

Country	1973	1979	1983	1985	Change, 1973–85
	(megajoules per 1980 dollar of GNP)				(percent)
Australia	21.6	23.0	22.1	20.3	− 6
Canada	38.3	38.8	36.5	36.0	− 6
Greece[1]	17.1	18.5	18.9	19.8	+16
Italy	18.5	17.1	15.3	14.9	−19
Japan	18.9	16.7	13.5	13.1	−31
Netherlands	19.8	18.9	15.8	16.2	−18
Turkey	28.4	24.2	25.7	25.2	−11
United Kingdom	19.8	18.0	15.8	15.8	−20
United States	35.6	32.9	28.8	27.5	−23
West Germany	17.1	16.2	14.0	14.0	−18

[1]Energy intensity increased as a result of a move toward energy-intensive industries such as metal processing.
SOURCE: International Energy Agency, *Energy Conservation in IEA Countries* (Paris: Organisation for Economic Co-operation and Development, 1987).

Energy efficiency data for centrally planned countries are more difficult to obtain, but available evidence indicates that these nations are lagging behind in the efficiency revolution. The Soviet Union has not bettered its record at all since the early seventies, and remains the least energy-efficient industrial economy. Without the discipline of market prices, Soviet industrial managers look at energy bills as just another cost to pass on to consumers; many families still use open windows to regulate the temperature in their centrally heated apartments, even in the dead of the Soviet winter.[6]

An energy efficiency gap has also opened among developing nations. Newly industrializing economies, such as Taiwan, South Korea, and Brazil, have begun to incorporate state-of-the-art industrial machines and processes, accompanied by a broad array of energy efficiency standards and financial incentives. But most of the Third World lags further and further behind the industrial world. Many nations are still going through the early, energy-intensive phases of industrialization, and energy intensity is rising rather than falling. Moreover, many countries subsidize energy prices, and have not yet implemented effective policies to restrain consumption. For most developing nations, imported oil continues to place a heavy burden on foreign exchange; lagging progress in efficiency will make it increasingly difficult to compete in international markets.

International economic competitiveness is not just an issue for the Third World. In 1986, the United States used 10 percent of its gross national product to pay the national fuel bill, but Japan used only 4 percent. Arthur Rosenfeld of Lawrence Berkeley Laboratory has calculated that, relative to Japan, the United States is effectively paying a $200-billion energy inefficiency tax,

leaving less to invest in other areas such as retiring the national debt. Japan is not only richer for its efficiency, it is also in position to dominate the world market for high-efficiency technologies.[7]

Another gap is developing between different sectors of society. Efficiency improvements have been most impressive in industry, with buildings and transportation trailing somewhat. Efficiency improvements depend on the structure of the market: Buildings, which actually have the most potential for efficiency gains, have progressed slowly due to the fragmented nature of the markets involved and the slow replacement rate of buildings compared with automobiles and industrial equipment. Energy-intensive industries like chemicals have improved remarkably, however. Similarly, the commercial aviation industry has been pushed by punishingly high fuel costs to invest heavily in wide-body aircraft, improved jet turbines, and lighter materials, increasing fuel efficiency by about half.[8]

In 1986, the United States used 10 percent of its gross national product to pay the national fuel bill, but Japan used only 4 percent.

How could the vast improvements that have occurred over the last 15 years have been so unobtrusive? Most of the changes are due to subtle shifts in the economy and to technological improvements, rather than to life-style changes or campaigns to turn down thermostats and buy tiny cars. Process and equipment changes make the average Japanese paper plant or steel mill 30–50 percent more efficient than it was a decade ago. A new American office building has about the same lighting levels and temperatures as older ones but uses less than half as much electricity. Even large luxury cars now get 20–25 miles per gallon, comparable to much smaller cars built in the mid-seventies.[9]

The main reason that efficiency has come so easily is that higher energy prices have spurred engineers, managers, and consumers to make operational changes and start using what had become a backlog of efficient technologies. Governments often sped the process. Efficiency standards have been enacted for buildings, appliances, and automobiles; tax credits and subsidies are available; and new institutions have been created to open new avenues of investment. Some utilities in the United States, for example, are now being rewarded by regulators for putting money into the efficiency of their customers' buildings.[10]

No country has even begun to tap the full potential for further improvements; a range of technologies now coming on the market are more efficient than experts thought feasible just a few years ago. Efficiency gains of at least 50 percent are available in every sector of the economy. Yet from wood stoves in African villages to office buildings in California, the limiting factor is not technical but rather institutional. (See Chapter 2.)

Increasing energy efficiency requires the orchestration of dozens of technologies, policies, and institutions—one reason that countries have differing degrees of success. Indeed, energy efficiency provides an interesting microcosm of economic organization. Centrally planned economies such as the Soviet Union's have shown virtually no improvement in energy efficiency, whereas market-oriented and highly organized economies such as Sweden's and Japan's have done unusually well.

Data available through mid-1987 indicate that energy efficiency continues to improve in most nations, despite the oil price collapse of 1986. Many of the investments made after the 1979–81 increases in oil prices are still "in the pipeline." It is only a matter of time, however, before lower oil prices slow the momentum. Around the world, government and private energy efficiency programs are being abandoned, and new investments are being curtailed. Without prompt action, trouble lies ahead.[11]

The key to cost-effective investment in energy efficiency is a concept known as "least-cost planning." Adopted by a growing number of American states, least-cost planning puts investments in energy supply and energy conservation on an equal footing. Whenever an investment in increased efficiency is more economical than one in energy supply, least-cost planning would give it priority. Several studies show that such an approach could lead to additional energy efficiency improvements worth billions of dollars. It is a principle that can be effectively used by government agencies, corporations, and consumers.[12]

BUILDING FOR EFFICIENCY

Winston Churchill once said "We shape our buildings and afterwards our buildings shape us." Churchill understood the crucial importance of the indoor environment to the human species. We have become an indoor breed, spending most of our lives inside walls we have built ourselves. We now also spend a substantial share of world energy resources heating, cooling, and lighting buildings: In 1985, buildings in the industrial market economies used the primary energy equivalent of 16.7 million barrels of oil per day, almost the entire daily production of OPEC that year. The economic and environmental implications of energy consumption on that scale are enormous. Indeed, a contemporary Churchill might say "We shape our buildings and afterwards our buildings shape our world."[13]

In industrial market economies, energy goes to buildings, industry, and transportation in almost equal parts. Centrally planned economies and many developing countries, on the other hand, devote over half their commercial energy to industry. In Eastern Europe and the Soviet Union, despite the prevalence of theoretically efficient apartment buildings and district heating, buildings tend to be leaky and poorly insulated.[14]

Better air conditioners make even more sense in Manila than in Manhattan.

Structures in developing countries present two starkly different images. In the countryside, buildings are Spartan, fuelwood is the dominant energy source, and the essential energy questions are those of bare needs. Because fuelwood use is currently so inefficient, total energy consumption measured in units of heat is actually quite high. (See Chapter 5.)

Cities across the Third World house the swelling urban underclass, who use fuelwood, charcoal, or more expensive fuels as changing prices dictate. Meanwhile, members of a relatively wealthy elite consume energy with the same profligacy as their industrial-country counterparts. For this modern sector, which takes the bulk of national commercial energy, high-efficiency technologies are crucial. Indeed, better air conditioners make even more sense in Manila than in Manhattan.[15]

In industrial market countries, an ever growing stock of buildings has used an almost constant amount of energy since the early seventies. Efficiency has filled the gap. Buildings in these countries use 25 percent less energy per person than they did in 1973, saving the equivalent of 3.8 million barrels of oil every day—more than the output of the North Sea. Gains to date, however, pale beside what new technologies make possible. Experience now proves that it is possible to construct buildings that use only one tenth to one third as much energy as today's structures.[16]

Already, Swedish homes are twice as well insulated as those in northern Minnesota, for example, and considerably better insulated than houses in other parts of Europe. Homes in London, for instance, use more energy than their counterparts in Stockholm but are much colder in the winter. "Retrofitting," renovating to save energy, can make a difference. In over 40,000 retrofits monitored by U.S. utilities, energy consumption fell by a quarter, and homeowners got a 23-percent annual return on their investment.[17]

Retrofits that are well conceived and executed pay for themselves in lower bills in less than five years. Many, however, are still poorly done, resulting in small energy savings. Such services must be improved. In addition, consumers often lack full information on the economic merits of retrofits or capital to carry them out. In rental housing, often the least efficient type, landlords pass electricity and gas bills on to renters, and so have no incentive to finance retrofits; tenants meanwhile have little interest in paying for improvements to someone else's property. These market failures perpetuate the waste of energy that occurs in existing homes.[18]

Boosting efficiency in new residences is also crucial. Energy efficiency is cheapest when built in from the start, so the efficiency potential in new buildings far exceeds that in existing ones. While average U.S. homes consume 160 kilojoules of heating energy per square meter of floor space per degree-day, new Swedish houses use just 65. Recently built super-efficient homes in Minnesota average 51 kilojoules, and some individual units in Sweden go as low as 18.[19]

The key to these savings is "superinsulation": doubling the normal insulation and building an airtight liner into the walls. In fact, superinsulated houses are so airtight that they require mechanical ventilation to remove indoor air pollutants. Heat radiating from people, stoves, and appliances warms the house, requiring little auxiliary heating. In summer, superinsulation also keeps warm air out.[20]

As much energy leaks through American windows every year as flows through the Alaskan pipeline.

Superinsulation adds about 5 percent to building costs, but the energy savings cover the extra expense in around five years. There are now more than 20,000 superinsulated homes in North America, with perhaps 5,000 more built every year. But this is not even 1 percent of new housing construction. Homebuyers tend to discount long-term costs like energy, so builders put their efforts into cosmetic selling points rather than efficiency. As one expert in energy-wise housing put it, when American homebuyers must choose between better insulation and a Jacuzzi whirlpool bath, "the Jacuzzi wins out most of the time."[21]

Commercial buildings—offices, hospitals, schools, and stores—use less total energy than residences in most countries, but their use is growing more rapidly. Efficiency investments in these structures tend to be very inexpensive, but commercial-building owners still tend to underinvest in this field. Since 1973, closer attention to heating, cooling, and lighting efficiency has already cut energy consumption in new U.S. office buildings from the extraordinarily wasteful level of 5.7 million kilojoules per square meter of floor space per year to 3.0. Commercial buildings in Sweden now average under 1.7, and the government enforces a maximum standard of 1.1 for new buildings. If all U.S. commercial buildings were that efficient, total U.S. energy consumption would be 9 percent lower.[22]

Survey data for the United States show no correlation between energy efficiency and construction costs in new office buildings, suggesting that efficiency improvements have been essentially free up until now. The cost of added insulation and window glazing is covered by the savings from smaller cooling and heating systems. The Oregon-based Bonneville Power Administration estimates that a further improvement of 30 percent would increase construction costs less than 1 percent. Energy savings from efficiency investments during construction are almost pure profit.[23]

The most important feature of efficient new commercial buildings is "intelligence." In existing structures, inflexible energy systems that are oblivious to outdoor temperatures often waste energy cooling air in winter and warming it in summer. "Smart buildings" monitor both outdoor and indoor temperatures, sunlight, and the location of people—sending heat, cooled air, and light where it is most needed. Analysts at Lawrence Berkeley Laboratory calculate that Los Angeles homes could halve their air conditioning bills just by changing the controls on air conditioners to measure temperatures outside and then ventilate rather than cool whenever possible.[24]

One intriguing technique now making a splash in the commercial building market is called "thermal storage," which holds heat or cold for later use. Some new office buildings in Sweden so effectively store heat from the people and equipment inside them that they use virtually no auxiliary heating, even in the middle of winter. And in Reno, Nevada, some buildings now operate through the summer without air conditioning, using cool night air to chill large chambers of water that keep indoor temperatures comfortable during the day.[25]

Many of the technologies used in efficient new commercial buildings are so cost-effective they are worth installing in existing buildings as well. A detailed analysis of commercial buildings in Austin, Texas, by Amory Lovins and his colleagues at the Rocky Mountain Institute identified potential savings of 1.8 billion kilowatt-hours per year, 73 percent of the buildings' current electricity use. Moreover, because the payoffs from these savings would be so great, realizing them would cost less than just operating most power plants.[26]

Window technology, crucial to both commercial and residential buildings, is improving rapidly. As much energy leaks through American windows every year as flows through the Alaskan pipeline. A special "heat mirror" film that doubles windows' insulation value by letting in light without letting out heat is moving well on the market. Further window improvements can be realized by creating a vacuum between the two parts of a double-pane window, effectively turning windows into thermos bottles. Advanced technologies that may be economical in the nineties could give windows the same insulation value as ordinary walls.[27]

Internal energy uses—appliances, furnaces, air conditioners, and lights—are also ripe for savings. For example, the average refrigerator-freezer in American homes consumes 1,500 kilowatt-hours of electricity every year. The average new model of that size does the same job

with 1,100, and the best model on the market, a Whirlpool, takes only 750. But further gains are possible: A Danish prototype consumes 530; a Californian custom model runs on 240; and one study suggests that the number could cost-effectively drop as low as 200 kilowatt-hours per year.[28] Similar stories could be told of most other appliances. (See Table 3–2.)

Efficient appliances generally have higher price tags, but the lower energy bills more than cover the difference. In 1986, the best refrigerator on the market cost $60 extra. But that investment paid itself off in 30 months, a 45-percent rate of return.[29]

A powerful measure of the economic merit of efficiency gains is called the "cost of saved energy." Every kilowatt-hour an American homeowner buys from a utility costs 7.8¢ on average, but every kilowatt-hour saved by the Whirlpool refrigerator costs the consumer less than two pennies. The pennies, of course, are not on the electric bill but in the higher purchase price of the more efficient model. These cost-of-saved-energy figures allow energy planners to compare efficiency investments with new supply options on a least-cost basis.[30]

Heating and cooling technologies can also be made far more efficient. Conventional gas furnaces, for instance, send a quarter of their heat up the chimney. But new condensing furnaces reabsorb much of that heat by cooling and condensing exhaust gases. They cut fuel use by 28 percent, reduce air pollution, and make chimneys obsolete, requiring only a small exhaust vent.[31]

Heat pump applications for both heating and cooling are proliferating. Electric heat pumps that heat in winter and cool in summer are already making inroads in home heating markets long dominated by oil and gas. Heat pump clothes dryers can be twice as efficient as conventional designs. Several heat

Table 3-2. United States: Energy Efficiency Improvements and Potential for Residential Appliances and Equipment, 1985

Product	Average of Those in Use	New Model Average	Best Commercial Model	Estimated Cost-Effective Potential[1]	Potential Savings[2]
	(kilowatt-hours per year)				(percent)
Refrigerator	1,500	1,100	750	200–400	87
Central Air Conditioner	3,600	2,900	1,800	900–1,200	75
Electric Water Heater	4,000	3,500	1,600	1,000–1,500	75
Electric Range	800	750	700	400–500	50
	(therms per year)				(percent)
Gas Furnace	730	620	480	300–480	59
Gas Water Heater	270	250	200	100–150	63
Gas Range	70	50	40	25–30	64

[1]Potential efficiency by mid-nineties if further cost-effective improvements already under study are made. [2]Percent reduction in energy consumption from average of those in use to best cost-effective potential.
SOURCE: Howard S. Geller, "Energy-Efficient Appliances: Performance Issues and Policy Options," *IEEE Technology and Society Magazine,* March 1986.

pump water heaters now on the market use half the power of conventional units. Howard Geller of the American Council for an Energy-Efficient Economy calculates that installing these in all American homes with electric water heaters would eliminate the need for 15 large power plants.[32]

Efforts to boost energy efficiency in buildings must eventually tackle all energy uses, but they might start with the light bulb. Lighting, which consumes about 20 percent of U.S. electricity, offers some of the largest and most economical savings now available. Arthur Rosenfeld of Lawrence Berkeley Laboratory believes that 40 large U.S. power plants could be given early retirement simply by fully applying available, cost-effective lighting technology.[33]

Lighting also has a psychological advantage as a starting point. Ever since Thomas Edison, the light has symbolized electricity—indeed, in much of Latin America the words are used almost interchangeably. Cutting energy used for lighting in industrial countries by three quarters, while extending efficient lighting into Third World villages where there has never been electricity before, would provide a fitting challenge. It could also serve as a test case for institutionalizing least-cost energy planning. Part of a global response to the mounting economic and environmental ramifications of fossil fuel dependence might grow, ironically, from the simple slogan "Better light bulbs."

Compact, screw-in fluorescent bulbs with special "warm light" coatings are beginning to replace traditional incandescent ones. One new 18-watt fluorescent provides the light of a 75-watt incandescent and lasts 10 times as long. The purchase price is high, but the cost of saved energy is generally under 2¢ per kilowatt-hour. They have an environmental bonus as well: Over their useful lives, compact fluorescent light bulbs each save 180 kilograms of coal and keep

130 kilograms of carbon out of the atmosphere.[34]

The bulbs are still somewhat bulky, not yet fitting into all standard fixtures, but engineers are improving them at breakneck speed. Major manufacturers have not aggressively marketed the bulbs, claiming that consumers' extreme sensitivity to purchase prices would make them unsalable. If utilities or energy conservation companies with ample capital were to invest in efficient lighting within people's homes and offices, and split the savings with them, compact fluorescents could sweep the market and electricity demand would drop.

One new 18-watt fluorescent provides the light of a 75-watt incandescent and lasts 10 times as long.

The lighting revolution does not stop with minifluorescents; researchers are making still greater improvements on full-sized tubes used in commercial buildings. High-frequency electronic ballasts (the devices in fluorescent fixtures that control the electrical current in the tube) cut energy use by 20–30 percent. High-frequency ballasts are now commercial and, because they are so economically attractive (with a cost of saved energy around 2¢ per kilowatt-hour), may capture half of fluorescent light sales by the mid-nineties.[35]

A package of measures already on the market, including better controls, reflectors, and spacing, as well as improved bulbs and ballasts, can reduce lighting energy required in commercial buildings by over 75 percent. The University of Rhode Island recently cut lighting energy consumption by 78 percent for only 1¢ per saved kilowatt-hour, chopping $200,000 off the university's annual electric bill. Advanced technical developments such as super-high-frequency ballasts are within a decade of maturity. Microelectronic sensors that measure sunlight and sense people entering and leaving rooms can cut energy use for lights in half yet again. Furthermore, every improvement in lighting efficiency lowers the generation of waste heat and therefore saves on air conditioning. The California Energy Commission calculates that in Fresno, every 100-watt savings on lighting means an additional 38-watt savings on air conditioning.[36]

If technical developments alone set the pace of efficiency improvements, buildings in much of the world would already be more than twice as efficient as they now are. But entrenched institutions and market failures perpetuate an economically irrational and ecologically wasteful status quo. Policies that reform institutions and correct market failures can open the vast efficiency gold mine. (See Chapter 2 for further discussion of energy policy questions.)

Providing buyers with full information may require energy ratings for new buildings along the lines of the automobile mileage ratings now common in many countries. Developing such ratings would be technically challenging, but initial work suggests it is possible. Overcoming consumers' sensitivity to initial costs may require special energy-saving financing. The diverging interests of tenants and landlords may require a variety of subtle responses from policymakers. And reforms in the construction industry will be required to build maximum efficiency in from the start. That is crucial because building practices shape energy demand for a century; power plants and oil wells last less than half as long.

THE FUEL ECONOMY CHALLENGE

Transportation is now the largest and most rapidly growing drain on the world's oil reserves. The United States uses fully 63 percent of its oil in transportation, more than the country produces. Worse, as auto sales grow, much of the world appears set on replicating this unhealthy condition. Already, passenger cars consume one of every six barrels of oil. Meanwhile, the by-products of human transport have become a force of nature: Fossil fuels burned to move people and cargo release more than 700 million tons of carbon into the atmosphere annually. Indeed, the average American car pumps its own weight in carbon into the atmosphere each year.[37]

The crux of the transportation energy predicament is overreliance on the automobile. It has led to neglect of railroads, halfhearted efforts at mass transit, and indifference to energy in urban planning. In a sense, the most significant transportation energy decisions are made by city planners. Suburban sprawl, for example, is both a by-product of the private car and the perpetuator of its dominion. Once sprawl sets in, as it has in much of the industrial world, cities are locked into auto-dependence. And as tightening gridlock slows traffic in many cities, the efficiency of auto-centered transport systems falls.

Young, rapidly growing cities, especially those in developing countries, have the opportunity to plan for enormous energy savings early on by designing residential and work areas that do not require people to travel long distances. But even mature cities can save energy by reducing dependence on the automobile. When policies encourage their full use, van pools, public cars, buses, and railroads require a quarter as much fuel to move each passenger a kilometer as private cars or airplanes do. Bicycling and walking not only take no fuel and release no pollution, they improve health simultaneously. Trains and ships, meanwhile, use less than a third as much fuel as trucks do to move a ton of freight. Only when walking, bicycling, and using public transit become the norm in the world's major urban complexes can oil dependence be cut substantially.[38]

Where the automobile culture is deeply ingrained, however, conversion to an energy-wise transportation system will take time. Institutions, life-styles, and the structures of many cities are built on the premise that "transportation" is synonymous with "automobile." Thus, improving auto fuel economy has to be a priority.

Worldwide, the average fuel efficiency of new cars has improved by at least 25 percent since 1973, but this has not prevented the overall oil requirements of cars from rising. New cars now average between 25 and 33 miles per gallon (MPG) in most countries, compared with the 1973 range of 13 MPG in the United States to 28 MPG in Italy. (See Table 3–3.) Fuel economy gains to date are dominated by simple weight reduction following the transition to smaller cars with front wheel drive. New American cars have nearly doubled their fuel economy since 1973, but still have not closed the efficiency gap with Europe and Japan.[39]

Today, a host of fuel-efficient technologies are being introduced in showroom models, and more exciting innovations can be found in research and development programs. Four-passenger cars with fuel economy close to 100 MPG have reached the test tracks of Europe and Japan. Indeed Europe and, especially, Japan are setting the pace in developing new fuel-saving technologies, while the United States falls further and further behind. By late 1987 the

Table 3-3. Urban Fuel Efficiency of New Passenger Cars Sold in Selected Countries, 1973 and 1985

Country	1973	1985	Change
	(miles per gallon)		(percent)
Denmark	26[1]	33	+27
West Germany	23	31	+35
Italy[2]	28	30	+ 7
Japan	23	30	+30
United Kingdom	21	31	+48
United States[3]	13	25	+92

[1]1975. [2]Average of all cars in use, not new cars. [3]Composite urban-highway figure. Figures for city driving would be lower.
SOURCE: International Energy Agency, *Energy Conservation in IEA Countries* (Paris: Organisation for Economic Co-operation and Development, 1987).

three leading American carmakers had dismantled much of their research programs on smaller, fuel-efficient cars. In Japan, meanwhile, advanced fuel economy technologies are moving steadily into production.[40]

Gains in fuel economy usually come piecemeal. Auto weight can be trimmed by incorporating more aluminum, new alloys of steel, recently developed engineering-grade plastics, and space age ceramics. Aerodynamic drag can be reduced by streamlining the body. Engines can be modified or completely redesigned to make fuller use of the energy released in combustion. Improved transmissions can match efficient engine speeds with drive power needs. Efficient air conditioners and other accessories allow reductions in engine size and auto weight. Microelectronics can fine-tune engine and transmission operation and can revolutionize steering.

Several innovative fuel-efficient models are already on the road, achieving over 50 MPG. (See Table 3–4.) Most are Japanese. The Honda CRX, a two-seater that runs like a sports car, has plastic body panels, aluminum parts, good aerodynamics, and a special lean-burning engine. The Suzuki Sprint engine is constructed largely of aluminum, and the Mitsubishi Mirage can turn extra cylinders on and off as needed. The Honda City has a hybrid manual-automatic transmission that in effect gives the car seven gears, keeping engine speed closer to the optimum.[41]

Subaru has replaced the gear box entirely in its tiny Justy, opting instead for a "continuously variable transmission" (CVT). In CVTs, a belt transfers engine power to the drive shaft as it runs around two self-adjusting pulleys, giving the car an unlimited number of gears. Subaru found that this technology improved fuel efficiency by 20 percent over a three-speed automatic and by 10 percent over a five-speed manual transmission.[42]

Prototype models have fuel economy levels far surpassing anything on the market. The most innovative prototype is Volvo's aerodynamic LCP 2000. Volvo

Table 3-4. Fuel Efficiency of Selected Four-Passenger Automobiles, 1987

Model	Fuel	Fuel Efficiency[1]
		(miles per gallon)
In Production		
Peugeot 205	gasoline	42
Ford Escort	diesel	53
Honda City	gasoline	53[2]
Suzuki Sprint	gasoline	57
Prototypes		
Volvo LCP 2000	diesel	71
Peugeot ECO	gasoline	73
Volkswagen E80	diesel	85
Toyota AXV	diesel	98

[1]Composite urban-highway figure. [2]City driving; composite would be higher.
SOURCE: Deborah Bleviss, *The New Oil Crisis and Fuel Economy Technologies: Preparing the Light Transportation Industry for the 1990's* (New York: Quorum Press, in press).

used lightweight materials extensively, including magnesium. The LCP weighs half as much as the average American car and has an advanced diesel engine that can accommodate alternative fuels. Furthermore, Volvo engineers plan to install a CVT and a flywheel energy storage system to boost mileage by an additional 20 MPG.[43]

Volvo has also kept the consumer in mind: The LCP 2000 withstands impacts more severe than many vehicles in use, meets air pollution standards, has better acceleration than the average new American car, and could be mass-produced at about the same cost as today's subcompacts. Toyota's prototype AXV is another standout, complementing an advanced diesel engine with a continuously variable transmission. It is spacious enough for use as a family car—a remarkable achievement considering its estimated fuel economy of 98 MPG.[44]

For most consumers fuel economy is a relatively low priority when fuel prices are not skyrocketing.

Any of a number of technologies could reshape future autos, bringing about even greater savings. Generally, improved aerodynamics and weight reduction promise the most gains today, but transmission advances are also rapidly maturing. New engines that may take over in the longer run include lean burn and stratified charge models, and those made wholly of ceramics.

There can be little argument about the technical potential for extraordinarily efficient automobiles, but marketers, especially in the United States, know that for most consumers fuel economy is a relatively low priority when fuel prices are not skyrocketing. Fortunately, fuel efficiency need not come at the expense of other important features. High-efficiency models can be safe, reliable, affordable, and even "sporty," as the Honda CRX and the Volvo LCP demonstrate.

Diesels are the most efficient engines to date, but their future is clouded by their air pollution emissions. Although they emit less carbon monoxide and hydrocarbons than gasoline engines do, diesels issue more nitrogen oxides and particulate matter. Both Mercedes Benz and Volkswagen have developed technologies to bring their diesels into compliance with California's particulate standards—the strictest in the world. Nevertheless, if these diesels were widely used, they would still result in some deterioration in air quality. Experts believe, however, that clean diesels can be developed. Alternatively, it may prove easier to achieve the same efficiency improvements using other technologies.[45]

All changes in auto design cost money, including those that go into periodic style changes. Although some efficiency technologies appear expensive, if they are mass-produced and integrated into modern assembly lines, the resulting vehicles may well cost about the same as today's models. Advanced materials like plastics require fewer welds and parts, and therefore cost less to manufacture. Moreover, the economics are far more favorable when technologies are introduced as a package rather than piecemeal. The U.S. Office of Technology Assessment estimated in 1982 that if fuel economy innovations were fully integrated into the normal cycle of turnover in plant and equipment, it would cost an additional $50–90 per automobile in the United States to bring most cars into the 38–53 MPG range by 1990. By 2000, cars could average 51–78 MPG for an additional $120–330 apiece (in 1980 dollars)—less than a good car stereo.[46]

Despite the modest cost of improving fuel efficiency, the market alone is unlikely to boost efficiency as significantly as necessary to head off growing oil dependence and greenhouse warming. Although the cost of saving gasoline (embedded in the higher price of a more efficient car) continues to be far below the cost of buying it, car buyers care less about fuel economy above a certain threshold. Attention shifts more to other factors like reliability and styling, because the expense of putting gas in the car becomes less significant than other costs, such as maintenance. At that threshold, which varies somewhat based on fuel prices, society's interests require policies such as standards and consumer incentives to continue to push fuel economy up.

NEW FRONTIERS FOR INDUSTRY

In most countries, industry has led the way in improving energy efficiency during the past 15 years. Overall, the energy intensity of the industrial sector in countries that belong to the Organisation for Economic Co-operation and Development has fallen a remarkable 30 percent since 1973. Denmark and Japan made unprecedented gains, with 7-percent annual savings between 1979 and 1984. In the United States, industrial energy use in 1986 was actually 17 percent lower than in 1973, despite a 17-percent increase in industrial production during the period. In some nations, including the United States, industry is no longer the largest energy user.[47]

Marc Ross, a physicist at the University of Michigan, has suggested that the lowered energy intensity of U.S. industry has two causes. About 45 percent, he estimates, is attributable to structural shifts in the economy toward the production of less energy-intensive materials and goods. Production of steel and cement, for example, has fallen, while electronic gadgets proliferate; some energy-intensive raw materials are now imported from newly industrializing countries. The other 55 percent of the improvement can be traced to new, more-efficient equipment and processes. In many industries, managers have aggressively reduced energy consumption to preserve their profit margins.[48]

Industry's use of oil has fallen particularly rapidly; petroleum has become a specialty fuel. Almost half the oil American industry consumes now serves as raw material rather than fuel. Use of natural gas and coal has also fallen in many cases, and even the utilities' loudly trumpeted "electrification of industry" has fallen flat: Electricity use has leveled off as efficiency gains consistently offset the introduction of electrical processes such as electric arc furnaces and robotics.[49]

Even after these advances, industry still uses 37 percent of the total energy supply of the industrial market economies, and as much as 60–70 percent in many developing nations. North American industry is still much more energy-intensive than the industries of Europe and Japan, and recent declines in oil prices may lull some industries into complacence, delaying additional improvements.[50]

The lion's share of industrial efficiency improvements in the United States so far has been in petroleum refining, chemicals, cement, metals, paper, glass, and clay—energy-intensive industries where competition required change. Other, less energy-intensive industries now use a growing share of industrial energy. Studies show that many companies continue to pass up many efficiency investments with short payback periods, while investing aggressively in means of boosting market share.[51]

Training managers how to identify and appraise opportunities to increase energy efficiency should be a high priority for corporate and national planners. Consideration of the potential to raise efficiency can make a particularly large difference when companies are adding new equipment, which affects the plant's energy use for decades. Many companies have appointed senior energy program managers with responsibility in this area—with rewards tied to success in lowering energy costs. Japan, which has made particularly large strides in reducing industrial energy use, requires by law that companies with high energy consumption designate full-time energy managers.

Industry's use of energy is varied, but a few widely used technologies hold immense potential for savings. In the United States, fully 95 percent of industrial electricity goes for electromechanical drives, electrolysis, and heating. (See Table 3–5.) Electromechanical drives, ubiquitous in industrial processes, can be improved in many ways, including the use of electronic speed controls that cut power needs by up to 50 percent. Sales of these devices have more than tripled in the United States since 1976, and can be expanded further. The Electric Power Research Institute estimates that variable speed drives alone are sufficient to offset the electricity that will be used by all 27 new electricity-using industrial technologies projected to be introduced between 1980 and 2000.[52]

Table 3-5. United States: New Technologies and Industrial Electricity Use

Electric Use	Share of Industrial Electricity[1]	Technologies to Improve Efficiency[2]	Probable Trend in Electric Intensity
	(percent)		
Electromechanical Drives	70	Efficient motors Adjustable speed drives Cogeneration	Down
Electrolysis	15	Improved cell efficiency Chloride process Membrane separation Electrochemical synthesis	Down
Electroheat	10	Plasma applications Electroslag casting Heating with: laser, electron beam, infrared, microwave. Ultraviolet curing	Up
Other	5	Robotics Improved space heating/cooling	Down

[1]As of 1983.   [2]Technologies likely to be widely employed by 2000.
SOURCE: Adam Kahane and Ray Squitieri, "Electricity Use in Manufacturing," in Annual Reviews Inc., *Annual Review of Energy, Vol. 12* (Palo Alto, Calif.: in press).

Production of chemicals is now the largest use of industrial energy in many countries, accounting for 22 percent in the United States. Improved processing techniques and heat recovery devices helped reduce the energy intensity of the U.S. chemical industry by 34 percent between 1972 and 1985. The cement industry is also a major and growing energy user. Efficiency improvements are under way, however, most notably the introduction of a dry production process that cuts energy requirements greatly.[53]

The steel industry, once a worldwide symbol of industrialization, has declined in importance but remains a significant user of energy. As total steel use has fallen, the industry has shut down its older, less efficient plants. In industrial countries, traditional open-hearth furnaces have largely been replaced by more-efficient basic oxygen furnaces and electric arc furnaces that recycle scrap steel and cut energy needs by half. The energy appetites of existing steel plants are being trimmed via the use of continuous casting, in which steel is formed directly into the desired shape, reducing waste.[54]

One of the greatest opportunities to improve industrial energy efficiency lies in cogeneration—the combined production of heat and electricity. By installing a small boiler and electric generator within a plant, the waste heat of electricity generation is available for industrial processes rather than lost, as in conventional power plants. Such systems are hardly new; they were widely used early in the century, but most were abandoned in the rush to build central power plants. In the United States, cogeneration reached a low of 10,476 megawatts in 1979; in Europe, it is still widely used in urban district heating systems. Since 1972, Denmark has encouraged cogeneration in all new power plants.[55]

Industrial cogeneration has grown explosively in the United States due to the Public Utility Regulatory Policies Act of 1978, which allows industry to sell power to utilities at a fair market price. As of 1985, total U.S. cogeneration had reached about 13,000 megawatts, but that number will grow rapidly in the next few years, as hundreds of new facilities are finished. Projects that would yield more than 47,000 megawatts of cogeneration—with as much generating capacity as 47 large nuclear plants and a market value over $40 billion—were registered with the Federal Energy Regulatory Commission as of October 1, 1987.[56]

In 1987 alone, about 13,000 megawatts of projects were registered. The cogeneration industry now includes most of the engineering and manufacturing firms that once served the utility industry, and is also well established financially, with extensive ties to the country's leading banks and institutional investors. Cogeneration projects range in size from 300,000-kilowatt facilities that serve petrochemical plants, to 20-kilowatt units in fast-food restaurants and apartment complexes. Manufacturers soon plan to make systems as small as 3–5 kilowatts, suitable for residential use. Some of the largest users include the oil industry, which taps such systems to produce steam for enhanced oil recovery; the chemical industry, which can use petroleum by-products as fuel; the food processing industry, which has large heat requirements; and the pulp and paper industry, which burns wood wastes.[57]

In the early eighties, conventional wisdom held that cogeneration would never make more than a small dent in centralized electric power systems. Today, however, as technologies advance, the potential uses for cogeneration have broadened to include a range of commercial and industrial facilities such as hospitals and hotels. Applied Energy Services, a cogeneration company, estimates that the U.S. market by the year 2000 could surpass that for nuclear power, reaching 100,000 megawatts—15 percent of the U.S power supply. The long-run potential is even greater.[58]

Industry as a whole is on a path to substantially decreased energy and materials intensity.

Cogeneration could have some problems, however, including the fact that about half the new U.S. projects rely on natural gas, a fuel that will probably not remain as inexpensive as it is today. Coal accounts for another 30 percent of planned U.S. cogeneration, which will tend to add to the problem of carbon dioxide buildup in the atmosphere. It is important to note, however, that many of the cogeneration projects will displace less-efficient central power plants fired by gas and coal. Industries that were once burning gas for process heat may now be using only slightly more gas and meeting all their electricity needs as well. Studies have shown that by using cogeneration, many factories can raise total plant energy efficiency from 50–70 percent to 70–90 percent. Nonetheless, with the rapid growth in cogeneration, its effect on total fuel requirements and on air pollutants and carbon dioxide needs careful consideration before major commitments are made.[59]

Industry as a whole is on a path to substantially decreased energy and materials intensity, rendering past projections obsolete. The world's largest economies appear to be in the midst of a structural shift away from the processing of basic materials, a shift that is caused only in small part by higher energy prices. Growing affluence, saturation of the market for energy-intensive materials, and the emergence of new high-technology products are helping to usher in this new era. On balance, most industrial market countries are unlikely to use as much industrial energy in the year 2000 as they did a quarter-century earlier.[60]

Although this is good news for the global environment, and for the economies of many nations, these benefits could well be offset by growing energy requirements in developing and centrally planned countries. Many Third World industries suffer from a damaging combination of subsidized energy prices, limited access to energy-efficient technologies, and poor management. All these can be overcome with policy changes, and can be sped with international technical assistance, but obstacles will prove insurmountable without a new commitment to energy efficiency.

Programs to improve the efficiency of basic industries in countries such as Kenya and South Korea have been quite successful, indicating the potential. Studies in India have found that efficiency can be improved in existing industries by 15–30 percent, largely by using simple "housekeeping" measures. Beyond such low-cost efforts, the rapid growth of industry in developing nations provides an opportunity for enormous strides in energy efficiency.[61]

As many of the world's energy-intensive basic materials industries shift to the Third World, it is essential that the frontier of technical innovation shift with them. Indeed, enhanced efficiency is essential for success in the tightening international competition that most Third World industries face.

THE LIMITS TO ENERGY GROWTH

The postwar era is commonly described as the age of oil. Petroleum fueled the engines of industrialization, and helped raise living standards around the globe. By similar logic, the current era is the age of energy efficiency. Since 1973, the world has saved far more energy than it has gained from all new sources of supply combined. The energy savings of the industrial market economies since 1973 exceed the combined energy use of Africa, Latin America, and South Asia. Efficiency made it possible for the world to climb out of the severe 1981–82 recession, and led to a 75-percent decline in the real price of oil between 1981 and 1986.[62]

The Club of Rome's 1972 warning that the world would run out of fuels and raw materials appears contradicted by the fact that the world today faces a glut rather than a shortage of fossil fuels. But that glut is itself a product of temporary shortages and soaring prices. Since the early seventies, the world has encountered a series of limits to growth and has so far shown remarkable adaptability, thanks to dramatic price increases not anticipated by the Club of Rome. But the global environmental limits now emerging may turn out to be the most stringent and dangerous of all, sorely testing the resolve of policymakers and citizens.[63]

Investment in energy efficiency is the most effective response to those limits, for it simultaneously leads to lowered oil dependence, reduced air pollution, and climate protection. Doubling the fuel efficiency of a typical European car, to 50 miles per gallon, lowers its annual fuel bill by almost $400; generally cuts emissions of nitrogen oxides, hydrocarbons, and carbon monoxide; and reduces carbon emissions by half, or 450 kilograms annually. A similar improvement for the world as a whole would cut carbon emissions by almost 200 million tons annually, a substantial contribution to climate protection.[64]

In 1986, oil imports in many countries rose for the first time in almost a decade—by more than 1 million barrels per day in the United States alone. If current trends continue, the United States will be importing more oil than ever by the mid-nineties. Meanwhile, the concentration of remaining petroleum reserves in the Persian Gulf grows ever more pronounced. By the late nineties, the United States and the United Kingdom are likely to be minor oil producers; a half-dozen Persian Gulf countries with at least 80 years' worth of remaining reserves will be in the driver's seat.[65]

These growing imbalances in the world oil market jeopardize the energy security of importing nations and the collective security of the world community. If Middle Eastern oil production reaches 80 percent of capacity—as it did in 1973 and 1979—it will take only a minor political or military conflict to send prices soaring. The increases that follow could well exceed those of the seventies. With world consumption now rising about 1 percent annually and production plummeting in the United States, the danger zone is likely to be reached in the mid-nineties.[66]

The only realistic means of avoiding another oil crunch in the nineties is to invest heavily in energy efficiency—largely in transportation. The potential of increased energy efficiency to reduce oil imports is demonstrated by the fact that efficiency largely caused the oil glut of the mid-eighties. One change alone—the increase in the average fuel efficiency of American automobiles from 13.1 MPG in 1973 to 17.9 MPG in 1985—cut U.S. gasoline consumption by 20 billion gallons per year, lowering oil imports by 1.3 million barrels per day, two thirds of the peak production from the rich oil fields of Alaska.[67]

Petroleum geologists agree that the United States is unlikely to find another oil field as large as Prudhoe Bay's, but the country could save another 1.9 million barrels per day by the year 2000 by raising new-automobile fuel efficiency to 45 MPG in 1995, according to a study by

Deborah Bleviss of the International Institute for Energy Conservation. This may be impractical, but most countries should strive for a minimum 1 MPG annual improvement in the fuel economy of new cars.[68]

After a decade of control efforts, air pollution remains a growing problem in most cities, and one that improved efficiency can help solve. Improved efficiency has the potential to reduce emissions of most dangerous pollutants, though this depends to some degree on the technologies employed. A 1987 study by the American Council for an Energy-Efficient Economy concluded that increased energy efficiency could cut electricity consumption in the Midwest by 15–25 percent, making it possible to reduce use of the region's dirtiest coal-fired power plants and so reduce acid rain. Because the efficiency savings are economical in their own right, the funds saved can be used to invest in additional pollution controls.[69]

Climate change looms as the ultimate environmental threat. Its impact would be global and, for all practical purposes, irreversible. As indicated in Chapter 2, improving worldwide efficiency by 2 percent annually would keep the world's temperature within 1 degree Celsius of current levels, avoiding the most catastrophic climatic effects.

Improving energy efficiency by 2 percent per year for several decades is challenging but probably feasible. Over 50 years it would reduce global energy intensity by almost two thirds. Some industrial market countries have been achieving this mark in the past 15 years. Sustaining this pace through decades of changing conditions and at times when fuel prices are not rising will be a difficult task however, requiring major institutional changes of the sort described in Chapter 2. Fortunately, many of the needed technologies are already in place, and some countries are showing the way. Buildings worldwide must become as efficient as Sweden's and industry must become as efficient as Japan's. Automobiles must become as efficient as the best prototype models now found in the engineering facilities of Europe and Japan.

Priorities in energy efficiency vary among countries. Industry is the top priority in the Third World and centrally planned nations since it is the largest energy user and is a key determinant of both environmental quality and economic competitiveness. In industrial countries, this sector probably needs less government attention than others.

Transportation efficiency is crucial for most countries. Improved automobile fuel economy could be accomplished with a package of consumer incentives for the purchase of more-efficient cars, fuel efficiency standards, industry R&D programs, and fuel taxes. Automobile fuel efficiencies will eventually reach some practical limits, at which point it will be important to have developed economical alternative fuels, such as ethanol, and be well on the way to more-efficiently designed communities that rely on human power and mass transit.

Buildings are the most wasteful energy users in industrial countries, and deserve the greatest attention from government programs. Improvements already made in these nations' buildings spare the atmosphere 225 million tons of carbon emissions annually, but heating, cooling, and lighting those buildings still pumps out over 900 million tons each year—17 percent of world carbon emissions from fossil fuels. Whereas the energy requirements of automobiles and industry could be halved with available technologies, building energy requirements can be reduced by 75 percent or more when new buildings are constructed. To sustain that 2-percent annual rate of improvement over the long run, building efficiency will have to compensate for diminishing returns in industry and transportation.[70]

The investments required to sustain a 2-percent rate of improvement in energy efficiency in the next decade or two are justified on purely economic grounds, but steps must be taken to make energy markets work much more effectively. The world has achieved over $300 billion worth of annual energy savings since 1973, mostly as a result of private investment decisions. Each additional 2 percent of savings will reduce bills by about $20 billion annually, at an incremental cost of $5–10 billion.[71]

In market economies, improved efficiency falls primarily to the private sector, which pays for the big-ticket items such as home weatherization and the modernization of industrial equipment. The world is now spending roughly $20–30 billion annually on improved efficiency, down somewhat from the peak of the early eighties. If governments were to create more incentives to invest in efficiency, this figure could productively be tripled by 2000. Government efficiency research, development, and demonstration programs in the industrial market economies absorb about $600 million annually.[72] Government R&D spending in these areas could also be tripled in most countries.

The United States and the Soviet Union will have to take leadership roles if the interrelated problems of energy efficiency and climate change are to be taken seriously. The United States is the world's largest energy consumer, and led other nations into the profligate energy practices of the postwar period. The Soviet Union is the least energy-efficient major industrial country, and its claim on global energy resources is among the fastest growing. Together the two countries account for 42 percent of the carbon now entering the atmosphere from fossil fuel use. A joint commitment to improved energy efficiency by the su-

perpowers would make a major contribution to climate protection, and might help mobilize action around the world.[73]

There are some indications that the Soviet Union may soon make improved energy efficiency a national priority. Senior officials have gone on record as saying that efficiency gains will be essential if perestroika (economic restructuring) is to be a success. Already, meetings have taken place with energy efficiency experts in the West, including representatives of the Rocky Mountain Institute and the U.S. National Academy of Sciences. Yevgeny Velikhov, vice president of the Soviet Academy of Sciences and an advisor to General Secretary Gorbachev, appears to have put his personal authority behind these new efforts.[74]

Buildings worldwide must become as efficient as Sweden's and industry must become as efficient as Japan's.

The Third World is also critical to any long-term energy scenario. Indeed, one of the most troubling features of most of the forecasts now in use is the assumption that today's industrial countries will continue to use a disproportionately large share of the world's energy, despite the fact that developing countries will soon have three quarters of the world's population. A 1981 study by the International Institute for Applied Systems Analysis was ostensibly attuned to global equity issues, yet it still assumed the Third World would use just 36 percent of the global energy supply in the year 2020.[75]

Such scenarios imply that while Third World energy use grows, per capita energy use will stagnate, presumably making it impossible for most developing countries to follow the modernization path taken by the newly industrializing nations in recent years. Although consistent with recent experience—many developing nations are burdened with unmanageable foreign debt and have been priced out of the oil market—it is a morally intolerable vision, inconsistent with the articulated goals of the international community. Poverty-induced conservation is not conservation at all. It is just plain poverty.

One of the greatest challenges will be to meet the energy needs of the poor without repeating the mistakes of the rich. Only rapid advances in energy efficiency and a decentralized, agriculturally based development path can allow the Third World to fuel improved living standards with limited energy supplies. In the poorer countries of Africa and Latin America, the rapid onset of an energy efficiency revolution is critical. Some Asian countries, including China, with the world's largest coal reserves, have sufficient fossil fuels to last for many decades but face a critical environmental choice. Using energy efficiency to displace coal may be essential to protecting human health as well as the climate.

One of the greatest challenges will be to meet the energy needs of the poor without repeating the mistakes of the rich.

A global energy study developed by an international team and published by the World Resources Institute in Washington, D.C., points up both the challenge and the promise of increased energy efficiency in the Third World. (See Table 3–6.) It concludes that the world energy supply in the year 2020 can hover just above the current level if energy efficiency is used both to halve per capita

Table 3-6. World Energy Consumption, by Region, 1980, With Scenarios for 2020

Region	1980	2020[1]	
		WRI	IIASA
		(terawatts)	
Developing Countries	3.3	7.4	9.2
Industrial Countries	7.0	3.8	14.6
World	10.3	11.2	23.8

[1]Scenarios developed by the World Resources Institute and the International Institute for Applied Systems Analysis; mid-range figures are given for IIASA.
SOURCE: José Goldemberg et al., *Energy for a Sustainable World* (Washington, D.C.: World Resources Institute, 1987).

energy use in industrial countries and to keep Third World per capita energy use steady while boosting living standards to European levels today. Some of the most dramatic improvements in Third World efficiency are projected for rural areas, as fuelwood cooking systems are replaced by more-efficient devices run on renewable fuels. (See Chapter 5.)[76]

This scenario is consistent with the goal of improving energy efficiency by 2 percent annually, would make a serious dent in global equity problems, and makes it possible to avoid the worst consequences of a global warming. But such scenarios are far easier to model on computers than to achieve in practice. If the story is to have a happy ending, Third World and industrial countries alike will have to overcome numerous political obstacles and begin ambitious efforts to improve energy efficiency.

To achieve its full potential, energy efficiency must emerge from the obscure corners of Energy Ministries. It must rise to the top of agendas throughout both government and industry. The very term energy efficiency must be transformed from a watchword of specialists to a centerpiece of national—and international—economic philosophy. Energy efficiency is an essential ingredient of economic and ecological progress; its status should be charted as closely as productivity or inflation. The Commission of the European Communities has suggested the need for such a commitment. At a 1986 meeting, national energy ministers agreed to an ambitious target of a 20-percent improvement in energy efficiency by 1995.[77]

Energy efficiency improvements are by nature fragmented and unglamorous: Thicker insulation and ceramic auto parts are not perhaps as intrinsically captivating as nuclear fusion or orbiting solar collectors. But infatuation with grandiose energy supply options got us into our current predicament; focusing on the mundane may be the only way to get out. Indeed, perhaps no other endeavor is as central to the goal of fostering sustainable societies. Without improved efficiency it is only a question of which will collapse first: the global economy or its ecological support systems. With greater energy efficiency, we stand at least a fighting chance.

4

Shifting to Renewable Energy

Cynthia Pollock Shea

When faced with a severe wood shortage due to overcutting, the ancient Greeks began to design their homes and cities so as to take advantage of the sun's ability to warm buildings in winter and cool them in summer. Through the ages many civilizations have learned to tap the multiple processes set in motion by the sun to garner useful energy. Uneven heating of the earth's surface produces wind, yesterday's winds are today's waves, and a season's worth of solar energy is trapped in plants whose residues can be burned as fuel.

Despite this knowledge, almost 15 years after the Arab oil embargo first wreaked havoc on the world's economies, efforts to tap the planet's myriad sources of renewable energy have met with mixed success. The 1986 oil price collapse further set back many renewables programs. If renewables are to offer a timely alternative to dwindling oil

supplies and to environmentally damaging coal combustion, policy support and financial backing need to be strengthened—now.

Renewables already provide about 21 percent of the energy consumed worldwide, of which 15 percent is biomass and 6 percent is hydropower. The distribution of this use is uneven: Some of the poorest developing countries derive more than 75 percent of their energy from biomass; others, well-endowed with water resources, obtain most of their electricity from hydro projects. Brazil, Israel, Japan, the Philippines, and Sweden are well on their way toward major reliance on renewable energy sources. In other countries, efforts on renewables ebb and flow with the political tide.[1]

An energy source is renewable if, with proper management, its sustained use will not permanently deplete supplies. Wind, sunlight, flowing water, plants, and forests are examples of seemingly perpetual energy sources. Unfortunately, the literature is replete with

An expanded version of this chapter appeared as Worldwatch Paper 81, *Renewable Energy: Today's Contribution, Tomorrow's Promise.*

failed projects that exceeded the renewable capacity of natural systems. An early calculation of environmental limits is thus an essential component of any renewable energy project.

Current uses of these energy sources range from small turbogenerators in free-flowing rivers, to boilers heated by agricultural residues, to computer-controlled solar concentrating systems that produce temperatures well over 3,000 degrees Celsius. For many applications, especially in remote areas and in developing countries with limited infrastructure, the simpler the technology the better. Simple does not, however, equate with inefficient, which has often been the case in the past. Some of the most exciting developments are technical advances that incorporate new ideas to make more energy for less money.

Half of all developing countries rely on imported oil for more than 75 percent of their commercial energy needs.

Despite erratic political and financial support, renewable sources of energy have made remarkable strides during the past decade and are well positioned to complement energy efficiency programs as the world moves beyond oil during the nineties. (See Chapter 2.) Investments in renewable energy technologies total some $30 billion annually. Two thirds is spent on hydroelectric projects financed by leading banks. Some sectors—small hydropower, geothermal energy, and biomass combustion—are growing rapidly. Others, such as the wind turbine and solar thermal equipment industries, are going through a difficult shakeout period during which marginal companies will fold. Major redirection of government policy is

needed to prepare countries for the growth spurt that is sure to accompany the next upward climb on the oil-price roller coaster.[2]

HARNESSING WATER'S POWER

Developments in hydropower are taking place at the two extremes of project size. In 1986, Venezuela completed the Guri dam, the largest in the world. With a 10,000-megawatt generating capacity, it can produce as much electricity as 10 large nuclear power plants. Brazil is in the process of building a hydroelectric plant with 20 percent more capacity than the Guri, and China is contemplating an even larger one. At the same time, many countries, particularly in the Third World, are installing generators thousands of times smaller on remote rivers and streams. (A generating plant is usually classified as "small" if it has a capacity of 15 megawatts or less.) The electricity is used to power isolated, sparsely populated communities and agricultural processing plants far from electric utility power lines.[3]

Before oil prices soared, nuclear economics soured, and the environmental constraints of coal burning became apparent, Third World governments were relatively content to import technologies and fuels from abroad. Half of all developing countries rely on imported oil for more than 75 percent of their commercial energy needs. But as the share of export earnings used to buy oil and repay foreign debts skyrocketed, interest in less expensive, domestic energy resources grew.[4]

Most hydro plants larger than 1,000 megawatts that are under construction or planned are located in developing countries or in remote areas of industrial nations. Industrial countries have already tapped their most promising hydro sites—areas with a steep, narrow gorge through which water can fall—and those locations that remain have generally been set aside as parkland or effectively excluded from consideration because of their natural beauty. Whereas North America and Europe had developed 59 and 36 percent of their hydropower potential, respectively, by 1980, Asia had harnessed just 9 percent, Latin America 8 percent, and Africa 5 percent.[5]

Brazil and China have the largest and most ambitious programs. China alone has 15,000 megawatts of large hydro projects under construction and plans to complete twice that much by the turn of the century. Brazil nearly tripled its hydroelectric generating capacity by adding 21,535 megawatts between 1973 and 1983; projects to tap the vast potential that remains are moving forward. New sites are farther from population centers and would thus incur higher transmission costs, but enthusiasm still runs high in some quarters.[6]

Yet many who have studied hydropower developments in Brazil claim that the construction program has developed a life of its own and that more rivers are being dammed than necessary. Part of the legacy of the military government, many dams now under construction would not be approved under today's stricter environmental regulations. The Balbina, for example, was ordered more than a decade ago, is not yet operational, and will flood an area of 1,554 square kilometers—half the size of Long Island and as much as required at another Brazilian dam (Tucurui) that produces 15 times as much power.[7]

These monster dams constitute some of the largest engineering projects in the world. The 12,600-megawatt Itaipu dam in Brazil is five miles long, and half as high as the Empire State Building. World Bank projections indicate that 223,560 megawatts of large hydro capacity will be added in developing countries between 1981 and 1995, more than half of it in Brazil, China, and India. This is equivalent to 225 large nuclear plants, or 82 percent of the world's nuclear capacity in 1986. Thirteen developing countries installed more than 40,000 megawatts of hydroelectric power between 1980 and 1985. (See Table 4–1.) But future growth is not likely to be as robust as anticipated because of the Third World debt crisis and the consequent shortage of investment capital.[8]

In the United States, which has the largest installed hydroelectric capacity, not a single new large dam was approved to receive federal funding between 1976 and 1986. For dams that receive federal dollars after 1986, local governments are having to put up half the money, a requirement that likely will cause many projects to be canceled and others to be reduced in size. After 85 years of building massive water projects in the western United States, the U.S. Bureau of Reclamation announced in 1987 that its mandate to tap new water supplies had virtually expired and that the agency would halve its work force over the next decade.[9]

Any large new supplies of hydroelectric power in the United States are likely to be imported from Canada. In 1986, transborder sales amounted to 12.7 billion kilowatt-hours, about 0.5 percent of U.S. electricity use. During the nineties, New Englanders may receive 7 percent of their electricity from Quebec, for a price of about $3 billion. Offers to sell additional hydroelectric power and to build new dams dedicated in part to exporting power have been made by British Columbia, Quebec, and Manitoba. The transactions hold special appeal to northeastern states with high electricity

Table 4-1. Thirteen Largest Additions to Hydroelectric Capacity in Developing Countries, 1980–85

| Country | Operating Capacity | | Increase |
	1980	1985	
		(megawatts)	
Brazil	27,267	42,762	15,495
China	20,318	25,788	5,470
Colombia	2,908	5,939	3,031
Romania	3,414	5,914	2,500
India	11,794	14,211	2,417
Mexico	6,491	8,626	2,135
Yugoslavia	6,115	7,841	1,726
Vietnam	330	1,800	1,470
Turkey	2,131	3,575	1,444
Pakistan	1,800	3,200	1,400
Zaire	1,077	2,477	1,400
Philippines	940	2,195	1,255
Nigeria	760	1,900	1,140
Total	85,345	126,228	40,883

SOURCE: World Bank, *A Survey of the Future Role of Hydroelectric Power in 100 Developing Countries* (Washington, D.C.: 1984).

prices and expensive nuclear plants.[10]

Huge dams can make substantial contributions to economic development in electricity-short developing countries, but as in any large electricity generating option there are trade-offs. Reservoirs inundate forests, farmland, and wildlife habitat and uproot entire communities of indigenous peoples. If China proceeds with its Three Gorges project—the world's largest at 13,000 megawatts—several million people will be displaced. An additional million people will be forced from their homes in central India if a project to build 3,000 dams in the Narmada Valley is pursued.[11]

Impounding a river radically changes the surrounding ecosystem. Nutrient-bearing sediments, instead of being deposited on agricultural floodplains and providing food for downstream fish,

accumulate behind turbines and diminish the capacity of reservoirs. Hydroelectric dams may also change the temperature and oxygen content of downstream waters, altering the mix of aquatic and riparian species. The use of ever higher dams—113 will exceed 150 meters by 1990—and the increased prevalence of seismic activity near reservoirs are leading many to believe that the combination of increased water pressure and unstable geological formations will result in more frequent and severe earthquakes. In tropical environments, reservoirs also expand the breeding grounds for the carriers of malaria, schistosomiasis, and river blindness.[12]

The reservoirs behind many large dams, especially those downstream from deforested watersheds, have silted up much faster than anticipated, substantially shortening the working life of projects, sometimes by decades, and altering their economics. (See Chapter 5 for further discussion of reservoir siltation.) In Colombia, an innovative program to transfer financial resources from the lowland beneficiaries of hydropower development to upland farmers is under way. A sales tax on electric power from major hydroelectric plants has been authorized to help stabilize upland watersheds through soil conservation and reforestation.[13]

Of 100 developing countries, 31 more than doubled their hydroelectric capacity between 1980 and 1985.

On a smaller scale, hydropower generation not connected to a central grid totaled nearly 10,000 megawatts worldwide in 1983. Most of these projects were in developing countries, but West Germany alone had 3,000 small units in operation. Frost & Sullivan, a market research firm, predicts that decentralized hydropower in stand-alone systems will generate 36,000 megawatts by 1991.[14]

A World Bank survey of 100 developing countries found that 31 had more than doubled their hydroelectric capacity between 1980 and 1985. At least 28 of these have small-hydropower programs. In Burundi, Costa Rica, Guatemala, Guinea, Madagascar, Nepal, Papua New Guinea, and Peru, small-hydropower potential exceeds total installed generating capacity from all sources in 1984. China leads the world in this field, with some 90,000 turbines supplying electricity to rural areas.[15]

Industrial countries are also starting to realize the contribution that small hydro projects can make. By 1985, private entrepreneurs in the United States had brought almost 1,000 megawatts of small hydropower on-line and electric utilities had installed more than twice that amount. Almost 60 percent of the total 3,200 megawatts came on-line during the eighties. Elsewhere, small dams that had fallen into disrepair are also being refurbished. Poland has begun to rehabilitate 640 small dams and in the Canadian province of Ontario, 570 formerly developed sites have been identified.[16]

As the manufacturers of turbine technology are found primarily in Europe and North America, hydro development in the Third World is often dependent on foreign equipment suppliers. These projects are capital-intensive, and foreign currency requirements mount rapidly. Limiting the tendency to overengineer projects can save several thousand dollars per kilowatt. To this end, China, Colombia, India, Indonesia, Nepal, Pakistan, and Thailand have all developed the capability to manufacture small turbines domestically. China also exports these turbogenerators to both industrial and developing countries.[17]

To operate well for many decades, hydro projects require sound management not just of equipment but of entire watersheds. Fragmented institutional structures impede enlightened management because each function of a watershed belongs to a different agency. As Brandeis University Professor Donald Worster writes in *Wilderness* magazine, "everybody wants a piece of [rivers], wants to siphon them off, dump wastes in them, drink from them, or move barges along them, but no one has ever been given overall charge of protecting their renewability."[18] Hydroelectric power will not be truly renewable until the functions of flood control, irrigation, transportation, power production, tree planting, fisheries management, and sanitation are coordinated with the goal of maintaining healthy and productive rivers.

NEW USES FOR BIOMASS

Biomass, derived directly or indirectly from plant photosynthesis, is a versatile fuel source capable of providing high-quality gaseous, liquid, and solid fuels as well as electricity. Primary sources include forestry and wood processing residues, crop residues and animal wastes, and energy crops. Though less than 1 percent of annual biomass growth is tapped for energy, it provides 15 percent of the energy used worldwide.[19]

An important distinction to make when assessing biomass-based systems is whether the process converts wastes and residues into fuel, which increases the efficiency of existing economic activity, or whether it instead requires the cultivation of biomass specifically for energy, which requires all the inputs of an agricultural or silvicultural production system.

Wood is the most widely used biomass energy source, with over half the wood cut each year being burned to produce energy. According to U.N. statistics, the world's largest fuelwood producers, in order, are India, Brazil, China, Indonesia, the United States, and Nigeria.[20]

Available energy potential from forest and timber industry residues was found by the International Energy Agency (IEA) to be highest in the United States. (See Table 4–2.) With proper management, a good number of countries can expand their fuelwood use without depleting natural forests. On average, about 25 percent of the wood entering the timber industry is available for conversion to energy.[21]

Many developing countries, on the other hand, are experiencing a severe wood shortage. In some regions, most notably sub-Saharan Africa, three quarters of harvested wood is burned, often inefficiently, for cooking. Unprece-

Table 4-2. Available and Recoverable Energy Potential from Agricultural, Forestry, and Timber Industry Residues, Selected Countries, 1979

| Country | Available Potential from Forestry and Timber Industry | Recoverable Potential | | Total | Share of Total Energy Requirements |
		Crop Residues	Animal Wastes		
	(million tons of oil equivalent)				(percent)
Turkey	5.9	5.4	1.5	12.8	41.7
Finland	8.6	0.4	0.2	9.2	36.8
Sweden	10.4	0.8	0.2	11.4	22.8
Canada	32.1	2.3	1.8	36.2	16.8
Austria	2.8	0.4	0.3	3.5	14.0
Spain	2.4	4.1	0.6	7.1	10.0
France	6.1	5.2	2.4	13.7	7.2
United States	68.5	20.2	5.0	93.7	5.2
West Germany	6.2	2.2	1.6	10.0	3.7
Japan	6.7	0.4	1.2	8.3	2.1

SOURCE: International Energy Agency, *Renewable Sources of Energy* (Paris: Organisation for Economic Co-operation and Development, 1987).

dented and unsustainable rates of forest clearing to provide agricultural and grazing land, timber supplies, and fuel have left nearly 100 million people suffering from an acute scarcity of fuelwood, and 1.2 billion more with unsustainable supplies. (See Chapter 5.) Wherever cutting exceeds regrowth, wood is no longer a renewable fuel.[22]

In the United States, industrial, commercial, and utility applications account for some two thirds of the wood used for energy. The remainder provides 10 percent of the nation's residential heating, warming 5.6 million homes exclusively and 21 million homes partially with wood. Almost half of all wood fuel is consumed by the pulp and paper industry, which meets more than 55 percent of its own energy needs. The second largest market is the lumber industry, and the fastest-growing sector is the non-forest-products industries. Users include electric utilities, industry giants such as Dow Corning and Proctor & Gamble, and companies formed specifically to take advantage of regional wood supplies by generating electricity and selling it to local utilities. (See Table 4–3.)[23]

Since 1983, four U.S. utilities have built wood-burning power plants each able to generate more than 45 megawatts of electricity; their combined output is enough to supply some 175,000 homes. According to a study conducted by the California Energy Commission, wood-fired boilers can be installed for about $1,340 per kilowatt, 20 percent less than a coal plant costs. Industrial-sector fuelwood users are greater in number and spread more evenly throughout the country. The largest market is in California, where almost two dozen 10–50 megawatt wood energy projects are on-line now and dozens more will be shortly. Nationwide, some 1,500 megawatts of power are already available or under construction.[24]

The untapped potential for using wood fuels remains great. One assessment found that each year the state of Virginia produces enough sawdust, logging residue, and unsalable low-quality trees to replace 42 percent of the oil and gas consumed in its industrial and commercial sectors. Thus far, little of this potential is harnessed, but industrial parks, colleges, hospitals, and a variety of other enterprises are likely to take the plunge once oil prices start creeping up again. Fuel costs are likely to remain low, especially if the supplier would otherwise be faced with mounting waste disposal charges.[25]

Wood-fired electricity is also being tried in smaller generating plants in the Third World. In the late seventies, 17 dendrothermal projects of 3 megawatts each were planned throughout the Philippines. Local farmers were to supply the fuel from leucaena plantations. Although British and French equipment for all 17 was delivered, only 4 plants were completed on schedule and just 2 are said to be operating reliably. The overly ambitious project was unable to garner sufficient financing, was blocked by bureaucratic infighting, and was based on excessively optimistic predictions of wood yields on marginal soils. A more modest effort might have succeeded.[26]

Crop residues and animal wastes are a substantial by-product of the food-producing agricultural sector, but diverse agricultural policies, marginal energy conversion economics, and alternative, nonenergy uses make assessing their potential difficult. An IEA study found that using the most energy-efficient processes available in 1979, agricultural wastes could contribute between 0.4 and 8.2 percent of total energy requirements in IEA member countries, with the exception of Turkey, where the contribution could equal 22.5 percent. Denmark, Greece, Ireland, Portugal, and Spain were considered able to meet at least 5

Table 4-3. United States: Selected Biomass-Fueled Electricity Generating Facilities

Project	Capacity	Fuel Source	Start-Up
	(megawatts)		
Forest Products Industry[1]			
Union Camp Corporation Franklin, VA	96	pulping waste, peanut shells	1937
Champion International Corp. Cantonment, FL	78	pulping waste, bark	1961
Manville Forest Products Co. West Monroe, LA	72	wood and pulping wastes	1961
Louisiana Pacific Corp. Antioch, CA	26	wood waste	1983
Electric Utilities			
Northern States Power Ashland, WI	72	forest residues[2]	1983
Burlington Electric Dept. Burlington, VT	50	forest residues	1984
Eugene Water & Electric Board Weyco Center, OR	46	mill residue	1983
Washington Water & Power Kettle Falls, WA	46	mill residues	1983
Independent Power Producers			
Ultrasystems Fresno, CA	27	forest, industry, and ag. residues	1988
Ultrasystems West Enfield, ME	27	forest residues	1986
Wheelabrator Energy Delano, CA	25	orchard prunings	1989
Alternative Energy Decisions Bangor, ME	17	forest and industrial residues	1986
Nontraditional Producers			
Lihue Plantation Kauai, HI	26	bagasse	1980
Dow Corning Midland, MI	22	wood chips	1982
Farmers Rice Milling Co. Lake Charles, LA	11	rice husks	1984
Proctor & Gamble Staten Island, NY	10	industrial residues, wood chips	1983

[1]Predominantly biomass-fueled. Sometimes supplemented with coal or natural gas.   [2]Multifuel capability, but has been burning mostly wood since 1983.
SOURCE: Worldwatch Institute, based upon Meridian Corporation, *Electric Power From Biofuels: Planned and Existing Projects in the United States* (Washington, D.C.: U.S. Department of Energy, 1985), news reports, and private communications.

percent of their total energy needs from crop residues and animal wastes.[27]

In the tropical Caribbean, where sugar is the major export crop but producers face depressed world markets, more efficient use of plant residues coupled with a switch to already tested fast-growing cane varieties that produce more biomass could significantly augment energy supplies. The amount of electricity available in Barbados, Cuba, the Dominican Republic, Guatemala, Guyana, and Honduras would increase severalfold. In Thailand, another sugar producer, cane residues could fuel 300 megawatts of electricity generating capacity and thereby add 25 percent to the annual value of the industry.[28]

The Hawaiian sugar industry started selling electricity in the late seventies and in 1985 supplied 58 percent of the power on the island of Kauai and 33 percent on the island of Hawaii. Sugar companies have installed at least 150 megawatts of capacity to burn bagasse, the residue after juice is extracted, and sell almost half of their power to the state's electric utilities. In the face of falling sugar prices, Hawaiian millers admit that without the revenues from electric power sales, their sugar production would have declined sharply by now. In the continental United States, another 80 megawatts' worth of bagasse-fired plants are operating in Florida and Louisiana.[29]

Researchers at Princeton University estimate that globally some 50,000 megawatts of gas turbine cogeneration units could be supported with the 1985 level of sugarcane production, based on recent advances in gas turbine technology. In the more than 70 developing countries that grow sugarcane, commercial use of gas turbines could provide as much electricity as the utilities in these nations now generate with oil. The cost of generating electricity with gas turbine cogeneration units would be lower than for most central-station alternatives.[30]

In most rice-growing developing countries, rice husks are the most abundant crop residue. Every five tons of rice milled produces one ton of husks with an energy content about the same as wood. At some mills, the residue is burned to generate mechanical energy and steam, but at many it is simply discarded. Using gasifiers or combustion systems, this byproduct can be used to power the mill, run irrigation pumps, electrify rural areas, or provide electricity to a central grid.[31]

Husk-fired steam power plants are operating in India, Malaysia, the Philippines, Suriname, Thailand, and the United States. A 10.5-megawatt plant in the Indian state of Punjab will operate year-round and burn 20 tons of rice husks per hour. As the world's second largest rice grower, India produces some 18 million tons of hulls annually, enough to justify investment in 500 megawatts of husk-fired generating capacity.[32]

Marginal land used to produce energy may be a boon in one setting, but deprive hungry people of land and food in another.

Vast paddy areas in Asia are not yet electrified, and mills in these areas depend on imported diesel engines and fuel. The total number of diesel engines used in small rice mills in developing countries probably exceeds 200,000, with almost 60,000 in Indonesia alone. A study at the Institute of Technology there calculated the country could save over $30 million each year by replacing relatively low-priced diesel fuel systems with newly developed husk gasifiers.[33]

Other crop residues that could be used more extensively include coconut shells, cotton stalks and ginning waste, peanut and other nut hulls, fruit pits, coffee and other seed hulls, and various sources of straw and fiber. Some food-processing plants already use these to provide on-site energy supplies, but there is vast untapped potential. Care must be taken when assessing the viability of these projects to consider the uses to which these materials would otherwise be put: Robbing the land of vital nutrients is counterproductive, whereas producing valuable energy from a by-product that would otherwise be discarded or attract pests is eminently sensible.[34]

Two additional sources of biomass include food surpluses and plants grown specifically to produce energy. The potential for fast-growing fuel plantations varies greatly among countries because of different resource endowments and sociopolitical systems. Marginal land used to produce energy may be a boon in one setting, but deprive hungry people of land and food in another.

The potential energy contribution of existing food surpluses is somewhat easier to determine, but difficult to extrapolate because of changing agricultural policies, market prices, and weather patterns. The IEA estimates that converting sugar surpluses in the European Community to ethanol would displace 2 percent of liquid petroleum fuels; in the United States, corn surpluses converted to ethanol could replace 7 percent of the country's gasoline consumption.[35]

Brazil and the United States have the two largest biomass-based ethanol programs in the world. In Brazil, sugarcane grown specifically for fuel was converted into 10.5 billion liters of ethanol in 1986, providing about half the country's automotive fuel. Most autos burn a gasoline-ethanol mixture that is 20-percent alcohol, but 29 percent of the nation's 10.6 million cars run on pure ethanol.[36]

The large alcohol-fuels program combined with successful offshore oil exploration has enabled Brazil, the largest Third World debtor, to curb its oil imports dramatically and conserve foreign exchange for investment and debt repayment. The program has created an estimated 475,000 full-time jobs in agriculture and industry, and indirectly another 100,000 jobs in commerce, services, and government. Mechanical power for cane crushers, electricity for on-site needs, and steam for alcohol distillation are provided by cogeneration units that burn the leftover bagasse.[37]

The United States, in contrast, relied on surplus corn and other grains for 90 percent of the 3 billion liters of ethanol it produced in 1987. More than 7 percent of the "gasoline" sold in the country was actually gasohol, a 1-to-9 blend. In the past, ethanol markets have been bolstered by generous tax advantages at the state and national levels and by regulations mandating the reduction of lead in gasoline. Ethanol can replace lead as an octane enhancer.[38]

Alcohol fuels are now gaining support as an air pollution control measure. More than 60 U.S. cities did not meet federal carbon monoxide and ozone standards by the end of 1987. Colorado is the first state to require motorists in its major cities to use gasohol during the winter, when pollution is worst. Officials expect carbon monoxide emissions to be cut by 12 percent. Federal legislation has been introduced that would require gasohol use nationally by 1992.[39]

Low prices for sugar and other food crops, a shortage of foreign exchange, and the desire for energy independence have prompted at least a dozen other countries to launch alcohol-fuels programs. Except for Canada and the Philippines, all projects to date are located in Latin America and Africa. Argentina has the world's third largest program, but is able to produce only one thirtieth as much ethanol each year as Brazil. In Europe, the primary factor behind increased interest in alcohol fuels is the region's tremendous agricultural surplus. Momentum is building to rechannel export subsidies into alcohol-fuels programs. France appears to be taking the lead, with Italy also carefully studying the possibility.[40]

POWER FROM THE SUN

Many techniques exist to collect, concentrate, and convert solar radiation into useful energy. The most basic methods use collectors to absorb relatively low-temperature heat and then transfer it to water or air. Somewhat more complicated are technologies that concentrate sunlight to produce higher temperature heat capable of producing steam or electricity. The third, most sophisticated use of solar power takes advantage of the photovoltaic effect to convert the sun's rays directly into electricity.

Northern Europeans started experimenting with solar collection devices in the seventeenth century to protect tropical plants brought home by explorers from distant lands. Two hundred years later, the first commercial solar product—a water heater—came on the market in the United States. From the early, bare water tanks placed in the sun, solar collector technology has advanced considerably. Today's models have transparent cover plates that trap heat without allowing it to be reradiated and that keep out cooling air currents. Once trapped, the heat is transferred to either water or air for immediate use or conveyed to a storage medium.

Water heating is still the most popular application of solar collectors. Swimming pools and residences are the largest markets, but commercial and industrial systems are becoming more common. In Cyprus, the world's largest solar energy user per capita, private industry has installed solar water heaters on 90 percent of the houses and on a significant portion of apartment buildings and hotels. In Israel, over 700,000 households, accounting for 65 percent of all domestic water heating, have simple systems that cost less than $500 per family to install. To encourage use of this low-cost technology and reduce dependence on imported petroleum, a 1980 law requires the use of solar water heating in all new residential buildings up to nine stories high.[41]

Four million solar water heaters are in use in Japan, including more-rudimentary devices produced in the sixties; 500,000 systems were sold in 1984 alone, the peak year for collector sales. And in the remote northwestern region of Australia, 37 percent of households rely on such systems.[42]

Through the mid-eighties, the world's largest collector market was in the United States, where 85 percent of 1984 sales were for residential applications— mostly in Sun Belt states. Unfortunately, by 1986 lower oil and gas prices and the elimination of residential renewable energy tax credits caused the bottom to fall out of the U.S. market. Sales volume dropped more than 70 percent from its 1984 level, and 28,000 of the estimated 30,000 employees in the industry lost their jobs.[43]

In Cyprus, private industry has installed solar water heaters on 90 percent of the houses.

The efficiency of flat-plate collectors has increased by 30 percent since 1977, but further gains, along with better materials, are being sought. Lightweight gels and polymer films for glazings and absorber components could cut collector mass sevenfold, thereby reducing production, distribution, and installation costs. If costs come down far enough, collectors to heat and cool air, which now account for only 10 percent of the market, may be more widely used.[44]

The second major category of solar technologies encompasses processes that concentrate the sun's rays to produce higher temperatures. Several approaches have been developed that achieve temperatures ranging from 85 to more than 3,000 degrees Celsius. The simplest systems, called solar ponds, rely on lined cavities filled with water and salt; as salt water is denser than fresh water, the salt water on the bottom absorbs heat while the water on the surface traps the underlying layer. The most complex systems incorporate thousands of mirrors that track the sun and reflect its light onto a central receiver through which passes a fluid that is used directly to produce heat or indirectly to turn a turbine and generate electricity.

Experimentation and some commercial development of these technologies is taking place in dozens of countries. Israel built the first small electricity generating solar pond in 1979 on the shores of the Dead Sea and in 1984 completed a larger, 5-megawatt pond. An Australian and an American company have each built smaller systems that came on-line in 1985 and 1986 respectively. Ormat Turbines, an Israeli firm, is involved in a project to build the world's largest solar pond, in southern California. The facility's 48-megawatt capacity would supply some 40,000 households with electricity.[45]

Other solar thermal energy technologies require significantly more equipment than ponds do. Each type depends on a differently shaped solar reflector to concentrate sunshine.

Trough systems use U-shaped mirrors to produce temperatures from 100 to 400 degrees Celsius. Concave parabolic dishes can yield temperatures as high as 1,700 degrees Celsius. Central receiver systems use computer-controlled mirrors to focus sunlight onto a tower. More than a half-dozen central receiver projects at least 1 megawatt in size have been built with government assistance. Trough and dish systems can be built in virtually any size, but central receivers are only likely to be economical for large-scale applications. (See Table 4–4.) (For further discussion of solar thermal technologies, see *State of the World 1985.*)

A trough system developed by Luz Engineering is enjoying the greatest commercial success. Five of their privately financed Solar Energy Generating Systems already operate in California's Mohave Desert and 14 more are scheduled to come on-line by 1992. The 30-megawatt plants supply enough electricity for some 10,000 U.S. homes, take only a year to construct, and with supplemental natural gas can consistently provide power during the peak afternoon hours, when utilities value it most. Capital costs have been halved since 1984 and are now comparable to those of recently built U.S. nuclear facilities. The Israeli government has signed a power purchase agreement for a 25-megawatt unit that will be built alongside other solar technologies at a demonstration test site. Serious negotiations are also under way to build a plant in the Indian state of Punjab.[46]

The third major category of solar technologies relies on the photovoltaic effect, discovered by Edmund Becquerel in 1839. This phenomenon causes electricity to be produced when light strikes certain materials. No moving parts or heat are required, just a parcel of light to jar an electron from its orbit, causing an electric current to flow. First used to

State of the World 1988

Table 4-4. Large Solar Thermal Electric Systems, Constructed or Planned, 1987

Project	Location	Technology	Capacity	Expected or Actual Completion Date
			(megawatts)	
Danby Lake[1]	California	Solar pond	48	—
Luz, SEGS 1	California	Trough Collector	14	1984
Luz, SEGS 2	California	Trough Collector	30	1985
Luz, SEGS 3	California	Trough Collector	30	1986
Luz, SEGS 4	California	Trough Collector	30	1986
Luz, SEGS 5	California	Trough Collector	30	1987
Luz, SEGS 6	California	Trough Collector	30	1988
Luz, SEGS 7–19	California	Trough Collector	450	1989–92
Luz, Eliat	Israel	Trough Collector	25	1990
Solar One	California	Central Receiver	10	1982
Mysovoye	Soviet Union	Central Receiver	5	1986
Bet Ha'Arava	Israel	Solar Pond	5	1984
Solarplant 1	California	Dish Receiver	4	1984
Themis	France	Central Receiver	2	1983
CESA-1	Spain	Central Receiver	1	1983
Sunshine 1	Japan	Central Receiver	1	1981
Sunshine 2	Japan	Hybrid	1	1981
Eurelios	Italy	Central Receiver	1	1981
Solntsye	Soviet Union	Central Receiver	1	1983

[1]Project on hold with no definite completion date.
SOURCE: Worldwatch Institute, based upon research reports, news articles, and private communications.

power spacecraft, the terrestrial market now dominates and grew at an average annual rate of 44 percent from 1980 to 1985. A 10-percent efficient photovoltaic (PV) cell about 100 square centimeters in size can produce 1 watt of electricity at noon on a clear day.[47]

In 1976, the average market price for a PV module was $44 per peak watt installed, and a half-million watts' (0.5 megawatts') worth were sold. Only a decade later, costs were down eightfold (in constant 1986 dollars) to $5.25 and shipments had climbed to 24.7 megawatts. (See Figure 4–1.)[48]

Half the photovoltaics sold in 1986 provide power to equipment or villages not hooked up to electric utility transmission lines. The communications industry accounts for the largest segment of this stand-alone market and relies on PV systems to relay radio, telephone, and television signals. Multinational communications companies, isolated villages, and researchers in the field all depend on this vital information link. Extending utility lines to these remote communication sites can cost between $23,000 and $46,000 per kilometer.[49]

Rural electrification projects that rely on photovoltaics are slowly spreading throughout the Third World. The greatest progress has taken place in the Dominican Republic and on islands in French Polynesia and Greece. Photovoltaics are used to provide refrigeration

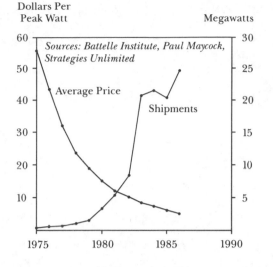

Dollars Per
Peak Watt   Megawatts

Sources: Battelle Institute, Paul Maycock,
Strategies Unlimited

Average Price

Shipments

**Figure 4-1. World Photovoltaic Shipments and
Average Market Prices, 1975-86**

for life-protecting vaccines, pumping for irrigation projects, and lighting and entertainment for homes. Worldwide, more than 15,000 homes receive their electricity from PV cells, and in West Germany a house was recently built with modules integrated into the roof tiles.[50]

The U.S. Coast Guard owns the largest number of stand-alone PV systems—10,525 used to power navigational aids. Each system saves taxpayers $5,000 because it eliminates the need to replace batteries at distant lighthouses and ocean buoys. The agency is seeking funding for another 6,400 units in 1988.[51]

The second largest, and newest, category of PV use is for consumer products. Sanyo, Sharp, and Fuji pioneered in this market, and in 1978 the world's first solar-powered calculator was sold. More than 200 million solar calculators were sold in 1987. Though still relatively novel, solar toys, clocks, and backyard lighting systems are all available commercially, a development made possible by the discovery of a radically new way of making PV cells. Japan has concentrated

on this new thin-film technology, and in 1985 surpassed the United States as the world's leading supplier of photovoltaic cells. Thin-film varieties have taken over one third of the market in just nine years.[52]

The United States produces thin-film cells primarily for power production. ARCO Solar, until 1986 the world's leading PV manufacturer, introduced the first thin-film power module in 1984. Japan only recently branched out into the power market, with systems designed for rural applications in developing countries. The United States, for the moment at least, retains its lead in sales of power generating equipment and provides most of the PV modules used by electric utilities and grid-connected customers—12 percent of the 1986 market.[53]

Photovoltaic sales will continue to grow at double-digit rates, but a dramatic and widespread increase in their use depends on continued progress in reducing costs, raising efficiencies, improving automated manufacturing techniques, and resolving degradation problems. At a June 1987 international meeting in California, experts concluded that at today's market price of $4–5 per watt, the annual worldwide market for photovoltaic cells was some $125 million. (Adding in the cost of other system components probably raises the 1986 sales figure to approximately twice that much.) These analysts speculated that when the price drops to $3, the market will go to $1.5 billion, and that when it dips below $1 per watt, sales would soar to about $100 billion annually.[54]

ARCO Solar is sufficiently convinced of the industry's growth potential that it is increasing the annual manufacturing capability at one of its plants to 5 megawatts. Another U.S. company, Chronar Corporation, recently announced plans to build a 10-megawatt production facility. When completed in late 1988, it will be the largest amorphous silicon PV manufacturing plant in the world.[55]

TAPPING THE WIND

Early in this century Danish industry relied on wind power for a quarter of its energy, and 150–200 megawatts of wind capacity were installed throughout the country. Cheap oil and gas and rural electrification displaced these early turbines, and wind energy did not make a resurgence until its rapid growth in the eighties. Electricity producing wind turbines (as opposed to windmills used for mechanical energy) are now installed in 95 countries from the tropics to the Arctic.[56]

Winds are created by the unequal heating of the earth's surface and atmosphere and by the regional differences in pressures that result. Local wind patterns are further influenced by the terrain. Most coasts on every continent and many inland areas are rich in wind resources that, if developed, could supply a major share of the world's electricity.

During the decade following the 1973 oil embargo, well over 10,000 wind machines were installed worldwide. Most of these units are small and used either to charge batteries or to produce minuscule amounts of electricity, usually less than 100 watts. The market in China for turbines in this size range has grown dramatically, from 1,282 units in 1982 to almost 11,000 in 1986. The demand was largely created by the recent availability of television reception nationwide but only a limited power grid. Five of the world's 10 largest manufacturers of small wind turbines in 1986 were Chinese.[57]

The international wind power generating market also expanded rapidly in the eighties, from 34 megawatts shipped in 1981 to 567 megawatts in 1985—a seventeenfold increase. By 1986, cumulative worldwide turbine sales reached $2.5 billion. The United States led in the installation of intermediate-size wind turbines, and in 1986 almost 90 percent of the wind energy produced worldwide was sold to the customers of two electric utilities in California. From 144 machines with a combined capacity of 7 megawatts in 1981, California had 16,769 turbines with an installed generating capacity of 1,463 megawatts by the end of 1987. (See Table 4–5.) These turbines were built in less time than required for traditional generating facilities, and, for the most recent machines, at a lower cost.[58]

Most of the turbines installed in the United States are in three mountain passes in California—Altamont, San Gorgonio, and Tehachapi. In Altamont and San Gorgonio, contrary to most other areas, wind speeds are highest in the summer, which coincides well with the peak seasonal demand placed on Sun Belt utilities. Seasonal variations and maximum wind speeds are important in assessing an area's wind power potential because the available power depends in part on the average wind speed. When it doubles, power output increases eightfold. Most systems are designed to operate in winds of 4–30 meters per second.[59]

Potential power output is also proportional to the area swept by each revolution of the turbine's rotor: Doubling the area doubles the output. Improved turbine design permitted the average rotor diameter of California's machines to reach 17 meters in 1984, resulting in a 50-percent increase in potential power output compared with the 1982 turbine models. Larger rotors effectively lower the capital costs of wind turbines because more electricity can be produced with fewer machines.[60]

Table 4-5. California Wind Farms, 1981–87

Year	Machines Installed (number)	Capacity Installed (megawatts)	Average Capacity (kilowatts)	Average Cost (dollars per kilowatt-hour)	Power Generated[1] (million kilowatt-hours)
1981	144	7	49	3,100	1
1982	1,145	64	56	2,175	6
1983	2,493	172	69	1,900	49
1984	4,687	366	78	1,860	195
1985	3,922	398	101	1,887	670
1986	2,878	276	96	1,250[2]	1,218
1987[2]	1,500	180	120	n.a.	1,600
Total	16,769	1,463	87	—	3,739

[1]Most wind machines are installed in the last half of a given year and do not produce substantial power until the next year. [2]Preliminary.

SOURCES: Pre-1985 from Paul Gipe, "An Overview of the U.S. Wind Industry," *Alternative Sources of Energy*, September/October 1985, based on California Energy Commission (CEC) data; 1985 and most 1986 from Sam Rashkin, CEC, Sacramento, Calif., private communication, October 6, 1987; preliminary estimates from Paul Gipe, American Wind Energy Association, Tehachapi, Calif., November 5, 1987.

During the early eighties many inexperienced manufacturers rushed to cash in on the heavily subsidized California market and built inadequately tested machines. Multiple repairs and major system overhauls soon bankrupted these firms. Those that remain have combined sturdy, reliable, proven windmill designs with new materials, knowledge, and manufacturing techniques to create more reliable products. In fact, today's turbines operate 80–98 percent of the time that the wind is blowing.[61]

The average size of turbines installed in California increased from 49 kilowatts in 1981 to 120 kilowatts in 1987. Many of the newest models have capacities of 150–750 kilowatts. Government-funded programs, however, started by promoting large, multimegawatt turbines. Eleven wind machines rated at 1,000 kilowatts or higher had been built as of 1985—seven in the United States, two in Sweden, and one each in Denmark and West Germany. Despite the dismal operating record of some large units, Canada, Denmark, the Netherlands, Sweden, the United Kingdom, and West Germany are building new multimegawatt machines. These governments, partly because of space constraints, are still advocating the use of large turbines, making them the centerpiece of R&D activity.[62]

The reverberations of the U.S. wind energy tax credit termination at the end of 1985 were felt by wind turbine suppliers worldwide. Outside the United States, Denmark was the hardest hit, as it supplies over half of California's turbines. In 1985, Danish manufacturers shipped more than 2,500 wind units to North America. Wind turbine exports, one of the country's most valuable, fell by half in 1986. U.S. suppliers also suffered setbacks and few U.S. manufacturers remain in business.[63]

The international wind turbine market peaked in 1985, and sales figures are unlikely to return to that level until the nineties. But despite the decline in the California market, interest in wind energy is growing rapidly in other areas of the world. The North American market is expected to gradually decrease in importance to about 50 percent of the global total by the early nineties. Europe will then account for 25 percent or more of the world market, absorbing at least 100 megawatts annually, and the remaining quarter will be geographically dispersed.[64]

Denmark, besides being the leading international supplier of intermediate-size wind turbines, with 7 of the world's top 10 manufacturers, has also built a domestic market. By mid-1987 installed capacity totaled 100 megawatts, including the first sea-based wind plant, on the east coast of Jutland. Although early wind development in Denmark relied almost exclusively on individual 55-kilowatt farm units connected to the central grid, the plan for the future is to build clusters of turbines in which each unit will be larger than 200 kilowatts. Elkraft and Elsam, the country's two utility power pools, expect to install an additional 100 megawatts' worth of turbines by 1991.[65]

The Chinese government is calling for wind farms with a total capacity of at least 100 megawatts to be built between 1990 and 1996. In the Netherlands, a five-year plan with the goal of installing 150 megawatts of capacity by 1992 is under way. By the end of the century, the government hopes to have 1,000 megawatts of capacity in place. Spain plans 45 megawatts by 1993 and Greece expects to install 80 megawatts' worth on islands. Smaller wind farms are also either installed or planned in Australia, Belgium, Israel, Italy, the Soviet Union, the United Kingdom, and West Germany.[66]

By far the most ambitious wind energy program belongs to the Ministry of Energy in India, which is pushing to have 5,000 megawatts of wind power generating capacity installed by both public and private developers by the year 2000. The country, which had virtually no wind turbines until 1985, now boasts as much installed capacity as California had in 1981 and is expected to be one of the most rapidly growing markets in the world. If the government achieves its goal, wind would supply more electricity by the end of the century than the country's somewhat optimistic nuclear program.[67]

Average costs for installed intermediate-size wind turbines have fallen by more than half since 1981, to some $800–1,200 per kilowatt. In many markets, such turbines are now competitive with traditional generating technologies. Costs are likely to be reduced further as more manufacturers start to mass-produce turbines.[68]

MAKING A CONTRIBUTION

Only periodically throughout history has reliance on renewable energy sources been interrupted by the discovery of apparently plentiful and cheap fuels, such as new deposits of coal, oil, natural gas, and uranium. But coal burning is warming the atmosphere and producing acid rain that is implicated in damaging 31 million hectares of forests in central Europe. Nuclear power is producing a legacy that will be hazardous for millennia. And oil wells are not replenishable on a human time scale.

Despite dwindling global supplies, many countries are increasing their dependence on the volatile Middle East. When oil prices resume their upward path, these nations may be more vulnerable to supply disruptions than they were in the seventies. A secure and stable energy future calls for an end to the squandering of a patrimony of hundreds of millions of years and a return to the elegance of renewable fuels.

A greater commitment to energy efficiency and expanded use of renewables are the most cost-effective approaches to mitigating these seemingly intractable problems. In addition, they will put the global economy on more stable footing. Building resilience into energy policies via efficiency and diversified, smaller scale supply options will help provide the flexibility needed to adapt to an unpredictable future.

Unfortunately, many energy policymakers, complacent after the oil price plunge of the mid-eighties, are not looking ahead. They became complacent as oil prices plunged in the mid-eighties. Developing countries are faced with the added constraint of large international debts and therefore little prospect to obtain financing for new energy projects.

A few countries appear to be moving in the right direction in their adoption of renewable energy. Brazil, for example, obtains almost 60 percent of its energy from a mix of renewables. In 1986, Brazil was the world's largest producer of alcohol fuels, the second largest producer of fuelwood, and the fourth largest producer of hydropower. Even the most modern sectors of the economy such as automobiles and steel production are dependent on these energy sources.[69]

Brazil demonstrates both the pitfalls and the promise of reliance on renewables. Many of the country's large hydro projects were approved without rigorous environmental assessments and without first tapping energy efficiency measures. In some cases residents were displaced and unique plant and animal species eradicated only to build generating capacity that went unused. Yet, other programs have resulted in real progress. One third of the steel manufactured in the country relies on charcoal for the smelting process. Fast-growing eucalyptus plantations provide most of the wood. Higher biomass yields and more efficient charcoal making and smelting processes will soon mean that just one

fifth as much land is required to support a given level of steel production as was required in the seventies.[70]

In India, slightly less than half the total energy is provided by renewables, but most of that is noncommercial, and often nonsustainable, use of fuelwood, agricultural wastes, and animal dung. The country's Department of Nonconventional Energy Sources recently developed a plan to increase the contribution of renewables by building 15,000 megawatts of renewably based electricity capacity by the year 2000. (This is in addition to the country's major commitment to large hydro plants.) Wind turbines and biomass technologies would make the greatest contributions, followed by small hydroelectric and solar thermal power stations and an even smaller share from biogas and municipal refuse facilities.[71]

In 1986, Brazil was the world's largest producer of alcohol fuels and the fourth largest producer of hydropower.

Several other countries also have plans to boost the share of energy they get from renewables. (See Table 4–6.) Denmark is pegging its hopes on wind turbines, Israel on solar technologies, and Japan on a range of renewables including solar, geothermal, and ocean technologies.

But success at this stage in the development of renewably based energy technologies cannot be judged simply on the share of energy provided or the number of megawatts installed. Technical improvements, including higher efficiencies, increased reliability, and the development of new designs and materials measure potential contribution. For many of the new technologies, monitor-

Table 4-6. Share of Total Primary Energy Requirements Supplied by Renewables in Selected Countries, 1984/85, With Projections to 2000

Country	1984/85	2000
	(percent)	
Brazil[1]	59.0	64.3
Norway	61.1	63.0
Japan	5.1	13.5
Australia	9.4	12.6
Israel	2.3	12.0
Denmark	2.0	10.0
Greece	5.9	8.9
United States	7.4	8.7
West Germany	2.5	5.5

[1]Figures for 1983 and 1993.
SOURCES: Ministry of Mines and Energy, "Energy Self-Sufficiency: A Scenario Developed as an Extension of the Brazilian Energy Model," Government of Brazil, Brasília, 1984; Strategies Unlimited, "International Energy and Trade Policies of California's Export Competitors," California Energy Commission, Sacramento, Calif., 1987; Scott Sklar, "International Trade Policy for the Renewable Energy Industries: An Assessment," *Solar Today*, March/April 1987; International Energy Agency, *Energy Policies and Programmes of IEA Countries: 1986 Review* (Paris: Organisation for Economic Co-operation and Development, 1987).

ing cost reductions also indicates how much work remains prior to achieving widespread commercial use.

The commitment that governments make to R&D on renewables can be measured in several ways. Looking strictly at the dollar figure gives an indication of the amount spent on technical advances. In the United States, still the leader in this category, research and development funding for renewables peaked in 1980 at $900 million (1986 dollars). Appropriations have since fallen 80 percent, with no rebound in sight.[72]

Total funding on renewable energy throughout IEA member countries has fallen 64 percent since its 1980 peak. Greece and Portugal are the only countries whose budgets have increased. In Japan, Switzerland, and Turkey the drop has been 25 percent or less; in Sweden, West Germany, and the United Kingdom, less than half.[73]

Widely fluctuating research and development support for new technologies thwarts progress. Without reliable funding, the needed long-term programs are difficult to plan and more complicated to implement. That is not to say that there should be no midcourse corrections. The learning process requires that new knowledge be accompanied by changes in R&D programs, but sudden cuts in ongoing research projects and staff can be devastating.

The share of total energy R&D funds going to renewables indicates their relative political support and perhaps the share of new energy supplies that they will contribute. Renewables have strong political backing in Greece, for example, which devotes 63 percent of its energy R&D budget to renewables and does not have a nuclear program. Japan, which does have a large nuclear program, devotes only 4 percent of its energy R&D budget to renewables, but nonetheless outspends Greece almost 10 to 1. (See Table 4–7.) Japan has 12 times as many people and an economy 17 times larger than Greece's.[74]

Perhaps the best measure for comparing overall government commitment to renewables in various countries is per capita expenditures. This factors out population size and funding support for other technologies. Sweden, which is out in front in this category, focuses its efforts on biomass—wood, energy crops, and agricultural surpluses. Because of a national referendum, Sweden must phase out all 12 of its nuclear plants by 2010.[75]

Following the nuclear accident at Chernobyl, government support for renewable energy technologies—particularly those that rely on solar power—has apparently increased in Italy, Japan,

Table 4-7. Government R&D Spending on Renewables in Selected Countries, 1986

Country	Renewables R&D Spending	Share of Energy R&D Budget	Spending Per Capita
	(million dollars)	(percent)	(dollars)
Sweden	17.3	21.8	2.06
Switzerland	10.2	14.7	1.57
Netherlands	17.0	10.6	1.17
West Germany	65.9	11.6	1.09
Greece	9.7	63.2	0.97
Japan	99.2	4.3	0.82
United States	177.2	7.8	0.73
Italy	29.5	3.9	0.52
Denmark	2.6	17.8	0.51
Spain	19.4	27.6	0.50
United Kingdom	16.6	4.4	0.29

SOURCE: International Energy Agency, *Energy Policies and Programmes in IEA Countries, 1986 Review* (Paris: Organisation for Economic Co-operation and Development, 1987); Population Reference Bureau, *1986 World Population Data Sheet* (Washington, D.C.: 1986).

Spain, and West Germany. The Swiss government's solar budget is expected to triple by 1990. Denmark and the Netherlands are pushing wind turbines, and Greece and India are launching broad-based renewable energy programs that will rely on a variety of sources.[76]

In Japan, the government and private sector work together closely in developing new technologies. Each contributes monetarily, the government often eases regulatory and fiscal restraints, and the private sector regularly reports—with one voice—on its progress and needs. The New Energy Foundation is a nonprofit organization that includes among its members virtually all the major Japanese manufacturers of photovoltaics. Besides assessing industry progress and pointing out obstacles to growth, it predicts plant and equipment investments needed to achieve cost goals over 10- and 20-year periods. Its recommendations carry significant weight in discus-

sions with the government concerning research priorities.[77]

A renewable source that has made remarkable strides in recent years because of R&D support is geothermal energy. Derived from the heat of the earth's core, its use is growing rapidly in many regions. New extraction techniques promise to expand the geographical range in which it can be used.

With some 5,000 megawatts of capacity installed worldwide, more than half of it since 1980, geothermal prospects look bright. Close to half the installed capacity is in the United States, followed by the Philippines, Mexico, Italy, and Japan. At least a dozen other countries have also built plants. More than 2,000 additional megawatts are planned to enter service by 1991, and a recent report by the Electric Power Research Institute found that North American capacity alone could reach from 4,200 to 18,700 megawatts by the year 2000.[78]

Some of the relatively young renewable energy technologies that have made substantial progress in recent years, but that have not achieved the overoptimistic goals set by many in the seventies, include advanced solar collectors, wind turbines, and photovoltaics. Solar collectors and wind turbines have recently become economical in many settings, but institutional barriers and a financial community whose perceptions lag several years behind technical advances are slowing their penetration of energy markets. In future decades, PV technologies are likely to play a major role.

Technologies with a long-term potential that require additional research to demonstrate their feasibility and reduce their cost include biochemical methods of converting biomass feedstocks, various solar thermal configurations, and systems that make use of the temperature difference between surface and deep ocean waters. Development of an economical chemical storage method, or battery, that could stockpile electricity for later use would also be a boon for renewables. Wind and sunlight are not always available when needed, but if their energy could be stored for later use, their intermittent nature would pose less of a problem.

The pace of development of many renewable energy technologies and the rate of adoption of efficiency measures will depend upon the level of R&D funds from both public and private sources, and upon institutional restructuring of the energy sector. (See Chapter 2.) Efficiency is capable of major energy savings today. Some renewable energy technologies, primarily hydropower and biomass, are also widely available commercially. Wind turbines will be internationally widespread before the turn of the century, and photovoltaics may be right on their heels.

A sustainable energy path will provide the flexibility to cope with an uncertain global future. Policymakers ready to make the change need to improve market pricing signals, open up the energy supply and energy savings business, and reinvigorate research and development programs. Educating their colleagues as well as consumers to see the true present value of future savings, and tailoring financial practices to reflect this vision, will be difficult. Nations that accept the challenge will be rewarded with increased energy security, more stable economies, and a healthier global environment.

5

Reforesting the Earth

Sandra Postel and Lori Heise

Before the dawn of agriculture, some 10,000 years ago, the earth boasted a rich mantle of forest and open woodland covering some 6.2 billion hectares. Over the centuries, a combination of land clearing for crop production, commercial timber harvesting, cattle ranching, and fuelwood gathering has shrunk the earth's forests to some 4.2 billion hectares—a third less than existed in pre-agricultural times.[1]

For centuries, this reduction in the earth's biological stock hindered human progress little, if at all. Indeed, the clearing of trees to expand food production and the harvesting of forest products were vital aspects of economic and social development. But the relentless loss of tree cover has recently begun to impinge directly on the economic and environmental health of numerous nations, mostly in the Third World. Combined with concerted efforts to protect remaining forests, large-scale reforestation—a seeming anomaly for a planet where woody vegetation still covers 40 percent of the land—now appears essential to improving the human prospect.

Most tree planting efforts over the last several decades have aimed at increasing supplies of marketable timber, pulp, and fuelwood for cities—forest products that yield obvious economic benefits. By contrast, reforestation for reasons that lie outside the monetized economy has been vastly underattended. Yet trees quite literally form the roots of many natural systems. With the inexorable march of deforestation, the ecological integrity of many areas is disintegrating—causing severe soil loss, aggravating droughts and floods, disrupting water supplies, and reducing land productivity.

Trees are also a vital component of the survival economy of the rural poor. Hundreds of millions of people rely on gathered wood to cook their meals and heat their homes. For them, lack of access to wood translates into reduced living standards and, in some cases, directly into malnutrition. In addition, trees and soils play a crucial role in the global cycling of carbon, the importance of which has been magnified by the emergence of carbon dioxide–induced climate change as arguably the most threatening environmental problem of modern times.

Efforts to slow deforestation certainly deserve redoubled support. But even if forest clearing miraculously ceased today, millions of hectares of trees would still have to be planted to meet future fuelwood needs and to stabilize soil and water resources. Increased planting to satisfy rising demands for paper, lumber, and other industrial wood products—an issue beyond the scope of this chapter—is also crucial. Expanding forest cover for all these reasons will reduce pressures on remaining virgin forest, helping to preserve habitats and thereby safeguard the earth's biological diversity. (See Chapter 6.) At the same time, it will mitigate the buildup of atmospheric carbon dioxide, which gives industrial countries sound reason to step up support for tree planting in the Third World.

Successfully reforesting large areas of degraded lands, however, will require much more than financial commitments from governments and international lending agencies. It will take a shift in emphasis from government foresters establishing and maintaining commercial plantations to the much more complex tasks of starting nurseries in thousands of villages, and encouraging the planting of multipurpose trees along roads, on farms, and around houses. Only by garnering the knowledge, support, and human energy of rural people themselves—and planting to meet their basic needs—is there any hope of success.

Tree Cover Trends

Dramatic changes in regional forest cover historically reflect powerful societal transformations. Beginning in the sixteenth century, the expanding agricultural and industrial needs of Renaissance societies spurred the clearing of large tracts of forest in Western Europe. France, once 80 percent forested, had trees covering only 14 percent of its territory by 1789. Both the French and the English so depleted their domestic forest resources that they were forced by the mid-seventeenth century to conduct a worldwide search for ship timbers in order to maintain their maritime superiority. Similarly, forest cover in what is now the contiguous United States totaled some 385 million hectares in 1630, about when the Pilgrims arrived. As colonization spread along the eastern seaboard and gradually westward, forests dwindled. By 1920, trees covered 249 million hectares, more than a third less than when European settlement began.[2]

Surprisingly little is known with certainty about the state of forest resources today.

Despite growing recognition of the importance of forests to the economic and ecological health of nations, surprisingly little is known with certainty about the state of forest resources today. Many countries have not fully inventoried their forests, and the data that do exist vary widely in quality. A 1982 study by the U.N. Food and Agriculture Organization (FAO) still provides the best information available on tropical forests, even though much of the data is more than a decade old. Combining FAO's estimates with those of a 1985 forest assessment by the U.N. Economic Commission for Europe and with various individual country reports yields a rough picture of the global forest resource base. (See Table 5–1.)

Closed forest, where the shade from tree crowns prevents substantial growth of grass, covers nearly 3 billion hectares worldwide. Another 1.3 billion hectares are open woodlands, including, for example, the wooded savannah of Africa and the cerrado in Brazil. Collectively,

Table 5-1. The Global Forest Resource Base, Circa 1980

Region	Closed Forest	Open Woodland	Total Forest	Forest Fallow and Shrubland	Total
	(million hectares)				
Asia (except China)	237	61	298	62	360
Africa	236	508	744	608	1,352
Latin America	739	248	987	313	1,300
North America	459	275	734	—	734
Europe	137	22	159	—	159
Soviet Union	792	137	929	—	929
China	122	15	137	—	137
Oceania	223	76	299	47	346
World	2,945	1,342	4,287	1,030	5,317

SOURCES: U.N. Food and Agriculture Organization/Economic Commission for Europe, *World Forest Resources 1980* (Rome: 1985); China data from China Scientific and Technological Information Research Institute, *China in the Year 2000* (Beijing: Science and Technology Documents Publishers, 1984).

forested lands cover approximately 4.3 billion hectares, an area almost triple that in crops. Shrubland and forest regrowth on temporarily abandoned cropland bring the total area supporting woody vegetation to more than 40 percent of the world's land.[3]

The most worrisome finding of FAO's assessment was that tropical trees were being cut much faster than reforestation or nature were replacing them. For tropical regions as a whole, 11.3 million hectares were cleared annually in the early eighties, while only 1.1 million hectares of plantations were established. Thus 10 hectares were being cleared for every 1 planted. In Africa, the ratio was 29 to 1; in Asia, 5 to 1. Even these alarming figures probably underestimate the extent of forest loss in particular regions, since tree planting is often highly concentrated, while cutting is widespread.[4]

Recent data for individual countries suggest that forest cover trends in some regions are even bleaker than FAO's sobering assessment indicates. Satellite imagery of five states in Brazil, for example, shows that deforestation in parts of the Amazon has proceeded much faster than estimates for the entire region suggest. Likewise, Landsat data released by the National Remote Sensing Agency of India reveal that India's forest cover declined from 16.9 percent in the early seventies to 14.1 percent in the early eighties, an average loss of 1.3 million hectares per year. FAO placed India's forest cover in 1980 at 17.4 percent—approximately 11 million hectares too high—and underestimated the true rate of deforestation almost ninefold.[5]

Fortunately, reforestation is also proceeding somewhat faster than official estimates suggest. Spontaneous tree planting by villagers around farm fields, as windbreaks, or along roadways is frequently not counted. Indeed, forestry statistics typically ignore "trees outside of forests," even though in many areas they are the primary source of fuelwood, fodder, and rural construction materials. In Kenya, for instance, the number of trees planted by villagers exceeds the number established in government plantations. And in Rwanda, scattered trees planted by rural people collectively cover some 200,000 hectares, more than the combined area of the country's remaining natural forest and all state and communal plantations.[6]

Nonetheless, the loss of forest cover in tropical countries remains rampant. Conversion of forest to cropland is by far the leading direct cause. Population growth, inequitable land distribution, and the expansion of export agriculture have greatly reduced the area of cropland available for subsistence farming, forcing many peasants to clear virgin forest to grow food. These displaced cultivators often follow traditions of continuous cropping that are ill suited to fragile forest soils. Eventually, the soils become so depleted that peasant colonists must clear more forest to survive.

Indigenous "shifting cultivators" clear new fields every few years, allowing forest regrowth to restore soil fertility before they return to clear and plant again several years later. But even this once-sustainable practice is being undermined as population pressures force farmers to recultivate land before it has recovered. FAO estimates that the breakdown of traditional shifting cultivation patterns is responsible for 70 percent of closed forest clearings in tropical Africa, nearly 50 percent in tropical Asia, and 35 percent in tropical America.[7]

Population pressures have also transformed fuelwood collection into an unsustainable practice. Given a choice, villagers generally gather dead wood and branches for fuel; they only cut live wood if nothing else is available or if they are converting wood to charcoal for urban markets. Fuelwood collection is thus an agent of forest destruction primarily in the arid woodlands of Africa, where population density is high and the natural growth rate of vegetation is low, and around large cities of Asia and Africa, where concentrated demand overtaxes available tree stock. Recent Landsat data show that in less than a decade forest cover within 100 kilometers of India's major cities dropped by 15 percent or more; Delhi lost a staggering 60 percent.[8]

Consumer demand in temperate countries fosters tropical forest depletion as well. Industrial countries' appetite for tropical hardwoods has encouraged many Third World governments to "mine" their forests to earn vital foreign exchange. As loggers selectively fell commercially valuable tree species—which sometimes account for less than 5 percent of any given hectare—they often destroy between 30 and 60 percent of unwanted trees as well. Roughly two thirds of the logging—and the damage—has occurred in Southeast Asia, although logging is likely to increase in Latin America as Asian forests become depleted.[9]

One additional agent of forest destruction operates in Latin America: the lure of cattle ranching. Between 1961 and 1978, pasture in Central America expanded 53 percent while forests and woodlands declined 39 percent. Much of this conversion was driven by U.S. demand for cheap beef, although in recent years Central American beef exports have dropped in response to declining U.S. beef consumption, escalating tensions in El Salvador, and the U.S. trade embargo against Nicaragua. Similarly, by the late seventies an estimated 1.5 million hectares of pasture had been established in the Brazilian Amazon. In 1979, Brazil eliminated some of the incentives that had spurred clearing for pasture; alas, forest clearing continues as a way of establishing claims in Brazil's highly speculative land market.[10]

Pressures on temperate forests have waned substantially following several centuries of clearing for agriculture. Forest cover in most European countries is now fairly stable; in some, it has even been increasing as marginal agricultural land reverts to woodland and as conscious efforts are made to plant trees. Since the early sixties, government and private plantings in the United Kingdom have increased net forest cover an average of 30,000–40,000 hectares per year. In France, forest area has risen substantially from its historic low of 14 percent in 1789; about a quarter of the country is now forested.[11]

Unfortunately, chemical stresses from air pollution and acid rain today place a substantial share of European forests at risk. Trees covering some 31 million hectares in central and northern Europe are showing signs of damage linked to air pollutants. (See Chapter 1.) Scientists do not know how extensive the damage will become, but it could substantially offset recent gains made in expanding the continent's forested area.[12]

As in Europe, forest cover in the contiguous United States was comparatively stable during most of this century, following the loss of 136 million hectares between 1630 and 1920. During the last two decades, however, forest area has declined as widening grain export markets encouraged conversion of forest to cropland and as urban and industrial development encroached on woodland. In 1982, forests covered 233 million hectares of the contiguous states—a 10-percent drop from 1963, and less than existed in 1920, the previous low point.[13]

Chemical stresses from air pollution and acid rain today place a substantial share of European forests at risk.

In the Third World, nothing in prospect suggests that forest cover will stabilize anytime soon, as it has in many industrial countries. The forces behind deforestation remain strong, and planting efforts are woefully inadequate to reverse the loss of tree cover.

MEETING FUELWOOD NEEDS

Energy planners in developing countries face a markedly different set of challenges over the coming decades than their counterparts in industrial countries. Much of the Third World remains tightly wedded to wood as a primary energy source, either in its raw form or after conversion to charcoal. As wood supplies in the countryside and around cities continue to dwindle, growing numbers face a deepening energy crisis. Even after more than a decade of increasing recognition of the problem, only halting progress has been made toward satisfying future fuelwood demands.

More than two thirds of all Third World people rely on wood for cooking and heating. Rural dwellers depend on wood almost exclusively, even in oil-rich Nigeria. In many countries—including most of Africa—wood not only dominates household energy use, it provides more than 70 percent of energy used for all purposes. (See Table 5–2.)[14]

Unfortunately, data characterizing the fuelwood gap are as out of date as those on tropical forest trends. According to FAO, in 1980 nearly 1.2 billion people in developing countries were meeting their fuelwood needs only by cutting wood faster than it was being replaced. Nearly 100 million people—half of them in tropical Africa—could not meet their minimum needs even by overcutting the woodlands around them. FAO projected that by the year 2000, the number of people lacking wood or overcutting would reach nearly 2.4 billion, more than half the projected developing-world population.[15]

Table 5-2. Share of Total Energy Use Provided by Wood, Selected Countries, Early Eighties

Country	Wood Share of Total Energy Use
	(percent)
Burkina Faso	96
Kenya	71
Malawi	93
Nigeria	82
Sudan	74
Tanzania	92
China	> 25[1]
India	33
Indonesia	50
Nepal	94
Brazil	20
Costa Rica	33
Nicaragua	50
Paraguay	64

[1]Includes agricultural wastes and dung in addition to wood and charcoal.
SOURCE: Worldwatch Institute, based on various sources.

The human and ecological costs of wood scarcity already are high. In rural parts of the Himalayas and the African Sahel, women and children spend between 100 and 300 days a year gathering fuelwood. Boiling water becomes an unaffordable luxury, and quick-cooking cereals replace more nutritious but slower-cooking foods, such as beans. Where fuelwood is critically scarce, people often have no choice but to divert dried dung and crop residues from fields to cookstoves, a practice that diminishes soil fertility and depresses crop yields. In Nepal, for example, this diversion reduces grain yields an estimated 15 percent.[16]

Rapid urbanization will only magnify the ecological consequences of increasing fuelwood scarcity. City dwellers tend to rely on charcoal rather than wood because its light weight makes it more economical to transport from the countryside. When wood is converted to charcoal in traditional earthen pits, more than half the primary wood energy is lost. This means that every villager who moves to a city and switches from wood to charcoal equals, in energy terms, two people. Even though urban areas have traditionally been less dependent on fuelwood, urbanization could soon make cities pivotal to national fuelwood strategies. Indeed, the World Bank estimates that by 2000, the urban areas of West Africa will account for 50–70 percent of the region's total fuelwood consumption.[17]

Experts generally agree that a successful strategy to meet the fuelwood needs of the Third World must include increasing the productivity of natural forests; making better use of wood now wasted, including logging residues and trees cleared for cropland; raising the efficiency with which wood is burned; and planting more trees. The World Bank has calculated that fuel substitution and the use of more efficient kilns and cookstoves could reduce fuelwood needs in the year 2000 by about a fourth. Eliminating the remaining gap between projected supply and demand would require planting the equivalent of 55 million hectares of high-yielding fuelwood plantations, or 2.7 million hectares per year, given a base year of 1980. If the needed number of trees were planted less intensively on farms, around houses, and in woodlots, planting efforts would involve an area at least four times as large. Actual planting for fuelwood has averaged about 550,000 hectares annually, a fifth of what is needed.[18]

More than a decade of experience with so-called communal and farm forestry projects has shown clearly that inspiring large-scale planting of trees is no easy task. The international donor community rightly recognized during the seventies that Third World villagers themselves formed the only labor force large enough to plant trees on the vast areas needed. In many cases, however, rural people were reluctant to participate in communal planting because they had no idea how the resulting benefits would be shared. Often their needs and ideas were not solicited, nor were they involved in the selection of tree species to be planted. Perhaps the greatest lesson of the first generation of fuelwood projects was that villagers rarely were motivated to plant trees exclusively for fuelwood.

To outsider observers, it seems irrational for people faced with an energy crisis to be reluctant to plant trees for fuel. But for most rural dwellers in the Third World, fruit, poles, fodder, and shade are higher priorities. They know that wood, in the form of trimmings and dead branches, will be a secondary benefit of plantings for these other purposes. Moreover, people do not always perceive the national "fuelwood gap" that so concerns energy planners. They may be cutting wood over and above a sustainable level, yet still not be experiencing an unacceptable shortage. And in rural areas where fuelwood is not part of the cash economy, the cost of increasing scarcity is measured in women's time, something that may have little value to male decision makers.

The key to mobilizing villagers is to promote multipurpose trees that meet their immediate needs while also increasing the woody biomass available for fuel. Particularly promising is the potential of agroforestry—the combined production of crops and trees—to raise crop yields while providing fuelwood and other useful products. Nitrogen-fixing trees planted in shelterbelts or interspersed with crops, for example, can enhance soil fertility, increase soil moisture, and reduce erosion.

Agroforestry programs offer a number of advantages over more traditional approaches to addressing the fuelwood crisis. They typically cost only 10–20 percent as much as government-established fuelwood plantations. Although yields per hectare may be higher in plantations, agroforestry often results in greater wood production per planted tree. Through pruning techniques known as coppicing and pollarding, a single tree can yield 5–10 times the wood volume that a plantation tree would yield upon felling. Since trees are grown on farms, agroforestry can cover significantly more area than plantations. And in contrast to communal woodlot projects, agroforestry does not pose problems with shared work loads, division of benefits, or the displacement of other productive uses of common land, such as grazing.[19]

Of course, agroforestry does not address the fuelwood needs of the millions of rural people who do not own land. Traditionally, they have had to collect wood from common lands or steal it from forest reserves. Providing fuel for the landless may well be the greatest energy challenge facing Third World governments today.

People do not always perceive the national "fuelwood gap" that so concerns energy planners.

In India, the government of West Bengal addressed this problem by allocating more than 5,000 hectares of denuded forestland to landless families for cash-crop tree farming. Though families were not ceded title to the land, they were granted ownership of the trees. To encourage participation, the Forest Department supplied free seedlings, fertilizer, technical assistance, and insecticide, and it offered small cash incentives based on the number of trees surviving after three years. The families harvested the wood for sale after five years, and with the proceeds bought small parcels of land suitable for farming. While the trees matured, villagers collected twigs and branches for fuel. Where a strong commercial market for wood exists and sufficient degraded forestland is available, such a strategy can bring nonproductive land into use while providing the landless poor with both fuelwood and added income.[20]

Meeting future fuelwood needs will depend as much on managing demand as on increasing supply. Many policies that could significantly reduce demand attack the broader economic and social conditions that underlie fuelwood shortages. If birth rates today in Africa were no higher than those in South Asia, for example, Africa's demand for fuelwood 40 years from now would be reduced by as much as 30 percent.[21]

Improving the efficiency of Third World cookstoves is also crucial. Such efforts will never solve the fuelwood crisis; population growth would soon outstrip even the most ambitious dissemination program. But improved stoves can benefit individual households while collectively relieving pressures on natural woodlands until tree planting programs take hold.

Particularly promising are prospects for reducing wood consumption in cities, where rising wood and charcoal prices provide a powerful incentive to invest in efficiency. An improved model of the traditional charcoal jiko in Kenya can halve fuel use. For the average Nairobi family spending 170 shillings (about $8.25) a month on charcoal, the stove pays for itself in just two months.[22]

In rural households, where wood is gathered rather than purchased, no direct economic advantage exists to boosting wood-burning efficiency. Yet women, who spend much time collecting wood, have an incentive to construct improved stoves if they can do so from free, locally available materials. A particularly successful program in Burkina Faso promotes an upgraded version of the traditional three-stone cookstove, surrounded by a cylindrical shield made of mud, dung, and chaff. The new model cuts wood use by 35–70 percent, takes only a half-day to make, and costs virtually nothing. By April 1986, more than 83,500 of these improved stoves were in use.[23]

STABILIZING SOIL AND WATER RESOURCES

"What do the forests bear? Soil, water, and pure air." So goes a slogan of India's Chipko movement, a nonviolent resistance campaign begun in the early seventies to save trees in the Himalayas. The motto reflects well a growing awareness of the role forests play in vital ecological functions: stabilizing soils, conserving nutrients, and moderating water supplies. Unfortunately, deforestation and poor land use practices in many parts of the Third World are undermining these support services at a rapid rate.[24]

Just how much ecological disruption forest clearing causes depends on a number of factors, including topography, rainfall patterns, soil characteristics, geologic conditions, and how the land is used and treated following clearing. In general, forests help anchor soils; thus the loss of tree cover—especially from steeply sloping hillsides—can lead to large losses of topsoil. Besides diminishing upland productivity, such erosion transfers sediment to river channels, which aggravates local flooding and can contribute to the premature silting of reservoirs downstream.[25]

The effects of forest clearing on water supplies seem much more variable and uncertain. In most cases, removing trees increases an area's available water supply, since the amount of water lost to the atmosphere through evapotranspiration decreases. If overgrazing or poor crop production practices follow forest clearing, however, soils can compact and lose some of their ability to absorb rainwater. In such cases, more water tends to run over the land surface rather than soaking into the subsurface, where it can be stored and released more gradually. In West Africa, for example, runoff rates recorded from some cultivated and bare soils exceeded those from forest twentyfold. Depending on the intensity and duration of rainfall, the loss of soil infiltration capacity can also increase flooding.[26]

In West Africa, runoff rates recorded from some cultivated and bare soils exceeded those from forest twentyfold.

Perhaps nowhere are the destructive effects of flooding and siltation more evident than in South Asia, especially in the heavily populated plains of the Ganges and Brahmaputra rivers. Sorting out human-induced hazards from natural causes in such a region is difficult. The Himalayas, where these rivers originate, are a geologically young and active mountain chain that is naturally prone to landslides and massive erosion. Even if the hills remained entirely cloaked in virgin forest, the intense monsoon rains undoubtedly would cause severe flooding in the plains below.[27]

Yet some observers believe flooding has worsened with forest destruction throughout the subcontinent. Researchers at the Centre for Science and Environment in New Delhi estimate that the flood-prone area in India now totals 59 million hectares, more than double a government estimate for the late sixties of 25 million hectares. Between 1913 and 1978, the peak flood level of the Brahmaputra at one monitoring point rose an average of 30.5 centimeters per decade, or nearly 2 meters over the 65-year period. According to these researchers, "We are no longer dealing with disaster events but disaster processes."[28]

Likewise, much of the sedimentation of river beds and reservoirs results from natural erosive activity. But careless tree felling and forest clearing in upland watersheds can exacerbate the problem. In the Philippines, researchers estimate that 1.4 million hectares of upland watershed have been denuded, primarily through uncontrolled logging and unsustainable shifting cultivation practices. Echo sounding measurements show that between 1967 and 1980, the sedimentation rates of the Ambuklao and Binga reservoirs more than doubled. (See Table 5–3.) By the late seventies, officials already were estimating

Table 5-3. The Philippines: Sedimentation Rates in Two Major Reservoirs, 1967–80

Reservoir	Annual Sedimentation Rate		Change
	1967	1980	
	(cubic meters per square kilometer)		(percent)
Ambuklao	3,647	8,071	+121
Binga	2,857	5,844	+105

SOURCE: Nicomedes D. Briones and Jose P. Castro, "Effective Management of a Tropical Watershed: The Case of the Angat River Watershed in the Philippines," *Water International*, December 1986.

that silting would halve the Ambuklao project's useful life.[29]

Similarly, in Central America, where forest cover has dwindled from 60 percent of the region's territory in 1960 to 40 percent in 1980, erosion is rampant in many upland watersheds. Heavy siltation has clogged hydroelectric reservoirs, irrigation canals, and coastal harbors. Revenue losses from sedimentation behind the 23-year-old Cachi hydroelectric dam in Costa Rica have reached between $133 million and $274 million.[30]

In semiarid regions, shelterbelts can substantially reduce wind erosion and boost crop yields.

Just how much land worldwide needs tree cover to stabilize soil and water resources is unknown. Forestry expert Alan Grainger estimates that 87 million hectares of tropical montane watershed (relatively moist and cool upland areas) have been deforested, one third of the estimated original area covered by montane forest. In 1985, an International Task Force of tropical forest experts judged that some 160 million hectares of upland tropical watershed have become severely degraded through clearing, overgrazing, poor crop production practices, and other unsustainable land uses.[31]

Neither estimate includes areas in need of tree planting to guard against wind erosion, an important cause of land degradation in some arid and semiarid areas. In India alone, wind erosion has degraded an estimated 13 million hectares; degraded areas at least as large probably exist in China and Africa. Planting to protect land from the wind often takes the form of shelterbelts, rows of trees that break the wind's erosive power. Only a small portion of such land—perhaps a tenth or a twentieth—would actually need to be planted in trees; the remainder would benefit from the shelter they provide.[32]

Some ecological stabilization undoubtedly could be achieved through means other than tree planting: Soil conservation measures, including construction of terraces and planting of grass, could anchor soils in some areas more cheaply. Nevertheless, at least 100 million hectares of tree planting worldwide appears necessary to restore and maintain the productivity of soil and water resources.

Reforesting so large an area—equivalent to the size of Egypt—presents a formidable set of challenges. The benefits of planting trees for ecological reasons are sometimes difficult to quantify, so rates-of-return on project investments may not appear attractive. Since many of the direct beneficiaries of upland watershed rehabilitation are located downstream, who should pay for and carry out the reforestation? Perhaps most important, the worst watershed problems exist not in remote regions, but in areas with intense population pressures. Thus even given adequate funding and resources, ecological reforestation schemes are bound to fail if they do not at the same time address the needs of the people with no alternative but to overtax upland areas.[33]

As indicated earlier, experience has shown that local people need economic incentives and the expectation of short-term gains to support and participate in tree planting efforts. A successful strategy for rehabilitating uplands in Nepal, for example, involved transferring control of forestland from the government to village organizations called panchayats, and paying local people to plant fodder grasses and trees, thus giving them an immediate incentive to join in. Such plantings not only stabilized soils on denuded slopes, they helped meet villagers' basic needs. Livestock were stall-fed, giving the slopes a chance to revegetate. The overall strategy proved successful by almost any measure: Local income increased, fodder became abundant, and fast-growing trees began providing fuel within a few years.[34]

An innovative project getting under way in Colombia tries to remedy the unequal distribution of benefits and costs inherent in many watershed projects. Revenues from a tax on electricity sales from hydropower facilities will pay for reforestation and soil conservation measures in upland watersheds. Lowland dwellers presumably will benefit from reduced flooding and the protection of their power supply, while farmers in the uplands gain from a more productive and stable ecosystem.[35]

Agroforestry holds much promise for stabilizing soil and water resources for many of the same reasons it has such strong potential for increasing fuelwood supplies. In one system, for example, nitrogen-fixing trees are established along the contours of steep slopes, and food crops that reduce sheet erosion are planted in between them. Soil collects behind the hedgerows of trees, forming natural terraces along the contours. Farmers in the highlands of Indonesia have a long tradition of planting the fast-growing legume leucaena in this way. By reducing soil erosion and increasing rainwater infiltration, such strategies enhance upland productivity while helping farmers meet their needs for wood, food, and fodder in a sustainable manner.[36]

In semiarid regions, planting trees to form shelterbelts around cropland can substantially reduce wind erosion, enhance soil moisture, and boost crop yields anywhere from 3 to 35 percent. Among the most notable windbreak projects is that in the Majjia Valley in Niger. Once heavily wooded, the hills surrounding the valley had become almost completely denuded by the mid-seventies. Winds approached 60 kilometers per hour during the dry season, and annual soil losses averaged 20 tons per hectare. In 1974, the villagers requested help from the government forestry officer to establish a nursery of neem, a deep-rooted tree native to Asia that produces wood good for both fuel and timber, oil useful as lamp fuel, and a natural insecticide that helps protect crops.[37]

Government foresters and Peace Corps volunteers selected the best locations for the windbreaks, but the farmers themselves did the planting. Although the trees occupied up to 15 percent of the cropland area, crop yields were a fifth above those of equal areas of unprotected land, more than compensating for the land taken out of cultivation. By 1985, some 330 kilometers of windbreak had been planted. In *The Greening of Africa*, Paul Harrison sums up the keys to this project's success: "The technology was appropriate and simple, the species well adapted to local conditions. The package delivered the protection that had been promised. The costs for the majority of farmers were slight. The benefit in increased crop production was rapid, and perceived by the farmers."[38]

Rehabilitating tens of millions of hectares of degraded land will require duplicating numerous times the successes of projects like those in Nepal and Niger. Such efforts—designed to benefit local people in the short term while stabilizing the resource base for the long term—illustrate that reforestation involves more than establishing plantations, and that trees do more than provide wood.

FORESTS AND CARBON DIOXIDE

Forests play a crucial role in the global cycling of carbon. The earth's vegetation and soils hold some 2,000 billion tons of

Table 5-4. Estimated Net Carbon Emissions from Tropical Forests, by Region, 1980

Region	Forest Cover	Estimated Net Carbon Emissions	Share of Total Carbon Emissions
	(million hectares)	(million tons)	(percent)
Tropical America	1,212	665	40
Tropical Asia	445	621	37
Tropical Africa	1,312	373	23
Total	2,969	1,659	100

SOURCE: R.A. Houghton et al., "The Flux of Carbon from Terrestrial Ecosystems to the Atmosphere in 1980 Due to Changes in Land Use: Geographic Distribution of the Global Flux," *Tellus,* February/April 1987; U.N. Food and Agriculture Organization, *Tropical Forest Resources,* Forestry Paper 30 (Rome: 1982).

carbon, roughly triple the amount stored in the atmosphere. When trees are cleared or harvested, the carbon they contain, as well as some of the carbon in the underlying soil, is oxidized and released to the air, adding to the atmospheric store of carbon dioxide (CO_2). This release occurs rapidly if the trees are burned, but slowly if they decay naturally.[39]

Since 1860, forest clearing has contributed some 90–180 billion tons of carbon to the atmosphere, compared with 150–190 billion tons from the burning of coal, oil, and natural gas. The annual release of carbon from the loss of forests probably exceeded that from fossil fuels until about mid-century, when the pace of industrialization and the use of oil rose markedly. By then, most clearing for agriculture in North America and Europe had ceased, and the forested area in those regions became fairly stable. Today the bulk of CO_2 added to the atmosphere by land use changes comes from the tropics.[40]

Estimates of the amount of carbon released through forest clearing have varied greatly in recent years. At present, deforestation is believed to add be-

tween 1.0 billion and 2.6 billion tons of carbon to the atmosphere annually, or between 20 and 50 percent as much as the burning of fossil fuels. The large range reflects uncertainties about the rates of forest conversion, the extent of forest regrowth after clearing, and the amount of carbon stored in the vegetation and soils of different types of forests. Only 100 million tons of the total comes from temperate and boreal forests; the rest derives from the tropics.[41]

Using the best available knowledge of forest clearing rates and carbon stocks, Richard Houghton of the Woods Hole Research Center in Massachusetts and his colleagues have painted a useful picture of the geographic distribution of carbon emissions from land use changes. (See Table 5–4.) Based on the midpoints of estimated ranges, 40 percent of the total net release of carbon from land conversion comes from tropical America, 37 percent from tropical Asia, and 23 percent from tropical Africa. Just five countries account for half of all net carbon releases from deforestation, and the loss of forests in Brazil alone contributes one fifth of the total. (See Table 5–5.)

Table 5-5. Estimated Net Carbon Emissions from Tropical Forests, by Country, 1980

Country	Net Carbon Emissions[1]	Share of Total
	(million tons)	(percent)
Brazil	336	20
Indonesia	192	12
Colombia	123	7
Côte d'Ivoire	101	6
Thailand	95	6
Laos	85	5
Nigeria	60	4
Philippines	57	3
Burma	51	3
Peru	45	3
Ecuador	40	3
Vietnam	36	2
Zaire	35	2
Mexico	33	2
India	33	2
Others	337	20
Total	1,659	100

[1]Figures are midpoints of estimated ranges; the estimated total net release from tropical forests ranges from 900 million to 2.5 billion tons.
SOURCE: R.A. Houghton et al., "The Flux of Carbon from Terrestrial Ecosystems to the Atmosphere in 1980 Due to Changes in Land Use: Geographic Distribution of the Global Flux," *Tellus*, February/April 1987.

Although the cutting and burning of forests clearly adds significantly to CO_2 buildup, the way remaining forests worldwide respond both to the buildup itself and to the resulting planetary warming could exert an even greater influence on the earth's future climate. Higher CO_2 levels might enhance the growth of trees, causing them to remove more carbon from the atmosphere, which in turn would dampen the warming. Greenhouse operators take advan-

tage of this fertilizing effect to boost crop production; they set the CO_2 concentration in greenhouse air two to three times higher than in the natural atmosphere. So far, however, no convincing evidence suggests that natural forests would respond in this way.[42]

A second way forests might respond has more ominous implications. Ecologist George Woodwell suggests that rising temperatures from the buildup of CO_2 and other greenhouse gases could substantially increase the respiration rates of trees, especially in the middle to higher latitudes where the temperature rise will be most pronounced. When respiration outpaces photosynthesis, trees release more carbon dioxide to the atmosphere than they remove, as those in seasonal forests do during autumn and winter when they lose their leaves. A temperature-induced increase in respiration could cause a significant additional release of CO_2, reinforcing the very buildup that initiated the warming.[43]

If respiration exceeded photosynthesis for an extended period, trees would stop growing, and ultimately die. New species better adapted to the altered climate eventually would replace the old ones, but for several decades trees might die off with little replacement. A large-scale forest die-off could release enormous amounts of carbon to the atmosphere—perhaps hundreds of billions of tons, Woodwell maintains, depending on the speed of the warming. According to Woodwell, "the sudden destruction of forests by air pollution, now being experienced in northern and central Europe and in the eastern mountains of North America, is but a sample of the destruction that appears to be in store."[44]

Woodwell's scenario might never become reality. Indeed, ecologists do not yet agree on how forests will respond to climate change, or even on whether that response will add CO_2 to the atmosphere or remove it. Another possibility, for example, is that higher temperatures would increase rates of organic decomposition, which in turn would release nutrients to the soil and thus potentially boost the productivity of trees. Since trees would be growing faster, they would remove more CO_2 from the atmosphere, thus mitigating the warming. The uncertainty about forests' response to the warming looms large, since the potential for a strong feedback—positive or negative—clearly exists.[45]

Since the ongoing loss of forest cover contributes significantly to the CO_2 buildup, concerted efforts to protect existing forests and to plant more trees could help slow it. It is unfair to expect developing countries to invest substantial resources in tree planting solely to ward off global warming. More immediate needs—including handling massive amounts of debt—command a higher priority. Yet satisfying rising fuelwood demands and stabilizing soil and water resources are among the pressing needs many countries face; planting trees for these purposes would have the added benefit of sequestering more carbon from the atmosphere.

Previous sections of this chapter provide ballpark estimates of reforestation needed for fuelwood and ecological rehabilitation of 55 million hectares and 100 million hectares, respectively. A larger area would actually be involved, since many of the trees presumably would be planted on and around farms as part of agroforestry systems rather than in concentrated plantations. Obviously, some planting to meet fuelwood needs would also serve to stabilize soil and water resources, but at this stage the extent of overlap is impossible to judge. Assuming 30 million hectares of overlap leaves the equivalent of 120 million hectares of planting.

One additional adjustment is necessary. Some of the trees planted for fuel-

wood would yield little carbon-fixing benefit, since the carbon they accumulate during growth would quickly be released to the atmosphere when they were burned. A large share of the estimated 55 million hectares of planting for fuelwood, however, aims to make fuelwood use sustainable by ensuring that new growth exceeds cutting. Extrapolating from FAO estimates of unmet demand for wood in 1980, it is reasonable to assume that 20 percent (about 10 million hectares) of fuelwood planting would be burned in the short term, while 80 percent (about 45 million hectares) would expand the resource base and thereby enhance carbon storage. Virtually all the area planted for ecological stabilization would yield carbon-fixing benefits. Thus the total area providing this service would be approximately 110 million hectares.[46]

How much would terrestrial carbon emissions be reduced as a result of these 110 million hectares? Too many uncertainties exist to answer this question accurately, but some back-of-the-envelope calculations can shed light on reforestation's potential role in mitigating the CO_2 buildup.

It is unfair to expect developing countries to invest substantial resources in tree planting solely to ward off global warming.

A fairly fast-growing tropical hardwood species yields on the order of 10–14 tons of biomass per hectare per year, depending on age and harvest schedule. Half that weight—about 6 tons per hectare—is carbon that has been assimilated from the atmosphere through photosynthesis. Reforestation would also increase the amount of carbon stored in soils. In shifting cultivation systems in tropical Asia, for example, soil carbon increases an average of about one ton per hectare per year during the fallow phase, the period of tree regrowth. Soils beneath trees planted for fuelwood or ecological stability would store a similar amount, but possibly somewhat less if litter were removed for fuel or fodder. Assuming conservatively that soil carbon storage would increase about a half-ton per hectare annually on reforested land, the total carbon-fixing benefit of tree planting would be 6.5 tons per hectare per year.[47]

At that rate, the equivalent of 110 million hectares of trees would sequester roughly an additional 700 million tons of carbon annually until the trees reach maturity, reducing net carbon releases from tropical terrestrial systems by 41 percent (assuming, that is, a current net release of 1.7 billion tons). Of course, concerted efforts to slow deforestation would also be a crucial component of any strategy to limit carbon emissions from tropical lands. Halving the CO_2 contribution from deforestation in Brazil, Indonesia, Colombia, and Côte d'Ivoire, for example, would cut total net carbon releases from tropical forests by more than a fifth. Together, that achievement and the carbon storage benefits from 110 million hectares of trees could reduce net carbon emissions from tropical lands by nearly two thirds. Stepped-up planting to meet industrial wood needs (a topic not addressed in this chapter) would mitigate the carbon dioxide buildup even further.

Houghton and his colleagues estimate that at present the only regions in which terrestrial ecosystems are accumulating more carbon each year than they are releasing are Europe and, possibly, Japan and South Korea. Abandonment of a significant share of cropland and the replanting and regrowth of trees has put Europe on the positive side of the terrestrial CO_2 ledger. Europe's estimated accumulation of carbon in 1980 nearly offset carbon releases from deforesta-

tion in India. Continued forest damage from air pollution and acid rain, however, could turn the region's terrestrial systems again into a net CO_2 contributor.[48]

In the United States, actions taken as a result of the Food Security Act of 1985 should augment the nation's terrestrial store of carbon. The act created a Conservation Reserve under which some 16 million hectares of cropland are to be taken out of production from 1986 through 1990 and planted in trees or grass. A hectare of temperate woodland or grassland stores on the order of 40–45 tons more carbon than a hectare of cultivated cropland. Assuming a yearly net carbon-fixing rate of 2 tons per hectare as the land undergoes conversion, the 16 million hectares placed in the reserve would assimilate a total of 32 million tons of carbon annually for the next couple of decades. As U.S. and Canadian lands were estimated to contribute 25 million tons of carbon to the atmosphere in 1980, the Conservation Reserve might make North American terrestrial systems a net sink for carbon.[49]

Incomplete knowledge of the carbon cycle necessarily makes these figures more illustrative than definitive. Nonetheless, they do suggest that efforts to preserve existing tropical forests and to plant trees—important for a host of other reasons—can make a positive contribution to mitigating the buildup of carbon dioxide in the atmosphere.

MOBILIZING FOR REFORESTATION

Nature employs a wide variety of methods for expanding tree cover: coconuts that float between tropical islands, aerodynamic seeds, and luscious fruits that attract animal carriers. Strategies equally diverse and ingenious are needed to mobilize human energy and financial resources for tree planting sufficient to satisfy fuelwood needs, stabilize soil and water resources, and slow the carbon dioxide buildup. As with nature's seed-dispersal strategies, the key to success is designing planting programs that fit the particular niche—the economic, social, and cultural setting—in which people live and work.

Tree planting programs are most effective when local people are involved in their planning and implementation and perceive their own interest in success. If fodder is a critical need, for example, a project that promotes a nonbrowsable species like eucalyptus will receive little popular support. Knowledge of villagers' access to cash, seasonal patterns of labor, and preferences for tree species is also crucial. Designing a reforestation project without local input is like letting a doctor prescribe treatment without asking the patient what hurts.

Not surprisingly, given their emphasis on grassroots participation, international nongovernmental organizations (NGOs) have orchestrated some of the most successful reforestation projects to date. Funneling more aid through them rather than official channels could improve reforestation's prospects. Groups such as CARE in the United States and Oxfam in the United Kingdom have flexibility and local-level experience that government forest departments often lack, making them useful agents for encouraging rural tree planting.

In one farsighted program, for instance, the U.S. Agency for International Development (AID) contracted with CARE and the Pan American Development Foundation to encourage agroforestry and tree farming in Haiti. The project's success—which included planting more than 27 million seedlings between 1982 and 1986—stemmed in part from the value and efficiency of working through NGOs that had grassroots networks already in place.[50]

Much could also be gained by reinforcing the efforts of small, local NGOs. Around the world, women's associations, peasant collectives, and church groups have taken up tree planting; in Kerala, India, alone some 7,300 organizations are involved. Because local groups reflect the true needs, abilities, and limitations of their community, their projects are more likely to succeed, given adequate resources and technical assistance. In Kenya, for example, the Greenbelt Movement—sponsored by the National Council of Women of Kenya—has involved more than 15,000 farmers and a half-million schoolchildren in establishing 670 community nurseries and planting more than 2 million trees.[51]

Understandably, international donors are reluctant to deal with numerous small organizations that can each absorb only limited funds. But the outstanding performance of groups like the Greenbelt Movement highlights the importance of supporting such efforts. One option is for donors to channel funds through an umbrella organization that in turn distributes money to local projects; KENGO (Kenyan Energy NGOs), a consortium of 60 smaller groups, plays just such a role.[52]

Even when aid goes through government channels, reforestation efforts could benefit from more innovative extension strategies. Most early projects were unsuccessful in transforming foresters into rural extension agents. It proved difficult to dispel the notion that foresters protect forests from villagers rather than encourage people's involvement in tree planting.

Experience in Asia suggests that village "motivators" or existing agricultural extension agents may be better positioned than foresters to advance rural tree planting, especially in the context of agroforestry. World Bank projects in Kenya, India, and Malawi now have foresters train agricultural workers about multipurpose tree species. In Thailand, AID has pioneered the use of nongovernmental "interface teams," groups of three people—including one woman and one ethnic minority—who go to live in a village as community organizers. The emphasis in this approach on reaching women is an essential yet often ignored aspect of forestry outreach.[53]

Even the best project designs, however, will not improve prospects for accelerated planting unless reforestation becomes a development priority. For decades, forestry has been the poor stepchild of development agendas emphasizing agricultural projects and capital-intensive energy schemes. Developing countries traditionally have undervalued forestry because national accounting schemes often ignore the ecological and social benefits of forests. A World Bank survey of more than 60 countries found that forestry budgets accounted for less than 2 percent of the combined government outlays for energy and agriculture. International donors likewise have shied away from forestry investments, preferring projects with quick, certain, easily quantifiable benefits. From 1980 through 1984, the major development banks allocated less than 1 percent of their annual financing to forestry, and the U.N. Development Programme (UNDP), only 2 percent.[54]

The late 1985 launch of the Tropical Forestry Action Plan, however, holds promise of elevating forestry to its rightful place among development priorities. Jointly sponsored by FAO, UNDP, the World Resources Institute, and the World Bank, the plan calls for accelerated investments of $8 billion over five years in tree planting projects and efforts to arrest deforestation. Development assistance organizations are to contribute half the needed funding ($800,000 a year), with the remainder coming from national governments and the private sector.[55]

For decades, forestry has been the poor stepchild of development agendas.

Already the Action Plan has stepped up global funding for forestry and spawned increased cooperation among development agencies. The World Bank, the Asian Development Bank, and several bilateral aid agencies plan to more than double their annual assistance to forestry. Collectively, global aid contributions to forestry are likely to increase from roughly $600 million in 1984 to over $1 billion in 1988.[56]

Ultimately, however, the response of developing-country governments will determine the impact of the Action Plan. International initiatives are only as strong as the national initiatives they inspire. Both South Korea and China have demonstrated that strong political commitment together with charismatic leadership and adequate resources are necessary prerequisites for successful national campaigns to increase tree cover. Yet recent trends in China suggest that even then, achieving an expansion of tree cover in the face of increasing demand for forest products presents a formidable challenge.

Official statistics claim that between 1948 and 1978, the Chinese successfully established trees on roughly 33 million hectares, and forest cover increased from 8.6 to 12.7 percent of the nation's land. During the eighties, however, this effort appears to have lost ground. Between 1979 and 1983, forest cover declined by 5 million hectares. Annual plantings of more than 4 million hectares apparently could not keep pace with the growing demand for timber sparked by the economic reforms of 1979. For the first time, rural people were allowed to build their own homes, and over half the rural households did. From 1981 through 1985, housing construction alone consumed a total of 195 million cubic meters of timber, about a year's growth from all of China's forests.[57]

In 1985, annual planting in China doubled to 8 million hectares, giving renewed cause for optimism. Tree survival rates that had averaged only 30 percent also may be improving, since the government now allows peasants to own the trees they plant. China seems unlikely to achieve its ambitious target of 20-percent forest cover by the year 2000, but the combination of increased planting and better management, if sustained, could mean the nation's tree cover resumes its upward trend.[58]

India's Rajiv Gandhi recently joined the ranks of political leaders who have elevated reforestation to the level of a national crusade. Recognizing that deforestation had brought his nation "face to face with a major ecological and socio-economic crisis," Prime Minister Gandhi assigned forestry a central place in his development agenda for 1985–90. He almost tripled funding for forestry, reorganized his Ministries to give forestry new prominence, and created a National Wastelands Development Board to spearhead a "peoples' movement for afforestation." Significantly, Gandhi recognizes that local people are India's greatest resource for reforestation. He has authorized the Development Board to distribute funds directly to schools, women's groups, and other NGOs for tree planting and peoples' nurseries.[59]

The positive effect of political leadership like Gandhi's could be multiplied by increased attention to basic forest research. Progress lies not simply in planting more trees, but in improving the productivity, usefulness, and survival of those that are planted. A focused effort on breeding multipurpose trees that endure droughts and grow well in marginal environments could greatly improve prospects for successful reforestation. Unfortunately, forestry research in the Third World is currently underdeveloped, underfunded, and highly skewed toward improving processed forest products. Relatively little effort goes to forest protection, ecosystem stability, or tree breeding.[60]

Indeed, what is needed in the coming decade is an effort somewhat akin to the agricultural Green Revolution of the sixties: a dedication to developing genetically improved tree species and to extending widely the technical and financial resources for reforestation. Forestry's Green Revolution, however, needs to promote indigenous tree species and diversified agroforestry systems, and must strive to benefit marginalized populations, including the landless. Accelerated planting that does not benefit the poor only masquerades as success.

6

Avoiding a Mass Extinction of Species

Edward C. Wolf

A dozen times in the last 600 million years, the earth's biological character has undergone abrupt changes. Fossil evidence reveals that large numbers of animal species disappeared from the evolutionary record during these episodes of "mass extinction."

Causes ranging from climate changes to cataclysmic asteroid impacts have been proposed to account for these prehistoric mass extinctions. But while scientists debate the causes, they agree that widespread extinctions are rare events, remote from human experience. Nearly 14 million years have passed since the last worldwide die-off of ocean-dwelling organisms. Even the most recent global extinction episode, during which mammals including woolly mammoths and saber-toothed cats went extinct, occurred millennia before the dawn of civilization.[1]

The earth is again poised on the brink

of a global extinction crisis. This one, however, is being set in motion by human activities. The human population, now over 5 billion, is expected to nearly double in the next four decades. Worse, most of the expansion to 10 billion and beyond will occur in developing countries, where human poverty and biological wealth seem locked in a tragic embrace.

Tropical forests, which harbor a disproportionate share of the earth's biological diversity, are the focus of concern about mass extinction today. The outright clearing of tropical forests by settlers in search of land for cultivation and by commercial logging operations producing timber for trade and domestic needs may directly cause the extinction of one fifth of all plant and animal species by destroying their habitat.

As roads, dams, and other forms of development fragment wilderness expanses such as the Amazon Basin and the vast watershed of the Zaire River, innumerable extinctions will occur. Habitat fragmentation is an indirect but per-

An expanded version of this chapter appeared as Worldwatch Paper 78, *On the Brink of Extinction: Conserving the Diversity of Life.*

vasive cause of extinction as small populations of plants and animals are isolated, and as inbreeding and other damaging genetic effects begin to take their toll. And the insidious degradation of forests and soils linked to acid rain and air pollution, already a widespread problem in industrial countries and a growing risk in parts of the Third World, compounds the stresses on species and dims the prospect for the recovery of diversity.

Designating parks—a static solution to a dynamic problem—is no longer enough to avert a mass extinction.

Many scientists believe that a larger share of the earth's plant and animal life will disappear in our lifetime than was lost in the mass extinction that included the disappearance of the dinosaurs 65 million years ago. It is likely to be the first time in evolution's stately course that plant communities, which anchor ecosystems and maintain the habitability of the earth, will also be devastated. The U.S. National Research Council warned in 1980 that "the ramifications of an ecological change of this magnitude are so far reaching that no one on earth will escape them."[2]

Creating parks and reserves free from human interference has long been considered the key to conserving plants and animals. Today, 425 million hectares of land in some 3,500 areas worldwide enjoy various degrees of protection. UNESCO's Man and the Biosphere Program coordinates a global network of 252 "biosphere reserves" in 66 countries. The network is intended to protect an intact example of each of the earth's ecological zones, called biogeographic or biotic provinces, and to reconcile their preservation with the economic needs of surrounding communities.[3]

But designating parks—a static solution to a dynamic problem—is no longer enough to avert a mass extinction. Perhaps as much as 1.3 billion hectares would have to be set aside to conserve representative samples of all the earth's ecosystems. Although additional land should be preserved, more scientific surveys of remaining wild areas must be undertaken to find out what species remain at risk. Degraded lands should be rehabilitated in an effort to reconstitute the diversity they have lost. An innovative strategy encompassing both preservation and active ecosystem restoration is needed to minimize the global extinction crisis.[4]

THE FRAYING WEB OF LIFE

Ecologists agree that a direct relationship exists between the area occupied by natural habitat and the number of species that habitat can sustain. This species-area relationship is a key concept of what biologists call "the equilibrium theory of island biogeography." First proposed to explain species changes observed on islands, the theory is being tested in many different ecosystems, and studies have confirmed that reducing habitat size increases species' risk of extinction. Thus, data on the distribution and abundance of known species can be analyzed using biogeographic theory to anticipate the disappearance of plant and animal species as natural habitats shrink.[5]

Although each ecosystem has a characteristic complement of species, within any one system—a forest, for example—more plant and animal species will be found in 100 hectares than in 10. The same relationship holds on islands, with

Table 6-1. Projected Plant Extinctions in Latin American Rain Forests

Scenario	Estimate of Forest Area	Equilibrium Number of Species	Share of Species Lost
	(million hectares)		(percent)
Original Forest	693.0	92,128	—
End of Century	366.0	78,534	15
Worst Case[1]	9.7	31,662	66

[1]Assuming only areas currently designated as parks and reserves remain intact.
SOURCE: Adapted from Daniel Simberloff, "Are We on the Verge of a Mass Extinction in Tropical Rain Forests?" in David K. Elliot, ed., *Dynamics of Extinction* (New York: John Wiley & Sons, Inc., 1986).

small ones containing fewer species than large islands do. But an island such as Puerto Rico holds fewer species than a Puerto Rico–sized patch in the midst of continuous Amazon rain forest. As that forest is reduced to isolated fragments by farmers and ranchers, the fragments lose species just as if the surrounding land were flooded.

Daniel Simberloff of Florida State University used biogeographic theory to consider whether we are on the verge of a mass extinction in tropical rain forests. His study dealt with the plants and birds of the Latin American tropics, for which reasonably thorough species lists have been compiled. Simberloff found that if Latin American forests contract to 52 percent of their original extent by the end of this century, as is consistent with current estimates of population growth and forest clearing, 15 percent of the forest plant species—about 13,600 kinds of plants—will be lost before a new biological equilibrium is reached. (See Table 6–1.) And the Amazon Basin would support 12 percent fewer bird species by then. If the worst case unfolds and only the forest in established parks and protected areas remains, as many as 66 percent of the plant species in the Latin American tropics and 70 percent of the bird species

in the Amazon will eventually be lost.[6]

Latin American forests, particularly those in the Amazon Basin, have so far sustained much less pressure and exploitation than other regions. The original forests of parts of Central America, Southeast Asia, and West Africa have already been more than 90 percent cleared. Thousands of their native species of insects, plants, and animals have undoubtedly already been lost, and tens of thousands more are immediately at risk. In these regions, the extinction crisis has already reached historical proportions.[7]

The same biological rules apply in temperate latitudes. In North America, for example, national parks considered the last refuge for some of the continent's most distinctive wildlife are proving inadequate to the task. Ecologist William Newmark surveyed these parks and found an alarming incidence of local extinctions of mammal species in all but the largest. (See Table 6–2.)

Like the fragments of forest in tropical latitudes, habitats in temperate zones lose species even when they are protected from the direct pressures of hunting or poaching. Many parks are simply too small to maintain populations sufficient to ensure species survival. As ecological theory predicts, the smallest

Table 6-2. Habitat Area and Loss of Large Animal Species in North American National Parks, 1986

Park	Area	Original Species Lost
	(square kilometers)	(percent)
Bryce Canyon	144	36
Lassen Volcano	426	43
Zion	588	36
Crater Lake	641	31
Mount Rainier	976	32
Rocky Mountain	1,049	31
Yosemite	2,083	25
Sequoia-Kings Canyon	3,389	23
Glacier-Waterton	4,627	7
Grand Teton-Yellowstone	10,328	4
Kootenay-Banff-Jasper-Yoho	20,736	0

SOURCE: Based on William D. Newmark, "A Land-Bridge Island Perspective on Mammalian Extinctions in Western North American Parks," *Nature*, January 29, 1987.

parks have lost the greatest share of their original mammal species, but even very large parks such as Rocky Mountain and Yosemite have lost between a quarter and a third of their native mammals.[8]

The disappearance of animals from national parks occurred so slowly that the local extinctions went unnoticed by park rangers. It is not clear to what extent bird and plant species will also be affected. According to Newmark, "The big question now is how many species can we expect to disappear and what is the time period."[9]

A GLOBAL SPECIES CENSUS

When Charles Darwin and his companions aboard H.M.S. *Beagle* made a landfall near Bahia, Brazil, in 1831, the coastal rain forest they encountered left a lasting impression. Darwin wrote in his journal: "Delight . . . is a weak term to express the feelings of a naturalist who, for the first time, has wandered by himself into a Brazilian forest. The elegance of the grasses, the novelty of the parasitical plants, the beauty of the flowers, the glossy green of the foliage, but above all the general luxurance of the vegetation, filled me with admiration."[10]

Darwin's successors have done much to augment that awe with scientific knowledge. Yet a century and a half after the *Beagle*'s voyage, vast areas of ignorance remain. Only 500,000 of the 1.4 million identified species of plants, animals, and other organisms worldwide are native tropical species. Yet biologists believe that a bare minimum of 3 million species live in the tropics alone. No more than one in six is known.[11]

Even more striking is the uncertainty surrounding the total diversity of life. Until just a few years ago, biologists believed that the earth sustained between 3 million and 5 million species of all living organisms. Recent studies in tropical forests suggest that there may be 30 *million* species of insects alone. According to Edward O. Wilson of Harvard University, "We do not know the true number of species on Earth even to the nearest order of magnitude."[12]

Because so many of the species facing extinction are completely unknown, their biological importance remains a mystery and their potential value to society, an open question. One isolated ridgetop in the Andean foothills of western Ecuador, only 20 square kilometers in size, lost as many as 90 unique plant species when the last of its forest was cleared to plant subsistence crops. The

Table 6-3. Known and Estimated Diversity of Life on Earth

Form of Life	Known Species	Estimated Total Species
Insects and Other Invertebrates	989,761	30 million insect species, extrapolated from surveys in forest canopy in Panama; most believed unique to tropical forests.
Vascular Plants	248,400	At least 10–15 percent of all plants are believed undiscovered.
Fungi and Algae	73,900	Not available.
Microorganisms	36,600	Not available.
Fishes	19,056	21,000, assuming that 10 percent of fish remain undiscovered; the Amazon and Orinoco Rivers alone may account for 2,000 additional species.
Birds	9,040	Known species probably account for 98 percent of all birds.
Reptiles and Amphibians	8,962	Known species of reptiles, amphibians, and
Mammals	4,000	mammals probably constitute over 95 percent of total diversity.
Misc. Chordates[1]	1,273	Not available.
Total	1,390,992	10 million species considered a conservative count; if insect estimates are accurate, the total exceeds 30 million.

[1]Animals with a dorsal nerve chord but lacking a bony spine.
SOURCES: Edward O. Wilson, Museum of Comparative Zoology, Harvard University, Cambridge, Mass., private communications, February 22, March 19, and March 20, 1987; Peter H. Raven, "The Significance of Biological Diversity" (unpublished), Missouri Botanical Garden, St. Louis, Mo., 1987; insect figures from Terry Erwin, National Museum of Natural History, Smithsonian Institution, Washington, D.C., private communication, February 13, 1987.

medicines and foods they may have harbored will never be known. Such unintentional extinctions are by far the rule, not the exception.[13]

Insects and plants account for four out of five species identified so far. (See Table 6–3.) Yet insects remain by far the most undercounted group. Mammals, which have been thoroughly inventoried, constitute just three tenths of 1 percent of all known organisms. All known vertebrates account for less than 3 percent. And despite the research devoted to organisms of direct interest to humanity, substantial gaps remain even among the best-known groups. Ten percent of all flowering plants and fishes have yet to be discovered and described. Since so little is known about the earth's biological fabric, the consequences of losing biological diversity cannot be forecast with confidence.

Comprehensive efforts are needed to identify and describe tropical species in the natural environment that remains to them. From a purely numerical standpoint, this means more extensive cataloging of insects, invertebrates, and plants. One scientist who has devoted his career to this work is entomologist Terry Erwin, director of the Biological Diversity Program of the Smithsonian Institution.

Because most forest insects live in treetops, Erwin developed new techniques to sample and record the nearly inaccessible canopy life of lowland rain forests in Central America and the Amazon Basin. He and his colleagues spray through the canopy a mist of pyrethrum, a biodegradable pesticide that kills insects without harming birds, mammals, or plants. The insects are collected on a tarpaulin as they fall to the ground. Once they are counted and identified, the percentage of new species is calculated. Using these methods, Erwin has found that one hectare of Peruvian forest can yield 41,000 species of insects, more than a quarter of them beetles.[14]

Similar studies conducted in lowland tropical forests in Panama led Erwin to estimate that there may be as many as 30 million species of insects in tropical forests worldwide. Collections from the tangled canopy of the Tambopata Wildlife Reserve in the Peruvian Amazon reveal that treetop insects there are often highly localized: Four out of five species collected live exclusively in a particular type of forest, and 13 percent are confined to one species of tree. Such specialization makes tropical insects extraordinarily vulnerable to extinction when their habitat is disturbed.[15]

The most ambitious insect survey to date was carried out recently on the Indonesian island of Sulawesi. The British Royal Entomological Society, in cooperation with the Indonesian Institute of Science, assembled 160 scientists from 17 countries to study and identify the insects in Dumoga-Bone Reserve. The scientists of Project Wallace, as the effort was called, collected insects from the canopy and forest floor throughout 1985, and devoted the following year to species identification and lab work.[16]

The lack of a global biological inventory remains a central gap in our understanding of the biosphere.

The forests of the Dumoga-Bone watershed act as a giant sponge controlling the water supply for a large rice irrigation project downstream. The reserve itself was created with the help of a World Bank loan in order to control siltation in the irrigation canals and protect the fields from flooding. Although the Bank's primary concern was the stability of water supplies, Project Wallace revealed intricate ecological connections between farm and forest that could shape Sulawesi's agricultural future as decisively as water availability.

Green leafhoppers, for example, carry viruses that can decimate rice harvests. Since leafhoppers' natural habitat is treetops, scientists looked there to study their behavior and find natural predators. Biological controls based on these predators might keep the leafhoppers in check and sustain rice harvests without incurring the risks and costs of chemical pesticides. (See Chapter 7.)[17]

Although the value of such local species surveys is evident, and pioneering techniques are pushing back the frontiers of knowledge about biological diversity, the lack of a global biological inventory—like surveys of the world's forests and soils—remains a central gap in our understanding of the biosphere. No country has yet conducted an exhaustive national biological survey, and Otto Solbrig of Harvard University points out that there is "no consensus as to what kind of data should be collected and how."[18]

In 1980, the Committee on Research Priorities in Tropical Biology of the U.S. National Academy of Sciences advocated a crash program of expanded training for systematic biologists, proposed increased financial support for inventories, and identified 11 tropical areas of special priority for study. These suggestions of the first modest steps toward a global species census, neglected for eight years, deserve renewed consideration by the world scientific community.[19]

STUDYING TROPICAL ECOSYSTEMS

As unknown species are discovered and named, and new findings flood the few journals devoted to tropical biology, scientists must piece observations together like a jigsaw puzzle to form a coherent picture of conservation priorities. Conservation biology, a discipline less than a decade old, has emerged to fill this role. This "science of scarcity and diversity" is an eclectic blend of genetics, ecology, and natural resource management designed to guide conservation decision making.[20]

Some pioneering projects in conservation biology are already reshaping scientists' ideas about extinction and its consequences. In the Amazon Basin near Manaus, Brazil, the World Wildlife Fund and Brazil's National Institute for Amazonian Research launched the Minimum Critical Size of Ecosystems project in 1979. As described in *State of the World 1985*, Brazilian law requires that half the land in new cattle ranches remain for-

ested; researchers worked with local ranchers as they cleared grazing land to create a set of forest reserves ranging in size from 1 to 10,000 hectares. This huge experiment allows biologists to monitor the process of extinction and species change when patches of habitat are isolated from once-continuous forest.[21]

The Minimum Critical Size project will reveal for the first time the rates and patterns of species loss as the ecosystem approaches new equilibrium populations of plants and animals. Studies in the various reserves focus on two key questions: Are species lost in any predictable order? Will fragments of the same size end up with the same array of species? Measurable changes have already occurred in the smaller reserves; as observations from the large fragments begin to fill in the picture, the studies will help scientists and policymakers collaborate on the design and location of preserves that can best protect the Amazon's spectacular diversity.[22]

Similar studies are needed in every type of habitat on every continent—a goal beyond the present capacity of the scientific community. Furthermore, once the biological changes in the largest forest fragments have been analyzed to the point that firm conclusions can be drawn, perhaps decades down the road, it may be too late to prevent comparable species losses in many areas.

Warning of "a permanent alteration in the course of evolution on a global scale through a drastic decline in genetic diversity," the National Academy of Sciences set an ambitious agenda for tropical research through 1990. As mentioned earlier, the Academy's report called on the worldwide scientific community to conduct biological inventories, establish research centers for integrated studies of tropical ecosystems, increase study of neglected tropical aquatic systems, and monitor deforestation. Despite this cogent appeal, the report's recommendations had little immediate impact on agencies that fund scientific research.[23]

Harvard University's Edward O. Wilson has called on the United States, still the largest funder of tropical research, to declare an International Decade for the Study of Life on Earth to focus scientific and financial resources on the pressing problems of biological diversity—a proposal for which the National Academy study could provide a substantive agenda.[24] Though such a high-profile initiative has yet to take shape, an ambitious research program called Decade of the Tropics now enjoys broad international support.

Decade of the Tropics was launched with little fanfare in 1982 by the Paris-based International Union of Biological Sciences (IUBS), consisting of 47 national academies of science and 66 professional societies. The program was prompted as much by the economic and social disparities that separate tropical and temperate countries as by the uncatalogued biological variety of the tropics. Much of the IUBS-sponsored research aims to discover ways to tap this biological abundance for the benefit of local populations without destabilizing tropical ecosystems.[25]

An ambitious research program called Decade of the Tropics now enjoys broad international support.

Since IUBS has no resources of its own to support a major research program, Decade of the Tropics' participants share results from existing national research efforts. Separate studies of tropical savannas, soil biology and fertility, mountain environments, human adaptations to tropical conditions, and species diversity are under way. Project leaders in Australia, the United Kingdom, the United States, Venezuela, and Zimbabwe manage the contributions of dozens of participating scientists and research stations.

In 1980, tropical biology research worldwide received about $35 million, excluding applied work in agriculture and forestry. As the urgency of tropical environmental problems has captured the attention of funders, the total may have risen to the $50–75 million range by 1986, according to Peter Raven of the Missouri Botanical Garden. But this growth in current dollars falls considerably short of the doubling in constant dollars that the National Academy of Sciences recommended.[26]

One way to strengthen research in critical tropical areas is to use development aid funds to train Third World students in conservation biology and help pay for national parks, species inventories, and natural resource management. But in the United States—a major source of such funds—development aid for scientific research faces an uncertain future. Pressures to use foreign aid to promote political objectives, along with budget constraints due to the federal deficit, reduced science and technology programs in the U.S. Agency for International Development (AID) more than 22 percent in fiscal years 1986 and 1987—a cut of $63 million.[27]

Given the growing importance of tropical studies as nations come to terms with an era of biological change, the need to attract sufficient resources to the field remains urgent. Stanford University biologist Paul Ehrlich proposes quadrupling the level of funding for research in ecology, taxonomy, and tropical studies through the National Science Foundation (NSF). Even at this level—roughly $200 million per year—tropical biology would remain a modest national science priority beside multibillion-dollar programs in biomedical research.[28]

In a 1987 report on biological diversity, the U.S. Office of Technology Assessment urged Congress to consider directing the NSF to establish a research program in conservation biology. The report also recommended that Congress designate a National Endowment for Biological Diversity, similar to the endowments for the arts and humanities, that would channel small grants to nongovernmental groups engaged in conservation research. With modest additional spending, such programs could give the field of conservation biology the professional prestige and security needed to sustain first-rate science.[29]

Tropical biology is constrained by a legacy of neglect. Yet the tropics and the whole earth face profound changes in the course of our lifetime. Research agendas and science budgets should address this challenge. Reweaving the fabric of biological diversity can scarcely begin as long as the strands remain uncounted and unknown.

ECOLOGICAL RESTORATION

No change in the biosphere is more dramatic than the degree to which human activities have reduced forested ecosystems to remnants. Less than 10 percent of the Brazilian coastal forest that Darwin admired remains today. Barely 2 percent of the tropical dry forest that once cloaked the Pacific Coast from Central America to the Gulf of California still stands. And as the more accessible forests have been cleared, pressures have shifted to rain forests, the last unexploited forest type. In the Amazon and Zaire basins, coastal West Africa, Central America, and the archipelagos of Southeast Asia, closed tropical forests

have already been cut back an estimated 44 percent from their original climatic range of 1.6 billion hectares.[30]

Many biologists believe that these official statistics vastly understate the extent of forest clearing. (See Chapter 5.) The World Commission on Environment and Development recently estimated that in addition to the outright clearing of between 7.6 million and 10.0 million hectares of tropical forests each year, another 10 million hectares are "grossly disrupted." Tropical forests may survive only in tiny stands in remote reaches of the Amazon and Zaire watersheds and parts of New Guinea a generation hence.[31]

In contrast to other forest types, the benefits of clearing rain forests have often proved short-lived or illusory. In the Amazon Basin, for instance, at least half of the 15–17 million hectares of forest converted to pasture and cropland are now abandoned. The soils that underlie these Amazon forests have often proved infertile, sustaining crops or cattle for no more than four to eight years. This land, worthless to conventional agriculture, today represents a deduction from the earth's reservoir of diversity.[32]

But even such severely degraded tropical land need not be written off as a total biological loss. Pennsylvania State University biologist Christopher Uhl believes nearly all the land deforested so far in the Amazon has the capacity to regenerate. If forests can be restored on once-cleared land in the Amazon and throughout the tropics, the implications for conservation are enormous. According to William R. Jordan III of the University of Wisconsin Arboretum, "The quality of the environment in the long run is going to depend not so much on the amount of land we are able to set aside and protect from disturbance as on our ability to achieve an equilibrium between the forces of degradation on the one hand and of regeneration on the other."[33]

The potential for human-managed regeneration is suggested by studies of how natural ecosystems repair themselves. For more than a decade, Uhl has been studying tropical forest recovery in southern Venezuela and in Brazil's Pará state in the Amazon Basin. In the San Carlos de Rio Negro region of Venezuela, just north of the equator, he documented the way forests return to small agricultural clearings. One measure of this recovery is the total biomass—the cumulative weight of living plant matter on a forested site. Uhl studied rates of biomass accumulation on farm sites that had been abandoned anywhere from 2 to 60 years and concluded that at least 150 years would be needed for complete forest recovery after slash-and-burn farming.[34]

Prolonged disturbances—for example, conversion to pasture rather than shifting cultivation—slow the recovery. As forests recede toward a distant horizon, fewer birds and mammals stray far enough from their forest refuge to bring seeds of the main forest trees. Leafcutter ants and mice devour the few seeds that arrive. Natural regeneration can be halted altogether by more severe disruption. Evaluating a site laid bare by a bulldozer, Uhl concluded that "close to 1,000 years may pass before biomass levels reach those of mature forest."[35]

Although tropical forests can slowly reclaim cropland and pasture, from the standpoint of biological diversity, slowly is not good enough. Once a tract of forest is reduced to isolated pockets, each of the fragments begins to lose species, as biogeographic theory predicts. Extinctions occur fairly quickly. If the fragments, particularly those amid abandoned lands, can instead be rejoined into larger areas quickly enough, at least some extinctions could be prevented.

Researchers are creating a new discipline of ecological restoration, based on lessons from the study of natural ecosystem recovery, that can speed the repair of damaged environments. Restoration aims to reestablish viable native communities of plants and animals. Advocates of restoration argue that the successful conservation of biological diversity depends less on keeping humans out of fragile ecosystems than on making sure they do the right things when they are there.

Degraded ecosystems cannot be restored to health haphazardly: Restoration requires natural ecosystems as models and seed sources. And just as modern medicine rests on a scientific foundation encompassing physiology, microbiology, and biochemistry, healing the land draws on the insights of conservation biology and the emerging scientific field of restoration ecology. Since putting ecosystems together is a good way to ask scientific questions about them, restoration offers valuable opportunities to test ecological theories as well as new ways to correct environmental damage.[36]

The wholesale conversion of tropical ecosystems today was foreshadowed a century ago on the vast grasslands of North America. The nearly 300 million hectares of tallgrass prairies that once blanketed the midwestern United States have now been reduced by farming, grazing, and the invasion of exotic plants to less than one tenth of 1 percent of their original expanse. This tiny remnant provided fertile ground for the first deliberate experiments in ecological restoration.

Wildlife ecologist Aldo Leopold conceived of prairie restoration in 1934. Leopold, then director of the University of Wisconsin Arboretum, sought to re-create the native plant communities that original settlers had encountered in Wisconsin. As he suspected, the process proved far more intricate than simply broadcasting seeds and hoping for the best. Native species have to be reintroduced in a pattern and sequence that sets natural succession in motion. The work is complicated by the presence of tenacious alien species that have been inadvertently introduced to the United States. "You do not get a prairie . . . today by fencing off a piece of land and waiting for the grass to grow back," writes Walter Truett Anderson in *To Govern Evolution*. "If you do that you get an interesting collection of weeds from all over the world."[37]

Once a tract of forest is reduced to isolated pockets, each of the fragments begins to lose species.

The University of Wisconsin's Center for Restoration Ecology carries on Leopold's work in a variety of ecosystems, and a number of other restoration projects have been launched in recent years. At the Fermi National Accelerator Laboratory (Fermilab) in Batavia, Illinois, native prairie has been restored to 180 hectares over 12 years, and the goal is a prairie that completely blankets the 240-hectare research facility. Unlike other experimental restoration sites, Fermilab offers enough space to sustain native animals as well as a flourishing array of native grasses and flowers. Managers at the site have already reintroduced trumpeter swans to "pothole" ponds in the prairie, and they plan to do the same with sandhill cranes, Franklin's ground squirrels, and a variety of native prairie insects.[38]

Near Manhattan, Kansas, researchers at the 3,500-hectare Konza prairie have found that the diversity of prairie plant and animal life depends on burning at appropriate intervals. Burning every four to six years results in more grass,

taller flowering plants, and more insects than other schedules would. Scientists have also reintroduced bison, elk, and pronghorn antelope to part of the prairie to compare the impact of their grazing with that of domestic livestock. Though Konza is not a *restored* prairie, lessons learned there will guide efforts to reestablish tallgrass elsewhere. A proposed National Tallgrass Prairie Preserve in Osage County, Oklahoma, could provide a major opportunity to test prairie restoration and management.[39]

Restoration of coastal and freshwater wetlands is also widely practiced in the United States, particularly on the eastern seaboard. Marshes, swamps, and seagrass beds, though less diverse than other native plant communities, play a critical biological role by providing spawning and feeding grounds for many fish species, and by acting as a living filter for wastewater. These natural wetlands have been polluted, drained, and buried by various forms of industrial and urban development.[40]

U.S. environmental law provides the incentive for restoration by requiring developers to replace what they degrade with natural habitat equivalent in size and character. Environmentalists charge that restoration seldom achieves this equivalence, and reports of poorly supervised restoration with inappropriate species are common. Despite the controversies, the legal and economic lessons learned in restoring wetlands have set precedents likely to guide restoration in other ecosystems.

The greatest challenges for restoration lie in the tropics, where numerous forest types are being converted to farmland and pasture or being degraded by poorly managed logging operations. Estimates of deforestation suggest that at least 10 hectares are cleared in the tropics for each hectare newly planted. Moreover, almost all reforestation in these areas consists of single-species plantations rather than diverse natural assemblages of forest species.[41]

The most ambitious tropical restoration project yet undertaken is in the dry tropical forest of northwest Costa Rica. Dry forest, like rain forest, is rich in species; unlike rain forest, its trees are deciduous and shed their leaves during the dry season. When Spanish conquistadores first reached Central America, dry tropical forest covered the Pacific Coast from Panama to northern Mexico. Today, less than 1 hectare in 50 remains of that original forest. The soils over much of the range of former dry forest are eminently suited to farming and grazing, unlike those beneath rain forests. Corn, cotton, and cattle have replaced the forest's rich web of plants, animals, and microorganisms.

The Guanacaste project reflects an overdue shift in thinking about how natural resources and ecosystems can be managed.

University of Pennsylvania biologist Daniel Janzen believes that dry tropical forest can be grown from scratch. Janzen works in the 10,500-hectare Guanacaste National Park in northwestern Costa Rica. He plans to use the few intact stands of tropical dry forest in Guanacaste, the largest that remain in Central America, as a graft to restore the surrounding lands to their pre-Columbian ecological health. With support from the Costa Rican government, the Nature Conservancy of Washington, D.C., and private donors, Janzen intends to purchase enough land from adjacent landowners to expand the park to 70,000 hectares—enough for its ecological communities to become self-sustaining once again.[42]

Despite the most aggressive conservation policy in the tropics, Costa Rica has been unable to slow the pace of deforestation outside the country's parks and preserves. Against the daunting array of pressures on forests, Janzen's effort appears quixotic. But the Guanacaste project reflects an overdue shift in thinking about how natural resources and ecosystems can be managed in the tropics. If successful, it will confirm that even intricate tropical forest ecosystems can be reassembled.[43]

Researchers at the University of Wisconsin's Center for Restoration Ecology have proposed an ambitious tropical restoration project in the Caribbean to be launched in 1992, the 500th anniversary of Columbus's first landfall in the West Indies. The primary goal of the Bosques Colón (Forests of Columbus) project is to recreate dry forest characteristic of Caribbean islands by reassembling constituent species that have survived only in small threatened stands.[44]

Native peoples in many tropical countries have traditions of artificial forest regeneration that could provide a point of departure for tropical forest restoration. A team of Mexican researchers led by Arturo Gomez-Pompa found that descendants of the Maya living on Mexico's Yucatan Peninsula protect and cultivate useful forest trees in managed stands called *pet kot*. The tended forests, composed of a variety of fruit and nut-bearing trees, so resemble surrounding rain forests in structure and appearance that Gomez-Pompa and his colleagues remark that they "in many cases are indistinguishable from them."[45]

Such tended rain forests are not unique to the Yucatan. Researchers have found and documented similar practices in Brazil, Colombia, Indonesia, Tanzania, and Venezuela. People in every tropical forest region have developed traditions of forest restoration. In some places these traditions reveal how useful products can be extracted from forests without disrupting ecological integrity. In Brazil, for example, rubber tappers, Brazil-nut gatherers, and others whose livelihoods depend on materials gathered from wild forests have lobbied the government to set up "extractive reserves."[46]

Though setting aside such forest reserves often arouses opposition from powerful vested interests who gain from cutting forests, the concept clearly shows that forest preservation and economic development can be reconciled. As nations recognize the potential economic contribution of such practices, interest in conservation and restoration will grow.

Land for restoration in the tropics is not scarce; the challenge will be deciding where to begin. The 8 million hectares of abandoned, unproductive pasture in the Amazon Basin suggest the dimensions of the opportunities, but every country contains eroded wasteland that could be used to test restoration's potential. The Indian government, for example, estimates that 175 million hectares—nearly half the country's land mass—is degraded land that produces far below its biological potential and sustains few of its native species.[47]

Indian Prime Minister Rajiv Gandhi established a National Wastelands Development Board in early 1985 to promote reforestation of 5 million hectares each year. Though the action plan emphasizes plantations of fuelwood and fodder trees to supply subsistence needs of India's poor, the Board's mission of "greening wastelands" could easily be broadened to include experimental ecological restoration on a small scale. As with fuelwood and fodder plantations, the key to sustained success would be the participation of local communities. (See Chapter 5.)[48]

Eventually, restoration will have to grow beyond pilot projects if it is to make a significant impact on conserving biological diversity. One opportunity to scale up restoration efforts lies in the United States. Under the Conservation Reserve mandated by the Food Security Act of 1985, some 16 million hectares of land now in the cropland base will be planted to grass or trees by 1990 in an effort to curb soil erosion and restrain surplus production. Farmers have already enrolled nearly 9 million hectares in the program, well ahead of schedule. Although this land is not all in adjacent parcels, it includes areas on which ecological restoration and soil conservation could go hand in hand.[49]

Scientists studying the restored prairie at Fermilab have found that prairie plants improved soil structure and water-holding capacity faster and more cheaply than domesticated pasture grasses planted on adjacent land. Native prairie might prove the best long-term rotation crop for some farm areas suffering erosion, soil compaction, and other consequences of intensive crop production. "Incorporating prairie into agriculture suggests an incentive for returning prairie to the landscape on a large scale, and so a major force for restoration," write ecologists Michael Miller and Julie Jastrow. "Perhaps before too long strips of prairie will again flourish on the gentle hills of Iowa and Illinois, a vision of the past pointing the way to our future."[50]

Restoration is not a substitute for vigorous efforts to preserve natural areas. It cannot be expected to recover the full range of natural diversity on converted lands. But restoration may help slow the effects of habitat fragmentation, and expand habitat to allow animals and plants maintained in zoos and botanic gardens to be reintroduced to the wild. By enhancing areas that border parks, biosphere reserves, and other remaining wildlands, restoration can help give some plant and animal species a reprieve from extinction.

EVOLUTION'S FUTURE

The next decade will be especially crucial in determining the ultimate severity of the extinctions that we have already set in motion. If deforestation unfolds according to projections, if biotic impoverishment proceeds unchecked, and if human populations double, future choices will be foreclosed. "No generation in the past has faced the prospect of mass extinction within its lifetime," writes environmental consultant Norman Myers. "The problem has never existed before. No generation in the future will ever face a similar challenge: if this present generation fails to get to grips with the task, the damage will have been done and there will be no 'second try.'"[51]

Avoiding a mass extinction will require a radical departure from deeply embedded policies and land use practices. But the necessary changes, if they are to come at all, must originate within existing institutions: Evolutionary responsibility will have to be accepted by the present set of agencies, international bodies, and nongovernmental organizations. Since the challenge is disproportionately severe in the Third World, development assistance from the industrial countries is today among the most important means of putting the preservation of diversity on government agendas.

In the United States, initiatives to conserve biological diversity at the international level have been pursued as part of foreign policy, and the main instrument has been the Agency for International Development. A series of amendments to the Foreign Assistance Act broadened AID's mandate to conserve biological diversity and reverse tropical deforestation in the 60 developing countries with AID missions.

In 1981, AID joined other U.S. government agencies to cosponsor a Strategy Conference on Biological Diversity. Two years later, Congress passed a landmark amendment to the Foreign Assistance Act that established the conservation of biological diversity as an explicit objective of U.S. foreign assistance. AID delivered a U.S. strategy for conserving biological diversity to the Congress in 1985, recommending 67 ways government agencies and private organizations could help developing countries reconcile conservation with their economic needs.[52]

By 1986, however, intentions and budgets collided. AID suffered severe funding cuts under the Gramm-Rudman-Hollings Deficit Reduction Act. AID's environmental programs were not well financed to begin with, but these programs received disproportionate cuts under Gramm-Rudman. For example, in fiscal year 1986 AID's total budget was cut 4.3 percent. But the Office of Forestry, Natural Resources, and the Environment, which helps administer activities related to biological diversity, was cut by 25 percent to maintain funding for other development assistance programs.[53]

Congressional sponsors of biodiversity initiatives, displeased by the way the Agency allocated cuts, earmarked $2.5 million of AID's appropriation for fiscal year 1987 to support conservation projects, and $4.5 million might be designated for biological diversity in fiscal year 1988. Although this level of support is small in relation to conservation needs, it represents the first congressional commitment to biodiversity and a precedent for more aggressive programs.[54]

The World Bank has gradually begun

to recognize the links between biological diversity and economic development. In 1986, the Bank adopted a new wildlands policy that for the first time establishes its role in the preservation of natural areas. Virtually all Bank-funded projects have an impact on the environment, but to date fewer than 1 percent have included an explicit effort to conserve natural areas.[55]

Long indifferent to environmental concerns, the Bank now acknowledges that intact natural areas are under severe pressure, and that remaining wildlands can contribute more to economic development in their natural state than if converted to some other use. The new policy is explicitly intended to "greatly reduce current extinction rates to much lower (perhaps almost 'natural') levels, without slowing the pace of economic progress"—the first development policy justified on the basis of its effect on extinction rates.[56]

The wildlands policy specifies that new development projects should be sited on lands already converted or degraded rather than on virgin lands, a requirement that could focus attention on the economic potential of abandoned land. When a project requires the clearing of more than 100 square kilometers of virgin land, an area of natural habitat equal in size and biological value must be protected. Thus the Bank will begin partly to compensate for the biological losses incurred by conventional development schemes.[57]

In May 1987, World Bank President Barber Conable announced the creation of an environment department that will contribute to the design and direction of development policies at the Bank's top level. New environmental offices in the four regional divisions will monitor Bank projects and promote innovative resource management. Acknowledging the Bank's past failures in the environmental area, Conable noted that "sus-tained development depends on managing resources, not exhausting them." The wildlands policy stands a better chance of aggressive implementation with this promise of institutional support. The African, Asian, and Inter-American Development Banks, which together with the World Bank lend $6.5 billion annually for agricultural projects that can put natural diversity at risk, should join this effort to reconcile conservation and development.[58]

Avoiding a mass extinction will require a radical departure from deeply embedded policies and land use practices.

In a landmark agreement linking conservation to international finance, Bolivia became the first tropical country to protect threatened ecosystems in exchange for partial debt relief. Conservation International, a Washington, D.C.-based environmental group, paid off $650,000 of Bolivia's outstanding debt. The debt had been discounted to $100,-000 by private creditors doubtful that they could recover the full payment from the country itself. For its part, the Bolivian government designated a 1.6-million-hectare buffer zone of forest and grassland around the Beni Biosphere Reserve in the Amazon Basin, and created an endowment fund in local currency to manage the area.[59]

Such debt-for-nature exchanges can currently only be arranged with private creditors, because the World Bank, the International Monetary Fund, and the industrial-country governments that hold most Third World debt have traditionally been unwilling to write down their loans. But new flexibility in these institutions, urged by some members of the U.S. Congress, could open conservation opportunities on an unprecedented scale. The Bolivian agreement, involving a tiny share of that country's $4-billion debt, only hints at that potential. As *Science* magazine observed, "ingenious ideas for turning at least part of the mountainous Third World debt into quid pro quos for conservation are far from exhausted."[60]

The objectives of development lenders and nongovernmental conservation groups are beginning to converge in a way that few conservationists or economists could have foreseen even a few years ago. While the World Bank is considering "wildland financing," some of the major international conservation groups now aim their activities squarely at economic development.

The World Wildlife Fund, for example, recently launched a program called Wildlands and Human Needs, which seeks to base small-scale rural development projects on the ecosystems that supply fodder, fuelwood, and fresh water supplies to local communities. Projects include an effort to provide secure land titles to small farmers in eastern Costa Rica in order to reduce the pressure to clear remaining forest, and a program to involve Zambian villagers in sustainable wildlife harvests for local needs from land adjacent to South Luangwa National Park. The program will expand in Africa, Asia, and Latin America with support from AID.[61]

Over 30 countries are preparing comprehensive national conservation strategies to identify environmental priorities and integrate sustainable management of natural resources into country development plans. These national initiatives are patterned on the World Conservation Strategy prepared in 1980 by the International Union for the Conservation of Nature and Natural Resources. Indonesia, Malaysia, and Venezuela, countries especially rich in biological diversity, are on the list; Brazil, Zaire, and the countries of West Africa that contain that continent's most threatened tropical forests are not. Though strategies are not binding, the attempt to integrate conservation plans into political and economic decision making signifies that some developing countries have begun to reverse their long-standing neglect of conservation.[62]

Major producers and consumers of tropical hardwoods are beginning to address the loss of tropical forests through the International Tropical Timber Agreement, ratified in 1985. The Agreement reflects an unprecedented consensus among sponsor countries about escalating pressures on forest ecology and the risks to timber production. As a report from Friends of the Earth points out, "It is the first time that a commodity agreement, or indeed any international trade agreement, has built the goal of environmental sustainability into its economic strategy."[63]

At the inaugural meeting of the International Tropical Timber Organization in April 1987, Japan led other donor countries in pledging $2 million for research on reforestation and sustainable management of tropical forests. Japan, the largest importer of tropical hardwoods, has long been criticized for practicing irresponsible logging in Southeast Asia. A change in that nation's attitude, backed up with expanded financial support for innovative forest management, could brighten the outlook for tropical Asia's threatened forests.[64]

Biologists estimate that as many as 2,000 species of mammals, reptiles, and birds will have to be bred in captivity to escape extinction as natural ecosystems are cleared and fragmented. Zoos, the key to this task, have become a kind of "millennium ark," sustaining animals for which wild habitat is no longer sufficient until the time that human demands on the biosphere stabilize.[65]

Zoos are now involved in "genetic

management" of increasing numbers of vulnerable species. In the late seventies, Species Survival Plans were drafted for a few animals and circulated among North American zoos to provide a comprehensive blueprint for breeding programs designed to maintain the genetic diversity of captive animal populations. The International Species Inventory System, set up to maintain records on captive populations, now tracks 2,500 species of mammals and birds kept in 223 European and North American zoos.[66]

Budgets, not natural constraints, limit the carrying capacity of zoos. William Conway, Director of the New York Zoological Society, estimates that if today's zoos aim to maintain viable populations of birds, mammals, reptiles, and amphibians unlikely to survive in the wild over the long term, they probably can afford no more than 900 species—less than half the 2,000 species in these groups that face this fate. And zoos can do almost nothing for the hundreds of thousands of insects and invertebrates threatened with extinction.[67]

Like zoos, botanical gardens could back up ecological restoration by maintaining threatened plant species off-site and strategically restoring them to natural settings. Botanical gardens in the United States now coordinate efforts to preserve threatened species in a program managed and funded by the Center for Plant Conservation in Jamaica Plain, Massachusetts. But conserving the full genetic range of threatened plant species in botanical gardens alone is an unattainable goal. "Although it may be theoretically possible for the botanic gardens of the world to grow the estimated 25,000 to 40,000 threatened species of flowering plants, cultivating sufficient populations to maintain diversity is unrealistic," warns the U.S. Office of Technology Assessment. "Consequently, protecting a diversity of wild species will rest on maintaining them in the wild."[68]

Still largely ignorant of their responsibility for the future course of evolution, policymakers are already negotiating the terms of humanity's coexistence with the millions of species with which we share the planet. But existing initiatives and institutions can be building blocks for a strategy to avert a mass extinction.

Though the consequences of continued evolutionary negligence loom large, the tools with which to exercise evolutionary responsibility are more numerous and more powerful than ever. To the extent humans learn to reverse the disastrous fragmentation of ecosystems and match human institutions to ecological realities, the global effort to avoid a mass extinction of species may one day be counted among the most enduring accomplishments of our age.

7

Controlling Toxic Chemicals

Sandra Postel

An uneasy counterpoint of benefits and risks marks the course of the chemical age. Events continue to reveal that "better living through chemistry" comes with serious costs, some of which have only recently come to light. Pesticides thought to degrade in soils turn up in rural drinking water wells. Underground plumes of toxic chemicals emanating from abandoned waste sites contaminate city water supplies. A gas leak at a chemical production plant in Bhopal, India, kills more than 2,000 people. Pesticides spilled into the Rhine River from a warehouse near Basel, Switzerland, destroy a half-million fish, disrupt water supplies, and cause considerable ecological damage. In many ways—some dramatic, others insidious—chemicals seem to be escaping society's control.

The use of pesticides in agriculture and the disposal of industrial chemical waste release hundreds of millions of

An expanded version of this chapter appeared as Worldwatch Paper 79, *Defusing the Toxics Threat: Controlling Pesticides and Industrial Waste.*

tons of potentially hazardous substances into the environment each year.[1] Strategies that reduce pesticide use and that minimize industrial waste generation offer cost-effective approaches to lessening risks from toxics. They differ markedly from current practices, requiring new ways of thinking. The quick fixes of pesticide spraying and end-of-pipe pollution control are replaced with new production systems aimed at reconciling economic profits and environmental protection.

With technologies and methods now available, pesticide use could probably be halved and the creation of industrial waste cut by a third or more over the next decade. Successful efforts to date suggest that farmers and manufacturers would benefit economically, while people and the environment would receive better protection. But existing policies fail to promote these new techniques; in some cases, they actually undermine them. Overall, public commitments to research and development, demonstration projects, training, and education in these methods are woefully inadequate to bring them into widespread use.

SHADOWS OF THE CHEMICAL AGE

Organic compounds, by definition, are those containing carbon. Unique among chemical elements, carbon easily bonds with itself to form chains and rings, and can combine in various ways with other common elements, including hydrogen, nitrogen, and chlorine. During recent decades, laboratory scientists learned to exploit carbon's properties not only to recreate chemicals found in nature, but also to fashion millions of entirely new compounds that have no natural analogs. In so doing, they paved the way for a host of new industrial and consumer products that have greatly changed the shape of society—from plastics and pesticides to birth control pills and polyester fibers.[2]

Both the volume and the number of manufactured chemicals have burgeoned since World War II. In the United States, annual production of synthetic organic chemicals rose fifteenfold between 1945 and 1985, from 6.7 million metric tons to 102 million. (See Figure 7-1.) Worldwide, some 70,000 chemicals are presently in everyday use, with between 500 and 1,000 new ones added to the list each year. No limit to the number of possible syntheses is in sight.[3]

Prior to the forties, farmers relied on a combination of mechanical, chemical, and biological methods to limit pest damage to crops. The discovery of DDT, however, ushered in an era of almost exclusive dependence on chemicals for pest control. DDT was safer and more effective than the arsenic, heavy metal,

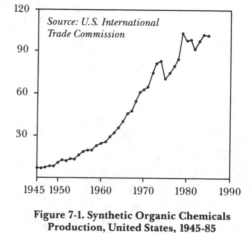

Figure 7-1. Synthetic Organic Chemicals Production, United States, 1945-85

cyanide, and nicotine compounds that had long been used. It was relatively inexpensive, remained active a long time in the soil, and was toxic to a broad spectrum of insects. Synthetic chemicals freed farmers from much of the worry and complexity of controlling insect pests. Demand for pesticides skyrocketed, and interest in nonchemical methods of pest control dwindled.[4]

In the United States, pesticide use in agriculture nearly tripled between 1965 and 1985. (See Figure 7–2.) Farmers applied 390,000 tons of pesticides to the nation's agricultural land in 1985, an average of about 2.8 kilograms (6.2 pounds) per hectare planted. Roughly 70 percent of all cropland (not counting land in alfalfa or other hay, pasture, or rangeland) receives some dosage of pesticides, including 95 percent of the area devoted to corn, cotton, and soybeans.[5]

Chemical pesticides are generally not used as widely or intensively in developing countries as they are in industrial ones. But in many, usage has been growing rapidly. Chemicals were part of the package of inputs promoted to boost Third World food production during the Green Revolution. The shift toward

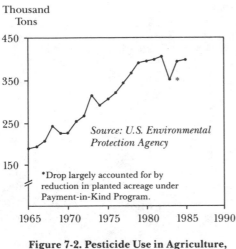

Thousand
Tons

Source: U.S. Environmental
Protection Agency

*Drop largely accounted for by
reduction in planted acreage under
Payment-in-Kind Program.

**Figure 7-2. Pesticide Use in Agriculture,
United States, 1965-85**

greater production of export crops also has spurred pesticide use, since investing in chemical inputs more often pays off for these higher valued crops. In India, pesticide use increased from about 2,000 tons annually in the fifties to more than 80,000 tons in the mid-eighties. Some 80 million hectares of India's cropland now receive treatment with chemical pesticides, compared with just 6 million in 1960.[6]

Unfortunately, data on the generation and disposal of chemical waste are much sketchier and more confusing than those for pesticides. Countries apply different definitions to what they variously call "hazardous," "special," or simply "industrial" waste, which obscures comparisons across countries. In many cases, current methods of managing industrial waste still reflect the "out of sight, out of mind" mentality of the fifties and sixties. Much waste is disposed of in or on the land through the use of injection wells, pits, ponds and lagoons, or landfills. Each of these practices risks contaminating groundwater, since experts claim that even the most carefully constructed landfill or surface impoundment will eventually leak.[7]

Many developing countries now industrializing their economies are generating growing volumes of hazardous waste, though the totals—impossible to specify —are still dwarfed by those in the West. Few have implemented regulations controlling this waste, and even fewer have the advanced technologies needed to do so adequately. Industries typically send it to unsecured domestic landfills, stockpile it, or dump it indiscriminately into the environment. In China, for example, where some 400 million tons of industrial waste and tailings are generated annually, much of it undoubtedly hazardous, mounds of potentially harmful waste reportedly occupy some 60,000 hectares of land today.[8]

CONSEQUENCES AND RISKS

The hazard to health posed by a chemical after it enters the environment depends primarily on two factors: its toxicity and the extent of human exposure to it. Unfortunately, knowledge of the harmful effects of synthetic organic compounds has lagged far behind their introduction to the marketplace.

The U.S. National Research Council (NRC) estimates that no information on toxic effects is available for 79 percent of the more than 48,500 chemicals listed in the inventory prepared by the Environmental Protection Agency (EPA). Fewer than a fifth have been tested for acute effects, and fewer than a tenth for chronic (for example, cancer-causing), reproductive, or mutagenic effects. Pesticides generally have received more extensive testing, but there, too, serious gaps remain. By allowing the production and release of these compounds without understanding their damaging effects, society has set itself up for unpleasant surprises.[9]

Pesticides account for only a small share of the 70,000 chemicals in common use, but they pose some of the greatest potential hazards. Unlike most industrial compounds, pesticides are purposely designed to alter or kill living organisms. Moreover, since they are spread widely over the land, they pose risks not only to farm workers but to the general population through residues in food crops and through contamination of drinking water.

Between 400,000 and 2 million pesticide poisonings occur worldwide each year, most of them among farmers in developing countries. The 10,000–40,000 such poisonings that are thought to result in death each year dwarf the 2,000 deaths caused by the toxic gas leak at the pesticide manufacturing plant in Bhopal, India, tragic though that accident was. No comparable estimates exist for deaths and disease caused by chronic, low-level exposures to farm chemicals, but the picture is far from comforting.[10]

Many older chemicals that industrial countries have restricted or outlawed are still widely used by farmers in the Third World. DDT and benzene hexachloride (BHC), both banned from use in the United States and much of Europe, account for about three quarters of total pesticide use in India. Residues of these compounds, both suspected carcinogens, were found in all 75 samples of breast milk collected from women in India's Punjab region. Through their mothers' milk, babies daily were ingesting 21 times the amount of these chemicals considered acceptable. Similarly, samples of breast milk from Nicaraguan women have shown DDT levels an astounding 45 times greater than tolerance limits set by the World Health Organization (WHO).[11]

Ironically, even though their own governments may have restricted or banned these chemicals from domestic use, consumers in industrial countries remain exposed to them through imported foods, completing what some have called a "circle of poison." In addition, a 1987 study by NRC suggested that pesticide residues in foods grown within the United States are of serious concern as well. In its worst-case estimate, the study calculated an increased risk of 5,800 cancer cases per million people over a 70-year lifetime, far higher than the 1 per million "acceptable" risk level that EPA often applies to cancer hazards. The NRC figure translates to roughly 1.4 million additional cases for the current U.S. population—or 20,000 additional cases per year. Nearly 80 percent of the estimated risk derived from just 15 foods, with tomatoes, beef, potatoes, oranges, and lettuce leading the list.[12]

Between 400,000 and 2 million pesticide poisonings occur worldwide each year, most of them among farmers in developing countries.

A third pathway of pesticide exposure—contaminated drinking water—is of rapidly growing concern. No nation has systematically monitored its water supplies for pesticides, so the full extent of contamination is unknown. Yet, again, the evidence available points toward some serious problems.

In the United Kingdom, preliminary survey results suggest widespread contamination of rivers and streams in the agricultural areas of eastern England. The herbicide atrazine, a suspected carcinogen, contaminates most surface waters in the region and has been found at levels nearly three times the maximum acceptable concentration for herbicides in drinking water set by the European Community.[13]

In the United States, routine agricultural practices have contaminated groundwater with more than 50 different pesticides in at least 30 states. The nation's two most widely used herbicides—alachlor and atrazine—have been among the pesticides most frequently detected. Tests have shown alachlor to cause cancer in laboratory animals, making it a probable human carcinogen. Surveillance efforts in Iowa, which has one of the best monitoring programs, indicate that more than a quarter of Iowans use drinking water contaminated with pesticides.[14]

The relative threat posed by pesticide poisonings, food residues, and contaminated drinking water varies with the type of pesticide used and the care taken during application. Organochlorine or DDT-type insecticides are not very acutely toxic. But their persistence, along with their ability to accumulate in fatty tissue, has led to their buildup in the food chain and to the high concentrations found in breast milk. Organophosphates degrade more readily, but are more acutely toxic. Many Third World farmers lack the training and equipment needed to apply such highly toxic chemicals safely, or cannot read well enough to understand the label instructions. A 1985 survey in one county of the Brazilian state of Rio de Janeiro found that 6 out of 10 farmers using pesticides had suffered acute poisonings, two thirds of them from organophosphates. Finally, many of the modern herbicides exhibit strong potential for leaching to groundwater, as the U.S. experience shows.[15]

Presumably greater pesticide use is justified if the benefits outweigh the costs and risks. But this case is getting harder to make. Insects and weeds now reduce crop production by about 30 percent, apparently no less than before the chemical age dawned. Because of stricter regulatory requirements and the greater complexity of modern chemicals, indus-

try now spends $20–45 million bringing a new pesticide to market, compared with about $1.2 million in 1956.[16]

More important, chemicals no longer provide the effective means of crop protection they once did. In response to heavier pesticide use, pests have evolved mechanisms of detoxifying and resisting the action of chemicals designed to kill them. In 1938, scientists knew of just seven insect and mite species that had acquired resistance to pesticides. By 1984, that figure had climbed to 447, and included most of the world's major pests. Resistance in weeds was virtually nonexistent before 1970. But since then, with the growth of herbicide use, at least 48 weed species have gained resistance to chemicals.[17]

Farmers and pesticide producers have thus locked themselves into a race with the rapid evolution of crop pests. Chemicals intended to enhance and stabilize agricultural production have in some cases done just the opposite. In Nicaragua, 15 years of heavy insecticide use on cotton were followed by four years in which yields fell by 30 percent. Pests had acquired resistance, the chemicals had killed pests' natural enemies, and new pests had emerged. As crop damage increased, desperate farmers reacted by applying more insecticide, which only aggravated the problem. In a classic case of the "pesticide treadmill," insect control costs rose to a third of total cotton production costs.[18]

Similarly, in Suffolk County, Long Island—the leading farm county in New York State—chemicals are losing the battle against the Colorado potato beetle. Growers spray up to 10 times per season, and pest control costs have climbed as high as $700 per hectare. Other cropping systems at risk from resistance problems include cabbage and rice in Southeast Asia, corn in the United States, potatoes in parts of Europe as well as the eastern United States, sugar beets in the United Kingdom, and cotton in many other parts of the world.[19] While an entrenched agrochemicals industry continues to propound the virtues and necessity of reliance on pesticides, the facts cry out for new solutions to pest problems.

As with pesticides, the consequences and risks from the burgeoning use of industrial chemicals have only begun to be characterized. Nearly a decade has passed since the Love Canal site in Niagara Falls, New York, spotlighted the insidious hazards posed by indiscriminate chemical waste disposal. Yet most countries still have only a vague idea of the magnitude of air, water, and soil contamination caused by industrial chemicals.

Farmers and pesticide producers have locked themselves into a race with the rapid evolution of crop pests.

Tens of thousands of active and abandoned waste disposal sites dot the landscapes of industrial countries. Corrosive acids, persistent organics, and toxic metals accumulated for decades with little thought about whether they would enter the environment. Preliminary estimates by the West German länder (states) suggest that as many as 35,000 problem sites exist nationwide. Efforts to assess how many pose serious risks are still going on, but officials expect corrective actions to require at least 18 billion German marks ($11 billion) over the next decade. In Denmark, which like West Germany relies heavily on groundwater, up to 2,000 sites are believed to be contaminated. Officials currently anticipate cleanup expenditures of some 1 billion Danish kroner ($158 million).[20]

In the United States, as of October 1987, EPA had placed 951 landfills, impoundments, and other waste sites on its National Priority List, which covers sites needing urgent attention. The agency estimates that the list will grow to not more than 2,500 sites and that cleanup costs may total some $23 billion. The Congressional Office of Technology Assessment (OTA) estimates, however, that the number of priority sites could climb to 10,000 and expenditures to $100 billion, roughly $400 for every U.S. resident.[21]

Meanwhile, no clear picture has emerged of the extent of groundwater contamination nationwide. Yet more than 200 substances have been identified in the nation's underground water supplies, including 175 organic chemicals. Thirty-two of these organics (including some pesticides) and five metals are known or suspected carcinogens. Equally unsettling, a substantial share of the contaminants frequently found have not even been tested for long-term health effects. Most remain unregulated and unmonitored: EPA has set drinking water standards for only about two dozen of the hundreds of substances detected in groundwater.[22]

Chemical wastes are not purposely spread over cropland the way pesticides are, but they can contaminate food nonetheless. Some drift through the air to lakes and farmlands, contaminating fish, crops, and grazing livestock. Researchers in Poland have found alarmingly high concentrations of heavy metals in vegetables in the heavily industrialized region of Upper Silesia, which harbors numerous smelters and metals factories. Soil samples taken from vegetable gardens in the region have contained levels of cadmium, mercury, lead, and zinc between 30 and 70 percent higher than levels considered safe by WHO.[23]

If good data on human exposure to contaminants were available, lack of knowledge about the toxic effects of most chemicals at various doses would still hinder an accurate assessment of health risks. The vast majority of chemicals have not been fully tested for toxicity, which requires animal experiments that can take several years and cost more than $500,000 per chemical. Even when animal data are available, very different risk assessments emerge, depending on the mathematical model to which the data are applied. One Stanford University researcher found that the estimated cancer risk arising from low-level exposure to the pesticide ethylene dibromide varied by a factor of 1 million depending on the model used.[24]

Epidemiology—the study of the incidence of disease within a population—offers a second approach to assessing health risks. In several ways, however, toxic chemicals pose an epidemiological nightmare. A cancer induced by a toxic chemical may appear decades after the exposure and will usually be indistinguishable from a cancer caused by other means. In addition, people usually are exposed to several contaminants simultaneously, which greatly frustrates efforts to ferret out cause-and-effect relationships.[25]

Despite these drawbacks, recent epidemiological work among more highly exposed population groups gives cause for concern. In 1986, scientists reported finding a sixfold increase in the risk of non-Hodgkin's lymphoma, a cancer of the lymphatic system, among Kansas farmers using certain herbicides—especially 2,4-D—for 20 days or more per year. They note that this greater risk among farmers could suggest increased risk to the general population exposed to low levels of these herbicides.[26]

Charles Benbrook, Executive Director of the Board on Agriculture at the National Academy of Sciences, commented on these findings: "For the first time there is clear and rather unequivocal evidence that the environmental exposure to pesticides at low levels causes cancer in man. It has taken a long time for that particular finding to emerge. It involves an old pesticide, one of the most widely used older pesticides, and one that is not really that potent of an oncogen [cause of tumors] if you look at the animal data. . . . I think that the emergence of the new epidemiological data is cause for very serious concern."[27]

BREAKING THE PESTICIDE HABIT

If chemicals were the only viable way to control crop-damaging insects and weeds, society would have little choice but to live with their associated risks. Fortunately, proven alternatives exist, and others await exploration. A commitment to break agriculture's unhealthy dependence on toxic chemicals is the first step toward realizing the potential of more ecologically sound, economically sustainable pest control methods.

A guiding philosophy known as integrated pest management (IPM) underlies most strategies to reduce pesticide use. IPM recognizes a field of crops as an ecosystem within which many natural forces affecting pests and weeds interact. It draws on biological controls (e.g., natural predators of pests), cultural practices (e.g., planting patterns), genetic manipulations (e.g., pest-resistant crop varieties), and judicious use of chemicals to stabilize crop production while minimizing hazards to health and the environment. The operating goal is not to eradicate insects and weeds but to keep them below the level at which damaging economic losses occur. Under this integrated approach, farmers use chemicals selectively and only when necessary, rather than as the first and primary line of attack.

IPM requires knowledge of a pest's life cycle, behavior, and natural enemies, of the way cropping patterns and chemical use affect pest and predator population levels, and of many other features of the crop ecosystem. As such, it differs greatly from the packaged variety of pest control provided by today's agrochemical industry. Research and extension are needed to design and implement an effective IPM program. It requires farmers to adopt a new way of thinking about pest management, along with new techniques. But the payoffs can be great. For some farmers, IPM provides an essential escape from the "pesticide treadmill." For most, it offers a welcome response to increasing concerns about chemical costs, health risks from pesticide exposure, and the threat of contaminating their own family's drinking water.

Perhaps no country has worked harder and accomplished more in nonchemical methods of pest control than China. This nation is well represented among the success stories in IPM and biological control. (See Table 7–1.) For the last three decades, a nationwide pest forecasting system has helped farmers identify, track, and control pest problems. Hundreds of data-collection stations around the country report to their respective provincial forecasting centers, which in turn transmit information on pest populations, the abundance of natural enemies, and weather conditions to some 500 agricultural production units. Between 1979 and 1981, Chinese scientists carried out surveys to locate organisms that could help farmers protect their crops, creating a rich resource base for expanding biological methods of pest control. Whether the nation will continue this emphasis on ecologically based pest control under its new market-oriented system of agricultural incentives remains to be seen.[28]

Over the last decade, Brazil also has advanced impressively toward integrated pest control in its production of soybeans, one of its major export crops. Soybeans are plagued by several insect pests, which variously eat the crops' leaves or suck nutrients out of the pods. With the help of U.S. scientists, an IPM program was developed and tested in trial plots in two of Brazil's leading agricultural states in the mid-seventies. By the early eighties, about 30 percent of Brazilian soybean growers had adopted IPM. Insecticide use by those growers in 1982 was 80–90 percent below the level in 1975, the year before the program began.[29]

Under integrated pest management, farmers use chemicals selectively and only when necessary, rather than as the first and primary line of attack.

Industrial countries also have much to gain from an integrated approach to pest control. Governments seeking to protect water supplies from pesticide contamination and to bolster ailing farm economies can do both simultaneously by investing in IPM. Price-depressing crop surpluses and growing amounts of farm debt make strategies that reduce input costs at least as important as ones that increase yields. Moreover, evidence to date strongly supports IPM as an economical enterprise.

In the United States as of 1984, IPM programs supervised by U.S. Department of Agriculture (USDA) extension personnel were under way for nearly 40 crops and collectively covered 11 million hectares, about 8 percent of the nation's harvested cropland area.[30] An evaluation of extension IPM programs published in 1987 showed clearly that farm-

Table 7-1. Selected Successful Applications of Integrated Pest Management and Biological Control

Country or Region	Crop	Strategy	Effect
Brazil	Soybean	IPM	Pesticide use decreased 80–90 percent over seven years.
Jiangsu Pr., China	Cotton	IPM	Pesticide use decreased 90 percent; pest control costs decreased 84 percent; yields increased.
Orissa, India	Rice	IPM	Insecticide use cut by a third to half.
Southern Texas, United States	Cotton	IPM	Insecticide use decreased 88 percent; average net return to farmers increased $77 per hectare.
Nicaragua	Cotton	IPM	Early to mid-seventies effort cut insecticide use by a third while yields increased.
Equatorial Africa	Cassava	BC	Parasitic wasp controlling mealybug pest on some 65 million hectares.
Arkansas, United States	Rice/ Soybean	BC	Commercially marketed, fungus-based "bioherbicide" controlling noxious weed.
Guangdong Pr., China	Sugarcane	BC	Parasitic wasp controlling stemborers at one third the cost of chemical control.
Jilin Pr., China	Corn	BC	Fungus and parasitic wasp providing 80–90 percent control of major corn pest.
Costa Rica	Banana	BC	Pesticide use was stopped; natural enemies reinvaded to control banana pests.
Sri Lanka	Coconut	BC	Parasite found and shipped for $32,250 in early seventies prevents pest damage valued at $11.3 million annually.

SOURCE: Worldwatch Institute, based on various sources.

ers adopting IPM strategies have benefited economically. Based on survey results on nine commodities from 15 different states, and considering practices on only one crop per state, farmers using IPM collectively earned $579 million more in profits than they would have otherwise. (See Table 7-2.)

IPM programs specifically aimed at reducing pesticide use, rather than just at increasing profits, have achieved some impressive results. U.S. IPM efforts, for example, were intensified in the early seventies on cotton, grain sorghum, and peanuts. By 1982, insecticide applications on these crops had dropped dramatically. (See Table 7-3.) In contrast, insecticide use on the areas planted in corn and soybeans—crops that received minimal IPM—slightly increased. As a result, corn replaced cotton as the crop receiving the greatest share of insecticides in the United States.[31]

Biological methods of pest control, either alone or as part of an IPM design, can provide some of the most elegant and long-lasting solutions to pest problems. In "classical" biological control, a beneficial organism is introduced into a pest-plagued area and, it is hoped, becomes a permanent part of the agroecosystem. The pest and the introduced natural enemy reach a population balance that keeps pest damage below the economic threshold. Since the 1860s, scientists have introduced some 300 organisms worldwide in classical control programs.[32]

Among the most exciting biological control efforts now under way is that to protect African cassava—a food staple for some 200 million people—from the ravaging effects of mealybugs and green spider mites. With no apparent natural enemies to keep them in check, both pests spread rapidly after the early seventies, when they were first detected. By 1982, the mealybug had infiltrated a large portion of the 34-country cassava belt. Together the two pests slashed cassava yields by 10–60 percent, causing losses estimated at $2 billion annually.[33]

Officials ruled out a massive pesticide program because the infrastructure was lacking to deliver chemicals to the subsistence farmers in need. Instead, the Nigeria-based International Institute of Tropical Agriculture (IITA) launched a major biological control effort with

Table 7-2. United States: Estimated Average Annual Economic Benefits from Use of IPM, Selected Cases, Early Eighties

State	Crop	Increase in Net Returns to IPM Users	
		Farm-level	Statewide
		(dollars per hectare)	(thousand dollars)
California	almonds	769	96,580
Georgia	peanuts	154	62,600
Indiana	corn	72	134,230
Kentucky	stored grain	<1	890
Massachusetts	apples	222	400
Mississippi	cotton	122	29,680
New York	apples	528	33,000
North Carolina	tobacco	6	780
Northwest[1]	alfalfa seed	132	2,420
Texas	cotton	282	215,830
Virginia	soybeans	10	2,570
Total			578,980

[1]Idaho, Nevada, Montana, Oregon, and Washington.
SOURCE: Virginia Cooperative Extension Service, Virginia Tech and Virginia State Universities, in cooperation with USDA Extension Service, *The National Evaluation of Extension's Integrated Pest Management (IPM) Programs* (Washington, D.C.: U.S. Department of Agriculture, 1987).

Table 7-3. United States: Effects of IPM on Insecticide Use, 1971–82

Crop	Use of IPM	Insecticide Use 1971	1982	Change
		(kilograms/hectare)		(percent)
Corn	minimal	0.38	0.41	+ 8
Soybeans	minimal	0.15	0.17	+13
Grain Sorghum	intensive	0.30	0.18	−41
Cotton	intensive	6.63	1.68	−75
Peanuts	intensive	4.48	0.86	−81

SOURCE: R.E. Frisbie and P.L. Adkisson, "IPM: Definitions and Current Status in U.S. Agriculture," in Marjorie A. Hoy and Donald C. Herzog, eds., *Biological Control in Agricultural IPM Systems* (Orlando, Fla: Academic Press, Inc., 1985).

funding from several foreign governments and technical support from the U.K.-based Commonwealth Institute for Biological Control. Extensive searching in Latin America, cassava's place of origin, turned up some 30 species of natural enemies of the mealybug. Several were quarantined and subsequently released in Africa.[34]

To date, a tiny wasp called *Epidinocarsis lopezi,* which parasitizes the mealybugs' eggs, has produced remarkable results. *E. lopezi* now effectively controls the mealybug over 65 million hectares in 13 countries of the cassava belt. African farmers are again growing cassava where mealybug damage had previously decimated the crop. So far, the effort has cost about $12 million, less than half the current cost of commercializing one chemical pesticide. Assuming *E. lopezi* provides the permanent control a successful introduction should, the annual benefits to African farmers will far exceed the project's costs.[35]

Another type of biocontrol strategy involves releasing large numbers of a pest's natural enemy during critical periods of the growing season to temporarily suppress the pest population, much the way chemical pesticides do. Probably the most widely used control agent of this type is *Trichogramma,* a tiny wasp that lives on the eggs of certain butterflies and moths, preventing them from developing into crop-damaging caterpillars. Useful in both temperate and tropical regions, *Trichogramma* now controls moth pests on an estimated 17 million hectares of cropland worldwide.[36]

So far, most IPM and biological control strategies have been directed at insect pests, and thus have reduced insecticide use. Of growing importance, however, are nonchemical methods of controlling weeds, the other major class of crop-damaging pests. The use of fungi, bacteria, and other disease-causing agents as "bioherbicides" shows perhaps the greatest near-term promise for supplanting chemicals in weed control. In recent years, two bioherbicides relying on a fungus as the working agent have entered the U.S. market. DeVine, produced by Abbott Laboratories, controls the milkweed vine in Florida citrus groves, and Collego, marketed by the Upjohn Company, has achieved 90 percent control of northern jointvetch, a troublesome weed in Arkansas rice and soybean fields.[37]

Altering cultural practices and cropping patterns can also help control weeds, just as it does insect pests. Research efforts under way include intercropping—for example, growing a nitrogen-fixing legume between rows of wheat. The legume competes with weeds, keeping them in check, besides adding nitrogen to the soil for the next season's crop. Planting cover crops that inhibit the germination or growth of weeds also shows promise. Such cropping patterns make use of a phenomenon known as allelopathy, the inhibition of one plant by another through the release of natural toxins. Researchers at Michigan State University have found, for example, that leaving residues of rye, sorghum, wheat, or barley on a field can provide up to 95-percent weed control for a month or two.[38]

The future of IPM, biological control, and other pesticide reduction practices, while promising, is clouded by several factors. New techniques in biotechnology could serve either to promote or to undermine nonchemical methods of pest management. Scientists can use gene-splicing methods, for example, to build pest resistance into crop varieties better and more quickly. Crops less damaged by pests and disease would need fewer chemicals applied to them. On the other hand, some two dozen chemical and biotechnology companies are researching ways to make crops resistant to chemical herbicides. Crops engineered to resist weed-killers could pave the way for broader use of chemicals.[39]

In recent years, several U.S. chemical companies have developed herbicides that apparently pose little risk to people, fish, and other animals, and that either break down rapidly in the environment or will not leach into groundwater. These seemingly safer chemicals could also undermine biological and other nonchemical techniques by offering a new and tempting quick fix. Indeed, the vast majority of corporate R&D in herbicide resistance is directed toward these newer compounds.[40]

Given the number of adverse chemical effects that have taken society by surprise, it seems unwise to place faith and resources solely in new products. Safer chemicals are certainly a welcome development, but they will best serve farmers and society if their use is integrated with other promising pest control methods.

RETHINKING INDUSTRIAL WASTE MANAGEMENT

For many countries taking on the challenge, locating and cleaning up all the leaking landfills and waste lagoons scattered across the industrial landscape will be among the highest priced items on their environmental agendas. Remedying the legacies of past mismanagement, however, only begins to address the toxics dilemma. Unless the wastes currently produced are better managed, new threats will simply replace the old ones, committing society to a costly and perpetual mission of toxic chemical cleanups. Moreover, without concerted efforts to reduce, recycle, and reuse more industrial waste, the quantities produced will overwhelm even the best treatment and disposal systems, and the goal of risk-minimizing, sustainable waste management will remain elusive.

Most countries still rely predominantly on land disposal methods—such as landfills, lagoons, and injection wells—for their hazardous wastes. But in several parts of Europe advanced technologies and effective institutional arrangements have combined to create management systems that appear to prevent most waste from being released into the environment in hazardous forms. Two such programs with comparatively long track records are those in Denmark and the West German state of Bavaria.[41]

In both regions, integrated treatment facilities equipped with incinerators, inorganic chemical treatment plants, and secure landfills form the technological backbone of hazardous waste management. A network of collection stations feeds wastes into regional facilities. With limited exceptions, Danish and Bavarian industries are required to send their wastes to a publicly controlled company that holds a monopoly on the waste management market.[42]

In sharp contrast to this public monopoly approach, the U.S. hazardous waste system is characterized by privately owned, competitive facilities operating with little or no public monies. About 95 percent of U.S. industry's hazardous waste is disposed of on the site where it is generated; scattered commercial facilities handle the rest. The U.S. government's role is strictly regulatory: It sets construction and operating standards with which the waste management facilities are to comply.[43]

Strategies to reduce waste differ markedly from the end-of-pipe treatment to which most industries have grown accustomed.

Neither approach will work best in all situations, since any institutional arrangement must mesh with the prevailing ideology and political culture. Yet more than a decade after passage of the U.S. hazardous waste law, a comprehensive, smooth-running system is not in place. Meanwhile, several other nations have adopted programs patterned after the Danish and Bavarian approaches, including Finland, South Korea, and Sweden. From available evidence, it seems that programs with a strong public sector management role have come closer to the goal of minimizing risks from chemical wastes entering the environment.[44]

Regardless of the type of management system established, greater efforts are needed to curb the amounts of waste being generated. Rising costs, scarce treatment and disposal capacity, and public opposition to siting new facilities plague hazardous waste programs virtually everywhere. In the United States, landfill prices have skyrocketed to $240 per ton, a sixteenfold increase since the early seventies. Incineration of organics now costs between $500 and $1,200 per ton. Waste management costs for Du Pont, the nation's largest chemical producer, now exceed $100 million annually. Paul Chubb, vice chairman of Du Pont's Manufacturing Committee, says that "an economical and environmentally acceptable" waste management plan may now "hold the key to the success or failure of many of our businesses."[45]

By not producing waste, industries obviously avoid all the costs and risks of treating, storing, transporting, and disposing of it. Strategies to reduce waste differ markedly from the end-of-pipe treatment to which most industries have grown accustomed. They focus on the production process itself, examining where wastes are generated and exploring how they can be reduced. Simple housekeeping measures, such as segregating wastes so they can more easily be reused, sometimes result in surprisingly large waste reductions. Other options include changing manufacturing processes, using different raw materials, and replacing hazardous products with safer substitutes.[46]

Numerous case studies of individual company efforts collectively attest to waste reduction's feasibility and cost-effectiveness. (See Table 7–4.) The Minnesota Mining and Manufacturing Company (3M) probably has the longest-standing commitment to waste reduc-

Table 7-4. Selected Successful Industrial Waste Reduction Efforts

Company/ Location	Products	Strategy and Effect
Astra Södertälje, Sweden	Pharmaceuticals	Improved in-plant recycling and substitution of water for solvents cut toxic wastes by half.
Borden Chem. California, United States	Resins; adhesives	Altered rinsing and other operating procedures cut organic chemicals in wastewater by 93 percent; sludge disposal costs reduced by $49,000 per year.
Cleo Wrap Tennessee, United States	Gift wrapping paper	Substitution of water-based for solvent-based ink virtually eliminated hazardous waste, saving $35,000 per year.
Duphar Amsterdam, The Netherlands	Pesticides	New manufacturing process cut toxic waste per unit of one chemical produced from 20 kilograms to 1.
Du Pont Barranquilla, Colombia	Pesticides	New equipment to recover chemical used in making a fungicide reclaims materials valued at $50,000 annually; waste discharges were cut 95 percent.
Du Pont Valencia, Venezuela	Paints; finishes	New solvent recovery unit eliminated disposal of solvent wastes, saving $200,000 per year.
3M Minnesota, United States	Varied	Companywide, 12-year pollution prevention effort has halved waste generation, yielding total savings of $300 million.
Pioneer Metal Finishing New Jersey, United States	Electroplated metal	New treatment system design cut water use by 96 percent and sludge production by 20 percent; annual net savings of $52,500; investment paid back in three years.

SOURCE: Worldwatch Institute, based on various sources.

tion of any major corporation. Through its "Pollution Prevention Pays" program, launched in 1975, the company claims to have halved its generation of wastes and saved nearly $300 million.[47]

As a creative, ongoing endeavor that essentially equates waste with inefficiency, waste reduction represents a new way of thinking. Its success hinges on top management making it a priority, since ideas can spring from all phases of a production process. 3M developed a videotape and brochure explaining the goals of its pollution prevention program to employees, and holds award ceremonies to recognize those who develop innovative projects. USS Chemicals rewards employees who develop waste-cutting ideas with a share of the money thereby saved. As of 1986, the company had distributed $70,000 in rewards for projects saving a total of $500,000.[48]

Despite signs of a shift toward waste reduction, the gains achieved so far represent a small share of their potential. A study of 29 U.S. organic chemical plants conducted by INFORM, an environmental research group in New York, found that the waste reductions achieved by the companies examined, while impressive, amounted to only a minute fraction of the total waste volume the facilities generated. EPA estimates that expanded use of existing techniques could reduce the total U.S. industrial waste stream by 15–30 percent. As the broad-based 3M program suggests, vigorous efforts could do much more.[49]

Along with reducing waste at its source, recycling and reusing waste can slow the volume of chemicals needing treatment and disposal and help keep toxics out of the environment. Many industries recycle a portion of their wastes internally, and to the extent that these quantities are excluded from statistics, recycling rates can be underestimated. Still, in most countries, recycling accounts for only a small fraction of the total volume of waste managed.

Japan seems to have advanced the furthest of any major industrial country toward recycling and reusing its industrial waste. Of the estimated 220 million tons of waste generated in 1983, more than half was recycled. (See Table 7–5.) Incineration, dewatering, and other treatment methods eliminated 31 percent of the waste stream, leaving just 18 percent for final disposal. Since these figures apply to all industrial waste, not just to those specified as hazardous or toxic, they are not strictly comparable to other national estimates. Japan's accomplishments are impressive nonetheless.

In Japan, North America, and Western

Table 7-5. Japan: Industrial Waste Management, 1983

Waste Disposition	Quantity	Share of Total
	(million tons)	(percent)
Total Generated	220.5	100
Recycled and Reused	112.7	51
Delivered Off-site for Reuse	(78.5)	(36)
Reused On-site	(34.2)	(15)
Reduced Through Treatment and Incineration	68.9	31
Disposed of	38.9	18

SOURCE: Clean Japan Center, *Recycling '86: Turning Waste into RESOURCES* (Tokyo: 1986).

Europe, waste exchanges have succeeded to varying degrees in promoting the recycling and reuse of industrial waste. Exchanges operate on the simple premise that one industry's waste can be another's raw material. Most of them serve as information clearinghouses, publishing catalogs of "waste available" and "waste wanted" listings to inform industries of trading opportunities. In Japan, exchanges have helped create markets for materials that previously had not been recycled, including sludges, slags, and waste plastics. Sixteen nonprofit exchanges currently operate in North America, and several have experienced healthy growth in recent years.[50]

DETOXIFYING THE ENVIRONMENT

Current efforts in integrated pest management and industrial waste reduction only hint at the long-term potential of these two strategies to detoxify the environment. Halving pesticide use in agriculture and cutting industrial waste by at least a third over the next decade would be reasonable targets for most countries. Yet for society to realize these gains, policies and funding priorities need to actively promote these new methods of production in agriculture and industry, rather than undermining them.

The private sector has little incentive to develop strategies relying on crop rotation or a permanent biological control agent.

Unraveling the near-total reliance farmers have acquired on chemicals will require much greater efforts from agricultural extension workers and researchers to advance nonchemical methods of controlling insects and weeds. In the United States the USDA Extension Service spent $48 million on IPM between 1973 and 1983. This modest public investment has increased farmers' profits, but so far apparently has not captured the potential societal benefits of reduced chemical use. Broadening the use of crop rotation, intercropping, and biological control requires that extension agents work closely with farmers, offering education, training, and demonstrations that these less familiar techniques work. Yet USDA Extension Service funding for IPM has remained at about $7.5 million per year since 1981, just 2 percent of the agency's total budget.[51]

In addition, greater public commitments to research and development are needed in the areas of biological, cultural, and genetic methods of pest control. The private sector has little incentive to develop strategies relying, for example, on crop rotation or a permanent biological control agent because they involve no marketable product. But the public sector is not adequately filling this R&D gap, despite evidence of the societal benefits. Currently, total direct federal funding in the United States for IPM research amounts to about $20 million annually—less than is needed to commercialize one chemical pesticide, and a mere one tenth of 1 percent of the $26 billion paid to farmers in crop subsidies in 1986.[52]

Revenues to expand research and extension efforts could come from a very modest tax on pesticide sales. Just a 2-percent tax on sales in the United States, which in 1985 totaled nearly $6.6 billion, would yield revenues sufficient to increase the annual federal IPM extension budget seventeenfold, the research budget more than sixfold, or the combined research and extension budgets nearly fivefold.[53] Such an increase in resources could go a long way toward meeting a target of halving pesticide use.

In developing countries, IPM and biological control offer promises of reduced poisonings and deaths from toxic pesticides, while simultaneously creating more sustainable crop production systems. A number of institutions are promoting nonchemical pest control methods for Third World farmers, but actual implementation of these strategies has lagged. As David Greathead, Director of the U.K.-based Commonwealth Institute of Biological Control, points out, alternatives to pesticides are still usually adopted only as a last resort—for example, when chemicals become too expensive or fail to work against resistant pests—rather than as an integral part of agricultural planning and development.[54]

An important first step for much of the Third World is to stop subsidizing chemical pesticides so heavily. Subsidies encourage farmers to apply more chemicals than is economically justified, undermine the development and use of nonchemical methods, and ultimately increase all the risks associated with toxic farm chemicals. In a study of nine developing countries—three each from Africa, Asia, and Latin America—the World Resources Institute of Washington, D.C., found that pesticide subsidies ranged from 19 percent of real retail costs in China to 89 percent in Senegal. By phasing subsidies out and devoting the public funds thereby freed to research and extension in IPM and biological control, governments could do much to promote more ecologically sound and sustainable pest control.[55]

Mounting concerns about pest resistance, chemical costs, groundwater contamination, and health risks have spurred a few governments to act to curb pesticide use. Indonesia achieved self-sufficiency in rice in 1984, but now finds that position threatened by the brown planthopper, an insect pest that has acquired resistance to every major rice pesticide. In November 1986, President Suharto banned the use of 57 insecticides on rice, and essentially made IPM national policy. By July 1987, extension workers had trained 31,000 farmers in IPM techniques. No other country has so strongly supported IPM at such a high official level. Indonesia's effort may set an example other nations trapped in the pesticide treadmill could follow.[56]

In Sweden, a program adopted in 1987 aims at cutting risks from pesticides by half over the next five years. Similarly, a new Danish program has targeted a 25-percent reduction in pesticide use by 1990 and a further 25-percent reduction by 1997. The government has imposed a 3-percent tax on pesticides to help pay for increased R&D and educational efforts in nonchemical pest control.[57]

In the United States, several states—including Iowa, Nebraska, and Vermont—have initiated efforts to reduce risks from pesticides. But IPM will not gain widespread use among U.S. farmers

until federal agricultural policies cease to indirectly promote pesticide use. Government programs offer farmers a guaranteed price for certain crops, and, to control crop surpluses, encourage them to idle a portion of their cropland. USDA economist Katherine Reichelderfer points out that the combination leads farmers to maximize yield—and thus guaranteed income—on the land kept in production. They do so with greater use of agricultural inputs, including pesticides, which partially or wholly offsets the pesticide reductions that result from idling land.[58]

By tying conservation priorities to farm programs, the Food Security Act of 1985 offered a unique opportunity to redress some of the negative consequences of agricultural practices. Arguably one of the strongest conservation initiatives in decades, the act created a "conservation reserve," which by 1990 will include some 16 million hectares of highly erodible cropland. Legislation introduced in the Senate in July 1987 would broaden the use of the reserve by making eligible for it cropland associated with the contamination of water supplies. By linking federal efforts to curb crop surpluses with state and local efforts to protect drinking water, such action would increase the societal benefits of the government's multibillion-dollar farm programs.[59]

Regarding industrial chemical wastes, virtually no country has yet designed an effective, long-term strategy. More vigorous research and development in waste-reducing technologies, technical and financial support to encourage investments in such technologies, and, in some cases, a tax on waste generated could probably cut problem wastes by at least a third in most countries over the next decade.

Several West European nations now show strong commitments to promoting "cleaner technologies" and other methods of curbing toxic pollution. The French government, for example, pays up to half the costs for research into widely applicable waste-minimizing technologies, and offers investment subsidies of 10 percent for demonstrations of pollution prevention techniques. Officials estimate that in 1984, government expenditures to promote cleaner technologies totaled 192 million francs ($35 million), inducing investments by private industry of several times that amount.[60]

In the Netherlands, a special Committee on Environment and Industry has aided some 200 clean technology research, development, and demonstration projects. The Dutch government spends about $8 million per year on such efforts, a large sum for a country of only 14.5 million people. Denmark and West Germany, widely lauded for their waste management systems, have recently stepped up their waste reduction efforts as well. Both have initiated pilot projects to promote clean technologies.[61]

Efforts in the United States pale in comparison to these European initiatives. EPA's 1988 budget request for waste minimization activities totals just $398,000—0.03 percent of its $1.5-billion operating program budget, and less than was spent in 1986.[62] With the nation already facing costs of from $20 billion to $100 billion to clean up old toxic waste sites, it seems foolhardy to ignore the timeworn truism that an ounce of prevention is worth a pound of cure. By investing modestly in waste reduction now, the government can avoid future problems and costs arising from waste mismanagement, shortfalls in treatment capacity, and public opposition to siting new facilities.

Legislation introduced in the U.S. Congress in June 1987 contains most of the elements needed for a successful national effort. It would create an Office of Waste Reduction within EPA, giving waste reduction a high-level institutional home and signaling a strong federal commitment. It authorizes up to $18 million for waste reduction activities: $8 million to operate the new office and $10 million for grants to the states. This would provide useful seed money, but greater funding for state efforts seems needed to get the waste reduction ball rolling effectively.[63]

A tax on waste generated could probably cut problem wastes by at least a third in most countries.

A handful of states already have their own programs, but they could benefit greatly from an infusion of federal funds. OTA analysts point out that spending $200 million over five years on state waste reduction grants could save industry billions of dollars in avoided management costs. Moreover, tax revenues from increased company profits likely would exceed the federal cost of the program.[64] If reallocating a small share of EPA's budget to pay for the program seemed infeasible, a minimal tax on waste—less than $1 per ton—would generate more than enough to launch a strong waste reduction initiative.

Few developing countries have even established the basic foundation of a hazardous waste management system. Most have no regulations governing toxic waste and no facilities capable of adequately treating and disposing of such materials. South Korea appears to be one exception, having fairly comprehensive legislation and two advanced treatment facilities slated to begin operation in 1987. An active exchange of information and experience between governments and industries in industrial countries with policymakers in developing countries could do much to advance the Third World's management of toxic chemicals. In a program announced in August 1986 three U.S. corporations—Dow Chemical, Exxon, and Mobil—will help train Indonesian environmental officials in industrial environmental management techniques, including hazardous waste management.[65]

Making industries assume responsibility for more of the societal costs and risks associated with hazardous substances is crucial to fostering a transition to safer chemicals and products. Government regulators often bear the burden of showing that a substance causes unacceptable harm before they can act to restrict or ban it. If, instead, industries had to prove suspect substances safe, and if they faced strict liability for damages caused from the manufacture, use, and disposal of their products, risks would diminish throughout the chemical cycle. Risky substances would be weeded out in industrial laboratories, rather than by a regulatory agency after many years of use.[66]

Voters in California overwhelmingly approved a referendum in 1986 that shifts at least some responsibility for chemical safety over to industry. It prohibits industries from releasing chemicals on a state list of those believed to cause cancer or birth defects in a manner that might allow them to enter drinking water. It also requires the labeling of products containing those chemicals, even in trace amounts. In court actions involving exposures to substances covered by the law, industry bears the burden of proving the contested exposure harmless.[67] If rigorously enforced, the new law in California should provide substantial incentive for the manufacture and use of safer chemicals and products.

A unique convergence of public and private interests now makes it a ripe time to promote alternative pest control methods and better management of industrial chemicals. Both farmers dependent on pesticides and generators of hazardous waste face rising costs and risks associated with their practices. Governments face the complex and expensive task of protecting people from contamination caused by agricultural and industrial chemicals. And a justifiably wary public wants assurance that its water, food, and surrounding environment are safe. Technologies and methods to minimize pesticide use and industrial waste tackle each of these concerns. For everyone's benefit, they deserve promoting.

8

Assessing SDI

William U. Chandler

The nightmare of nuclear weapons makes dreams of perfect defenses against them understandable. An all-out nuclear exchange would almost certainly end Soviet and American societies as we know them. Even a limited nuclear war would kill an estimated 30 million Americans and Soviets, throw both economies into indefinite decline, and cause millions of cancer deaths and genetic defects. Thus, when President Reagan's Strategic Defense Initiative (SDI) seemed to offer an alternative to Mutual Assured Destruction, it received serious attention.[1]

President Reagan at first proposed a goal of "eliminating the threat posed by strategic nuclear missiles." His original SDI plan was to develop a near-perfect defense of the entire U.S. territory. But it has become increasingly clear that defending populations against nuclear attack by a determined foe is virtually impossible. Any ballistic missile defenses deployed this century would not protect people directly; they would protect weapons.[2]

Defending weapons, according to SDI proponents, would reduce the threat of nuclear war and therefore benefit everyone. SDI critics counter that less-than-perfect defenses would, at best, cost billions of dollars and benefit no one. At worst, they argue, missile defenses on one side would create a first-strike advantage, thus increasing the temptation for both sides to launch attacks in a serious crisis.[3]

A defense deployment in the absence of new arms control measures would in any case guarantee a new arms race. The Soviets would try to catch up with the United States—and vice versa—by adding defenses of their own or, more likely, enough new warheads to overwhelm any defense. Former Secretary of Defense Caspar Weinberger voiced this likelihood when he said in 1984 that "even a probable [Soviet] territorial defense would require us to increase the number of our offensive forces."[4]

Concern that a costly SDI deployment could erode the superpowers' economic security has arisen alongside strategic matters. Some critics, for example, worry that an expensive arms race would divert capital and attention from problems of declining U.S. competitiveness and Soviet economic inefficiency. Their concerns have some merit, for early deployment might cost Americans each year during the nineties as much as they currently invest in manufacturing.[5] Similarly, early deployment would burden the Soviet Union at a time when it might otherwise place highest priority on liberalizing its economy—perhaps the best opportunity for improving Soviet-American relations since the dawn of the nuclear age. Because SDI's direct costs and its opportunity costs are both very large, its advocates must persuade policymakers that it could substantially diminish the threat of war.

THE ILLUSION OF PERFECT DEFENSE

If the superpowers could make strategic defenses work perfectly, they would escape from the mutual hostage condition of nuclear deterrence. They could, in Ronald Reagan's words, "defend rather than avenge." But a growing scientific chorus holds that SDI is highly unlikely to provide a near-perfect defense at any cost. This realization arises from the strategic and technical realities of deterrence.[6]

President Kennedy's secretary of defense, Robert S. McNamara, believed that the United States had to deter Soviet conventional force with conventional force, and its nuclear force with nuclear force. This approach led to the concept of mutual assured destruction, the capability of destroying Soviet society even after suffering a nuclear surprise attack. McNamara defined this as the ability to destroy 25 percent of the Soviet population and 50 percent of Soviet industry, in part because studies showed that larger attacks would yield diminishing results. The superpowers now have many times this power. (See Table 8–1.)[7]

The Nixon administration, perhaps because the U.S. arms buildup had provided far more weapons than were needed for the McNamara goal, initiated what became known as warfighting strategies. In the event of Soviet provocation, the U.S. president was to be presented with a variety of retaliatory options, including various "withholds."

Table 8-1. Superpower Nuclear Weapons Capability, 1987[1]

Delivery System	Force Available Relative to Force Needed[2]	
	United States	Soviet Union
	(ratio[3])	
Land-Based Missiles	4	14
Submarine-Based Missiles	3	5
Airplanes	8	1

[1]Extreme caution should be used in interpreting these ratios. For example, U.S. missiles are more accurate than Soviet missiles, a fact that is of great importance for missions other than Mutual Assured Destruction.   [2]Defined as destroying 25 percent and 50 percent of the opponent's population and industry, respectively. It is assumed that 300 equivalent megatons is sufficient for this task. [3]The capability given is for arsenals *before* an attack by an opponent. A surprise attack would reduce the number of times one side could destroy the other by two thirds or more.
SOURCE: Worldwatch Institute, based on International Institute for Strategic Studies, *The Military Balance* (London: 1986), and on "U.S.–Soviet Strategic Nuclear Forces." Center for Defense Information, Washington, D.C., September 1987.

For example, the president could refrain from attacking all Soviet cities or targets that would create an especially large number of civilian casualties.

The president might want to attack only the same types of targets that the Soviets had destroyed, so that if U.S. missiles and bomber bases had been hit, surviving weapons and submarine missiles would be used against comparable military targets. The idea was that the United States should not be left with only the option of attacking Soviet cities, an escalation that would leave the Soviet leadership little choice but to respond in kind, thus converting a catastrophic war into an apocalyptic one.

More recent advocates of warfighting strategies reiterate that it is not credible to threaten Armageddon for every nuclear attack, and that the president should not be forced to choose between doomsday and surrender for lack of options. That is, if the Soviets have only attacked U.S. missile silos, attacking the entire Soviet society would be the final folly. They add that targeting innocent civilians for mass murder is immoral.

Critics, however, contend that planning for these warfighting contingencies makes war more likely by making it more thinkable. They argue that limited nuclear war is impossible and will inevitably escalate out of control, and therefore any planning that makes the use of nuclear weapons more likely is unethical and dangerous. They maintain that, in any case, a "limited" attack that killed 15 million Americans would not likely be met by a limited response.

McNamara himself now argues that nuclear weapons are useless except for deterring the use of nuclear weapons themselves, not for achieving other military goals. Other analysts, such as Princeton physicist Frank von Hippel, submit that the world would be safer, relatively speaking, with mutual assured destruction as the prevailing strategy

than with warfighting strategies.[8]

Most people in the United States, according to surveys, share McNamara's attitude. For that reason, Americans are sometimes surprised to learn that U.S. policy follows exactly the kind of warfighting strategy many find absurd. With Presidential Directive 59, Jimmy Carter expanded the number of sets of targets and seemed to pursue the capability of waging and winning a protracted nuclear war. The Reagan administration strongly embraced this policy.[9]

President Reagan ostensibly launched SDI as a way out of these nuclear straits, as a means of mutual assured survival. Unfortunately, perfect defense against nuclear weapons is technically impossible for three reasons. First, no system can be tested against the real contingency in which it must perform, and therefore can never be considered perfectly reliable. Second, technology has not advanced to the point where perfect defenses could work cheaply enough to be feasible. Third, a determined offense can use a number of countermeasures to overcome a defense against ballistic missiles.[10]

Confidence is a prerequisite for investing in technological systems. It is unimaginable that the United States or the Soviet Union would stake deterrence on the ability to retaliate with weapons they have not tested. Ballistic missiles, for example, are tested dozens of times for reliability and accuracy. Aircraft and pilots are continuously tested under the most realistic conditions possible. A system of space-based lasers directed by computer programs millions of lines long would be unlikely to work perfectly, or even well, the first time. Corrections entered in computer code are estimated to generate new errors between 15 and 40 percent of the time.[11]

The most important constraints to achieving the perfect SDI shield are technical. The exotic technologies that have received so much attention since President Reagan's "Star Wars" speech in 1983 are generally decades away from maturity. The "directed-energy" systems such as lasers and particle beam guns being studied by the Strategic Defense Initiative Office would destroy missiles by attacking them in launch, or boost, phase.

Boost phase is the first of the three stages of ballistic missile flight; it refers to the 150–300 seconds required for today's missiles to achieve the momentum needed to propel their warheads over distances of 10,000 kilometers (6,000 miles). Missiles in this phase are simple to detect because the bright plumes of their rockets give infrared signals that are easy for satellite monitors to identify and track. Destroying missiles before they deploy their multiple warheads—up to 10 on each Soviet SS-18 missile and potentially 100 decoys—also makes the task easier for the defense. Unfortunately for the defense, boost phase is not only short, but can be cut to just 100 seconds.[12]

The Soviets could always add missiles to reestablish the former strategic balance for much less than Americans would have to spend.

Directed-energy systems would in any event have to be vastly scaled up in power and size. The hydrogen fluoride laser, for example, is the most mature of these technologies, and it would have to be a hundred times more powerful than current technology permits in order to destroy Soviet missiles effectively.[13]

Other directed-energy systems would suffer similar difficulties. X-ray lasers, for example, would destroy missiles much more quickly because they provide higher power. But since nuclear explosives provide the "pumping" energy for X-ray lasers, they could not be retargeted if they missed. Because they incorporate nuclear warheads, American "defensive" weapons are unlikely to be cheaper than Soviet "offensive" weapons, particularly since expensive detection and tracking equipment will be required. It is highly unlikely that such sophisticated equipment could be deployed in space at an acceptable cost, and even less that it could be kept perpetually ready to fire.

Some might argue that cost should not matter because a defense against nuclear-tipped missiles would be worth any price. But cost does matter: A laser weapon costing $1 billion could destroy perhaps as many as 20 missiles.[14] Twenty missiles would at most cost only half as much as the laser. Thus, the Soviets could always add missiles to reestablish the former strategic balance for much less money than the Americans would have to spend to regain the new balance. It would be like trying to "keep up with the Joneses" when the Joneses get a 50-percent discount on everything they buy.

Any space-based weapon would also be exceedingly vulnerable to attack. Space mines can be deployed against them. Even sand placed in the orbit of sensitive mirrors could destroy them. And "defensive" directed-energy weapons on one side can destroy directed-energy weapons on the other.

If a ballistic missile defense could work perfectly, it would still not remove the potential for a determined enemy to attack the United States with nuclear weapons. Both the United States and the Soviet Union have bombers and cruise missiles equipped to deliver nuclear explosives, with either side having sufficient force in strategic aircraft alone to destroy the other's society. If the Soviet Union felt really threatened, it could smuggle cargoes past U.S. borders—as drug dealers do every day—and hide nuclear weapons inside them. The hope of a perfect defense against nuclear weapons thus seems, at best, a fantasy. That is why SDI has already taken on new, less-than-perfect missions, with goals that derive from traditional nuclear warfighting strategies. This reality has in fact moved the director of SDI research, Lt. Gen. Dean Abrahamson, to say, "Nowhere have we stated that the goal of the SDI is to come up with a 'leakproof' defense."[15]

SDI's New Missions

The original Reagan version of SDI envisioned protecting cities against nuclear warheads. But a less-than-perfect ballistic missile defense would serve traditional military goals of deterrence. Its objective would be outwardly similar to that of many strategic weapons systems: to reduce the incentive for the other side to strike first with nuclear warheads. It would most likely protect the U.S. Minuteman and MX intercontinental ballistic missile forces or the command, control, and communications systems necessary for actually using the U.S. arsenal.

Though many people assume that only a madman or an accident would launch a nuclear attack, war is conceivable if one side can perceive some advantage in shooting first. The theory of mutual assured destruction is based on the ability to deny any such advantage. If the Soviets, say, were utterly convinced—mistakenly or otherwise—that the United States were about to launch a nuclear war, and that they could attack U.S. missiles and thus avoid complete destruction of Soviet society, they might be tempted to do so even if they would suffer many millions of deaths in the

counterstrikes that would certainly follow. In the elementary psychology of nuclear security, this means attacking—or protecting—the nuclear sword itself.

In the late eighties, it is conceivable if unlikely that the Soviets could destroy just over 80 percent of U.S. intercontinental ballistic missiles in a surprise attack. After such an attack, the Soviets would still face 400 surviving warheads on Minuteman alone, not to mention the strategic air command and over 3,000 submarine-based warheads that could destroy Soviet cities several times over. Though it is difficult to believe the Soviets could find much advantage in striking first under such conditions, some strategic planners point to increasing Soviet missile accuracy and worry that the chance of a disarming first strike on Minuteman is increasing.[16]

As Secretary of Defense, Caspar Weinberger said that one goal of less-than-perfect ballistic missile defense would be to ensure the survival of a minimum number of Minuteman missiles, with the number depending on the intended targets for retaliation as well as the capability of the defensive system. American military planners will probably want to ensure that a sufficient number of warheads on Minuteman and MX missiles alone survived to destroy, say, half of Soviet industry and a quarter of its population—the criteria for assured destruction. This would require some 200–400 equivalent megatons of nuclear explosive.[17]

A similar number would enable the United States to strike a significant set of military targets deemed useful under a warfighting doctrine. Given the average number of warheads per U.S. missile, a goal of 200 surviving missile silos is likely. The number offers a scenario for evaluating issues and priorities bearing directly on the Strategic Defense Initiative.[18]

The question of whether SDI will

"work" can be assessed by comparing the cost of defensive versus offensive strategies—the cost-exchange. The cost to the Soviet Union of defeating a U.S. ballistic missile defense must be higher than the cost to the United States of deploying it; otherwise, a tit-for-tat arms competition would ensue that the United States could not win.[19]

Any ballistic missile defense capable of operating in the nineties will require conventional missile interceptors that attack warheads in their terminal, or reentry, phase. In boost phase, the United States would have no way of knowing which Soviet missiles were targeted on the silos it wanted to protect. The midcourse phase of ballistic missile flight offers much more time for intercept than either the boost or terminal phase, but simple countermeasures would make midcourse interception exceedingly difficult. The Soviets, for example, could throw many thousands of light-weight decoys at the United States along with several thousand warheads.

Terminal-phase silo defense would rely on so-called High Endoatmospheric Defense Interceptors (HEDI), which could destroy incoming weapons at an altitude of 30 kilometers, high enough to avoid blast damage to the unprotected antiballistic missiles. The interceptors would be guided by relatively invulnerable, accurate sensors based in aircraft permanently stationed around the sites to be defended. The warheads would be non-nuclear, directed by homing infrared interceptors, and could destroy targets by hitting them directly or with exploding fragments.[20]

The cost-exchange ratio for a HEDI designed to protect 200 Minuteman silos would depend on interceptor reliability, efficiency, and cost, on the number of warheads that the U.S. defense can force the Soviets to "spend" on each defended target, and on the cost of Soviet weapons. The United States might,

for example, deploy 1,000 interceptors to protect 250 silos and keep secret which ones were to be defended. Each preferentially defended silo would have four interceptors protecting it. The Soviets might then conclude that to destroy all 1,000 silos they would have to add four interceptors to each target, because they would not know which silos were to be defended. Thus if warheads cost the same as interceptors, the Soviets would have to outspend the United States four to one to keep up with U.S. deployments.[21]

But the Soviets would not target U.S. missile silos so simplemindedly. They could exploit the Achilles' heels in the defense such as the need to deploy interceptors in clusters to save money on land, utilities, and personnel. Each cluster of interceptors would represent what amounts to a single target, and it is doubtful that they could defend themselves against a sequence of more than three warheads. The warheads could be "salvage-fused," meaning that they could be set to explode upon contact, and the resulting nuclear effects would seriously degrade defensive detection and tracking capabilities. If four warheads were targeted on a cluster of any number of interceptors, it is likely that one would penetrate to destroy the cluster.[22]

The likely outcome of either side deploying a ballistic missile defense is an expensive new arms race.

The Soviets might feel uncomfortable with the notion of launching warheads in timed sequences or of depending on their ability to blind U.S. radar. If so, they could opt for a simpler but only slightly less favorable strategy of targeting one new warhead on each new interceptor. Because the clusters would represent the most valuable targets from the Soviets' point of view, and because the United States would be forced to defend its interceptor clusters against each warhead, the exchange ratio would be one. The cost-exchange, then, would simply depend on the cost of warheads and interceptors.

A silo defense might be cost-effective if one interceptor were deployed per warhead and if U.S. interceptor costs fell well below $6 million each, the cost per Soviet warhead. Under the assumptions just described, however, a cost-exchange ratio clearly favorable to the defense would not occur for deployments up to 10,000 interceptors. At worst, the Soviets could indefinitely add warheads to match the defense without a losing cost-exchange. At best, the United States would gain a cost advantage so slight it would fall within the range of errors caused by rounding numbers.[23]

The likely outcome of either side deploying a ballistic missile defense is an expensive new arms race. If, for example, the United States initially built 2,000 interceptors to protect Minuteman missiles, it would spend about $25 billion. But the total cost to the Soviet Union to neutralize the deployment by adding new warheads would come to only about $13 billion. If the United States then responded by adding more interceptors to try to recapture the advantage given by its initial deployment—to catch up with the Joneses, as it were—the Soviets could again match the deployment for roughly half the U.S. cost.

Conceivably, a spiral of defensive deployments to protect missiles, offensive countermeasures, and new deployments could cost the superpowers over $100 billion. (See Figure 8–1.) The result would be little change in deterrence, while thousands of additional Soviet

warheads would be aimed at U.S. territory.

A second less-than-perfect mission for ballistic missile defense, according to former Secretary Weinberger, would be to reduce the vulnerability of the U.S. command and control systems for nuclear weapons. Concern that the Soviet Union could "decapitate" the U.S. nuclear arsenal with a preemptive nuclear strike against this network has grown recently, at least among military analysts.[24]

Command, control, and communications systems—ranging from Presidential bunkers through command aircraft to antennae towers—are much more vulnerable targets than missile silos. They are far less hardened against explosive force, and they are not concentrated where they might be protected. Some analysts fear that Soviet destruction of a few vital command targets alone might cause the temporary loss of control of the U.S. arsenal. These installations thus might present tempting targets in a crisis, a possibility that looms large among those who worry that a Soviet strike that delayed or otherwise disorganized a U.S. retaliation would place the United States in danger of capitulation. Analysts who

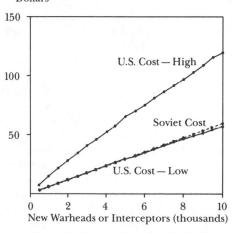

Figure 8-1. Capital Costs for Silo Defense

accept this scenario often find merit in a cost-effective ballistic missile defense that could protect—albeit less than perfectly—certain command and control targets.[25]

Defending command, control, and communications systems under any assumption presents a more difficult problem than defending missile silos. Warning time would be shorter—because they would be attacked by off-shore submarines instead of land-based missiles, and the targets to be protected would be less blast-resistant and far more widely distributed. The systems' proximity to cities would further complicate deployment, for residents would be unlikely to want interceptor missiles based "in my backyard." However, boost-phase intercept of submarine-launched missiles would protect both command installations and bomber bases.

Increases in military expenditures have already heavily burdened the U.S. economy.

The most plausible near-term concept for intercepting Soviet submarine-launched missiles in boost phase would be a system of chemical rockets clustered on orbiting space platforms. The rockets would by necessity be very small and would be guided by separate battle-station satellites in addition to on-board homing infrared detectors. The interceptors would seek the hot plume of an accelerating missile and maneuver to collide with the rocket body.[26]

To be cost-effective, the maximum allowable bill for a 100-percent accurate interceptor would be about $175,000, assuming slower Soviet missiles, and only $40,000 assuming fast-burn boosters. But interceptors are not likely to cost less than $1.7 million each, even if

produced in large quantities. And this does not include the expense of placing interceptors in orbit or the costs associated with the platform or the battle satellites. This scheme thus faces a hopeless cost-exchange. Even the Reagan administration's unrealistic target for interceptor costs, $100,000 each, would not be sufficiently low. The total U.S. bill could run to over $600 billion, 10 times what it would cost the Soviets to neutralize it.[27]

The possibility that interceptor platforms could be mined greatly reduces confidence that the defensive weapons could even survive to begin their mission. The Soviet Union—with existing technology—could launch into orbit devices that would explode on command or upon attack.[28] Thus, if a system were to meet all cost hurdles, a plausible method of self-defense would have to be devised. On the basis of cost or survivability, it would seem that the space-based SDI command and control defense notion is unrealistic.

There is the additional problem of the vulnerability of communications systems and air bases to cruise missile attack. Though cruise missiles can take hours longer to reach targets than ballistic missiles launched by submarine, an early, coordinated attack could be just as disabling. No SDI system is likely to be capable of intercepting these low-flying weapons.

A major problem with the space-based concept is that it could be construed by the Soviets as an attempt to achieve a U.S. first-strike capability. The systems would, in fact, provide at least the potential for intercepting the "ragged" Soviet retaliation that would follow a U.S. first strike. Though silo defense with terminal-phase interceptors would give no such capability, a space-based interceptor system capable of destroying submarine-launched missiles could destroy most of the Soviet missiles that would survive the U.S. strike.

The sudden vulnerability this entails for two thirds of the Soviet nuclear triad would be destabilizing, especially because the remaining leg—the strategic air force—is the weakest superpower nuclear force. The result would likely be an increase in Soviet ballistic missile deployment, strategic defense, or air force, or in all three. Thus, after billions of dollars in investments in defense, the United States would find itself in the same relative strategic balance with the Soviet Union. But, as in the earlier scenario, thousands of additional warheads would now be aimed at U.S. territory.

MILITARY VERSUS ECONOMIC SECURITY

Although SDI will rise or fall primarily on how it affects nuclear security, its price tag ensures another kind of debate. Neither the United States nor the Soviet Union could even in the best of times spend hundreds of billions of dollars without sacrificing vital opportunities. But both superpowers are suffering relative decline in their civilian economies. These problems, perhaps more than the nations' military competition with each other, threaten their positions of leadership in the world.

On its present course, the U.S. economy will in 10 years be as indebted to foreigners as Brazil is today. This scenario does not include the expense of an SDI deployment, which could add as much as $750 billion to U.S. government revenue requirements over the next decade. The global financial crisis that ensued after Brazil, Mexico, and other developing countries accumulated large debts should give pause to anyone who considers what might happen if the

world's largest economy were so imperiled. Nations that cannot maintain balanced trade accounts (without trade barriers) will inevitably suffer declining living standards.[29]

Ability to compete in international markets depends directly on macroeconomic policy—living within one's means. Competitiveness is strongly affected by the strength of the dollar, which increased by 50 percent from 1979 to 1984. This factor alone probably caused three fifths of the prodigious U.S. trade deficit. When the dollar increased in strength, Japanese had to spend more yen to buy an American computer, but Americans could spend fewer dollars to buy a Japanese car. This meant fewer U.S. exports to Japan, and more Japanese exports to the United States. And even with the dollar's recent decline, several years will be required to correct the distortions of overvaluation.[30]

The major reason for the increase in the strength of the dollar was the growing U.S. federal deficit. Since President Reagan took office, the annual federal deficit has increased from about $75 billion to about $200 billion. At the same time, the U.S. trade deficit surged from $20 billion to $170 billion per year. The deficit naturally increased the demand for dollars, which in turn raised their value. This situation was self-reinforcing, since U.S. managers reduced investment—in capital as well as R&D—because the strength of the dollar handicapped them against the Japanese.

The relevance for SDI policy has less to do with laboratory research than with the decision to deploy ballistic missile defenses. That is, the economic problem is the projected cost of an SDI system. Increases in military expenditures have already heavily burdened the U.S. economy, driving the federal budget into deficit. The consumption stimulated by deficit spending also drove the trade accounts deeply into the red. (See Figure

8–2.) If a $750-billion ballistic missile defense is added to this burden, the United States could find itself in deep financial trouble. And testing outside the laboratory may be tantamount to a decision to deploy.

Japan already invests twice as much capital per worker as the United States does. As a result, Japanese labor productivity in the critical automobile and electronic industries exceeds that of the United States. The Japanese pay for high rates of investment—and the jobs that come with them—with lower living standards in the short term. Japan does enjoy the luxury of the protection of the U.S. military. But this fact simply amplifies the more fundamental one that military expenditures are pure consumption, and they detract from sustainable development in the same way that eating seed corn reduces future harvests.[31]

The Soviet Union can also ill afford the diversion of resources from economic performance that a new arms race would cause. General Secretary Gorbachev has undertaken revolution-

ary economic reforms to get an ossified economy moving, and such reform is a delicate and frustrating undertaking even in the best of circumstances. For a nation struggling with vast inefficiency, one with little excess surplus to commit to anything but the prodigious economic task before it, ballistic missile defense would present an unfortunate diversion.

Worse, it could squander the best opportunity the United States has seen in decades for reducing superpower tensions: liberalization of the Soviet Union. This liberalization should lead to greater trade, exchanges, and tourism—things that break down suspicions and tension. After all, as Harvard professor Albert Carnesale points out, the United Kingdom also has enough nuclear-armed missiles to destroy the United States, but no one feels a particular need to erect a defensive umbrella against that nation. Only by reducing the major differences between U.S. and Soviet societies can a basic transformation in superpower relations be achieved.[32]

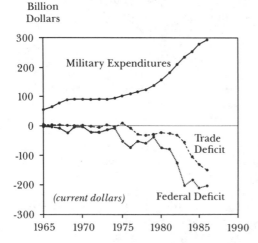

Billion Dollars

Figure 8-2. U.S. Deficits and Military Spending, 1965-86

SDI AND SCIENCE POLICY

"SDI means jobs," President Reagan told the American people in 1986. He was implying that research and development for SDI would provide spin-off technologies for competitiveness. The research might well yield new developments in radar and sensing technology. But these will have limited application to international manufacturing markets, the key source of decline for the U.S. trade position. Military R&D is heavily weighted to development, meaning that most funds go into building prototypes and making demonstrations, not into basic science, which is far more likely to lead to new inventions and commercial products. Recently, less than 3 percent of U.S. military research has gone for basic science.[33]

Nevertheless, a dramatic shift to military matters in research priorities, pushed in part by SDI, has alarmed some observers. The military share of U.S. federal R&D funds increased from roughly 50 percent in 1978 to 68 percent in 1986.[34] (See Figure 8–3.) Though the constant-dollar value of military research has just surpassed the commitment levels of the mid-sixties, this shift has occurred during a period of new challenges for the nation, not just in economic competitiveness, but in public health and the environment as well. It is logical to ask whether defense priorities are undercutting civilian priorities by devouring most scientific resources.

Ability to compete does depend on technology, and consequently on research and development for productivity. Economist John Kendrick has estimated that about two thirds of labor productivity increases in the United States between 1960 and 1973 came

from technological advances. The price and quality of an internationally traded good depends on the capital invested in it, the skills of the laborers who make it, and the cost of the natural resources that go into it.[35]

Technology touches each of these factors of production, for it is not just the efficiency of the machine tool that makes a product, but the training and motivation of the worker and the efficiency of the use of energy and materials. Each factor affects cost and quality. And each can be made more efficient by investment—in plant, the education of workers, the conservation of resources, and the science to improve the contribution of each factor. Research and development can thus also be considered an investment and a factor of production itself.[36]

These trends, coupled with the very high rate of growth in Japanese investment in research and development, have spurred calls in Washington for responses ranging from creation of a Department of Science to a halt to Japanese imports. The United States compares poorly with Japan in R&D committed to nonmilitary ends. (See Table 8–2.) Washington concentrates public research and development funds on high-technology military ends; Tokyo concentrates public funds in neglected areas

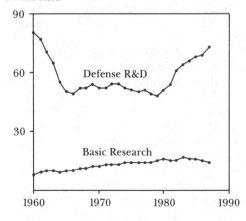

Percent of
Public R&D

Figure 8-3. Selected Trends in U.S. Research Priority, 1960-87

Table 8-2. Nonmilitary Research Expenditures, Selected Countries, 1983

Country	Share of GNP
	(percent)
Japan	2.6
West Germany	2.5
United States	1.9
France	1.7
United Kingdom	1.6

SOURCE: National Science Foundation, *Science Indicators 1985* (Washington, D.C.: 1985).

of lower technology and social and organizational sciences.[37]

Interestingly, the United States experiences its highest trade deficit in low-technology areas, in textiles, for example. And it has lost markets most dramatically in technology requiring more modest amounts of research and development. These are the very areas where government subsidies for research are most justified, in fragmented industries where the motivation for and ability of a single company to conduct R&D is limited, though both the private and social returns could be high. But they are the most neglected in the United States.[38]

Insofar as competitiveness is concerned, it is interesting also to note that almost all Japanese industrial research and development is sponsored by Japanese industry itself.[39] This fact suggests that misplaced U.S. research priorities may not be at the bottom of the competitiveness predicament.

The problem is more deeply rooted in macroeconomic woes, as described earlier, and perhaps in industrial management. The Japanese automobile industry may be more competitive than its U.S. counterpart because it has more competition. That is, some nine automakers in Japan compete for markets while three essentially dominate the U.S. field. Similar observations can be made about the electronics and computer industries.

A recent National Academy of Sciences study concludes that civilian employers have had no more difficulty recently hiring scientists and engineers than during the seventies. One reason for this is that the number of engineering graduates in the United States has doubled over the last decade. Just over 10 percent of engineers work on defense-related projects, while only about 3 percent of scientists are so engaged.[40]

Though the military budget is not nec-essarily "stealing" engineers and scientists from other fields, a connection between science and military priorities does exist. And that is simply one of priorities and the competition for the attention of American leadership. A new set of problems—environmental in essence—now competes with strategic and economic problems for the attention of U.S. and Soviet leaders.

These environment and development problems threaten economies on a global scale. Climate change, energy-use inefficiency, unsanitary water supply, child mortality, population growth—each needs a major injection of scientific resources. The conjuncture of these problems, and the perception that science policy can help resolve them, calls for a fresh look at societies' priorities for science and technology.

But these problems are not accorded the urgency they deserve; leaders are too distracted by the pressing need to avoid nuclear war. The $3.2 billion allocated to the U.S. Strategic Defense Initiative in 1987 was 20 times the federal energy conservation research budget, which declined by almost 7 percent. The Environmental Protection Agency, the Agency for International Development, and the Education Deparment have also experienced declines in research funding.[41]

None of this suggests that research on ballistic missile defense should be abandoned by the superpowers. Indeed, because a one-sided defensive deployment would cause the highest tensions, it is important that neither side place itself in the situation of being unable to match technically the sudden "breakout" or deployment of the other. That is, laboratory research on ballistic missile defenses may be necessary for superpower stability. This goal can be accomplished, however, only as long as all sides keep research strictly limited to the laboratory. Testing interceptors or directed-energy devices pushes systems closer to deployment.

THE REAL WORLD OF SDI

Nuclear weapons are so powerful and diplomacy so weak that the United States and the Soviet Union stand ready to commit murder-suicide on a national—perhaps global—scale in order to avoid domination. Would that it were true that a strategic defense initiative could end for all time the terrible realities of the nuclear age.

But the Reagan vision of perfect defense is an illusion. The technology is too remote, the mission too complex, the possibilities for defeating or circumventing ballistic missile defenses too numerous. The original mission for SDI is no longer taken seriously by mainstream analysts.

The new missions that SDI has taken on are more troubling, however. They raise the spectre of new arms races and imbalances that could make crises much more dangerous. Early U.S. deployment of SDI to defend nuclear weapons would void the Anti-Ballistic Missile Treaty and push the Soviets to add their own defense, many new offensive warheads, or both. The United States and the Soviet Union would be obligated to spend hundreds of billions of dollars each. The result would, at best, make Americans and Soviets poorer.

At worst, an early deployment of SDI would create a far more dangerous world. It could make Soviet submarines vulnerable for the first time. The United States could even achieve the ability to intercept Soviet land-based missiles surviving a U.S. first strike. The possibility that the Soviet Union would be unable to retaliate after a U.S. attack would make the Soviets more trigger-happy, more

likely to find advantage in a nuclear first strike. Now that the superpower relationship has thawed a bit, the negotiation of nuclear arsenals may be both useful and possible. The removal of medium-range missiles from Europe and Asia is a modest step forward. The 50-percent reduction in strategic weapons discussed at the Reykjavik summit could also improve superpower relations, ease tensions, and reduce risks of war somewhat, though no one should imagine that such a reduction would make Mutual Assured Destruction obsolete. Until wiser heads can find a way to circumvent the need for nuclear weapons altogether, balance and accommodation between the nuclear powers is essential. As Princeton foreign policy analyst Daniel Deudney has recently pointed out, too little attention is being given to such options.[42]

The Reagan vision of a perfect defense is an illusion.

The singular act of reaffirming the Anti-Ballistic Missile Treaty of 1972 would avoid the arms race that an SDI deployment would cause. The treaty was drafted and signed to avoid exactly these kinds of instabilities and risks. It states in plain English that testing of new devices outside the laboratory is prohibited.[43] This constraint was the goal—indeed the language—of the U.S. negotiators. The Soviets did object to the restriction, but, more important, they signed the treaty and have obeyed it in that regard.

The Soviets have indeed violated the treaty by building a phased-array radar at Krasnoyarsk, well within their territorial boundary. The treaty prohibited such radars, which could be used to direct an SDI-like system, except on the borders where they would be less effective for use in ballistic missile defenses. Still, in an exchange of thousands of warheads when perhaps only one would destroy the radar (and therefore a ballistic missile defense system dependent on it), the radar poses little threat to U.S. security.

The deployment of SDI technologies would affect the other nuclear powers, but how is not clear. If a defense worked well enough that one superpower could not destroy the arsenals of the other, but imperfectly enough that cities could be attacked, then France, India, Israel, Pakistan, and the United Kingdom would be more equal with the United States and the Soviet Union in nuclear might. That is, their nuclear threats would be more on a strategic par with those of the superpowers.

More important, perhaps, a new arms race caused by SDI-like deployments could threaten the renewal of the Nuclear Non-Proliferation Treaty, signed in 1968 to restrict the spread of nuclear weapons. Many nations were persuaded to forgo arms development in part in return for a commitment by the superpowers to reduce their own arsenals. The treaty expires in 1992; renewal will be difficult enough because the United States and the Soviet Union have vastly expanded their arsenals. If arms expansion were to accelerate, renegotiation of this important treaty could be problematic.

At bottom, the best hope for avoiding nuclear war lies in changing fundamentally the connection between the United States and the Soviet Union. The relationship might actually mature if General Secretary Gorbachev succeeds in liberalizing the Soviet Union, and if American leaders become astute enough to recognize and capitalize on the opportunity. Deploying an SDI system could extinguish this hope.

9

Planning the Global Family

Jodi Jacobson

Thirty-three-year-old Socorro Cisneros de Rosales, a Central American mother of 13, is neither a demographer nor an economist. But in describing her own plight and that of her country as "an overproduction of children and a lack of food and work," Mrs. Cisneros speaks authoritatively on the conflict between high birth rates and declining economies that faces many in the Third World.[1]

Over the past two decades, steadily declining birth rates have contributed to significant improvements in the health and well-being of millions of people and to the growth of national economies. To date, however, only a handful of countries have reduced fertility rates enough to make these gains universal or to ensure that their populations will stabilize in the foreseeable future. Countries that remain on a high fertility path will find that meeting basic subsistence needs will be increasingly difficult in the years to come.

An expanded version of this chapter appeared as Worldwatch Paper 80, *Planning the Global Family.*

Despite lower fertility levels for the world as a whole, population increased by 83 million people in 1987, surpassing a total of 5 billion. Although birth rates continue to fall in many developing countries, the pace has slowed markedly. And declining death rates have balanced out the modest reductions in fertility of the past few years. Furthermore, slower economic growth in developing countries plagued by debt, dwindling exports, and environmental degradation means that governments can no longer rely on socioeconomic gains to help reduce births. This uncertain economic outlook raises important questions. Can governments successfully encourage fertility reductions in the face of extensive poverty? What mix of policies is likely to promote smaller families, thereby reducing fertility and raising living standards?

Encouraging small families requires a two-pronged strategy of family planning and social change. Few countries, however, have put family planning and reproductive health care at the top of their agendas. In most industrial nations, widely available contraceptive technologies enable couples to choose the number and spacing of their children. But for the majority of women in many developing countries, contraceptive methods remain unavailable, inaccessible, or inappropriate. Surveys confirm that half the 463 million married women in developing countries outside of China want no more children. Millions more would like to delay their next pregnancy. Meanwhile, the number of women in their childbearing years is increasing rapidly.[2]

With few exceptions, governments have not changed policies or invested in programs sufficiently to weaken the social conditions underlying high fertility. These conditions include, most significantly, the low status of women and the high illiteracy, low wages, and ill health that customarily accompany it. Until societal attitudes change, national fertility rates are unlikely to decline significantly.

For the majority of women in many developing countries, contraceptive methods remain unavailable, inaccessible, or inappropriate.

International support for family planning has been considerably weakened in recent years by changes in U.S. policy. By the time the world's population surpassed 5 billion in 1987, the United States had abdicated its role as a leading supporter of reproductive rights worldwide. Political and societal disputes have converged with fiscal constraints to cut funding for contraceptive research and for both domestic and international family planning. This policy change has set worldwide efforts to reduce fertility back by several years, dimming hopes of achieving population stabilization by the end of the next century.

Reducing birth rates to speed the development process is a goal that deserves the immediate attention of the world community—one that will benefit every segment of society. For women, bearing fewer children means better health for themselves and their offspring. For countries, reducing average family size increases per capita investments and alleviates pressures on the natural resources that underpin national economies. For the world, slower population growth enhances the prospects for widespread security and prosperity.

FERTILITY TRENDS WORLDWIDE

Childbearing trends are most clearly represented by total fertility rates, defined as the average number of children a woman will bear at prevailing levels of fertility. A country that has achieved replacement-level fertility of about 2.1 births per woman is well on the road to a stable population size. Once this level has been reached, births and deaths eventually balance out. A population at or below replacement level may continue to grow for two or three generations, however, if the group reaching childbearing age is larger than that reaching old age and dying.

With few exceptions, total fertility rates in the industrial world are at or below replacement level. In France, the United Kingdom, and the United States, for example, the rate is 1.8 births per woman; in Denmark, Italy, and West Germany, it is below 1.5. As a result of low birth rates and populations distributed about evenly among age-groups, these countries will stop growing in the near future. The United Kingdom, for example, is projected to stabilize at 59 million people, about 5 percent above its current population.[3]

Developing countries can be divided into two groups. In the first, fertility rates declined significantly over the past two decades, although few have reached replacement level. In the second group, mostly countries in sub-Saharan Africa, fertility rates have not declined at all.

Twenty countries for which there are reliable data show fertility declines of more than 20 percent since 1960. (See Table 9–1.) The most dramatic change took place in several East Asian nations and in Cuba, where fertility levels dropped by as much as 75 percent. Only one Middle Eastern country (Turkey) and two African ones (Egypt and Tunisia) have experienced fertility declines of more than a fifth since 1960. China reduced fertility rates by 56 percent since the sixties; Chile, Colombia, and Costa Rica, by more than 50 percent each. Significant reductions were also achieved in Brazil, Indonesia, Mexico, and Thailand. Nevertheless, fertility rates remain moderately high, above 3.5 children per woman, in several of these countries.

Despite some impressive gains, only 4 of the 20 countries listed in Table 9–1 achieved replacement-level fertility: Cuba, Singapore, South Korea, and Taiwan. These four have also made tremendous economic strides. In demographic terms, however, they are responsible for only a minuscule fraction of annual increases to the global population.

Trends in the more populous countries are much more important to global population growth. Between 1987 and 2007, five countries in Table 9–1—Brazil, China, India, Indonesia, and Mexico—will account for 37 percent of total world population growth. Cumulatively, these five will add nearly 700 million people, slightly fewer than India's current population. By 2020, India will rival China as the world's largest nation, with

Table 9-1. Fertility Declines in Selected Countries, 1960–87

Country	Total Fertility Rate		Change
	1960	1987	
	(average number of children per woman)		(percent)
Singapore	6.3	1.6	−75
Taiwan	6.5	1.8	−72
South Korea	6.0	2.1	−65
Cuba	4.7	1.8	−62
China	5.5	2.4	−56
Chile	5.3	2.4	−55
Colombia	6.8	3.1	−54
Costa Rica	7.4	3.5	−53
Thailand	6.6	3.5	−47
Mexico	7.2	4.0	−44
Brazil	6.2	3.5	−44
Malaysia	6.9	3.9	−43
Indonesia	5.6	3.3	−41
Turkey	6.8	4.0	−41
Tunisia	7.3	4.5	−38
Sri Lanka	5.9	3.7	−37
India	6.2	4.3	−31
Philippines	6.6	4.7	−29
Peru	6.6	4.8	−27
Egypt	6.7	5.3	−21

SOURCE: 1960 data from Ansley Coale, "Recent Trends in Fertility in Less Developed Countries," *Science*, August 26, 1983; 1987 data from Population Reference Bureau, *1987 World Population Data Sheet* (Washington, D.C.: 1987).

about 1.3 billion people. And Mexicans will then number 138 million, more people than are in all of Central America and the Caribbean today. China, with a current fertility rate of 2.4 births per woman, is the only one of these demographic giants likely to achieve replacement-level fertility in the near future.[4]

Fertility is declining much more slowly

now, and in some countries appears to have reached a standstill. A recent report from the Indian National Academy of Science shows that the total fertility rate there declined by about 16 percent between 1972 and 1978, from 5.6 births per woman of reproductive age to 4.7. But the pace has slowed markedly since then. In 1987, Indian women bore on average 4.3 children, only 8 percent below the figure in 1978. Egypt, the Philippines, and Tunisia show similar trends.[5]

Pockets of extremely high fertility—above six children per woman—still exist throughout Africa and the Middle East. (See Table 9–2.) Sub-Saharan Africa faces the highest fertility rates and population growth rates in the world. Nigerian women, for instance, bear nearly seven children on average. Most Middle Eastern countries also maintain high fertility levels, as do Bangladesh and Pakistan.

A tradition of large families in countries where young people are predominant means these nations will experience massive population increases over the generation ahead. Pakistan's population will more than double over the next 30 years, from 105 million to well over 240 million; Nigeria's will reach 274 million, up from its current population of 109 million; and Bangladesh's 104 million will grow to 200 million.[6]

Lowering birth rates will help ease the transition from persistent poverty to sustainable development by reducing pressure on national resources. For example, a 1985 analysis by Kenya's National Council for Population and Development projected the country's future population size under two scenarios. It showed that at current fertility rates, Kenyans—now 22 million—would number 57 million in 2010, as opposed to 38 million if total fertility dropped by half, to four children per woman. With the smaller population size, corn require-

Table 9-2. Countries With High Fertility, 1987

Country	Total Fertility Rate	Population Growth Rate
	(average number of children per woman)	(percent)
Kenya	8.0	3.9
Afghanistan	7.6	2.6
Jordan	7.4	3.7
Tanzania	7.1	3.5
Zambia	7.0	3.5
Saudi Arabia	6.9	3.1
Ethiopia	6.7	2.3
Senegal	6.7	2.8
Nigeria	6.6	2.8
Pakistan	6.6	2.9
Sudan	6.5	2.8
Zimbabwe	6.5	3.5
Iran	6.3	3.2
Bangladesh	6.2	2.7
Zaire	6.1	3.1

SOURCE: Population Reference Bureau, *1987 World Population Data Sheet* (Washington, D.C.: 1987).

ments would be eased by 3.2 million tons, twice the amount that Kenyan farmers produced in 1980.[7]

THE ROLE OF FAMILY PLANNING

Family planning has played an important role in reducing fertility throughout the world. Countries such as China, Mexico, and Thailand have devoted extensive government resources to expanding services and supplying contraceptives. In Brazil, the efforts of private voluntary organizations have been key to declining birth rates. Nevertheless, in a substantial number of high fertility countries, family planning programs are weak or nonexistent, in part because governments have been slow to allocate the necessary resources. But the recent experiences of several nations suggest a close relationship between effective voluntary family planning programs, rising levels of contraceptive use, and declining fertility, even in the absence of broad-based economic gains.

Programs on family planning primarily affect fertility by raising contraceptive prevalence—the share of married women of reproductive age who use modern contraception to prevent pregnancy. Modern birth control methods like the pill and intrauterine device (IUD) are far more effective at preventing pregnancy than their traditional counterparts, such as withdrawal. The cost, availability, and effectiveness of birth control dictate the difference between the number of children a couple wants and the number they actually have. Significantly, the demand for contraceptive information and supplies is rising among groups traditionally resistant to family planning,

namely the urban and rural poor.

Unmet need, defined as the gap between the number of women who express a desire to limit fertility and the number who actually are able to do so, exists to varying degrees in virtually every developing country. This gap results from inadequate access to or knowledge of family planning methods, even where programs already exist. According to data from the World Fertility Survey (an international reproductive trends survey sponsored by the United Nations between 1974 and 1984), 40–50 percent of women of reproductive age in 18 developing countries desire no more children but have no access to family planning. Fertility rates could be reduced by 30 percent in these countries if unwanted births were prevented.[8]

In India, half the couples contacted in the 1980 All-India Family Planning Survey wished to limit family size, but only 28 percent were using a modern method of birth control. (See Table 9–3.) The gap between desired and actual family size spotlights the inadequacy of family planning programs.

Two thirds of the couples surveyed

Table 9-3. Unmet Need for Family Planning in Egypt, India, Peru, and Rural Ghana

Country	Share of Women of Reproductive Age		
	Wanting No More Children	Using Contraception	Unmet Need
	(percent)		
India	50	28	22
Egypt	56	30	26
Peru	70	25	45
Ghana, Rural Areas near Accra	90	10	80

SOURCE: Peruvian and Indian data from *International Family Planning Perspectives,* September 1984 and March 1986; Hussein A.A.H. Sayed et al., *Fertility and Family Planning in Egypt 1984* (Columbia, Md.: Egypt National Population Council/Westinghouse Public Applied Systems, 1985); Robert M. Press, "Family Planning Gains Some Favor in Africa," *Christian Science Monitor,* January 7, 1987.

felt three children was ideal, although most couples in India have four or more. Similarly, a 1985 survey showed that while 56 percent of Egyptian women wanted no more children, only 30 percent were using contraceptives. These surveys actually define a minimum level of unmet need: Because a significant share of respondents have never even heard of a family planning method, they are unlikely to identify a need for one even if they desire smaller families.

Not surprisingly, the countries with the strongest commitment to family planning are making the greatest strides in reducing fertility, regardless of their level of development. In Indonesia, a predominantly rural country with a per capita income of $530, a well-organized national family planning program has been in operation since 1969. A 1987 government survey indicates that between 1980 and 1985 contraceptive prevalence increased from 27 to nearly 41 percent of married women of reproductive age. A striking 42-percent decline in the number of births per woman of reproductive age occurred between 1970 and 1985, with the most significant drop after 1980. Due to the government's efforts to make family planning universally available, over 80 percent of Indonesian contraceptive users rely on modern methods.[9]

Examining data from the World Fertility Survey, University of Michigan sociologist Ronald Freedman showed that contraceptive use varies little among Indonesians in different social and economic groups. Couples with low living standards are almost as likely to use contraception as those with the highest standards. Professional and clerical workers are only slightly ahead of farmers with small landholdings. And villages without modern amenities like electricity have contraceptive prevalence levels about as high as those with such facilities.[10]

In Bangladesh, a deteriorating agrarian economy has raised the ante on large families just when a growing family planning program is making birth control cheaper. Agricultural wages today are below those of 150 years ago in constant dollars. Demographer Samuel Preston notes that much of the decline in real wages occurred since the fifties, a period of rapid population growth. The number of landless families has mushroomed. Parents do not see a very bright future for their children: Land scarcity has undermined traditional inheritance practices, while rising educational costs have foreclosed employment options outside the agricultural sector.[11]

One study based on data from three government surveys found that the adoption of family planning methods in Bangladesh has accelerated gradually in recent years in response to greatly improved services. Between 1969 and 1983, the share of married women who said they did not want additional children increased slightly, from 52 to 57 percent. Over the same period, contraceptive use increased steadily among both rural and urban women of all educational levels and all family sizes. In 1969, fully 93 percent of Bangladeshi women who wished to end childbearing were not using contraceptives; by 1983, this unmet need had declined to 71 percent, albeit still a high level. The study concludes that deteriorating economic and environmental conditions "may have influenced couples . . . to believe that large families are burdensome."[12]

The lowest contraceptive prevalence rates (and the highest fertility rates) are found in sub-Saharan Africa, where the use of modern methods of birth control is rising quite slowly. Until recently, most African governments firmly opposed family planning programs on the grounds that curtailing population growth would limit the region's ability to recognize its economic potential. The low status of women has made childbearing the only rite of passage for girls. And lack of funds and poor service delivery systems hinder the dissemination of information and methods outside major urban areas. Surveys show that fewer than a fifth of Nigerian women have ever heard of a modern method of birth control. In Kenya, less than 40 percent of women familiar with at least one modern contraceptive method knew of a supply source; fewer than half of these women could reach the source on a 30-minute walk.[13]

Despite these constraints, the desire both to space and limit births is increasingly evident in some African countries, particularly among educated women and those living in urban areas. Evidence of fertility decline due to strong family planning programs exists in sub-Saharan Africa. In 1982, a government survey showed that contraceptive prevalence in Zimbabwe stood at 14 percent for both modern and traditional methods. That year, Prime Minister Robert Mugabe committed his government to a strong family planning effort to slow population growth and promote economic development. The program was immediately incorporated into the Ministry of Health, linking it with training and outreach for maternal and child health care. Zimbabwe made a financial commitment unparalleled among sub-Saharan nations, allocating $24 million to the program. By 1984, total contraceptive prevalence reached 38 percent (27 percent for modern methods), a remarkable increase for any country.[14]

By reducing fertility levels, and hence the total amount of per capita social expenditures necessary just to maintain the economic status quo, family planning programs can help raise living standards. Between 1972 and 1984, for example, every peso spent on family planning by Mexico's urban social security system (IMSS) saved nine pesos that would otherwise have been spent on maternal and infant health care. During this time, IMSS spent 38 billion pesos ($165 million) to provide nearly 800,000 women with contraceptive supplies, thus averting 3.6 million births and 363,000 abortions. Net savings for IMSS equaled 318 billion pesos ($1.4 billion), which was rechanneled into pension payments and expansion of general health care services.[15]

Programs to increase the use of birth control are not a substitute for investments in education or efforts to raise per capita incomes. But reducing fertility is integral to any economic development strategy, allowing governments to raise per capita investments in health, education, and other social services. The growing desire for smaller families shows that family planning has a major role to play in virtually every nation. Developing countries that encourage family planning may be the first to experience rapid and widespread social and economic advances.

FAMILY PLANNING AND HEALTH

Family planning is among the most basic of preventive health care strategies, though it is rarely recognized as such. Encouraging fewer and safer births among women in developing countries will reduce unacceptably high rates of maternal mortality from complications of childbirth and abortion. Moreover, by distributing condoms and increasing the public's understanding of reproductive health issues, family planning programs can help control the spread of acquired immunodeficiency syndrome (AIDS), a major threat to Third World health and economic survival.

Each year, at least a half-million women worldwide die from pregnancy-related causes. Fully 99 percent of these deaths occur in the Third World, where complications arising from pregnancy and illegal abortions are the leading killers of women in their twenties and thirties. World Health Organization (WHO) officials caution that maternal deaths—those resulting directly or indirectly from pregnancy within 42 days of childbirth, induced abortion, or miscarriage—may actually be twice the estimated figures. What is more, for every woman who dies, many more suffer serious, often long-term, health problems. That bearing life brings death to so many women is a distressing irony. It is even more distressing given that family planning and preventive medicine could substantially reduce these losses.[16]

Family planning programs can help control the spread of AIDS, a major threat to Third World health and economic survival.

In the Third World, maternal mortality accounts for some 25 percent of deaths of women aged 15 to 49. More than 3,000 maternal deaths occur per 100,000 live births annually in parts of Ethiopia and Bangladesh. (See Table 9–4.) By contrast, the figures in the United States and Norway are only 10 and 2, respectively. Each year, over 20,-000 women die from pregnancy or related complications in Bangladesh, compared with about 500 women in the United States, a country with more than twice as many people.[17]

Illegal abortion is one of the major direct causes of maternal death. Rough estimates indicate that only half the estimated 54 million abortions performed annually around the world are legal. Most illegal abortions are carried out under unsanitary conditions by unskilled attendants, leaving women vulnerable to serious complications and infection. By contrast, modern abortion procedures, carried out under proper medical supervision in countries where they are legal, cause fewer maternal deaths than pregnancy or oral contraceptives do.[18]

Forty-four percent of women in the developing world (outside of China) live in countries where abortion is allowed only to save the mother's life. Another 10 percent live in countries where abortion is totally prohibited. Sadly, millions of women unable to obtain a legal abortion on the basis of life-threatening circumstances have subsequently died from the complications of an illegal abortion. Those who advocate restrictive abortion policies rarely acknowledge this toll on women's lives.[19]

Estimates of the annual number of deaths due to abortion complications range from 155,000 to 204,000 women worldwide. Abortion-related deaths are especially common among poor and illiterate women living in countries with strict abortion laws. In Latin America, where legal abortion is generally restricted to cases of rape or endangerment of the woman's life, up to half of maternal deaths appear to be due to illegal abortions.[20]

Pregnancy itself takes a greater toll on a woman's body in regions where malnutrition and poor health are the norm. In the Third World, pregnancy is associated with a higher incidence of health-threatening infection, vitamin and mineral deficiencies, and anemia.

Table 9-4. Maternal Mortality Ratios, Selected Countries

Country	Maternal Mortality Ratios (deaths per 100,000 live births)	Study Region and Year
Ethiopia	3,500[1]	Urban, 1984
Bangladesh	3,000[2]	National, 1983
Senegal	700[1]	Rural, 1983
India	400–500[2]	National, 1984
Egypt	190	Rural, 1981–83
Romania	175	National, 1982
Mexico	103	National, 1978
Thailand	81	National, 1981
Chile	73	National, 1980
United States	10[1]	National, 1979
Norway	2	National, 1981

[1]Unknown whether deaths from abortions included.   [2]Deaths from abortions not included.
SOURCE: World Health Organization, *Maternal Mortality Rates: A Tabulation of Available Information* (Geneva: 1985).

Due to reduced immunity, common diseases such as pneumonia and influenza cause 50–100 percent more deaths in pregnant than in nonpregnant women.[21]

Three groups of women face the highest risk of pregnancy-related deaths—those at either end of their reproductive cycle, those who bear children in rapid succession, and those who have more than four children. Due to biological factors, women under 19 or over 35 are more susceptible to complications of pregnancy. Women giving birth to children spaced less than a year apart are twice as likely to die from pregnancy-related causes than those who have children two or more years apart. In Matlab Thana, Bangladesh, health workers recorded three times as many deaths among women giving birth to their eighth child as among those giving birth to their third.[22]

At least half of all maternal deaths can be averted through a combined strategy of family planning, legal abortion, and primary health care. According to researchers Beverly Winikoff and Maureen Sullivan of The Population Council, a fertility rate reduction of 25–35 percent resulting from more widely available family planning would also lower maternal mortality by one fourth. Making abortions legal and safe could reduce the toll an additional 20–25 percent. Making all pregnancies safer through increased investments in prenatal health care and reducing the number of high-risk pregnancies would prevent another 20–25 percent of deaths. Winikoff and Sullivan point out that while, theoretically, this three-pronged strategy could reduce maternal mortality by three fourths, a 50-percent decrease is a more realistic expectation, given prevailing social and political conditions, such as large desired family size and the opposition to legalizing abortion.[23]

Establishing integrated family planning and health strategies will be well worth the investment. Village-based paramedics and midwives can teach women the benefits of birth spacing, breast-feeding, prenatal care, and contraceptive use. Small-scale maternity centers—on the order of one for every 4,000 people—could promote simple solutions to some of the most pervasive maternal health problems, by providing, for instance, iron supplements to treat anemia. Linked with regional facilities run by doctors, such clinics would constitute a pivotal link between rural populations and the often urban-based medical community. Assuming that maternal deaths run as high as 1 million per year, family planning and health care would save at least 500,000 women's lives annually, and improve the health of millions more.[24]

Family planning and health care would save at least 500,000 women's lives annually, and improve the health of millions more.

Ironically, new health threats may push family planning services to the top of national agendas. By October 1987, the total number of reported AIDS cases worldwide (of persons who have tested positive for the virus) had exceeded 68,000, more than one sixth of whom were in developing countries. Although the United States leads the world, with nearly 45,500 documented cases as of November 1987, the potential devastation from AIDS appears to be a far greater threat in developing countries. WHO estimates that between 5 million and 10 million people around the world may now be infected with the virus that can lead to AIDS, and that at least 2 million of them are in Africa. Approximately 6,000 cases have been found in Latin America and the Caribbean thus far. Current health care problems may only foreshadow far more serious public health burdens.[25]

As transmission of this new virus through sexual contact is the single greatest route of infection, AIDS prevention and education can effectively be carried out by family planning and related health programs. Next to total abstinence, condoms offer the best protection against the spread of sexually transmitted diseases. Yet, primarily for cultural reasons, condoms are rarely used in most of the Third World. Excluding China, fewer than one third of the world's 45 million condom users live in developing countries.[26]

Increasing the availability of condoms and linking their use with better health may slow the spread of AIDS. Instructing health care workers on the dangers of reusing needles and of performing routine procedures with unsanitary implements, and securing adequate supplies of medical equipment, will ensure that the health care community itself is not responsible for spreading the virus.

Scientists currently believe that between 25 and 50 percent of those infected with the virus that can lead to AIDS will die in the next 10 years. In developing countries, this disease will primarily afflict individuals aged 20 to 49. Both pregnancy- and AIDS-related deaths thus strike at people in their prime, taking a tremendous toll in human life and productive capacity. The need for public education about reproductive health is stronger than ever.[27]

CHANGING CONTRACEPTIVE TECHNOLOGIES

Nearly 30 years after the introduction of oral contraceptives, millions of couples in the developing world remain without the means to plan their families. Poor supply and distribution networks are part of the problem. But contraceptive prevalence in the Third World remains low, in part, because few of the methods currently available fit the life-styles or the pocketbooks of potential users. Today's menu of technologies is not versatile enough, nor is it changing quickly enough, to meet the needs of a highly diverse and growing world population.

About 372 million of the 860 million married couples of reproductive age worldwide use modern contraceptives, a prevalence rate of 43 percent. (See Table 9–5.) Among couples in developing countries outside of China, use of modern methods is much lower than the world average. Although more than half indicate a desire to practice family planning, only 27 percent actually do.

At least nine reversible contraceptives are on the market, including hormonal methods and less effective barrier devices. Their distribution is highly skewed to particular regions or countries. Eighty-three million women have IUDs, the most prevalent reversible method; nearly three fourths of them are in China. By contrast, the 64 million users of oral contraceptives are more evenly divided between the Third World and industrialized countries. Nearly 60 million people, about two thirds of whom live in the industrial world, rely primarily on condoms, diaphragms, and sponges.

Contraceptives vary significantly in their effectiveness, depending on the skill and consistency with which a given method is used. As a group, hormonal

Table 9-5. Estimated Use of Effective Birth Control Methods, 1986

Birth Control Method[1]	China	Other Developing Countries	Industrial Countries	World
	(million)			
Female Sterilization	53	45	15	113
Intrauterine Devices	59	13	11	83
Oral Contraceptives	9	28	27	64
Condoms	5	12	28	45
Male Sterilization	17	18	8	43
Other Effective Methods[2]	3	8	13	24
Total Users	146	124	102	372
Total Couples at Risk[3]	200	463	197	860
	(percent)			
Contraceptive Prevalence (users as share of those at risk)	73	27	52	43
	(million)			
Abortions	12	16	26	54

[1]Effective or modern methods excludes natural family planning (rhythm), withdrawal, abstinence, and breast-feeding.   [2]Includes diaphragms, sponges, injectables, and implants.   [3]Number of married couples of reproductive age at risk of pregnancy; does not include those currently pregnant or sterile for other than contraceptive reasons.
SOURCE: Population Crisis Committee, "Access to Birth Control: A World Assessment," Briefing Paper No. 19, Washington, D.C., October 1987.

methods, including implants and injectables, have the lowest failure rates. Birth control pills—the most established hormonal method—have the widest failure range in that group. The effectiveness of these oral contraceptives, which must be taken every day, depends on a high level of individual motivation and an understanding of self-administered drugs.

Injectable contraceptives have been on the market for about a decade and are among the most effective hormonal methods. Approximately 6.5 million women around the world use injectables, one sixth of whom are Chinese. The injectable Depo-Provera, approved in 90 countries, prevents conception for three months. Injectables effective for one month are used primarily in China and Latin America.[28]

At the other end of the scale of effectiveness, natural family planning—also known as the rhythm method or periodic abstinence—has consistently high failure rates. Worldwide, between 10 million and 15 million people use rhythm, most of whom live in industrial countries. This technique requires a woman to time her ovulatory cycle by charting bodily functions, such as basal temperature, on a daily basis. Because a significant proportion of women everywhere experience highly variable menstrual cycles, fertile periods may be hard to calculate, and reliance on this method can often lead to unwanted pregnancy. Apart from other drawbacks, periodic abstinence requires a degree of cooperation between husband and wife that is unusual in many cultures.[29]

No one contraceptive can fit the needs of every couple any more than one eyeglass prescription can correct all vision problems. In many cultures, for example, the diaphragm is considered undesirable because women are uncomfortable with inserting it. It may also be impractical where water for washing is in short supply. Though the pill is relatively inexpensive, it may be a highly ineffective method where primary health care is poor and contraceptive supplies uncertain. And unexpected or unpleasant side effects can cause considerable anxiety among women in countries where medical advice is hard to come by.

First-year discontinuation rates between 20 and 40 percent among new pill and IUD users in the Third World indicate that these methods will not be effective in meeting the needs of most women in these countries. Advances in contraceptive technology that address concerns about safety and side effects will help speed the transition from high to low fertility around the world.[30]

It can take 15 years or more under good conditions for a new contraceptive to move from laboratory to market availability.

Long-acting, inexpensive methods of birth control are more likely to serve the needs of low-income consumers in developing countries. In this category, recently developed hormonal implants show considerable promise. One such product, NORPLANT, is the most effective reversible contraceptive yet developed, offering protection against pregnancy for five years. Small permeable rods filled with timed-release hormones are implanted under the skin of the upper arm in a simple surgical procedure. The rods can be removed at any time. NORPLANT has already been approved in 10 countries, including China, Colombia, Finland, Indonesia, Sweden, and Thailand, and is still undergoing evaluation in 26 others. A two-year implant, NORPLANT-2, is under study in several countries. The price tag for NORPLANT runs about $2.80 per year of protection, a cost that can be significantly reduced as production increases.[31]

It can take 15 years or more under good conditions for a new contraceptive to move from laboratory to market availability. Contraceptives evolve from a lengthy process of basic and applied research, product development, testing, marketing, and safety evaluation. In order to be registered in the United States and most other countries, experimental methods must pass muster through a series of animal and human clinical studies that usually take more than a decade to complete. Relatively few of the many leads scientists follow result in a marketable product. Not surprisingly, contraceptive development is an expensive and uncertain undertaking.[32]

Several new hormonal methods aimed at Third World consumers are in varying stages of development. WHO is investigating two new monthly injectables, Cycloprovera and HRP102, both of which will be tested in clinical trials beginning in 1988. Biodegradable injectables and implants, which break down over time and do not require surgical removal, are in the early stages of testing. All of these are more effective and have fewer side effects than their currently available counterparts. Market introduction of more revolutionary methods, like a two-year pregnancy vaccine, a reversible contraceptive for men that reduces sperm count, and chemicals for nonsurgical female sterilization, is still far off. How quickly these methods become available hinges on the amount of money and scientific effort invested in contraceptive R&D.[33]

Each new contraceptive technology results in an increase in the total number of users worldwide, which in turn translates into lower fertility rates. Unfortunately, the prospects for developing and disseminating new methods are not bright. Measured in constant dollars, global funding for overall reproductive research—including basic nondirected research, contraceptive research and development, and safety evaluation—peaked in 1973. (See Figure 9–1.)[34]

Since 1973, European contributions to the field have declined in both constant and current dollars. The U.S. expenditure, averaging roughly 75 percent of the total since 1965, has declined by 23 percent in real terms since 1978. China and India alone among Third World countries have spent more than $1 million annually in these areas. Moreover, cutbacks in public support for contraceptive research funding come at a time when the private sector is moving away from developing new methods, placing the burden of contraceptive evolution on often cash-poor, nonprofit research institutions. (See Table 9–6.)[35]

Reduced funding and an inhospitable political climate are delaying the development and introduction of contraceptive technology just as the demand for new methods is multiplying. About $100 million is needed annually through 2000 to take new products out of the lab and put them onto the market. Creating an international consortium of public and private groups to promote cooperation on contraceptive research and recom-

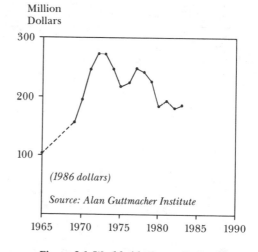

Million
Dollars

(1986 dollars)

Source: Alan Guttmacher Institute

Figure 9-1. Worldwide Expenditures for Reproductive Research, Contraceptive R&D, and Safety Evaluation, 1965-83

Table 9-6. Annual Average Public and Private Expenditures for Contraceptive Product Development, 1980–83

Method	Total Expenditures	Share from	
		Private Sector	Public Sector
	(million dollars)	(percent)	
Established Methods			
Oral Contraceptives	6.75	97	3
Barrier Methods	1.63	39	61
Intrauterine Devices	1.06	52	48
Spermicides	1.05	51	49
Natural Family Planning	0.21	17	83
Condoms	0.07	100	—
New Methods			
Postovulatory	6.89	81	19
Nonsteroid Ovulation Inhibitor	5.54	57	43
Male Contraceptives	3.65	35	65
Vaccines	2.26	9	91
Implants	1.92	—	100
Injectables	1.27	29	71
Vaginal Rings	0.99	—	100
Tubal Sterilization	0.43	—	100
Other	2.72	100	—
Multiple[1]	15.12	—	100
Total	51.56		

[1]Grants given for research on several different methods, which could not be broken down.
SOURCE: Adapted from Linda Atkinson et al., "The Next Contraceptive Revolution," *International Family Planning Perspectives*, December 1985.

mend uniform regulatory standards among countries would speed that development process.[36]

THE INGREDIENTS OF SUCCESS

Without fertility declines, many governments cannot hope to make the invest-

ments necessary to improve human welfare and encourage economic development. But a number of political and social obstacles remain for countries wishing to reduce fertility, improve health, and raise living standards. Attaining these goals will depend on fundamental changes in several areas, including the way governments shape population policies, the degree to which they make contraceptive supplies and information accessible, and the steps they take to improve the status of women and increase their access to education. Governments can use a mix of policies to hasten the transition to lower fertility. Population-related policies, such as laws governing minimum age at marriage, delivery of family planning services, and the importation or manufacture of contraceptive methods, directly affect the determinants of fertility. Official sanction of family planning efforts in the form of revised policies and legal codes is likely to increase acceptance of these services and help dispel widespread myths and misconceptions about contraception. Public policies concerning development indirectly affect fertility by influencing economic opportunities, social services, literacy, mortality, and the status of women.

A transformation in the laws, attitudes, and beliefs that directly and indirectly encourage high fertility will be essential to achieving population stabilization. Over the past decade, there have been promising changes in the attitudes of African officials toward population policy and family planning. Thirteen of the 42 sub-Saharan countries have issued explicit population policies, and 11 of them have incorporated in their development plans policies specifically aimed at population problems. In discussing demographic trends, leaders have cited environmental degradation, unemployment, and the difficulty of raising living standards among their growing concerns. In the words of one Kenyan official, "If more and more people keep pouring into a country that can only deliver so much, you can expect political unrest, serious shortage of food and everything else that people need to live, and in general, chaos."[37]

Realistic goals are an essential aspect of any national population policy. Programs that attempt to enforce norms—such as a two-child family—upon society before they have some cultural acceptance usually do not succeed. Sociologist

Ronald Freedman notes that "setting a goal of a two child family as soon as possible may be a necessary and rational [long term] policy goal. [But] to press for only two, when the real potential for decreasing fertility [in the short run] is to encourage reducing desired family size from six children to four, makes the effort appear alien and ridiculous."[38]

Countries that do not start now to reduce fertility may face stark choices later, however. The conflicts between individual desires and societal goals that result from excessive population growth are evident in China's one-child family program, perhaps the best known and most controversial of all fertility reduction campaigns.

Programs that attempt to enforce norms before they have some cultural acceptance usually do not succeed.

In 1953, the first census taken in China revealed a rapidly growing population of about 582 million. But Mao Zedong, Communist Party Chairman at that time, did not see China's expanding millions as a problem. Less than 30 years later the Chinese numbered 1 billion, more than a fifth of the world's population living on 7 percent of the world's arable land. By the late seventies, years of famine, poverty, and political upheaval had convinced the leaders in Beijing of the need for a rigorous family planning campaign.[39]

Today's one-child family program evolved out of a series of strategies that began in the early seventies with the Wan Xi Shao (Later, Longer, Fewer) program. This strategy encouraged delayed marriage, longer birth intervals, and smaller families. Even so, China's population continued to grow rapidly.

As a result, policymakers enacted the one-child family policy in the hope of holding the population to about 1.2 billion just after the turn of the century.[40]

The policy, intended to last through 2000, offers a series of incentives and disincentives. Substantial pay increases, better housing, longer maternity leaves, and priority access to education are among the benefits offered to one-child families, while heavy fines and social criticism await couples who bear more than one. China's original policy, often seen as monolithic in its application, actually allows certain segments of the population to have more than one child. Urban couples are generally expected to adhere to the policy. But ethnic minorities and rural couples—80 percent of the nation's population—are allowed two or more.[41]

Several other countries have turned to incentives in their attempts to influence fertility trends. Most such programs have targeted individuals or couples, such as the programs in India and Bangladesh offering financial incentives for sterilization. Several have experienced uneven success, and in some cases have incited charges of coercion.

On the other hand, experimental incentive programs aimed at overall community participation and development have shown some promise. A pilot program in northeastern Thailand tested the effects of community-level incentives on contraceptive prevalence. Loan funds of $2,000 each were set up in several villages in conjunction with a family planning and health program. Initially, loans to individuals were based on character, credit-worthiness, and the project to be carried out. After the program became established, preference was given to applicants who were practicing family planning. Members of the loan fund received shares and dividends on the basis of the contraceptive method used; more effective methods had higher values. As the level of contraceptive prevalence within a village increased, so did the total amount of the loan fund.[42]

The Thai program was designed to prevent coercion. Money was not subtracted from a loan fund if contraceptive prevalence fell; shares in the loan fund and the right to borrow were not taken away from those who chose not to continue using contraceptives. At the end of two years, loans totaling $72,000 had been granted for small-scale income-generating projects, such as pig and silk farming and cassava cultivation. During that period, contraceptive prevalence in the experimental villages rose from 46 to 75 percent; in control villages, it went from 51 to 57 percent. By mixing small-family incentives with programs to increase community self-sufficiency, this experiment demonstrated the link between lower fertility and higher standards of living.[43]

Women hold a paradoxical place in many societies. As mothers and wives, they often bear sole responsibility for childrearing and domestic duties. In many cultures, they are bound by custom and necessity to contribute to household income; in some, they are the only breadwinners. Despite these roles as the linchpins of society, women—particularly in the developing world—have few rights under the law regarding land tenure, marital relations, income, or social security.

In traditional African societies, women are required to be economically self-sufficient but remain legally and socially dependent on husbands and parents. On average, African women are completely responsible for child care, cooking, cleaning, and food processing. They are responsible for at least half the effort needed to care for animals, repair homes, and market surplus products. They are almost entirely responsible for water and fuel supplies and food production, and are therefore most closely affected by ecological disruptions such as water shortages, deforestation, and loss of land productivity due to soil erosion.[44]

Subsistence agriculture is the responsibility of African women, while land-ownership rights are held by men. Under the terms of customary marriage agreements, a man "buys" the labor of his bride and the couple's future offspring from her family. A woman's economic and social standing rises with the number of children she bears, particularly since children represent extra hands to help with farming, marketing, and other tasks. Each additional child affirms a woman's place within her marriage, ensures her access to land, and fulfills her "obligations" to her husband and her own family. But a woman's claim to her children is nonexistent: In the case of a divorce, a mother generally must leave her children behind.[45]

Such attitudes toward familial relationships dim the prospects of reducing fertility rates in African societies until the status of women improves. Prices paid for brides in expectation of high fertility increase the wealth of a woman's family. Odile Frank and Geoffrey McNicoll, in a study on population policy in Kenya, note that because men bear little financial or domestic reponsibility for basic subsistence, the costs of large numbers of children are invisible to them. As a result, they write, "even an emerging land shortage is not necessarily felt by men as a reason to limit fertility." Policies aimed at capping and regulating bride-price payments as well as those recognizing and enforcing a woman's right to lay claim to land may serve to at least partially counteract the social forces that underlie high fertility.[46]

Improving the status of women, or, more specifically, reducing their economic dependence on men, is a crucial aspect of development. Until female education is widespread—until women gain at least partial control over the resources that shape their economic lives—high fertility, poverty, and environmental degradation will persist in many regions.

FILLING THE GAP

Policymakers concerned with population dynamics are faced with two objectives: reducing the unmet need for family planning in intermediate fertility countries and, in high fertility countries, providing an environment in which small families can become the norm. Helping couples achieve that norm will require a major commitment to family planning from both the international community and the Third World. But uncertain economic prospects, competing investment needs, and international politics have subverted the growing support for family planning in developing countries. Without the resources needed to back that commitment, the trend of declining fertility in developing countries may be reversed.

Over the past two decades, about $10 billion has been spent on family planning programs in developing countries, with $4 billion coming from donor countries and the rest from developing countries themselves. The current budget from public and private sources for family planning and population activities in developing countries is about $2.5 billion per year. The Chinese government alone spends about $1 billion, while the Indian government spends roughly $530 million.[47]

The international community, particularly the United States, has traditionally played a significant role in international family planning, giving political as well as financial support to reducing fertility and charting demographic trends. Donor countries have been spending about $500 million per year in this area. Recently, however, the United States—the largest dollar contributor in absolute terms—has scaled back its commitment to international population assistance. U.S. funding fell 20 percent between 1985 and 1987, from $288 million to $230 million.

More significantly, the United States no longer contributes to the U.N. Fund for Population Activities (UNFPA) or to the International Planned Parenthood Federation. At the International Conference on Population in Mexico City, the Reagan administration set in motion a policy denying funds to any international organization that alerted women that abortion might be one of their options. UNFPA funds were withdrawn as a result of U.S. opposition to grants it made to China. More than 340 million couples in 65 countries are affected by this shortsighted policy.[48]

The United States has scaled back its commitment to international population assistance.

Instead of cutting back on international family planning assistance, the United States and other industrial countries need to increase their contributions. Dr. Joseph Speidel of the Population Crisis Committee of Washington, D.C., estimates that in order to achieve population stabilization by the end of next century, global expenditures must rise to $7 billion annually over the next decade. Industrial countries could contribute at least $2 billion of this total.[49]

An increase in international donor assistance can be used to strengthen family planning in several key areas. First, improving the statistics-gathering and ana-

lytical capabilities of Third World governments is essential to charting and responding to trends more accurately. Second, priority should be given to the poorest, most rapidly growing countries, such as those in sub-Saharan Africa and parts of Asia, where services are scant, but sorely needed. Third, donors can augment funding for programs in countries where current efforts are inadequate. And new approaches to family planning and social change in these countries deserve more support. India and Mexico, for example, are both using the popular media to spread information and promote the concept of smaller families.

Developing countries themselves need to make a greater commitment to family planning. At the moment, the Third World spends more than four times as much on weaponry and upkeep of military forces as it does on health care—$150 billion in 1986, compared with $38 billion. Increased government funding of family planning and primary health care programs is essential as part of the effort to speed fertility rate declines.[50]

Contraceptive supplies, educational materials, prenatal health care, and information on family health are desperately needed in rural areas throughout the developing world. New approaches to contraceptive marketing and distribution, such as those that rely on local residents and shopkeepers to disseminate information and supplies, are now being tried in a number of countries, and should be considered in others.

The primary goals of a family planning program are to reduce unmet need for fertility control, to improve maternal and child health through birth spacing, and eliminate the need for illegal abortion. But an integrated development strategy that combines family planning with income generation for women, reforestation efforts, small-scale agricultural projects, and improvements in water supply and sanitation will simultaneously reduce births and improve the quality of life.

Although national leadership is needed, encouraging the development of regional, district, and village programs that are responsive to local needs is essential too. Programs patterned after the Thai loan experiment, relying on village leaders to help develop and introduce new ideas, may be the most successful. The private sector should also be involved. Initiatives in Africa and elsewhere have shown that it is cost-effective for employers to offer primary health care and family planning services, which result in better overall health and higher productivity. In Kenya, a group of 50 companies and plantations is the second largest provider of family planning. Likewise, in Nigeria, Gulf Oil and Lever Brothers Co. are planning to introduce such programs.[51]

Three decades of international family planning experience hold important lessons for designing effective programs and for creating a social environment receptive to smaller families. Countries such as China, India, Mexico, and Thailand can serve as models for different approaches. Sub-Saharan African countries may find that region-wide cooperation on family planning, in the form of training and outreach programs through perhaps a new consortium on population growth, will strengthen the efforts of individual countries.

As the interdependence of nations becomes increasingly clear, so too does the knowledge that the fate of even the richest nation is intertwined with that of the most destitute. Planning families to reduce the number of births, improve health, and raise living standards is a universal responsibility. No nation should exempt itself from this global effort.

10

Reclaiming the Future

Lester R. Brown and Edward C. Wolf

Putting the world on a sustainable development path will not be easy, given the environmental degradation and economic confusion that now prevail. Modest increases in energy efficiency investments or family planning budgets will not suffice. Getting on such a path depends on a wholesale reordering of priorities, a fundamental restructuring of the global economy, and a quantum leap in international cooperation on the scale that occurred after World War II. Unless the desire to ensure a sustainable future becomes a central concern of national governments, the continuing deterioration of the economy's natural support systems will eventually overwhelm efforts to improve the human condition.

A sustainable future requires that a series of interlocking issues be dealt with simultaneously. Stabilizing population will prove difficult until poverty is reduced. It may be impossible to avoid a mass extinction of species as long as the Third World is burdened with debt. Perhaps most important, the resources needed to arrest the physical deterioration of the planet may not be available unless the international arms race can be reversed.

If the world stays on the current path,

crises will compound and accelerate until they overwhelm the capacity of institutions to respond. Time is of the essence: Species lost cannot be recreated. Soil washed away may take centuries, if not millennia, to replace even under careful husbandry. Once the earth gets warmer there will be no practical way of cooling it.

Scientists, political leaders, and the general public are beginning to recognize that world population and energy trends are disrupting the natural systems and resources on which humanity depends. But the policy adjustments required to return the world to a sustainable economic path are lagging far behind. The commitment to action is negligible in many national capitals, and political leaders remain preoccupied with day-to-day crises at the expense of long-term sustainability.

With the notable exception of the United States, efforts to protect the earth's thin layer of topsoil, for example, range from inadequate to nonexistent. Other than South Korea and China, developing countries have done little to reverse their deforestation. Of even more concern is the need to stabilize and restore the forests of the tropics. Scores of

[handwritten margin note: can't cure pop problem while there's still poverty, + vice versa]

developing countries have yet to confront this challenge.

In industrial countries, evidence of forest damage from air pollution and acid rain continues to accumulate, with 19 nations now reporting extensive forest deterioration. Yet while new areas of damage come to light and scientific scrutiny increases, not one industrial country has designed, let alone enacted, a credible plan to reverse the deterioration.[1]

The effort to protect the earth's ozone layer provides a welcome precedent for cooperative action on global threats.

Close to half the world is succeeding in the effort to halt population growth. But that means just over half is failing. Neglect of the population issue is pushing many Third World governments into a corner where they soon must choose between frantic efforts to reduce family size, with the risk of coercion, and intolerable declines in living standards.

Some progress, albeit inadvertent, has been registered in slowing the growth of carbon dioxide emissions, but not a single government has adopted an energy policy that takes climate change into account. Fossil fuel use leveled off during the eighties, but it did so because higher fuel costs spurred investments in efficiency, nuclear power, and the use of renewables.

The effort to protect the earth's ozone layer, signaled by the 24-nation protocol on chlorofluorocarbons signed in Montreal, provides a welcome precedent for cooperative action on global threats. But what is needed is a groundswell of public support for such innovative diplomacy. Today, most of the battles to protect the planet's health are being lost.

Some have not yet even been effectively joined.[2]

UNSUSTAINABLE DEVELOPMENT

As noted in earlier editions of *State of the World,* a sustainable society is one that satisfies its needs without diminishing the prospects of future generations. The concept of sustainability originated with ecologists concerned about the long-term consequences of excessive pressures on natural support systems, such as forests and soils. Though inspired by ecology, sustainable development can only be achieved through economic and political decisions.

Although forest stocks and soil reserves do not appear in national economic accounts, economies depend on them. Even the most advanced society depends on the photosynthesis that occurs in its forests, grasslands, and croplands. If the biological productivity of the land is continually degraded through mismanagement, society will eventually pay a price.

The line between an activity that is sustainable and one that is not is often a thin one. Sustainability can be evaluated at the level of individual ecosystems, sectors of the economy, or geographic regions. The Peruvian anchovy fishery remains one of the most clear-cut examples of how excessive demand can destroy an ecosystem. Glowing economic reports accompanied the expansion of the Peruvian anchovy fishery as the catch rose from 4 million tons in 1960 to 8 million tons in 1965 and then to 13 million tons in 1970. Ecologists, having estimated that the fishery could sustain a yield of 9 million tons, reacted with alarm. Their warnings were vindicated during the early seventies, when the anchovy catch plummeted to less than 2 million per year, where it has since remained.[3]

Analyses of individual sectors of the global economy also reveal unsustainable patterns. Economic reports on world food output during the mid-eighties describe food production that has outpaced effective demand, leading to surpluses and a price-depressing buildup in world grain stocks. Ecological analyses, by contrast, point out that production has expanded in part by plowing highly erodible land that cannot sustain cultivation over the long term. This ecological interpretation is reflected in the U.S. program designed to convert 40 million acres (16 million hectares) of rapidly eroding cropland, roughly 11 percent of the U.S. total, to sustainable uses such as grass or tree production. Highly erodible land will likely be withdrawn from production in scores of other countries in the years ahead, either because it is converted to sustainable, less intensive uses or because it becomes wasteland.[4]

Signs of unsustainable trends in the energy sector are unmistakable. The ever expanding use of fossil fuels is, by definition, not sustainable. But even before reserves are exhausted, fossil fuel use may be curtailed because it is acidifying and destroying local forests and fisheries, and because it is leading to a planetary warming.

In terms of geographic regions, the yearly addition of 17 million people and over 5 million cattle, sheep, and goats in Africa is destroying vegetation and degrading land, making the lesson that environmental degradation can undermine economic progress especially painful. The first indication that Africa was in trouble came when per capita grain production turned downward after 1967, eventually leading to a decline in real incomes as well. Not only are per capita

food output and income continuing to decline, but nothing in prospect is likely to reverse this deterioration.[5]

The economic future of the Indian subcontinent is similarly threatened. As Indian scientists have gathered more accurate data on deforestation, soil erosion, and land degradation, official concern has turned to alarm. India has been remarkably successful in expanding the harvest from its irrigated land using high-yielding varieties of wheat and rice, but it is now experiencing severe local shortages of water, fodder, and firewood. In the absence of a major effort to reverse the wholesale deterioration of the Indian subcontinent, officials fear that living standards there may turn downward within the next few years, following the trend in Africa.

Latin America, though more advanced economically, faces a similar situation. The combination of rapid population growth, environmental degradation, and mounting external debt has reduced living standards in most Latin American countries well below the levels of 1980. As in Africa, living standards are likely to be lower at the end of this decade than they were at the beginning. Even if ways can be found to ease the debt burden, continued deterioration of the region's environmental support systems could well overwhelm future efforts to reverse the decline.

The immediate effects of population growth and land degradation are largely local, but the climate alteration linked to fossil fuel combustion is incontestably global. Just as land degradation can threaten local efforts to raise living standards, so too climate alteration can overwhelm progress at the global level. Efforts to adjust the global economy to a much warmer earth—with the accompanying changes in rainfall patterns, evaporation rates, and sea level—eventually could absorb all available investment capital.

CONSERVING SOIL AND PLANTING TREES

Restoring two of the earth's life-support systems—its soil and trees—will require heavy capital investments and strong commitments by political leaders. Estimating the costs of securing these support systems is a speculative undertaking, handicapped by the lack of reliable data both on how rapidly they are deteriorating and how much it will cost to restore them. Further complicating the calculation, no consensus exists on the most appropriate measures to reverse the deterioration. The expenditures sketched here are rough estimates at best, intended only to convey the magnitude of the effort needed.

It is appropriate to begin with soils, the foundation not only of agriculture but of civilization itself. When world grain prices surged in the mid-seventies, farmers around the world plowed large areas of highly erodible land and they adopted more intensive, often erosive, agricultural practices. Although soil erosion data do not exist for most countries, detailed data on U.S. soil erosion and recent expenditures to control it provide a basis for estimating a worldwide investment in soil conservation.

As of the early eighties, American farmers and the U.S. Department of Agriculture (USDA) together were spending just over $1 billion per year to control erosion on cropland, with expenditures divided almost equally between the two. Despite this effort, a detailed soil survey conducted in 1982 showed farmers were losing 3.1 billion tons of topsoil annually from water and wind erosion, with some 2 billion tons believed to exceed tolerable levels of soil loss. For every ton of grain they produced, American farmers were losing six tons of their topsoil.[6]

Congress responded to this clearly documented threat and the runaway costs of farm price-support programs (which resulted in large measure from the excessive production due to the plowing of highly erodible lands) with a landmark program, the Conservation Reserve, that was incorporated into the Food Security Act of 1985. For the first time, policy was designed to control excessive production *and* to cut soil losses by idling land.[7]

For every ton of grain they produced, American farmers were losing six tons of their topsoil.

One key provision calls for the conversion of at least 40 million acres of highly erodible cropland to grassland or woodland (1 acre equals 0.4 hectares). In 1986 and 1987, the USDA accepted farmers' bids to enroll 23 million acres, well above the rate needed to reach the 40-million-acre goal in five years. The USDA agreed to pay farmers an average of $48 per acre each year for land enrolled in the Reserve, to compensate them for net income from the crops the land would otherwise have produced.[8]

If it is assumed that the average bid to retire the entire 40 million acres is a slightly higher $50 per acre, it will cost the U.S. Treasury $2 billion per year once the full area is retired, beginning in 1990. If the $1 billion already spent each year on erosion control is continued but targeted on the remaining cropland that is eroding excessively, the cost of a comprehensive U.S. government program to secure topsoil can be estimated. (See Table 10–1.)

Erosion on the land planted to grass or trees during the first year of the cropland conversion program was estimated to decline from an average of 29 tons per acre to 2 tons. If this rate prevailed on all

Table 10-1. United States: Estimated Expenditures to Secure Topsoil on Cropland, 1986–2000

Year	Cropland Conversion	Adoption of Conservation Practices	Total
	(billion dollars)		
1986	0.4	1.0	1.4
1987	0.8	1.0	1.8
1988	1.2	1.0	2.2
1989	1.6	1.0	2.6
1990	2.0	1.0	3.0
1995	2.0	1.0	3.0
2000	2.0	1.0	3.0

SOURCE: Worldwatch Institute estimates derived from USDA data.

the land to be enrolled in the reserve, excessive erosion would be reduced by over 1 billion tons. This would leave just under 1 billion tons to be eliminated on that remaining 30 percent of the cropland still eroding excessively. Much of this would be controlled by a provision in the Food Security Act that required farmers with erodible land to develop an approved soil conservation program by 1990 in order to remain eligible for price-support payments, crop insurance, and other farm program benefits.[9]

In summary, annual expenditures of roughly $3 billion would be required for the United States to stabilize the soils on its cropland once the program is fully in place by 1990. These data for the world's leading food producer provide a point of departure for estimating the cost of stabilizing topsoil on all the world's cropland.

First, it is assumed that the share of world cropland that cannot sustain cultivation with any economically feasible soil-conserving agricultural practices is one tenth—roughly the same as in the United States. This would equal some

128 million hectares worldwide. Applying the cost of converting such land to grassland or woodland in the United States as a first approximation, the global cost would be $16 billion per year by 1994. (See Table 10–2.) If expenditures to conserve topsoil on the remaining erosion-prone cropland are comparable to those in the United States (disregarding for the purpose of illustration the vast differences in land tenure and farming methods that characterize farming in different regions), a global program of conservation practices enacted by 1994 would cost an additional $8 billion annually.

When both the cropland conversion program and the full range of needed soil-conserving practices are in place, global expenditures to protect the cropland base would total some $24 billion per year. Although this is obviously a large sum, it is less than the U.S. government paid farmers to support crop prices in 1986. As an investment in future food supplies for a world expecting 3 billion to 5 billion more people, $24 billion is one that humanity can ill afford not to make.[10]

Table 10-2. Estimated Global Expenditures to Secure Topsoil on Cropland, 1990–2000

Year	Conversion of Cropland to Grassland or Woodland	Adoption of Conservation Practices	Total
	(billion dollars)		
1990	3.2	1.3	4.5
1991	6.4	2.7	9.1
1992	9.6	4.0	13.6
1993	12.8	5.3	18.1
1994	16.0	8.0	24.0
1995	16.0	8.0	24.0
2000	16.0	8.0	24.0

SOURCE: Worldwatch Institute.

Constructing a comparable global estimate of the additional investment in tree planting needed to restore tree cover is more difficult. Few people dispute the need to plant more trees. Whether to satisfy growing firewood needs in the Third World or to stabilize soil and water regimes in watersheds where land degradation and disruptions of the hydrological cycle are undermining local economies, adding trees to the global forest stock is a valuable investment in our economic future.

Over a billion people live in countries that are already experiencing firewood shortages. Unless corrective action is taken, that number will nearly double by the year 2000. An estimated 55 million hectares of tree planting will be needed to meet the fuelwood demand expected at the turn of the century. In addition, anchoring soils and restoring hydrological stability in thousands of Third World watersheds will require tree planting on some 100 million hectares. (See Chapter 5 for a discussion of both these goals.)[11]

Considering that some trees would serve both ecological and fuelwood objectives, a total of 120 million hectares might need to be planted. An additional 30 million hectares will be needed to satisfy demand for lumber, paper, and other forest products. If this tree planting goal is to be achieved by the end of the century, the effort would need to proceed somewhat along the lines outlined in Table 10–3, with annual plantings gradually expanding over the next several years.

Estimating the cost of reforesting an area equivalent to 150 million hectares faces two problems. First, no one expects plantations to satisfy more than a small share of the rural demand for fuelwood in the Third World. The need for fuel is dispersed, not centralized, and the only labor force capable of planting trees on the scale needed to meet fuel needs and to restore barren land is that found in local communities. In reality, most of the new trees will appear not in orderly plantations, but rather on hillsides, next to dwellings, and in borders around fields, or will be interplanted with crops. The principal resource in this effort is thus not capital, but labor.

Table 10-3. Estimated Tree Planting to Supply Fuelwood, Lumber, and Pulpwood and to Stabilize Soil and Water Regimes, 1990–2000

Year	Firewood Supply	Soil and Water Conservation	Lumber and Pulpwood	Total Plantings	Estimated Cost
	(million hectares)				(billion dollars)
1990	2	3	1	6	2.4
1991	3	4	1	8	3.2
1992	4	5	2	11	4.4
1993	5	6	2	13	5.2
1994	5	6	3	14	5.6
1995	6	6	3	15	6.0
1996	6	7	3	16	6.4
1997	6	7	3	16	6.4
1998	6	7	4	17	6.8
1999	6	7	4	17	6.8
2000	6	7	4	17	6.8

SOURCE: Worldwatch Institute.

Second, reestablishing tree cover on severely degraded land is not an easy matter, often requiring watering and protection from roaming animals. Seedlings can be produced for a fairly modest sum, but tree survival rates are often low. The planting itself is sometimes a minor part of the effort required to establish a stand of trees. In many cases, a catchment must be built for each tree or a terrace cut around a mountainside to trap water, soil, and nutrients. Once established, the stand of trees helps maintain itself through self-reinforcing cycles of soil building and natural seeding, but the initial intervention requires a major investment in human time and talent.

The cost of restoring the earth's tree cover varies widely, according to the approach taken. Numerous studies by the World Bank and other development agencies show costs ranging from $200 to $500 per hectare for trees planted by farmers as part of agroforestry activities and up to $2,000 or more for commercial plantations. Farmers' costs are lower mainly because the labor to plant, maintain, and protect the trees is contributed by the family. The effort is seen as an investment in family welfare, much as home gardening uses family labor to reduce food expenditures.[12]

One purchase that is common to all tree planting efforts is the seedlings, usually reckoned at $40 per 1,000. A typical planting rate of around 2,000 seedlings per hectare would amount to $80 per hectare for seedlings alone. In estimating the cost of establishing tree cover, it is assumed that the great bulk of the 150 million hectares will be planted by local villagers and that the average cost will be $400 per hectare including seedling costs. At this rate, tree planting expenditures would total some $60 billion, just under $6 billion per year over the remainder of this century. The tree planting to restore watersheds, thereby conserving soil and water, complements the expenditures on soil erosion by farmers on their cropland that were discussed earlier.[13]

SLOWING POPULATION GROWTH

The success of efforts to save topsoil and restore tree cover both depend heavily on slowing population growth. Indeed, countries with populations expanding at 2 to 4 percent per year may find it almost impossible to restore tree cover, protect their soils, and take other steps toward a sustainable development path. The economic and environmental future of these countries is inextricably entwined with their ability to alter reproductive tradition and dramatically reduce family size.

Providing family planning services in response to unsatisfied demand is often the quickest and most cost-effective step countries can take to secure life-support systems. World Bank surveys show that from 50 to 90 percent of the women interviewed in a broad sample of Third World countries either want to stop childbearing altogether or to delay the birth of another child, suggesting an enormous unsatisfied demand for contraceptive services. (See Chapter 9.) The Bank estimates that providing family planning services to all those in need would entail expenditures of roughly $8 billion per year by the end of the century. (See Table 10–4.)[14]

In effect, this level of expenditures would help shift global population from a total now headed toward 10 billion to one on the way toward 8 billion. Two hundred million fewer births than expected between now and the end of the century would put the world on this lower demographic path.

Table 10-4. Estimated Expenditures on Family Planning and Related Activities in Third World to Stabilize World Population Size at Roughly 8 Billion by 2050

Year	Family Planning Services	Social Improvements	Financial Incentives	Total
	(billion dollars)			
1990	3.0	6.0	4.0	13.0
1991	3.5	8.0	6.0	17.5
1992	4.0	10.0	8.0	22.0
1993	4.5	11.0	10.0	25.5
1994	5.0	11.0	12.0	28.0
1995	5.5	11.0	14.0	30.5
1996	6.0	11.0	14.0	31.0
1997	6.5	11.0	14.0	31.5
1998	7.0	11.0	14.0	32.0
1999	7.5	11.0	14.0	32.5
2000	8.0	11.0	14.0	33.0

SOURCE: Worldwatch Institute estimates derived from World Bank data.

Fertility declines most rapidly when family planning services are introduced into a society already enjoying broad-based economic and social gains. The social indicator that correlates most closely with fertility decline is the education of women. Simply put, the more schooling women achieve, the fewer children they choose to bear. There are occasional exceptions, but this general relationship holds over a wide spectrum of cultures. A second social indicator that correlates closely with declines in birth rates is infant mortality. It is rare for birth rates to drop sharply if infant survival remains low.

Although educating girls and women achieves social and economic progress and reduces fertility, there are still many countries, such as Bangladesh, Senegal, and Uganda, where barely half the girls of primary school age are attending classes. Although almost all governments have adopted universal primary education as a goal, many have seen their educational systems overwhelmed by the sheer number of children enter-

ing school. In India, the world's second most populous country, scarcely three quarters of primary school-age girls are actually in school. The governments of high fertility societies cannot realistically hope to rein in population growth without broadening access to education and thus providing women with options beyond childbearing.[15]

The more schooling women achieve, the fewer children they choose to bear.

Fulfilling this social condition for a more rapid fertility decline will require a heavy investment in both school building and teacher training. Providing elementary education for the estimated 120 million school-age children not now in school would cost roughly $50 each, or $6 billion per year. Providing literacy training for those women who are illiterate and beyond school age would require an additional estimated $2 billion per year.[16]

Substantial gains in reducing infant mortality can be achieved with relatively modest investments. Immunizing the 55 percent of the world's children not now protected from diphtheria, measles, polio, and tuberculosis would cost roughly $2 billion per year, for example. Training mothers in the oral rehydration therapy used to treat infants with diarrhea, in basic hygiene, and in the health advantages of breast-feeding would cost another $1 billion per year. Although immunization and the training of mothers will fall far short of the basic health care needed to reduce infant mortality rates to those of industrial nations, these efforts would markedly lower infant deaths and in the process stimulate interest in reducing family size.[17]

Even when family planning services are available, when literacy is high, and when infant mortality rates are falling, as they have been in East Asia for example, birth rates may not fall quickly enough. In these circumstances, governments often turn to financial incentives. Indeed, incentives have played some part in almost every country that has quickly lowered fertility. South Korea, for instance, provides free medical care and educational allowances to all families with no more than two children in which one parent agrees to be sterilized.[18]

In China, which has one of the most comprehensive systems of incentives and disincentives in this area, provincial governments are encouraged to work out their own detailed programs appropriate to local circumstances. Sichuan province, for example, makes monthly payments to couples who agree to limit their family to one child. In the early eighties, payments of 5 yuan per month made until the child reached age 14 added up to some $420, an amount that might exceed the earnings from a farmer's annual harvest. Financial incentives that can be used to provide the old age security once sought in large numbers of children are invariably among the more successful inducements to reduce family size.[19]

STABILIZING THE EARTH'S CLIMATE

The worldwide warming that threatens to raise the earth's average temperature by 1.5–4.5 degrees Celsius (2.7–8.1 degrees Fahrenheit) by 2050 is generating some of the most difficult questions political leaders have ever had to deal with. Faced with enormous uncertainty and the possibility of catastrophic consequences, the central issue is whether to follow a business-as-usual energy policy and risk having to adapt the global economy to the changed climate, or to take steps to slow the warming. Unfortunately, the costs of adapting to the global warming could one day siphon off so much investment capital that economic progress would come to a halt and living standards would begin to decline.

As a first step toward devising intelligent policy, leaders need broad estimates of the cost of economic adjustments that may be demanded by higher concentrations of carbon dioxide and other industrial gases. At present, modelers cannot predict precisely how the climate will change in particular regions. Nor is there consensus about how the world's climate will change on the geographic scale at which decisions are made. Ironically, it may be easier to estimate the costs of adjusting to some of the global effects of climate change, such as sea level rise, than to local or national changes.

The most costly adjustments now anticipated would be those needed to protect coastal areas from the rising sea. Some sense of the magnitude of these expenses is offered by the Netherlands, nearly 60 percent of which is below sea level. Each year, the Dutch spend a larger proportion of their gross national product to maintain a complex set of dikes, sea walls, and other structures to protect them from the sea—roughly 6 percent—than the United States spends on military defense.[20]

An indication of the human costs borne by countries that cannot afford massive engineering projects is offered by Bangladesh. A low-lying country, with millions of its people living only a few feet above sea level, it is vulnerable to storm surges from the Bay of Bengal. Unlike the Netherlands, it cannot afford a series of costly dikes. Consequently, Bangladesh has paid a heavy toll in human lives. In 1970, some 300,000 people were killed in a single cyclone; 10,000 people were killed and 1.3 million affected by a storm surge in 1985. The willingness of Bangladeshis to resettle in such high-risk areas reflects a keen land hunger, one that will intensify if the population increases as projected from 106 million in 1988 to 305 million late in the next century.[21]

No one knows how many of the rice-growing river deltas and floodplains in Asia or of the world's low-lying cities will be inundated over the next century. The coastlines where protection might prove necessary in decades to come could easily total thousands of kilometers. In the Netherlands, a single 4-kilometer barrier completed in 1986 to provide extra protection against storm surges cost $3.2 billion. The costs of trying to protect productive land and cities from the rising sea would thus likely be measured in the trillions of dollars.[22]

The many costs of adjusting the world economy—country by country and sector by sector—cannot yet be calculated, but the experience of countries like the

Netherlands suggests that they could be astronomical. If leaders decide instead to slow the warming of the planet and delay or prevent these costly adjustments, how much should they be prepared to invest in energy efficiency and in the development of renewable energy resources in the years immediately ahead? Twice present levels? Five times as much? Ten times as much?

Bangladesh, unlike the Netherlands, cannot afford a series of costly dikes.

One thing is clear: If the projected warming is to be minimized, the buildup of carbon dioxide and the trace gases that contribute to the greenhouse effect must be slowed, and quickly. One small step in the right direction is the goal of halving emissions of chlorofluorocarbons, as called for in the September 1987 Montreal accords. And as earlier chapters have argued, carbon emissions can be reduced by raising the efficiency of energy use, by shifting from fossil fuels to renewable energy sources, and by reversing deforestation. In 1987, fossil fuel combustion emitted some 5.4 billion tons of carbon into the atmosphere, while deforestation released on the order of 1 billion to 2.6 billion tons.[23]

Two benchmarks can help evaluate the potential for raising world energy efficiency. One is the level of efficiency attained by the most energy-efficient countries. The second is the levels achieved by the most energy-efficient technologies now used in transportation, food production, heating, lighting, industrial processes, and so on.

The efficiency with which energy is used varies widely among countries. (See Chapter 3.) Japan, for example, the world's third largest economy, is one of the most efficient simply because both government and industry have emphasized energy efficiency to make their resource-poor country more competitive in world markets. The United States uses twice as much energy to produce a dollar's worth of goods and services as Japan does. The Soviet Union, with one of the world's least efficient economies, uses three times as much as Japan. Even Japan does not come close to fully exploiting available technologies.[24]

Replacing existing technologies with more efficient ones is merely the first step. Beyond this, economic systems can be redesigned so that some sectors can be sustained with relatively little energy. For example, although fuel-inefficient cars can be replaced with more efficient ones, the large gains in transport efficiency will come from designing communities where residents do not depend on automobiles.

Over the longer term, many countries can aim to reduce carbon emissions by shifting away from fossil fuels to other generating sources. Developing countries can neither afford the investment nor manage the risks inherent in reliance on nuclear power. Renewable energy sources are better matched to their needs. These sources include hydropower, fuelwood, agricultural wastes, wind power, solar water heaters, photovoltaic cells, agriculturally based alcohol fuels, and geothermal energy. (See Chapter 4.) Assuming the forests supplying fuelwood are managed on a sustainable-yield basis, none of these raises atmospheric carbon dioxide.

The potential for renewable energy development varies widely among countries. With hydropower, the industrial regions of North America and Europe have developed their most promising sites. But Asia, Africa, and Latin America have developed less than one tenth of their potential, leaving enormous opportunities for both large-scale and small-scale hydropower. Although large projects involve difficult environmental and social trade-offs, they typically provide power at less cost than small ones.[25]

Some sources of renewable energy, such as wind power and photovoltaics, are in the early stages of global development, but the local rate of development is in some cases astonishing. Within a four-year span, California developed more than 1,000 megawatts of wind-powered generating capacity at roughly half the cost per megawatt of nuclear power. India now plans to develop 5,000 megawatts of wind power by the end of the century. If the entire world were to systematically harness its wind power potential, thousands of megawatts could undoubtedly be generated.[26]

Even in exploiting a technology as simple as solar water heaters, there are enormous variations among societies, variations that reflect different levels of social commitment to the technology. In Israel, an energy-poor country attempting to reduce its dependence on imported fossil fuels, some 65 percent of all residences have solar water heaters. Israeli energy planners expect that eventually nearly all residential water will be heated by the sun. Japan, also committed to reducing oil and coal imports, has some 4 million solar water heaters in use.[27]

As market reforms penetrate the Soviet economy, energy efficiency will climb sharply.

Countries that rely heavily on renewable energy typically use several different sources. Among the largest is Brazil, a country that relies heavily on hydropower for electricity, alcohol fuels for transport, and charcoal for steel smelting. Altogether, renewable energy sources account for some 60 percent of Brazil's total energy use, making it the first large industrializing economy to rely primarily on renewables. The Philippines, which now gets half its energy from renewables, has also made major strides over the past decade in substituting indigenous renewable energy for imported oil, concentrating on the development of hydropower, firewood, geothermal energy, and the use of agricultural wastes.[28]

A third activity that could help slow the pace of climate change is the tree planting discussed earlier in this chapter. As noted, South Korea is the only developing country that has successfully reversed the trend toward deforestation. China, with a renewed commitment to tree planting in the eighties, may be on the verge of doing so. If India can reach its recently adopted goal of planting 5 million hectares per year, which it is not yet close to doing, it too will turn the tide on forest loss.[29]

At the national level, a few initiatives could dramatically reduce global carbon emissions. At the top of the list are the economic reforms launched by Mikhail Gorbachev in the Soviet Union. As market reforms penetrate the ossified Soviet economy, energy efficiency will climb sharply, eliminating some of the extraordinary waste associated with its centralized planning and management. The vast potential these reforms hold for reducing carbon emissions gives the entire world a stake in their success.

A second significant national initiative on this issue would be a renewed commitment to automobile fuel-efficiency standards in the United States. Between 1974 and 1987, the fuel efficiency of new cars in the United States nearly doubled, increasing from 14 to just over 26 miles per gallon, largely because of legislation passed in 1976. If the United States were to double fuel-efficiency standards for vehicles again by the end of the century—a level that can be achieved with cars now on the market—global carbon emissions would drop measurably.[30]

Brazil ranks fourth in carbon dioxide emissions not because it is a heavy user of fossil fuels, but because it is burning its vast Amazon rain forest to make way for cattle ranching and crop production. Accumulating scientific evidence suggests that preserving the Amazon forests is in Brazil's interests as much as the world's. At the moment, these forests support a few million people on a sustainable basis, including indigenous tribes and rubber tappers. If the forest is burned off, soils can deteriorate quickly, creating a wasteland incapable of supporting even cattle. There is also a risk within Brazil, where the vast Amazon rain forest helps shape continental climate patterns, that unrestrained forest clearing would adversely affect rainfall and temperatures in the important agricultural regions to the south.[31]

Pressure on the Amazon forests can be relieved only if the government of Brazil slows population growth and institutes meaningful land reform. Neither alone will suffice. Bringing population growth to a halt without land redistribution will ensure continued settlement of the Amazon region. Similarly, an effective land reform program on its own will reduce, but not eliminate, pressures to clear the Amazon for farming.

Up until now, no national government has explicitly attempted to design an energy policy intended to reduce carbon emissions. The time to do so has arrived. Just as some countries banned various uses of chlorofluorocarbons in the late seventies, thereby laying the groundwork for the September 1987 agreement signed in Montreal, so leadership by individual countries in cutting carbon emissions could hasten a broader international consensus on actions to slow the global warming.

Expenditures in energy efficiency and

renewable energy sufficient to head off the warming cannot easily be estimated, in contrast to those on soil conservation and population stabilization. Having only a sense that the costs of climate change are enormous, we recommend a tripling in the annual investment in energy efficiency during the nineties and a doubling in investment in developing renewable energy resources. These investment levels, which offer immediate environmental and economic gains, should be viewed as minimal. If the economic disruption associated with the global warming passes the threshold of political acceptability, then investments far greater than those outlined here will be made to reduce fossil fuel use.

INVESTING IN ENVIRONMENTAL SECURITY

For four decades, security has been defined largely in ideological terms. The East-West confrontation has dominated international affairs, setting priorities in the use of public resources. It has spawned an arms race and put the world economy on a more or less permanent war footing. Although this deadlock and the ever present risk of nuclear war continue to threaten human security everywhere, the deterioration of the biosphere now also threatens the security of not only this generation but future ones as well.

To continue with a more or less business-as-usual attitude—to accept the loss of tree cover, erosion of soil, the expansion of deserts, the loss of plant and animal species, the depletion of the ozone layer, and the buildup of greenhouse gases—implies acceptance of economic decline and social disintegration. In a world where progress depends on a complex set of national and international economic ties, such disintegration would bring human suffering on a scale that has no precedent. The threat posed by continuing environmental deterioration is no longer a hypothetical one. Dozens of countries will have lower living standards at the end of the eighties than at the beginning. We can no longer assume that economic progress is automatic anywhere.

The momentum inherent in population growth, the forces of land degradation, and the changing chemistry of the atmosphere make it difficult to get the world on a sustainable development path. The inertia of our political institutions further complicates the task. The scale of these challenges and the urgency with which they must be addressed requires that they be moved from the periphery to the center of governmental agendas.

As preceding sections have outlined, investments above and beyond current expenditures are needed to stabilize topsoil, restore tree cover, get the brakes on population growth, and foster development of energy efficiency and renewable power sources quickly enough to slow the global warming. (See Table 10–5.) Efforts to retire Third World debt, discussed later in this section, are also essential. The numbers used in this table are rough estimates, bounded by wide margins of uncertainty. Though based on specific experiences wherever possible, the figures in Table 10–5 are not intended to be authoritative. Instead, they are meant as a point of departure to stimulate thinking about what it will take to put the world on a sustainable path.

For the purposes of this discussion, these expenditures are treated as outlays only, but in reality they would yield substantial net savings over the longer term. Each $1 invested in energy efficiency in the United States, for example, trims an estimated $2 from electricity bills. The

Table 10-5. Rough Estimates of Additional Expenditures to Achieve Sustainable Development, 1990–2000

Year	Protecting Topsoil on Cropland	Reforesting the Earth	Slowing Population Growth	Raising Energy Efficiency	Developing Renewable Energy	Retiring Third World Debt	Total
	(billion dollars)						
1990	4	2	13	5	2	20	46
1991	9	3	18	10	5	30	75
1992	14	4	22	15	8	40	103
1993	18	5	26	20	10	50	129
1994	24	6	28	25	12	50	145
1995	24	6	30	30	15	40	145
1996	24	6	31	35	18	30	144
1997	24	6	32	40	21	20	143
1998	24	7	32	45	24	10	142
1999	24	7	32	50	27	10	150
2000	24	7	33	55	30	0	149

SOURCE: Worldwatch Institute.

same can be said about family planning expenditures. In societies where population pressures are excessive, the relatively modest expenditure to avoid an additional birth is not only repaid several times over, it may be essential to reversing a decline in living levels.

In addition, not all the expenditures outlined in Table 10–5 are "investments" in the strict sense; both soil conservation and population stabilization entail substantial recurrent costs, while spending for energy efficiency and renewable energy commonly represents one-time capital outlays that yield long-term benefits. The need for these investments will not end at the turn of the century; rather, these priorities represent a first substantial step toward restructuring the global economy along lines that will sustain progress.

The priorities in Table 10–5 reflect a common goal of restraining carbon emissions, which they achieve in a variety of ways. Once erodible land is planted to grass or trees, for instance, it begins to absorb carbon from the atmosphere. Tree planting along the lines suggested earlier to supply fuelwood, lumber, and other forest products, and to stabilize soil and water regimes, will fix large quantities of carbon. Combined with the planting of highly erodible cropland to grassland or trees—already under way in the United States—this will fix close to a billion tons of carbon annually in the late nineties as young stands of trees mature.

If remaining forests are better managed and new plantings begin to meet a substantial share of human needs, stabilizing the earth's forested area could reduce global carbon emissions by some 1.5 billion tons, more than a fifth of 1986 emissions. Meanwhile, the energy saved during the nineties through the proposed tripling of annual investments in energy efficiency, plus the new supplies from a doubled investment in renewables, could meet much of the projected growth in energy demand between now and the end of the century.

Together, these forestry and energy initiatives could actually reduce carbon emissions by the year 2000, helping to minimize the global warming. The likelihood of investments being made depends on the threat of disruptive climate change being taken seriously by enough governments and the ability of these governments to work together to forge a common strategy.

Through decisions about existing and prospective energy technologies, humanity has far more control over the rate of global warming than is commonly recognized. In addition to direct influence over the activities that produce carbon dioxide and the land uses that sequester carbon from the atmosphere, accelerating progress toward population stabilization can reduce the numbers dependent on activities that put climate stability at risk. The many factors that will shape future energy demand and the pattern of human activities in generations to come cannot be forecast with any certainty, but investing some $150 billion per year in areas that broaden human options in the face of enormous uncertainty would be a reasonable down payment on an environmentally sustainable global economy.

A world where living standards are continually falling in some regions and continually rising in others is unacceptable.

Two barriers now stand in the way of ensuring that capital and political will are available on the scale needed. One is the profound misallocation of capital implicit in global military expenditures of $900 billion each year. The other is the unmanageable Third World debt that burdens the world economy. Unless these obstacles are overcome, funds on

the scale needed to ensure sustainable development will not be available.

The external debt of the Third World, now totaling roughly $1 trillion, is growing at some $60 billion a year. Interest payments of some $80 billion per year have reversed the traditional net flow of capital from the industrial to the developing countries, leading to a net capital transfer from poor countries to rich of nearly $30 billion annually. Five years have passed since Third World debt emerged as a major international issue, and all the prescribed remedies have failed.[32]

The economic and social progress that normally drives the demographic transition, leading to slower population growth, has been replaced in many countries by falling incomes. As a result, rapid population growth continues, destroying the environmental support systems on which future economic progress depends. A world where living standards are continually falling in some regions and continually rising in others is an unacceptable prospect.

The economic advantages to the entire world of easing the stranglehold of external debt on international development and trade are evident. World Bank president Barber Conable has pointed out that the heavily indebted middle-income developing countries reduced their imports from $165 billion in 1980 to $110 billion in 1985. And this at a time when they normally would have increased their imports to $220 billion.[33]

Recognizing that this situation is untenable, numerous experts have proposed ways of dealing with a level of debt that has grown beyond all reasonable hope of repayment. One possibility would be to set up a fund jointly managed by the International Monetary Fund and the World Bank, perhaps called a Debt Retirement Fund (DRF), with the intention of retiring enough Third World debt to restore economic progress. The 1987 restructuring of the World Bank, including a new emphasis on the primacy of environmental concerns in development planning, puts it in a position to provide leadership in formulating sustainable development strategies. A fund to retire outstanding debt could complement such strategies.[34]

Japan, with its enormous trade surpluses, could take the lead in organizing such a fund with a major contribution of its own, much as the United States assumed the leadership with the Marshall Plan in rebuilding war-torn countries after World War II. Canada has already taken a bold step in the right direction, by canceling the $581 million official debt owed it by African countries.[35]

Debt relief would be handled by the fund on a country-by-country basis, with funds going to countries that could devise a credible sustainable development strategy, including efforts to increase energy efficiency, develop renewable energy sources, stabilize population, replant forests, and conserve soils. When a country agreed to take the needed steps, the DRF would convene a meeting of the relevant bilateral aid agencies of the donor countries. Officials of the new fund would design a package that would include forgiveness of all or part of the debt held by the bilateral agencies.

The new fund could agree to purchase a portion of the country's external private debt at the rate at which its debt issues were trading on the secondary market, roughly half face value. For purposes of illustration, assume an outstanding external debt of $10 billion. With $2 billion of its resources, the DRF could purchase $4 billion worth of debt. If bilateral aid agencies collectively canceled $1 billion of debt, only $5 billion of outstanding debt would remain, a level that the country should be able to manage. Such a move would also reestablish confidence in the economy, encouraging both a return of capital and

new foreign investment. The goal would not be to eliminate a country's outstanding debt, but to reduce it to a level that would restore economic progress.

Estimating how much debt reduction would be needed to restore economic progress is not easy, particularly since the debt continually grows. At a minimum, it would be necessary to eliminate the annual net outflow of roughly $30 billion, replacing it with a net inflow of at least the same magnitude. Even if the $1 trillion of the Third World debt does not rise further, it will require some $800 billion in interest payments in the nineties if interest rates hold at around 8 percent. The estimated capital needed to reduce the debt to manageable levels in the Third World during the next decade could be as much as $300 billion, enough to retire $600 billion of debt discounted at 50 percent of face value.

With the estimates of debt retirement we now have the principal components of the overall expenditures needed to get the world onto a sustainable development path. As indicated in Table 10-5, our rough estimate of the investments needed to reduce Third World debt to a manageable level and to protect environmental support systems and stabilize climate is roughly $45 billion in 1990, with an increase to nearly $150 billion per year by the mid-nineties.

This capital could be obtained either by increasing taxes or by reordering existing expenditure priorities. It may make more sense for most governments to divert resources from the military than from elsewhere for two reasons. First, many governments will be reluctant to reduce expenditures in other major sectors, such as health or education. Second, and perhaps more important, such a reordering of priorities would be part and parcel of efforts to reduce international tensions. Without this, the cooperation needed to put the world on a sustainable environmental and economic path is not likely to be forthcoming.

In a business-as-usual world, global military expenditures would probably continue at something like $900 billion annually, where they seem to have leveled off in the late eighties. A shift of resources from the military sector into investments in sustainability might resemble the pattern of priorities in Table 10–6. A reduction in military expenditures of nearly one sixth could rejuvenate moribund national economies. The Soviet Union has already indicated an interest in a plan to shift resources from its military sector to aid developing countries.[36]

Such a shift in expenditures from the military sector to sustainable development activities is not without precedent. China has followed precisely this path over the past decade. Ten years ago, the government spent nearly 13 percent of its gross national product on military purposes, one of the highest in the world. Since then, a one-tenth reduction of military expenditures in a rapidly expanding economy has reduced the military share by nearly half, dropping to an estimated 7 percent in 1986. At the same time, investments in family planning, reforestation, and food production have expanded dramatically. These shifts, accompanied by economic reforms, have helped China dramatically lower its birth rate and raise per capita food production by half within a decade. It is precisely such a combination that can yield the greatest progress for the rest of the world during the years ahead.[37]

ENTERING A NEW ERA

As increasing human numbers and advancing technologies have expanded the scale of human activity, we find ourselves in a new era, one in which the environ-

Table 10-6. Two Possible Global Security Budgets, 1990–2000

Year	Global Security Defined in Military Terms	Global Security Defined in Sustainable Development Terms		
	Current Military Expenditures Continued	Military Expenditures	Expenditures to Achieve Sustainable Development	Total Security Expenditures
	(billion dollars)			
1990	900	854	46	900
1991	900	825	75	900
1992	900	797	103	900
1993	900	771	129	900
1994	900	755	145	900
1995	900	755	145	900
1996	900	756	144	900
1997	900	757	143	900
1998	900	758	142	900
1999	900	750	150	900
2000	900	751	149	900

SOURCE: Worldwatch Institute.

mental effects of economic activities spill far beyond national borders. Governments assume responsibility for supplying energy at home, but not for the acid precipitation that destroys forests in nearby countries or for the carbon dioxide buildup that will warm the earth. Deforestation in Nepal can aggravate flooding in Bangladesh. The manufacture of chlorofluorocarbons in Japan can influence skin cancer rates in Argentina. The list of such connections is endless.

The link between cause and effect has been severed by the nature of today's international political system.

The world is now facing a crisis of governance resulting from the mismatch between the international and sometimes global environmental consequences of domestic economic policies and the national interests that shape these policies. The link between cause and effect has been severed by the nature of today's international political system. Unless this can be remedied by creating new international institutions or by expanding the authority of existing ones, no mechanism will exist to promote responsible behavior. To leave processes that will directly influence the future habitability of the planet to chance is risky beyond reason.

In some important respects, the world situation today resembles that during the mid-forties. For 15 years the world had been in the grip of economic depression or war. The collective effect of national monetary and trade policies adopted during the early thirties to serve short-term national interests had brought the world economy to its knees. The unilateral pursuit of economic goals by national governments proved to be a

prescription for disaster. A similar crisis paralyzed international diplomacy. With the failure of the League of Nations in the early twenties, there was no institutional forum within which to address Hitler's expansionist policies in Europe.

The scale of human suffering as a result of the Great Depression and World War II gave the international community the resolve to address the weaknesses inherent in the system. In 1944, monetary authorities from 44 countries met in Bretton Woods, New Hampshire, to organize the International Monetary Fund (IMF), charging it with the responsibility to secure international monetary cooperation. As part of its mandate, the IMF established a capital fund that countries deficit in their international accounts could draw upon rather than adopt protectionist trade policies of the sort that had deepened and prolonged the Depression.

The following year, diplomats met in San Francisco to approve a charter for the United Nations. With the horrors of war freshly imprinted in their minds, national representatives established within the United Nations a Security Council endowed with the authority to intervene in regional conflicts, with force if necessary, upon approval of its members. In contrast to the IMF, which has played a central role in the international economic system, the Security Council was hamstrung almost from its inception by the ideological conflict between the United States and the Soviet Union, the two most powerful of its five permanent members.

This period of crisis produced some visionaries, leaders who were able to engineer an effective response to the new threats to progress. One was General George Marshall, U.S. Secretary of State from 1947 to 1949. When he proposed in 1947 that the United States launch a massive international assistance plan to rebuild Europe, including Germany, the conventional image of postwar relationships was turned upside down. Instead of plundering the defeated enemy, the United States held out a helping hand, launching a massive reconstruction of victors and vanquished alike, an effort that led to a generation of European prosperity.

Within Europe, leaders confronted with the rubble of World War II recognized that European civilization could not survive another Franco-German war of the kind that had historically plagued the region. Individuals like Belgium's Paul-Henri Spaak and France's Jean Monnet pushed for creation of the European Coal and Steel Community in 1950, later expanded into the European Economic Community or Common Market. As a result of their efforts, few worry today about the outbreak of war between France and West Germany, or indeed between any West European nations. Such an event has become an anachronism in the late twentieth century.

Initiatives of comparable boldness are needed in the late eighties. Whether any Marshalls or Monnets will emerge remains to be seen. The world may not have the financial resources to both sustain the arms race and make the investments needed to return the world to a sustainable development path. The agreement between the United States and the Soviet Union to eliminate all medium- and short-range nuclear missiles is a promising step. If the two superpowers can transcend their ideological differences and work together within the U.N. Security Council, as they began to do in late 1987 to end the Iran-Iraq war, then that forum could become the peace-enforcing agency intended by its founders. Such a clear vote of confidence in international conflict resolution would not only reinforce progress on arms control by the superpowers, it would allow a reduction in the size of national military establishments every-

where, freeing up resources to invest in sustainability.[38]

With the stage set for a major reordering of national priorities, governments could focus their energies on protecting and restoring natural support systems, and begin to consider the vast challenge posed by climate change. The international community could concentrate on reversing the environmental deterioration and economic decline now affecting so many Third World countries.

The parallels between the world situation in the late eighties and the mid-forties suggest a need for new mechanisms of international cooperation. Then, the need was to deal with the devastation of war. Now, the need is to address the environmental devastation caused by a destructive energy path and failed population policies. These trends can be clearly identified. Whether they can be reversed in time to avoid serious economic disruptions in the global economy and a sustained decline in living standards beyond Africa is an open question.

The deterioration of the earth's life-support systems is threatening, but the psychological toll of failing to reverse it could also be high. Such a failure would lead to a loss of confidence in political institutions and would risk widespread demoralization—a sense that our ability to control our destiny is slipping away.

If, on the other hand, the world can mobilize along the lines discussed here, the trends that threaten to undermine the human future can be reversed. If widespread concern motivates political action, and if the needed changes in national priorities, national policies, and individual life-styles take root, then— and only then—can we expect sustained improvement in the human condition. If our future is to be environmentally and economically sustainable, many adjustments will have to be made. It will not be enough that we care. We must also act.

Notes

Chapter 1. The Earth's Vital Signs

1. West German data from Der Bundesminister Für Ernährung, Landwirtschaft, und Forsten, "Neurartige Waldschäden in der Bundesrepublik Deutschland," Bonn, West Germany, October 1983; International Co-operative Programme on Assessment and Monitoring of Air Pollution Effects on Forests, "Forest Damage and Air Pollution: Report on the 1986 Forest Damage Survey in Europe," Global Environment Monitoring System, U.N. Environment Programme (UNEP), Nairobi, mimeographed, 1987.

2. For evidence that warming is under way see P.D. Jones et al., "Global Temperature Variations Between 1861 and 1984," *Nature*, July 31, 1986, and B. Vaugh Marshall and Arthur Lachenbruch, "Changing Climate: Geothermal Evidence from Permafrost in the Alaskan Artic," *Science*, November 7, 1986; V. Ramanathan et al., "Trace Gas Trends and Their Potential Role in Climate Change," *Journal of Geophysical Research*, June 20, 1985.

3. Shirley Christian, "Pilots Fly Over the Pole Into Heart of Ozone Mystery," *New York Times*, September 22, 1987; "Ozone Hole Deeper Than Ever," *Nature*, October 8, 1987; for effects, see U.S. Environmental Protection Agency (EPA) and UNEP, *Effects Of Changes in Stratospheric Ozone and Global Climate, Volume 1: Overview* (Washington, D.C.: 1986).

4. Four fifths figure derived from U.S. Department of Agriculture (USDA), Economic Research Service (ERS), *An Economic Analysis of USDA Erosion Control Programs* (Washington D.C.: U.S. Government Printing Office, 1986), and from Norman A. Berg, "Making the Most of the New Soil Conservation Initiatives," *Journal of Soil and Water Conservation*, January/February 1987.

5. Michael Weisskopf, "Nations Sign Agreement to Guard Ozone Layer," *Washington Post*, September 17, 1987.

6. Paul Lewis, "Rare Unity Brings Smile to 'Toothless Tiger,'" *New York Times*, September 20, 1987.

7. U.N. Food and Agriculture Organization (FAO), *Tropical Forest Resources*, Forestry Paper 30 (Rome: 1982); Centre for Science and Environment, *The State of India's Environment 1984–85* (New Delhi: 1985).

8. FAO, *Tropical Forest Resources*.

9. International Co-operative Programme, "Report on the 1986 Forest Damage Survey in Europe."

10. USDA Soil Conservation Service and Iowa State University Statistical Laboratory, *Basic Statistics 1977 National Resources Inventory*, Statistical Bulletin No. 686 (Washington, D.C.: 1982); Lester R. Brown and Edward C. Wolf, *Soil Erosion: Quiet Crisis in the World Economy*, Worldwatch Paper 60 (Washington, D.C.: Worldwatch Institute, September 1984).

11. Gandhi quote from national broadcast of January 5, 1985, as quoted in Government of India, "Strategies, Structures, Policies: National Wastelands Development Board,"

New Delhi, mimeographed, February 6, 1986.

12. Number of chemicals in use from "The Quest for Chemical Safety," *International Register of Potentially Toxic Chemicals Bulletin*, May 1985.

13. H. Jeffrey Leonard, "Hazardous Wastes: The Crisis Spreads," *National Development*, April 1986.

14. Jean Pierre Lasota, "Darkness at Noon," *The Sciences*, July/August 1987.

15. James Bovard, "A Silent Spring in Eastern Europe," *New York Times*, April 26, 1987.

16. Cass Peterson, "Ozone Depletion Worsens; Hazard to Researchers Seen," *Washington Post*, October 28, 1987; Walter Sullivan, "Ozone Hole Raising Concern for Scientists' Safety," *New York Times*, October 28, 1987.

17. F. Sherwood Rowland, Department of Chemistry, University of California at Irvine, and Michael B. McElroy, Department of Earth and Planetary Sciences, Harvard University, Testimonies at Hearings, Committee on Environment and Public Works, U.S. Senate, October 27, 1987.

18. See Charles D. Keeling et al., "Measurements of the Concentration of Carbon Dioxide at Mauna Loa Observatory, Hawaii," in William C. Clark, ed., *Carbon Dioxide Review* (New York: Oxford University Press, 1982).

19. FAO, *Fuelwood Supplies in the Developing Countries*, Forestry Paper 42 (Rome: 1983).

20. Example from Ecuador from Paul Warpeha, Peace Corps volunteer, seminar given at Worldwatch Institute, 1978; example from Sahel from Bina Agarwal, *Cold Hearths and Barren Slopes: The Woodfuel Crisis in the Third World* (Riverdale, Md.: The Riverdale Co., Inc., 1986).

21. Government of India, "National Wastelands Development Board."

22. Southern African Development Coordination Conference, *SADCC Agriculture: Toward 2000* (Rome: FAO, 1984).

23. Government of India, "National Wastelands Development Board."

24. Barber B. Conable, President, World Bank, address delivered to the World Resources Institute, Washington, D.C., May 5, 1987.

25. Robert Mann, "Development and the Sahel Disaster: The Case of The Gambia," *The Ecologist*, March/June 1987.

26. J. Bandyopadhyay and Vandana Shiva, "Drought, Development and Desertification," *Economic and Political Weekly*, August 16, 1986.

27. Ibid.

28. USDA, ERS, *World Indices of Agricultural and Food Production 1950–1987* (unpublished printout) (Washington, D.C.: 1987).

29. For a discussion of Chinese military spending see Lester R. Brown, "Redefining National Security," in Lester R. Brown et al., *State of the World 1986* (New York: W.W. Norton & Co., 1986); Chinese agriculture statistics from USDA, ERS, *China: Situation and Outlook Report* (Washington, D.C.: 1986).

30. According to Worldwatch estimates based on data from American Petroleum Institute and U.S. Department of Energy (DOE), fossil fuel consumption increased from 3 billion tons of coal equivalent in 1950 to 12 billion tons in 1986. Gross world product increased from $2.9 trillion (1980 dollars) in 1950 to $13.1 trillion in 1986; see also Herbert R. Block, *The Planetary Product in 1980: A Creative Pause?* (Washington, D.C.: U.S. Department of State, 1981). According to USDA data, grain production increased from 624 million tons in 1950 to 1,423 million tons in 1980; for a discussion of petroleum use by farmers see Lester R. Brown, "Sustaining World Agriculture," in Lester R. Brown et al., *State of the World 1987* (New York: W.W. Norton & Co., 1987). For a dis-

cussion of all these trends, see Lester R. Brown and Sandra Postel, "Thresholds of Change," in ibid. World auto production from Motor Vehicle Manufacturers Association, *World Motor Vehicle Data Book, 1982 Edition* (Detroit, Mich.: 1982); United Nations, *World Energy Supplies* (New York: 1976); United Nations, *Yearbook of World Energy Statistics* (New York: 1983).

31. British Petroleum Company, *BP Statistical Review of World Energy* (London: 1987).

32. Ibid.; DOE, Energy Information Administration (EIA), *Monthly Energy Review*, July 1987.

33. "Coal-Fired Power to Reach 670 GW by 2000, Says IEA," *Energy Daily*, October 6, 1987; World Bank, *China: The Energy Sector* (Washington, D.C.: 1985).

34. Ralph Rotty, University of New Orleans (formerly of Institute for Energy Analysis, Oak Ridge Associated Universities, Oak Ridge, Tenn.), private communications, June 16 and November 4, 1987; sulfur data from Swedish Ministry of Agriculture, *Proceedings: The 1982 Stockhom Conference on Acidification of the Environment* (Stockholm: 1982); nitrogen data from P.J. Crutzen and M.O. Andreae, "Atmospheric Chemistry," in T.F. Malone and J.G. Roederer, eds., *Global Change* (New York: Cambridge University Press, 1985).

35. EPA, *National Air Pollutant Emission Estimates 1940–85* (Research Triangle Park, N.C.: 1987).

36. John McCormick, *Acid Earth* (Washington, D.C.: International Institute for Environment and Development, 1985); *Acid Magazine*, Vol. 1, 1987.

37. 1982 West German data from Der Bundesminister Für Ernährung, Landwirtschaft, und Forsten, "Neurartige Waldschäden"; 1986 data from International Cooperative Programme, "Report on the 1986 Forest Damage Survey in Europe."

38. Observations about relative damage from "Auswirkungen des Waldsterbens und Stand der Gegenmaßnahmen in Europa," *Holz-Zentralblatt*, October 26, 1987; Bovard, "A Silent Spring in Eastern Europe."

39. Hon. Tom McMillan, "Canada's Perspective on Global Environment and Development," speech before the 42nd session of the U.N. General Assembly, New York, October 19, 1987.

40. Rain data from James N. Galloway, "Acid Rain: China, United States, and a Remote Region," *Science*, June 19, 1987; forest damage from "Acid Rain Harms Southwest Forests," *Beijing Review*, October 19, 1987.

41. Svante Arrhenius, "On the Influence of Carbonic Acid in the Air Upon the Temperature of the Ground," *Phil. Magazine*, Vol. 41, 1896.

42. Rotty, private communications; R.A. Houghton et al., "The Flux of Carbon from Terrestrial Ecoystems to the Atmosphere in 1980 Due to Changes in Land Use: Geographic Distribution of Global Flux," *Tellus*, February/April 1987; Irving M. Mintzer, *A Matter of Degrees: The Potential for Controlling the Greenhouse Effect* (Washington, D.C.: World Resources Institute, 1987); Charles D. Keeling, Scripps Institution of Oceanography, La Jolla, Calif., private communication, November 11, 1987.

43. World Meteorological Organization (WMO), *A Report of the International Conference on the Assessment of the Role of Carbon Dioxide and of Other Greenhouse Gases in Climate Variations and Associated Impacts*, Villach, Austria, October 9–15, 1985 (Geneva: WMO, International Council of Scientific Unions, and UNEP, 1986).

44. Malone and Roederer, *Global Change*; Mintzer, *A Matter of Degrees*.

45. Mintzer, *A Matter of Degrees*.

46. WMO, *Assessment of Role of Carbon Dioxide and Greenhouse Gases in Climate Variations*.

47. Jessica Tuchman Mathews, "National Security, Global Survival," presentation given at the Comittee for National Security's

Fifth Women's Leadership Conference, Washington, D.C., June 25, 1987.

48. Michael C. MacCracken and George J. Kulka, "Detecting the Climatic Effects of Carbon Dioxide: Volume Summary," in Micheal C. MacCracken and Frederick M. Luther, eds., *Detecting the Climatic Effects of Increasing Carbon Dioxide* (Washington, D.C.: U.S. Government Printing Office, 1985).

49. S. Manabe and R.T. Wetherald, "Reductions in Summer Soil Wetness Induced by an Increase in Atmospheric Carbon Dioxide," *Science,* May 2, 1986; WMO, *Assessment of the Role of Carbon Dioxide and Greenhouse Gases in Climate Variations.*

50. Cynthia Rosenzweig, "Potential CO_2-Induced Climate Effects On North American Wheat-Producing Regions," *Climatic Change,* Vol. 7, 1985; Cynthia Rosenzweig, "Climate Change Impact on Wheat: The Case of the High Plains," paper presented at the Symposium on Climate Change in the Southern United States: Future Impacts and Present Policy Issues, sponsored by the Office of Policy, Planning, and Evaluation, EPA, New Orleans, La., May 28–29, 1987.

51. See Sandra Postel, "Stabilizing Chemical Cycles," in Brown et al, *State of the World 1987.*

52. EPA projections cited in *Glaciers, Ice Sheets, and Sea Level: Effect of A CO_2-Induced Climatic Change,* report prepared for the DOE on a workshop held in Seattle, Wash., September 13–15, 1984 (Washington D.C.: U.S. Government Printing Office, 1986).

53. Erik Eckholm, "Significant Rise in Sea Level Now Seems Certain," *New York Times,* February 18, 1986. See also Tom Goemans and Tjebbe Visser, "The Delta Project: The Netherlands Experience with a Megaproject for Flood Protection," *Technology in Society,* Vol. 9, 1987.

54. Maumoon Abdul Gayoom, speech before the 42nd Session of the U.N. General Assembly, New York, October 19, 1987.

55. Graham S. Giese and David G. Aubrey, "Losing Coastal Upland to Relative Sea-Level Rise: 3 Scenarios for Massachusetts," *Oceanus,* Vol. 30, No. 3, 1987.

56. World Commission on Environment and Development, *Our Common Future* (New York: Oxford University Press, 1987).

57. Weisskopf, "Nations Sign Agreement to Guard Ozone Layer."

58. Information on banning CFC production in Belgium and Nordic countries from embassies, Washington, D.C., private communications; "Vermont Says No To Plastic Plates," *New York Times,* September 13, 1987; " 'Mac' Backs CFC Attack," *World Environment Report,* August 20, 1987.

59. For a discussion of Africa see Lester R. Brown and Edward C. Wolf, *Reversing Africa's Decline,* Worldwatch Paper 65 (Washington, D.C.: Worldwatch Institute, July 1985).

60. Conable, address before the World Resources Institute.

61. World Commision on Environment and Development, *Our Common Future.*

Chapter 2. Creating a Sustainable Energy Future

1. Carbon emissions from Ralph Rotty, University of New Orleans (formerly of Institute for Energy Analysis, Oak Ridge Associated Universities, Oak Ridge, Tenn.), private communication, June 16, 1987.

2. British Petroleum Company (BP), *BP Statistical Review of World Energy* (London: 1987).

3. International Energy Agency (IEA), *Energy Policies and Programmes of IEA Countries, 1986 Review* (Paris: Organisation for Economic Co-operation and Development (OECD), 1987).

4. U.S. Environmental Protection Agency, "National Air Pollutant Emission Estimates,

1940–1985," Washington, D.C., January 1987.

5. American Council for an Energy-Efficient Economy (ACEEE), *Acid Rain and Electricity Conservation* (Washington, D.C.: 1987).

6. Irving M. Mintzer, *A Matter of Degrees: The Potential for Controlling the Greenhouse Effect* (Washington, D.C.: World Resources Institute, 1987).

7. William U. Chandler, "The Case of China," Worldwatch Institute, Washington, D.C., unpublished, 1987, and William U. Chandler, *Energy Productivity: Key to Environmental Protection and Economic Progress*, Worldwatch Paper 63 (Washington, D.C.: Worldwatch Institute, January 1985); Mintzer, *A Matter of Degrees.*

8. Worldwatch Institute estimates based on Rotty, private communication, on J. A. Edmonds and J. M. Reilly, "A Long-Term Global Energy-Economic Model of Carbon Dioxide Release from Fossil Fuel Use," *Energy Economics*, April 1983, and on United Nations, *1985 Energy Statistics Yearbook* (New York: 1987).

9. Christopher Flavin, *Reassessing Nuclear Power: The Fallout From Chernobyl*, Worldwatch Paper 75 (Washington, D.C.: Worldwatch Institute, March 1987).

10. U.S. Department of Energy (DOE), Energy Information Administration (EIA), *Monthly Energy Review*, May 1987.

11. Ibid.; American Petroleum Institute, *Basic Petroleum Data Book, Vol. 5* (Washington, D.C.: 1985).

12. IEA, *Policies and Programmes, 1986;* Mohan Munasinghe and Jeremy J. Warford, *Electricity Pricing: Theory and Case Studies* (Baltimore, Md.: The Johns Hopkins University Press, 1982).

13. John Lichtblau, remarks at Seminar on Oil and America's Energy Security, Brookings Institution, Washington, D.C., October 15, 1987.

14. DOE, *Energy Security* (Washington, D.C.: 1987).

15. BP, *Statistical Review of World Energy.*

16. Worldwatch Institute estimate based on DOE, *International Energy Annual 1986* (Washington, D.C.: 1987), on Youssef Ibraham, "New Pipelines are Reducing Persian Gulf's Strategic Role," *New York Times*, October 7, 1987, and on Amory B. Lovins and L. Hunter Lovins, "The Avoidable Oil Crisis," *The Atlantic*, December 1987.

17. DOE, *International Energy Annual.*

18. Ibid.

19. James Clad, "That Was the Week," *Far Eastern Economic Review*, September 10, 1987.

20. IEA, *Policies and Programmes, 1986;* IEA, *Energy Policies and Programmes of IEA Countries, 1983 Review* (Paris: OECD, 1984); "Austrian Dispute Over Energy Tax," *European Energy Report*, October 30, 1987.

21. Christopher Flavin et al., "The Oil Rollercoaster," Fund for Renewable Energy and the Environment, Washington, D.C., 1987.

22. IEA, *Policies and Programmes, 1986.*

23. Lee Schipper et al., *Coming in from the Cold: Energy-Wise Housing in Sweden* (Washington, D.C.: Seven Locks Press, 1985); on South Korea, see Howard Geller, "End-Use Electricity Conservation: Options for Developing Countries," Energy Department Paper No. 32, World Bank, Washington, D.C., 1986; studies on European standards cited in IEA, *Energy Conservation in IEA Countries* (Paris: OECD, 1987).

24. "Energy Department Sued for Not Issuing Appliance Standards," *Energy Daily*, November 4, 1983.

25. "California Adopts Efficiency Standards," *Energy Daily*, December 20, 1984; John McCaughey, "Long-Running Appliance Standards Battle is Settled," *Energy Daily*, August 15, 1987; "Senate Approves Bill on Ap-

pliance Efficiency," *New York Times*, February 18, 1987.

26. Howard S. Geller, "Energy and Economic Savings from National Appliance Efficiency Standards," ACEEE, Washington, D.C., 1987; carbon emissions is Worldwatch Institute estimate based on ibid. and on Rotty, private communication.

27. Stalon quoted in John McCaughey, "Stalon Backs Plan To Deregulate Generation of Electricity," *Energy Daily*, September 10, 1987.

28. Federal Energy Regulatory Commission (FERC), *Small Power Production and Cogeneration Facilities: Regulations Implementing Section 210 of the Public Utility Regulatory Policies Act of 1978* (Washington, D.C.: 1980).

29. Edison Electric Institute, "1985 Capacity & Generation, Non-Utility Sources of Energy," Washington, D.C., 1987; value of industry is Worldwatch Institute estimate based on 4,000–5,000 megawatts of completed projects annually and an estimated average construction cost of $1,000 per kilowatt; plant orders from North American Electric Reliability Council, "1986 Reliability Review," Princeton, N.J., 1986.

30. California Energy Commission, "Relative Cost of Electricity Production," Sacramento, Calif., April 1987.

31. William Mead, "Competitive Bidding and the Regulatory Balancing Act," *Public Utilities Fortnightly*, September 17, 1987.

32. "More Large, Fewer Small Projects Planned During First Half of 1987," *Cogeneration and Small Power Monthly*, July 1987.

33. Larry Stoiaken, "The PURPA Hearings: What's Next," *Alternative Sources of Energy*, July/August 1987; "Excerpts from a FERC Staff Analysis of the Regulation of Independent Power Producers," *Cogeneration and Small Power Monthly*, October 1987.

34. Bill Rankin, "FERC Competitive Bidding Plan Splits The Utility Industry," *Energy Daily*, September 9, 1987.

35. Renewable share from FERC, "The Qualifying Facilities Report," Washington, D.C., January 1, 1987, and private communication, November 4, 1987.

36. Danish information from Jørgen Nørgaard, Technical University of Denmark, Lyngby, Denmark, private communication, October 28, 1987; "Greek Legislation Frees Electricity Market," *European Energy Report*, July 26, 1985; Andrew Holmes et al., *Power on the Market: Strategies for Privatising the UK Electricity Industry* (London: Financial Times Business Information, 1987); New Zealand information from David Pate, Energy Consultant, private communication, November 30, 1987.

37. Martin Klepper, Lane and Edson, Washington, D.C., private communication, October 21, 1987; Martin Klepper, "Issues in Performance Contracting: An Agenda for the Next Ten Years," in Mike Weedall et al., eds., *Financing Energy Conservation* (Washington, D.C.: ACEEE, 1986); Eric Hirst et al., *Energy Efficiency in Buildings: Progress & Promise* (Washington, D.C.: ACEEE, 1986).

38. Wes Birdsall, General Manager, Osage Municipal Utility, Osage, Iowa, private communication, November, 10, 1987.

39. Douglas Cogan and Susan Williams, *Generating Energy Alternatives, 1987 Edition* (Washington, D.C.: Investor Responsibility Research Center, 1987).

40. George Reeves and Marilyn Brown, "General Public Utilities: Buying Residential Conservation," and Harold Schick and Leslie E. McMillan, "Bonneville Power Administration's Purchase of Energy Savings," in Weedall et al., *Financing Energy Conservation*.

41. Lindley Peaco, Purchased Power Administration, Central Maine Power Co., Augusta, Me., private communication, October 21, 1987.

42. IEA, *Policies and Programmes, 1986*.

43. Ibid.

44. Value of industry is Worldwatch Institute estimate based on Strategies Unlimited, "International Market Evaluations: Wind Energy Prospects" and "International Energy and Trade Policies of California's Export Competitors," California Energy Commission, Sacramento, Calif., 1987; IEA, *Policies and Programmes, 1986;* IEA, *Renewable Sources of Energy* (Paris: OECD, 1987).

45. R. Lynette & Associates, "The Lessons of the California Wind Farm: How Developing Countries Can Learn From the American Experience," Redmond, Wash., May 1987.

46. Howard Geller et al., "The Role of Federal R&D in Advancing Energy Efficiency: A Fifty Billion Dollar Contribution to the U.S. Economy," in Annual Reviews, Inc., *Annual Review of Energy, Vol. 12* (Palo Alto, Calif.: in press).

47. Ibid.

48. Ibid.

49. Energy Conservation Center, "Energy Conservation in Japan 1986," Tokyo, February 1987.

50. IEA, *Policies and Programmes, 1986.*

51. Ibid.

52. U.S. General Accounting Office, "Energy R&D: Changes in Federal Funding Criteria and Industry Response," Washington, D.C., February 1987; DOE, Inspector General, "The Coordination of Long-Term Energy Research and Development Planning," Washington, D.C., November 1986.

53. IEA, *Policies and Programmes, 1986.*

Chapter 3. Raising Energy Efficiency

1. International Energy Agency (IEA), *Energy Conservation in IEA Countries* (Paris: Organisation for Economic Co-operation and Development (OECD), 1987). In this chapter the term energy is meant to include only commercial energy; fuelwood and similar developing-country subsistence energy supplies are not included.

2. National energy efficiency is measured in energy consumption per dollar of gross national product, based on data in IEA, *Energy Conservation in IEA Countries;* economic savings from efficiency from Arthur H. Rosenfeld, Director, Center for Building Science, Lawrence Berkeley Laboratory, "Energy-Efficient Buildings: The Case for R&D," Testimony in Hearing on Conservation and Renewables, Subcommittee on Energy Research and Development, Committee on Energy and Natural Resources, U.S. Senate, March 26, 1987.

3. Energy Policy Project of the Ford Foundation, *A Time to Choose: America's Energy Future* (Cambridge, Mass.: Ballinger, 1974); U.S. Department of Energy (DOE), Energy Information Administration (EIA), *Monthly Energy Review,* February 1987.

4. For a discussion of various energy forecasts, see John H. Gibbons and William U. Chandler, *Energy: The Conservation Revolution* (New York: Plenum Press, 1981); on nuclear power, see Christopher Flavin, *Reassessing Nuclear Power: The Fallout From Chernobyl,* Worldwatch Paper 75 (Washington, D.C.: Worldwatch Institute, March 1987).

5. IEA, *Energy Conservation in IEA Countries.*

6. Ed A. Hewett, *Energy, Economics, and Foreign Policy in the Soviet Union* (Washington, D.C.: Brookings Institution, 1984).

7. Arthur H. Rosenfeld, "Conservation and Competitiveness," Testimony in Hearings on Economic Growth Opportunities in Energy Conservation Research, Task Force on Community and Natural Resources, Budget Committee, U.S. House of Representatives, July 15, 1987.

8. Eric Hirst et al., *Energy Efficiency in Buildings: Progress & Promise* (Washington, D.C.: American Council for an Energy-Efficient Economy, 1986); aviation industry status

from Boeing, Inc., Seattle, Wash., private communicatons, September 1987.

9. Arthur H. Rosenfeld and David Hafemeister, "Energy-Efficient Buildings: Davids vs. Goliath," *Scientific American*, forthcoming; "EPA Mileage Test Results," *Washington Post*, September 21, 1987.

10. Douglas Cogan and Susan Williams, *Generating Energy Alternatives, 1987 Edition* (Washington, D.C.: Investor Responsibility Research Center, 1987).

11. Efficiency data from IEA, *Energy Conservation in IEA Countries*.

12. Roger W. Sant et al., *Creating Abundance: America's Least Cost Energy Strategy* (New York: McGraw-Hill, 1984); Alan K. Meier et al., *Saving Energy Through Greater Efficiency* (Berkeley: University of California Press, 1981); for current progress in U.S. least-cost planning, see Energy Conservation Coalition, "A Brighter Future: State Actions in Least-Cost Energy Planning," Washington, D.C., December 1987.

13. Churchill quoted in K.E. Goodpaster and K.M. Sayre, *Ethics and the Problems of the Twenty-First Century* (Notre Dame, Ind.: University of Notre Dame, 1979); IEA, *Energy Conservation in IEA Countries*.

14. For industrial market countries, see IEA, *Energy Conservation in IEA Countries;* for Third World, see, for example, Oscar Guzmán et al., *Energy Efficiency and Conservation in Mexico* (Boulder, Colo.: Westview Press, 1987); for centrally planned economies, see William U. Chandler, *The Changing Role of the Market in National Economies*, Worldwatch Paper 72 (Washington, D.C.: Worldwatch Institute, September 1986).

15. Howard S. Geller, "End-Use Electricity Conservation: Options for Developing Countries," Energy Department Paper No. 32, World Bank, Washington, D.C., 1986; José Goldemberg et al., *Energy for Development* (Washington, D.C.: World Resources Institute, 1987).

16. IEA, *Energy Conservation in IEA Countries;* Hirst et al., *Progress & Promise*.

17. Lee Schipper et al., *Coming in from the Cold: Energy-Wise Housing in Sweden* (Washington, D.C.: Seven Locks Press, 1985); on United Kingdom, see "The 56 Church Road Syndrome: Nice but not Efficient," *Energy Economist* (Financial Times Business Information, London), August 1987; Charles Goldman, "Measured Energy Savings from Residential Retrofits: Updated Results from the BECA-B Projects," in American Council for an Energy-Efficient Economy (ACEEE), *Proceedings of the 1984 ACEEE Summer Study on Energy Efficiency in Buildings, Vol. B* (New and Existing Single Family Residences) (Washington, D.C.: 1984).

18. Hirst et al., *Progress & Promise;* Deborah Bleviss and Alisa Gravitz, *Energy Conservation and Existing Rental Housing* (Washington, D.C.: Energy Conservation Coalition, 1984); "Issue Brief: Alliance Efforts to Improve Residential Energy Audits," Alliance to Save Energy, Washington, D.C., September 1987.

19. A degree-day is a measure of wintertime severity; indexing efficiency to degree-days takes account of different heating requirements. These homes are all traditionally heated, not employing passive solar techniques. José Goldemberg et al., "An End-Use Oriented Global Energy Strategy" in Annual Reviews, Inc., *Annual Review of Energy, Vol. 10* (Palo Alto, Calif.: 1985).

20. Schipper et al., *Coming in from the Cold;* William A. Shurcliff, "Superinsulated Houses" in Annual Reviews, Inc., *Annual Review of Energy, Vol. 11* (Palo Alto, Calif.: 1986).

21. Les Gapay, "Heat Cheap in Cold Country," *Public Power*, July/August 1986; Liz Fox quoted in Peter Tonge, "Energy Efficiency vs. Frills," *Christian Science Monitor*, September 18, 1987. On residential efficiency in general, see ACEEE, *Proceedings from the ACEEE 1986 Summer Study on Energy Effi-*

ciency in Buildings, Vol. 2 (Small Building Technologies) (Washington, D.C.: 1986).

22. In these energy consumption figures, electricity is expressed in energy content of the fuel required in generation rather than the energy content of the electricity itself. Roughly two thirds of fossil fuel energy is lost in electricity generation. Rosenfeld and Hafemeister, "Davids vs. Goliath." U.S. savings potential is a Worldwatch Institute estimate based on ibid. and on DOE, EIA, *Monthly Energy Review,* May 1987. On commercial building efficiency in general, see ACEEE, *1986 Summer Study, Vol. 3* (Large Building Technologies).

23. Rosenfeld and Hafemeister, "Davids vs. Goliath"; Kate Miller, Commercial Building Energy Conservation Office, Bonneville Power Administration, Portland, Ore., private communication, August 28, 1987.

24. Herb Brody, "Energy-Wise Buildings," *High Technology,* February 1987; Hashem Akbari et al., "Undoing Uncomfortable Summer Heat Islands Can Save Gigawatts of Peak Power," *ACEEE 1986 Summer Study, Vol. 2.*

25. Arthur H. Rosenfeld and David Hafemeister, "Energy Conservation in Large Buildings," in David Hafemeister et al., eds., *Energy Sources: Conservation and Renewables,* Conference Proceedings No. 135 (New York: American Institute of Physics, 1985).

26. Rocky Mountain Institute, "Advanced Electricity-Saving Technologies and the South Texas Project," Old Snowmass, Colo., 1986. These estimates have undergone scrutiny and been corroborated by a review performed for a Massachusetts utility; see Boston Edison Review Panel (William Hogan, chair), *Final Report, Vol. 2,* Appendix 6 (Boston, Mass.: Boston Edison Company, 1987).

27. Brody, "Energy-Wise Buildings"; Stephen Selkowitz, "Window Performance and Building Energy Use: Some Technical Options for Increasing Energy Efficiency," in

Hafemeister et al., *Energy Sources: Conservation and Renewables.*

28. All the models discussed here are comparably sized, 16 to 18 cubic feet, except for the Danish-built model, which is 20 cubic feet. Jørgen Nørgaard, Technical University of Denmark, Lyngby, Denmark, private communications, October 28–29, 1987; Howard S. Geller, "Energy-Efficient Residential Appliances: Performance Issues and Policy Options," *IEEE Technology and Society Magazine,* March 1986; David B. Goldstein and Peter Miller, "Developing Cost Curves for Conserved Energy in New Refrigerators and Freezers," ACEEE, *1986 Summer Study, Vol. 1* (Appliances and Equipment).

29. Geller, "Energy-Efficient Residential Appliances."

30. Cost-of-saved-energy figures are calculated by dividing the annualized cost (an efficient model's extra purchase price) by the annual energy savings; see Meier et al., *Saving Energy Through Greater Efficiency.*

31. Hirst et al., *Progress & Promise.*

32. The term large power plant is meant to imply a 1,000 megawatt plant; Geller, "Energy-Efficient Residential Appliances."

33. Rosenfeld and Hafemeister, "Davids vs. Goliath."

34. Ibid.; Geller, "Energy-Efficient Residential Appliances."

35. William R. Alling, Electronic Ballast Technology, Inc., Testimony in Hearings on Economic Growth Opportunities in Energy Conservation Research, Task Force on Community and Natural Resources, Budget Committee, U.S. House of Representatives, July 15, 1987; Arthur Rosenfeld, Lawrence Berkeley Laboratory, Berkeley, Calif., private communication, October 25, 1987.

36. New England Energy Policy Council, "Power to Spare: A Plan for Increasing New England's Competitiveness Through Energy Efficiency," Boston, Mass., 1987; Boston Edison Review Panel, *Final Report;* Samuel Ber-

man, "Energy and Lighting" in Hafemeister et al., *Energy Sources: Conservation and Renewables;* California Energy Commission cited in Rocky Mountain Institute, "South Texas Project."

37. IEA, *Energy Conservation in IEA Countries;* DOE, *International Energy Annual 1984* (Washington, D.C.: 1985); DOE, *Annual Energy Review 1985* (Washington, D.C.: 1986); Office of Conservation, "FY 1988 Energy Conservation Multi-Year Plan," DOE, Washington, D.C., 1986; estimate of worldwide carbon emissions from transportation based on fossil fuel carbon emissions model of Ralph Rotty, University of New Orleans (formerly of Institute for Energy Analysis, Oak Ridge Associated Universities, Oak Ridge, Tenn.), private communication, June 16, 1987; carbon emissions for American car based on Jim MacKenzie, "Relative Releases of Carbon Dioxide from Synthetic Fuels," World Resources Institute, Washington, D.C., unpublished memorandum, June 10, 1987.

38. A public car (also called a "jitney") is a private vehicle like a taxi that runs on well-traveled routes, transporting several passengers at once. The efficiency of mass transit is primarily determined by how fully it is used. Empty buses and trains are no more efficient than autos. For comparisons of different modes, see William U. Chandler, *Energy Productivity: Key to Environmental Protection and Economic Progress,* Worldwatch Paper 63 (Washington, D.C.: Worldwatch Institute, January 1985), which shows efficiency of European transit modes, where buses and trains tend to be well used. But compare Mary C. Holcomb et al., *Transportation Energy Data Book, Edition 9* (Oak Ridge, Tenn.: Oak Ridge National Laboratory, 1987), which shows the relatively minor differences among modes in the United States, where mass transit is underutilized.

39. IEA, *Energy Conservation in IEA Countries.* Fuel economy ratings are composite figures, calculated as a weighted average of 55 percent urban driving and 45 percent highway driving. All figures are either from U.S. Environmental Protection Agency (EPA) or are normalized to EPA's standard test (except in Table 3–3, which is normalized to the European urban test). Although EPA ratings were once consistently above actual road performance, adjustments of their techniques now improve their accuracy. To convert from MPG to liters per 100 kilometers, divide 235 by the MPG figure.

40. Deborah Bleviss, *The New Oil Crisis and Fuel Economy Technologies: Preparing the Light Transportation Industry for the 1990's* (New York: Quorum Press, in press).

41. Ibid.

42. Ibid.

43. Ibid.

44. Ibid.

45. Ibid.; Jack Paskind, California Air Resource Board, Sacramento, Calif., private communication, August 27, 1987; Jeff Alson, Assistant to the Director, Emissions Control Technology Division, EPA, Ann Arbor, Mich., private communication, September 29, 1987.

46. Bleviss, *The New Oil Crisis;* U.S. Congress, Office of Technology Assessment (OTA), *Increased Automobile Fuel Efficiency and Synthetic Fuels: Alternatives for Reducing Oil Imports* (Washington, D.C.: U.S. Government Printing Office, 1982).

47. IEA, *Energy Conservation in IEA Countries;* DOE, EIA, *Monthly Energy Review,* April 1987; DOE, "Energy Conservation Indicators 1984 Annual Report," Washington, D.C., 1985; Lee Baade, EIA, DOE, Washington, D.C., private communication, October 8, 1987.

48. Marc Ross, "Current Major Issues in Industrial Energy Use," prepared for Office of Policy Integration, DOE, October 24, 1986.

49. Ibid.; Adam Kahane and Ray Squitieri, "Electricity Use in Manufacturing," in Annual Reviews, Inc., *Annual Review of Energy, Vol. 12* (Palo Alto, Calif.: in press).

50. IEA, *Energy Conservation in IEA Countries;* Guzmán et al., *Energy Efficiency and Conservation in Mexico.*

51. Marc Ross, "Industrial Energy Conservation," *Natural Resources Journal,* August 1984.

52. Kahane and Squitieri, "Electricity Use in Manufacturing"; Electric Power Research Institute, "Electrotechnology Reference Guide," Palo Alto, Calif., April 1986.

53. Ross, "Major Issues in Industrial Energy"; Chandler, *Energy Productivity.*

54. Ross, "Industrial Energy Conservation"; Marc Ross, "Industrial Energy Conservation and the Steel Industry," *Energy, The International Journal,* October/November 1987.

55. OTA, *Industrial Energy Use* (Washington, D.C.: U.S. Government Printing Office, 1983); Edison Electric Institute, "1985 Capacity & Generation, Non-Utility Sources of Energy," Washington, D.C., 1987; Nørgaard, private communications.

56. Edison Electric, "1985 Capacity & Generation"; Federal Energy Regulatory Commission (FERC), "The Qualifying Facilities Report," Washington, D.C., January 1, 1987.

57. FERC, "Qualifying Facilities Report"; "Cogeneration," *Power,* June 1987; "GE Plays the Cogeneration Card," *Energy Daily,* August 6, 1985; Donald Marier and Larry Stoiaken, "Financing a Maturing Industry," *Alternative Sources of Energy,* May/June 1987; Mueller Associates, Inc., "Cogeneration's Retail Displacement Market," *Alternative Sources of Energy,* June/July 1986; Donald Marier and Larry Stoiaken, "Surviving the Coming Industry Shakeout," *Alternative Sources of Energy,* May/June 1987.

58. Roger Naill, Applied Energy Services, Arlington, Va., "Cogeneration and Small Power Production," presentation to Energy Policy Forum, Airlie, Va., June 16, 1987.

59. Breakdown of cogeneration from FERC, "Qualifying Facilities Report"; OTA, *Industrial Energy Use.*

60. Robert Williams et al., "Materials, Affluence, and Energy Use," in Annual Reviews, *Annual Review of Energy, Vol. 12.*

61. Geller, "Options for Developing Countries"; Lee Schipper and Stephen Meyers, "Energy Conservation in Kenya's Modern Sector: Progress, Potential and Problems," *Energy Policy,* September 1983; G. Anandalingam, "The Economics of Industrial Energy Conservation in the Developing Countries," in R.K. Pachauri, ed., *Global Energy Interactions* (Riverdale, Md.: The Riverdale Co., Inc., 1987).

62. Based on IEA, *Energy Conservation in IEA Countries.*

63. Donella H. Meadows et al., *The Limits to Growth* (New York: Universe Books, 1972).

64. Worldwatch Institute calculations based on data from IEA, International Road Federation, and Rotty, private communication.

65. British Petroleum Company, *BP Statistical Review of World Energy* (London: 1987); DOE, EIA, *Monthly Energy Review,* May 1987; Christopher Flavin et al., "The Oil Rollercoaster," Fund for Renewable Energy and the Environment, Washington, D.C., 1987.

66. Flavin et al., "The Oil Rollercoaster."

67. DOE, EIA, *Monthly Energy Review,* April 1987; U.S. oil savings, Worldwatch Institute estimate based on ibid.

68. Flavin et al., "The Oil Rollercoaster"; Bleviss, *The New Oil Crisis.*

69. ACEEE, *Acid Rain and Electricity Conservation* (Washington, D.C.: 1987).

70. Worldwatch Institute estimate based on data from IEA and Rotty, private communication.

71. Worldwatch Institute estimate based on Rosenfeld, "Conservation and Competitiveness."

72. Current global expenditures on efficiency improvements is Worldwatch Institute estimate, based on Rosenfeld, "Conservation and Competitiveness"; R&D budgets from IEA, *Energy Policies and Programmes of IEA Countries, 1986 Review* (Paris: OECD, 1987).

73. Carbon data from Rotty, private communication.

74. Dennis Miller, Energy Engineering Board, National Academy of Sciences, Washington, D.C., private communication, November 6, 1987; Amory Lovins, Rocky Mountain Institute, Old Snowmass, Colo., private communication, November 4, 1987.

75. International Institute for Applied Systems Analysis, *Energy in a Finite World: Paths to a Sustainable Future* (Cambridge, Mass.: Ballinger Publishing Co., 1981).

76. José Goldemberg et al., *Energy for a Sustainable World* (Washington, D.C.: World Resources Institute, 1987).

77. Directorate-General for Energy, *Energy in Europe: Energy Policies and Trends in the European Community* (Luxembourg: Commission of the European Communities, 1987).

Chapter 4. Shifting to Renewable Energy

1. Global contribution of renewables from World Commission on Environment and Development, *Our Common Future* (New York: Oxford University Press, 1987); Third World biomass figure from D.O. Hall et al., *Biomass for Energy in Developing Countries* (Elmsford, N.Y.: Pergamon Press, 1982).

2. Investment figure is Worldwatch Institute rough estimate, assuming investments of $20 billion in hydropower, $6 billion in biomass, $2.5 billion in geothermal, $550 million in solar collectors, $500 million in R&D, $400 million in wind power, and $250 million in photovoltaics.

3. Guri dam information from "Price Decline is Harmful For Development of Energy Resources," *OPEC Bulletin,* May 1987; Peter T. Kilborn, "Brazil's Hydroelectric Project," *New York Times,* November 14, 1983; Catherine Caulfield, "The Yangtze Beckons the Yankee Dollar," *New Scientist,* December 5, 1985; Strategies Unlimited, "International Market Evaluations: Small-Scale Hydropower Prospects," California Energy Commission (CEC), Sacramento, 1987.

4. Third World reliance on imported oil from U.S. Agency for International Development (AID), *Decentralized Hydropower in AID's Development Assistance Program* (Washington, D.C.: 1986).

5. T.W. Mermel, "Major Dams of the World-1986," *Water Power & Dam Construction,* July 1986; World Energy Conference, *Survey of Energy Resources, 1980* (Munich: 1980).

6. "The World's Hydro Resources," *Water Power & Dam Construction,* October 1986; Gary Aderman, "China Turns to Hydropower," *Journal of Commerce,* October 1, 1987; Ministry of Mines and Energy, "Energy Self-Sufficiency: A Scenario Developed as an Extension of the Brazilian Energy Model," Government of Brazil, Brasília, 1984.

7. Marlise Simons, "Dam's Threat to Rain Forest Spurs Quarrels in the Amazon," *New York Times,* September 6, 1987; Philip M. Fearnside, National Institute for Research in the Amazon, Manaus, Brazil, private communication, May 29, 1987; Catherine Caulfield, "Dam the Amazon, Full Steam Ahead," *Natural History,* July 1983.

8. Kilborn, "Brazil's Hydroelectric Project"; World Bank, *A Survey of the Future Role of Hydroelectric Power in 100 Developing Countries* (Washington, D.C.: 1984); Don Winston, U.S. Council on Energy Awareness, Wash-

ington, D.C., private communication, October 7, 1987.

9. Donald Worster, "An End to Ecstasy: What Will the Dam Builders Do Now?" *Wilderness*, Fall 1987; Philip Shabecoff, "U.S. Bureau for Water Projects Shifts Focus to Conservation," *New York Times*, October 2, 1987.

10. "Canadian National Energy Board Rejects H-Q Hydroelectric Sale to New England," *International Solar Energy Intelligence Report*, June 23, 1987; "Canadians Size Up U.S. Hydro Export Market," *Alternative Sources of Energy*, July/August 1987; Bill Rankin, "Manitoba Hydro Plans Large Exports of Electricity to the U.S.," *Energy Daily*, January 8, 1986.

11. Catherine Caulfield, "Environmentalists Warn of Damage from Planned Dam in China," *Christian Science Monitor*, December 9, 1985; Claude Alvares and Ramesh Billorey, "Damming the Narmada: The Politics Behind the Destruction," *The Ecologist*, May/June 1987. For furthur information, see Bruce Rich, Environmental Defense Fund, Testimony in Hearings on Environmental Performance of the Multilateral Development Banks, Subcommittee on International Development Institutions and Finance, U.S. House of Representatives, April 8, 1987.

12. Edward Goldsmith and Nicholas Hilyard, *The Social and Environmental Effects of Large Dams* (San Francisco, Calif.: Sierra Club Books, 1987); Philip B. Williams, "Damming the World," *Not Man Apart*, October 1983; Caulfield, "Environmentalists Warn of Damage"; Robert Goodland, *Environmental Assessment of the Tucurui Hydroproject* (Brasília: Electronorte, 1978).

13. International Task Force, *Tropical Forests: A Call for Action, Part I: The Plan* (Washington, D.C.: World Resources Institute, 1985).

14. Frost & Sullivan cited in Don Best, "Remote Power Market Is Predicted to Swell," *Renewable Energy News*, July 1985.

15. World Bank, *Survey of Hydroelectric Power;* Strategies Unlimited, "Small-Scale Hydropower Prospects"; Larry N. Stoiaken, "The Chinese Hydro Imports: Testing the North American Marketplace," *Alternative Sources of Energy*, July/August 1983.

16. Edison Electric Institute, "1985 Capacity & Generation, Non-Utility Sources of Energy," Washington, D.C., April 1987; Douglas Cogan and Susan Williams, *Generating Energy Alternatives, 1987 Edition* (Washington, D.C.: Investor Responsibility Research Center, 1987); Donald Marier and Larry N. Stoiaken, "An Industry in Transition: The Hydropower Industry Looks Ahead," *Alternative Sources of Energy*, July/August 1987; "Poland Restarts Small Hydro Plants," *European Energy Report*, July 24, 1987; Ian Lewis, "Small Hydro Playing Key Role in Ontario's Economy," *Alternative Sources of Energy*, October 1986.

17. AID, *Decentralized Hydropower;* Strategies Unlimited, "Small-Scale Hydropower Prospects"; Maria Elena Hurtado, "Hydro Power: China's Marriage of Convenience," *South*, January 1983.

18. Worster, "An End to Ecstasy."

19. International Energy Agency (IEA), *Renewable Sources of Energy* (Paris: Organisation for Economic Co-operation and Development (OECD), 1987); World Commission on Environment and Development, *Our Common Future.*

20. Gordon T. Goodman, "Biomass Energy in Developing Countries: Problems and Challenges," *Ambio*, Vol. 16, No. 2–3, 1987; United Nations, *1985 Energy Statistics Yearbook* (New York: 1987).

21. IEA, *Renewable Sources.*

22. Goodman, "Biomass Energy"; U.N. Food and Agriculture Organization, *Fuelwood Supplies in the Developing Countries*, Forestry Paper 42 (Rome: 1983).

23. National Wood Energy Association, "Wood   Energy—America's   Renewable

Source," fact sheet, Washington, D.C., September 1987; American Paper Institute, "U.S. Pulp, Paper and Paperboard Industry Estimated Fuel & Energy Use, Full Year 1986, 1985 and 1984," New York, April 1987; Robert P. Kennel, "Biomass for Cogeneration (A Better Option Than You Expected)," presented at Co-energy '86, Boston, Mass., September 3–4, 1986; Solar Energy Industries Association, *Energy Innovation: Development and Status of the Renewable Energy Industries, Vol. 2* (Washington, D.C.: 1985).

24. Meridian Corporation, *Electric Power From Biofuels: Planned and Existing Projects in the United States* (Washington, D.C.: U.S. Department of Energy (DOE), 1985); Everett Jordan, Eugene Water & Electric, Eugene, Ore., private communication, September 3, 1987; Thomas Carr, Burlington Electric Department, Burlington, Vt., private communication, August 12, 1987; Gerry Anderson, Northern States Power Company, Minneapolis, Minn., private communication, September 2, 1987; George Parks, Washington Water & Power, Kettle Falls, Wash., private communication, September, 1987; CEC, "Relative Cost of Electricity Production," Staff Report, Sacramento, Calif., April 1987; Robert P. Kennel, "Comments of the National Wood Energy Association on Cogeneration and Small Power Production," before the U.S. Federal Energy Regulatory Commission, April 30, 1987.

25. Dean Mahin, "Wood-Fuel Users Report Cost Savings in Virginia," *Renewable Energy News*, October 1985.

26. Frank H. Denton, *Wood for Energy and Rural Development: The Philippines Experience* (Manila: Frank H. Denton, 1983); Christopher Flavin, "Bio-Energy in the Philippines," Worldwatch Institute, unpublished memorandum, December 1985.

27. IEA, *Renewable Sources.*

28. Al Binger, President, Biomass Users Network, Washington, D.C., private communication, October 1, 1987; Bill Belleville, "Renewable Energy Promises Much As Caribbeans Look to the Future," *Renewable Energy News*, October 1985; Eric Larson, Center for Energy and Environmental Studies, Princeton University, Princeton, N.J., private communication, November 12, 1987; information on Thailand from RONCO Consulting Corp., "The Sugar Industry in the Philippines," Arlington, Va., December 1986.

29. Information on Hawaii from Charles Kinoshita, Hawaiian Sugar Planters Association, Honolulu, Hawaii, private communication, November 24, 1987, and from RONCO, "Sugar Industry in the Philippines"; information on continental capacity from Michael D. Devine et al., *Cogeneration and Decentralized Electricity Production* (Boulder, Colo.: Westview Press, 1987).

30. Eric D. Larson et al., "Steam-Injected Gas-Turbine Cogeneration for the Cane Sugar Industry: Optimization Through Improvements in Sugar-Processing Efficiencies," Center for Energy and Environmental Studies, Princeton University, Princeton, N.J., September 1987.

31. AID, "Power From Rice Husks," *Bioenergy Systems Report*, April 1986.

32. Ibid.; Bob Schwieger, "Rice-hull-fired Powerplant Burns a Nuisance Waste, Sells Electricity, Ash," *Power*, July 1985.

33. AID, "Power From Rice Husks."

34. Per Johan Svenningsson, "Cotton Stalks as an Energy Source for Nicaragua," *Ambio*, Vol. 14, No. 4–5, 1985; Amory B. Lovins et al., "Energy and Agriculture," in Wes Jackson et al., eds., *Meeting the Expectations of the Land* (San Francisco, Calif.: North Point Press, 1984).

35. IEA, *Renewable Sources.*

36. Dr. Marcos M. Soares, Technical Assistant, National Executive Commission of Alcohol, Government of Brazil, Brasília, pri-

vate communication, June 25, 1987; "Fuel Consumption High Despite Price Hike," *Gazeta Mercantil,* January 26, 1987; National Executive Commission of Alcohol, "The National Alcohol Program," Ministry of Industry and Commerce, Government of Brazil, Brasília, 1984.

37. Robert H. Williams, "Potential Roles for Bioenergy in an Energy-Efficient World," *Ambio,* Vol. 14, No. 4–5, 1985; Howard S. Geller, "Ethanol Fuel From Sugar Cane in Brazil," in Annual Reviews Inc., *Annual Review of Energy, Vol. 10* (Palo Alto, Calif.: 1985).

38. Information Resources, Inc., information packet, Washington, D.C., 1987; A. Barry Carr, Congressional Research Service, Testimony at Hearings on Possible Effects of Legislation Mandating Use of Ethanol in Gasoline, Subcommittee on Energy and Power, U.S. House of Representatives, June 24, 1987; Richard B. Schmitt, "Gasohol Backers See Ban on Lead Boosting Sales," *Wall Street Journal,* September 26, 1985; Sarah McKinley, "Ethanol Enjoys Good Times, But Is There A Hangover Ahead?" *Energy Daily,* August 21, 1985.

39. Cities not meeting U.S. pollution standards from Brock Nicholson, U.S. Environmental Protection Agency, Research Triangle Park, N.C., private communication, November 9, 1987; Mark Ivey and Ronald Grover, "Alcohol Fuels Move Off the Back Burner," *Business Week,* June 29, 1987.

40. Meridian Corporation, "Worldwide Review of Biomass Based Ethanol Activities," Falls Church, Va., 1985; Information Resources, Inc., *Alcohol Outlook,* various issues; Alan Friedman and George Graham, "Ferruzzi Plans to Produce Ethanol at Plant in Northern France," *Financial Times,* July 10, 1987; David Lindahl, U.S. Department of Energy, Washington, D.C., private communication, August 27, 1987; "Alcoholic Problems in Italy," *European Energy Report,* August 21, 1987.

41. IEA, *Renewable Sources;* Ross Pumfrey and Thomas Hoffman, "Incentives for the Use of Renewable Energy: The Experience in Brazil, Cyprus, India, the Philippines, and California," International Institute for Environment and Development, Washington, D.C., 1985; D. Groues and I. Segal, *Solar Energy In Israel* (Jerusalem: Ministry of Energy & Infrastructure, 1984).

42. IEA, *Renewable Sources;* Strategies Unlimited, "International Market Evaluations: Solar Thermal Energy Prospects," CEC, Sacramento, Calif., 1987.

43. U.S. Department of Energy, *Solar Collector Manufacturing Activity 1986* (Washington, D.C.: 1987); U.S. Department of Energy, *Solar Collector Manufacturing Activity 1984* (Washington, D.C.: 1985); Scott Sklar, Solar Energy Industries Association, Testimony at Hearings, Subcommittee on Energy Research and Development, Committee on Science, Space and Technology, U.S. House of Reprsentatives, March 11, 1987.

44. IEA, *Renewable Sources.*

45. Michael Edesedd, "On Solar Ponds: Salty Fare for the World's Energy Appetite," *Technology Review,* December 1982; "Bet Ha'Arava Solar Pond Power Plant Inaugurated," *Sun World,* Vol. 8, No. 1, 1984; "Solar Ponds Performing Well, Several Countries Advance Plans," *Solar Energy Intelligence Report,* April 28, 1987; Robert L. Reid and Andrew H.P. Swift, "El Paso Solar Pond First in U.S. to Generate Electricity," *Solar Today,* January/February 1987; "California Looks to Salt Water and the Sun," *New Scientist,* July 3, 1986.

46. Luz International Limited, information packet, Los Angeles, Calif.; Trudy Self, Luz International Limited, private communication, July 23, 1987; "Solar Energy Strikes Gold in California," *International Power Generation,* December 1986/January 1987; David W. Kearney and Henry W. Price, "Overview of the SEGS Plants," presented to the Solar '87 Conference, Portland, Ore., July 1987.

47. Christopher Flavin, "Electricity from Sunlight: The Emergence of Photovoltaics," U.S. Department of Energy, Washington, D.C., December 1984; R.L. Watts and S.A. Smith, "Photovoltaic Industry Progress from 1980 through 1986," Pacific Northwest Laboratory, Battelle Memorial Institute, Richland, Wash., June 1987; IEA, *Renewable Sources.*

48. Pre-1981 shipments and cost data from Strategies Unlimited, *1980–81 Market Review* (Mountain View, Calif.: 1981); post-1980 shipments data from Watts and Smith, "Photovoltaic Industry Progress"; post-1980 cost figures from Paul Maycock, "PV Technology, Performance, Cost, and Market Forecast to 1995," PV Energy Systems, Casanova, Va., November 1986.

49. Watts and Smith, "Photovoltaic Industry Progress"; "Communication Systems: Photovoltaics is Preferred Power Source," *ARCO News,* Summer 1986.

50. Herbert Wade, U.N. Pacific Energy Development Programme, Fiji, "The Socio-Economic Benefits of PV Applications in the Pacific," presented to the Photovoltaics: Investing in Development Conference, organized by U.S. Department of Energy, New Orleans, La., May 4–6, 1987; "French Polynesia - World's Largest Market for Small PV Systems?" *PV News,* May 1987; William Meade, "Caribbean Project Opportunities," Renewable Energy Institute, Washington, D.C., May 1987; Richard Hansen, Enersol Associates, Somerville, Mass., private communication, September 23, 1987; IEA, *Renewable Sources.*

51. "Solarex Wins U.S. Coast Guard Contract," *Photovoltaic Insider's Report,* July 1987; Paul Maycock, presentation to Society for International Development Energy Luncheon, Washington, D.C., July 2, 1987.

52. Paul Maycock, "Consumer Products—PV's Fastest Growing Segment," *PV International,* November 1987; Watts and Smith, "Photovoltaic Industry Progress."

53. Watts and Smith, "Photovoltaic Industry Progress."

54. "The Bad News and Good News for Photovoltaics," *Solar Today,* May/June 1987.

55. "Solarex, ARCO Solar Sue Each Other, Charging Thin Film Technology Patent Infringement," *Photovoltaic Insider's Report,* June 1987; "Chronar, Pension Fund Sign Letter of Intent on 10-MWp a-Si PV Plant," *International Solar Energy Intelligence Report,* October 20, 1987.

56. IEA, *Renewable Sources;* Thomas Jaras, *Wind Energy 1987: Wind Turbine Shipments and Applications* (Great Falls, Va.: Stadia, Inc., 1987).

57. Jaras, *Wind Energy 1987.*

58. Ibid.; IEA, *Renewable Sources;* R. Lynette & Assoc., Inc., "The Lessons of the California Wind Farms: How Developing Countries Can Learn From the American Experience," Redmond, Wash., 1987.

59. IEA, *Renewable Sources.*

60. Strategies Unlimited, "International Market Evaluations: Wind Energy Prospects," CEC, Sacramento, Calif., 1987; IEA, *Renewable Sources.*

61. Lynette & Assoc., "Lessons of California"; Tom Gray, American Wind Energy Association, Testimony at Hearings, Subcommittee on Energy Research and Development, Committee on Science, Space and Technology, U.S. House of Representatives, March 11, 1987; IEA, *Renewable Sources.*

62. Average wind turbine size derived from information provided by Sam Rashkin, CEC, Sacramento, Calif., private communication, October 6, 1987, and in Paul Gipe, "An Overview of the U.S. Wind Industry," *Alternative Sources of Energy,* September/October 1985; Lynette & Assoc., "Lessons of California"; IEA, *Renewable Sources;* Strategies Unlimited, "Wind Energy Prospects"; Kevin Porter, Renewable Energy Institute, Washington, D.C., private communication, October 22, 1987.

63. Strategies Unlimited, "Wind Energy Prospects"; Strategies Unlimited, "International Energy and Trade Policies of California's Export Competitors," CEC, Sacramento, Calif., 1987.

64. Jaras, *Wind Energy 1987*.

65. Information on Danish manufacturers from Thomas Jaras, quoted in "Top Ten Listings Prove Third World Growth," *Windpower Monthly*, September 1987; Torgny Møller, Publisher, *Windpower Monthly*, Knebel, Denmark, private communication, September 9, 1987; Cathy Kramer, "The Ebeltoft Sea-Based Wind Project," *Alternative Sources of Energy*, December 1985; Strategies Unlimited, "International Energy and Trade Policies."

66. Strategies Unlimited, "Wind Energy Prospects"; IEA, *Renewable Sources;* Jaras, *Wind Energy 1987;* Costis Stambolis, "Danwin Snares Large Export Contract to Supply Windmills to Soviet Union," *International Solar Energy Intelligence Report*, September 29, 1987; "International Roundup," *International Solar Energy Intelligence Report*, September 22, 1987.

67. Strategies Unlimited, "Wind Energy Prospects"; Jaras, *Wind Energy 1987;* Gipe, "Overview of U.S. Wind Industry"; "World List of Nuclear Power Plants," *Nuclear News*, February 1986.

68. Gipe, "Overview of U.S. Wind Industry"; Lynette & Assoc., "Lessons of California"; Philip C. Cruver, "Windpower: Electrical Power Source for the Future," *SunWorld*, Vol. 11, No. 3, 1987.

69. Ministry of Mines and Energy, "Energy Self-Sufficiency: A Scenario Developed as an Extension of the Brazilian Energy Model"; United Nations, *1985 Energy Statistics;* DOE, Energy Information Administration, *International Energy Annual 1986* (Washington, D.C.: 1987); José Goldemberg et al., *Energy for Development* (Washington, D.C.: World Resources Institute, 1987).

70. Goldemberg et al. *Energy for Development.*

71. Ross Pumfrey et al., "India Trade and Investment Laws Relating to Renewable Energy," Renewable Energy Institute, Washington, D.C., March 1987; Judith Perera, "Indian Government Draws Up Plans to Exploit Renewable Energy," *Solar Energy Intelligence Report*, August 11, 1987.

72. IEA, *Energy Policies and Programmes of IEA Countries, 1986 Review* (Paris: OECD, 1987).

73. Ibid.

74. Population Reference Bureau, *1986 World Population Data Sheet* (Washington, D.C.: 1986); World Bank, *World Development Report 1987* (New York: Oxford University Press, 1987).

75. Sweden's per capita R&D spending derived from IEA, *Policies and Programmes*, and from Population Reference Bureau, *1986 World Population Data Sheet;* information on Swedish biomass programs from IEA, *Policies and Programmes*, from "Green Power: Biofuels are a Growing Concern," *Scientific American*, August 1984, and from Allerd Stikker, President, Trans-form Foundation, London, private communication, September 28, 1987; information on Sweden's nuclear policy from "Swedish Plan for Nuclear Phase-out," *European Energy Report*, May 29, 1987.

76. Strategies Unlimited, "International Energy and Trade Policies"; "Swiss Program Reflects Interest in Indigenous, Non-Polluting Energy," *Solar Update*, May 1987; Strategies Unlimited, "Wind Energy Prospects"; IEA, *Policies and Programmes;* Perera, "Indian Government Draws Up Plans."

77. Strategies Unlimited, "International Energy and Trade Policies."

78. IEA, *Renewable Sources;* Ronald DiPippo, Southeastern Massachusetts University, private communication, June 29, 1987; Ronald DiPippo, "Geothermal Power Plants, Worldwide Status—1986," *Geothermal*

Resources Council Bulletin, December 1986; 1991 capacity figure and Electric Power Research Institute study cited in Donald Finn, "Expanding Geothermal Industry," Alternative Sources of Energy, October 1987.

Chapter 5. Reforesting the Earth

1. Preagricultural number from E. Matthews, "Global Vegetation and Land Use," Journal of Climate and Applied Meteorology, Vol. 22, 1983, pp. 474–487; current number from R. Persson, unpublished report to the Swedish International Development Authority (1985) as cited in World Resources Institute/ International Institute for Environment and Development, World Resources 1986 (New York: Basic Books, 1986).

2. John F. Richardson, "World Environmental History and Economic Development," in William C. Clark and R. E. Munn, eds., Sustainable Development of the Biosphere (New York: Cambridge University Press, 1986); International Institute for Environmental Studies, European Environmental Yearbook 1987 (London: DocTer International UK Ltd., 1987); Robert G. Albion, Forests and Sea Power: The Timber Problem of the Royal Navy 1652–1862 (Cambridge, Mass.: Harvard University Press, 1926); U.S. Forest Service, U.S. Department of Agriculture (USDA), Timber Resources for America's Future, Forest Resources Report No. 14 (Washington, D.C.: U.S. Government Printing Office, 1958).

3. Total world land area equals 13,081 million hectares, excluding Antarctica, Greenland's tundra, and inland water bodies. Area in crops equals 1,477 million hectares, according to U.N. Food and Agriculture Organization (FAO), 1985 Production Yearbook (Rome: 1986).

4. FAO, Tropical Forest Resources, Forestry Paper 30 (Rome: 1982).

5. Philip Fearnside, "Spatial Concentration of Deforestation in the Brazilian Amazon," Ambio, Vol. 15, No. 2, 1986; Philip Fearnside, "Deforestation in the Brazilian Amazon: How Fast Is It Occurring?" Interciencia, Vol. 7, No. 2, 1982; Centre for Science and Environment, The State of India's Environment 1984–85 (New Delhi: 1985); FAO, Tropical Forest Resources.

6. Kenya example from Peter A. Dewees, Forest Economist, Nairobi, Kenya, private communication, July 7, 1987; Rwanda example from R. Winterbottom, Rwanda Integrated Forestry and Livestock Project, Report of the Rural Forestry Preparation (Phase II), FAO/ World Bank, Washington, D.C., 1985.

7. FAO, Tropical Forest Resources.

8. B. Bowander, "Deforestation Around Urban Centres in India," Environmental Conservation, Vol. 14, No. 1, Spring 1987.

9. Sandra Postel, "Protecting Forests," in Lester R. Brown et al., State of the World 1984 (New York: W.W. Norton & Co., 1984). For a listing of studies documenting secondary damage from selective logging, see Norman Myers, The Primary Source: Tropical Forests and Our Future (New York: W.W. Norton & Co., 1984); Robert O. Blake, "Moist Forests of the Tropics—A Plea For Protection and Development," Journal '84, World Resources Institute, Washington, D.C., 1984.

10. Norman Myers, "The Hamburger Connection: How Central America's Forests Become North America's Hamburgers," Ambio, Vol. 10, No. 1, 1981; H. Jefferey Leonard, Natural Resources and Economic Development in Central America (Washington, D.C.: International Institute for Environment and Development, 1987); Philip M. Fearnside, "Land-Use Trends in the Brazilian Amazon Region as Factors in Accelerating Deforestation," Environmental Conservation, Summer 1983.

11. F.C. Hummel, "In the Forests of the EEC," Unasylva, No. 138, 1982; International Institute for Environmental Studies, European Environmental Yearbook 1987.

12. International Co-operative Programme on Assessment and Monitoring of Air Pollution Effects on Forests, "Forest Damage and Air Pollution: Report on the 1986 Forest Damage Survey in Europe," Global Environment Monitoring System, United Nations Environment Programme, Nairobi, mimeographed, 1987.

13. Loss between 1630 and 1920 from U.S. Forest Service, *Timber Resources for America's Future*. Forest area in 1982 adapted from U.S. Forest Service, *America's Renewable Resources: A Supplement to the 1979 Assessment of Forest and Rangeland in the U.S.* (Washington, D.C.: USDA, 1984); note that figure cited in text omits forest area for Alaska and Hawaii. Total forest area of United States in 1963 was approximately 307 million hectares according to USDA, U.S. Forest Service, *Timber Trends in the U.S.*, Forest Resource Report No. 17 (Washington, D.C.: U.S. Government Printing Office, 1965); forest area of contiguous states in 1963 was estimated by subtracting the 48 million hectares of forest listed for Alaska and an additional 804,000 hectares to approximate the forest area of Hawaii. For a description of U.S. forest cover trends, see "The Evolving Use and Management of Our Forests, Grassland and Croplands," in Council on Environmental Quality, *Environmental Quality 1985* (Washington, D.C.: U.S. Government Printing Office, 1987).

14. Gordon T. Goodman, "Biomass Energy in Developing Countries: Problems and Challenges," *Ambio*, Vol. 16, No. 2–3, 1987.

15. FAO, *Fuelwood Supplies in the Developing Countries*, Forestry Paper 42 (Rome: 1983).

16. Bina Agarwal, *Cold Hearths and Barren Slopes: The Woodfuel Crisis in the Third World* (Riverdale, Md.: The Riverdale Co., Inc., 1986); Nepal figure from Robert Winterbottom and Peter T. Hazelwood, "Agroforestry and Sustainable Development: Making the Connection," *Ambio*, Vol. 16, No. 2–3, 1987.

17. The energy efficiency of traditional charcoal-making processes tends to be about 30 percent. Although some efficiency will be recouped because charcoal stoves are slightly more efficient (at 25 percent) than wood-burning stoves (at 18 percent), the overall efficiency will probably still be close to 50 percent. See Gerald Foley, *Charcoal Making in Developing Countries* (Washington, D.C.: International Institute for Environment and Development, 1986), and Goodman, "Biomass Energy." West African urban figure from William Floor, "A Strategy for Household Energy in West Africa" (draft), World Bank, Washington, D.C., June 1987.

18. John Spears, Senior Forestry Advisor, World Bank, Washington, D.C., private communication, September 24, 1987.

19. Dennis Anderson and Robert Fishwick, *Fuelwood Consumption and Deforestation in African Countries*, Staff Working Paper No. 704 (Washington, D.C.: World Bank, 1984); John Spears, "Replenishing the World's Forests: Tropical Reforestation, An Achievable Goal?" *Commonwealth Forestry Review*, Vol. 62, No. 3, 1983.

20. Keynote Paper, Bellagio Strategy Meeting on Tropical Forests, Lake Como, Italy, July 1–2, 1987; Gerald Foley and Geoffrey Barnard, *Farm and Community Forestry* (Washington, D.C.: International Institute for Environment and Development, 1984); Dr. Kamla Chowdry, "Wastelands and the Rural Poor: Essentials of a Policy Framework," *Forest News*, Vol. 14, No. 2, 1987.

21. Paul Harrison, *The Greening of Africa* (New York: Viking/Penguin, Inc., 1987).

22. Ibid.

23. Paul Harrison, "A Tale of Two Stoves," *New Scientist*, May 28, 1987.

24. Jayanta Bandyopadhyay and Vandana Shiva, "Chipko: Rekindling India's Forest Culture," *The Ecologist*, January/February 1987.

25. Lawrence S. Hamilton and Peter N. King, *Tropical Forested Watersheds: Hydrologic*

and *Soils Response to Major Uses or Conversions* (Boulder, Colo.: Westview Press, 1983).

26. West Africa figure from Eneas Salati et al., "Amazon Rainfall, Potential Effects of Deforestation, and Plans for Future Research," in Ghillean T. Prance, ed., *Tropical Rain Forests and the World Atmosphere* (Boulder, Colo.: Westview Press, 1986).

27. Jack D. Ives, "The Theory of Himalayan Environmental Degradation: Its Validity and Application Challenged by Recent Research," and K.G. Tejwani, "Sedimentation of Reservoirs in the Himalayan Region—India," *Mountain Research and Development,* Vol. 7, No. 3, 1987.

28. Centre for Science and Environment, *The Wrath of Nature: The Impact of Environmental Destruction on Floods and Droughts* (New Delhi: 1987).

29. Nicomedes D. Briones and Jose P. Castro, "Effective Management of a Tropical Watershed: The Case of the Angat Watershed in the Philippines," *Water International,* December 1986; National Environmental Protection Council, *Philippine Environmental Quality 1977,* First Annual Report (Manila: 1977).

30. James Nations and H. Jeffrey Leonard, "Grounds of Conflict in Central America," in Andrew Maguire and Janet Welsh Brown, eds., *Bordering on Trouble: Resources and Politics in Latin America* (Bethesda, Md.: Adler & Adler, Inc., 1986).

31. Alan Grainger, "Estimating Areas of Degraded Tropical Lands Requiring Replenishment of Forest Cover," *International Tree Crops Journal,* Vol. 5, No. 1/2, 1987; International Task Force (ITF), *Tropical Forests: A Call for Action, Part I: The Plan* (Washington, D.C.: World Resources Institute, 1985).

32. India figure from D.R. Bhumbla and Arvind Khare, "Estimate of Wastelands in India," Society for Promotion of Wastelands Development, New Delhi, undated.

33. U.S. Congress, Office of Technology Assessment (OTA), *Technologies to Sustain Tropical Forest Resources* (Washington, D.C.: U.S. Government Printing Office, 1984).

34. ITF, *Tropical Forests: A Call for Action, Part II: Case Studies* (Washington, D.C.: World Resources Institute, 1985).

35. ITF, *Tropical Forests, Part I.*

36. OTA, *Technologies to Sustain Tropical Forest Resources;* P.K.R. Nair, *Soil Productivity Aspects of Agroforestry* (Nairobi: International Council for Research in Agroforestry, 1984).

37. Crop yield increases from ITF, *Tropical Forests, Part II;* Harrison, *Greening of Africa.*

38. Harrison, *Greening of Africa.*

39. A.M. Solomon et al., "The Global Cycle of Carbon," in John R. Trabalka et al., *Atmospheric Carbon Dioxide and the Global Carbon Cycle* (Washington, D.C.: U.S. Government Printing Office, 1985).

40. Ibid.; Richard A. Houghton, "Estimating Changes in the Carbon Content of Terrestrial Ecosystems from Historical Data," in John R. Trabalka and David E. Reichle, eds., *The Changing Carbon Cycle: A Global Analysis* (New York: Springer-Verlag, 1986).

41. R.A. Houghton et al., "The Flux of Carbon from Terrestrial Ecosystems to the Atmosphere in 1980 Due to Changes in Land Use: Geographic Distribution of the Global Flux," *Tellus,* February/April 1987.

42. Sylvan H. Wittwer, "Rising Atmospheric CO_2 and Crop Productivity," *Hortscience,* October 1983; A.M. Solomon and D.C. West, "Potential Responses of Forests to CO_2 Induced Climate Change," in Margaret R. White, *Characterization of Information Requirements for Studies of CO_2 Effects: Water Resources, Agriculture, Fisheries, Forests and Human Health* (Washington, D.C.: U.S. Department of Energy, 1985).

43. George M. Woodwell, "Forests and Climate: Surprises in Store," *Oceanus,* Winter 1986/87.

44. Ibid.

45. R.A. Houghton et al., "Carbon Dioxide Exchange Between the Atmosphere and Terrestrial Ecosystems," in Trabalka et al., *Atmospheric Carbon Dioxide;* Richard Houghton, Woods Hole Research Center, Woods Hole, Mass., private communication, September 1987; Sandra Brown, University of Illinois at Champaign-Urbana, private communication, October 1987.

46. According to FAO, in *Fuelwood Supplies in Developing Countries,* of the people who were not using fuelwood sustainably in 1980, roughly 8 percent could not find enough wood, even by overcutting. The other 92 percent were able to find enough wood, but only by depleting the resource base. The assumption in this chapter is that by the year 2000, the proportion of people living in acute scarcity may increase to 20 percent. Therefore, 20 percent of the fuelwood planted would be burned immediately to satisfy unmet needs and the other 80 percent would become part of an expanded resource base that could sustainably service remaining demand.

47. Figure for fast-growing hardwoods from Sandra Brown et al., "Biomass of Tropical Tree Plantations and its Implications for the Global Carbon Budget," *Canadian Journal of Forest Research,* Vol. 16, No. 2, 1986. Percentage of biomass that is carbon from Houghton et al., "Carbon Dioxide Exchange." Soil carbon increase from Houghton et al., "The Flux of Carbon from Terrestrial Ecosystems." Observation about removal of litter from Sandra Brown, University of Illinois at Champaign-Urbana, private communication, November 7, 1987.

48. Houghton et al., "The Flux of Carbon from Terrestrial Ecosystems."

49. Subtitle D, "Conservation Reserve," of the U.S. Food Security Act, *Congressional Record–House,* December 17, 1985; assumptions drawn from data in Houghton et al., "The Flux of Carbon from Terrestrial Ecosystems."

50. For a discussion of the role of nongovernmental organizations in development, see OTA, *Continuing the Commitment: Agricultural Development in the Sahel—Special Report* (Washington, D.C.: U.S. Goverment Printing Office, 1986); Winterbottom and Hazelwood, "Agroforestry and Sustainable Development."

51. "A Vulnerable Seedling: India's Movement for Social Forestry," *Development International,* March/April 1987; Louis Sweeney, "The Greening of Kenya," *Christian Science Monitor,* October 7, 1986.

52. Jodi Jacobson, "Agroforestry: An Old Idea Shows New Promise," *VITA News,* April 1985.

53. Cynthia Mackie, "Forestry in Asia: U.S. AID's Experience," Division of Energy and Natural Resources, U.S. Agency for International Development, unpublished, November 1986; "World Bank Financed Forestry Activity in the Decade 1977–86: A Review of Key Policy Issues and Implications of Past Experience to Future Project Design," Agriculture and Rural Development Department, World Bank, Washington, D.C., December 1986.

54. World Bank survey cited in Harrison, *Greening of Africa;* funding statistics from ITF, *Tropical Forests, Part I.*

55. In 1985 two groups, an international task force convened by the World Resources Institute (WRI) and one called by FAO, issued separate but similar documents calling for a global initiative to arrest deforestation and promote tree planting. In June 1987, these efforts were merged into the Tropical Forestry Action Plan, a framework for action jointly sponsored by FAO, WRI, the United Nations Development Programme, and the World Bank. Activities under the Action Plan actually began in 1985 although the final joint document was not released until June 1987.

56. "The Tropical Forestry Action Plan: Background Information and Update,"

World Resources Institute, Washington, D.C., mimeographed, September 1987; funding figures are from survey conducted by World Resources Institute.

57. China Scientific and Technological Information Research Institute, *China in the Year 2000* (Beijing: Science and Technology Documents Publishers, 1984) (available from National Technical Information Service, Springfield, Va., as JPRS-CEA-86–023). Chinese forest cover statistics from *Zhongguo Tongji Nian Jian* (Chinese Statistical Yearbooks) (Beijing: Zhongguo Tongji Chubanshe, 1981, 1983, 1984, 1985, and 1986). Housing data and planting statistics from USDA, Economic Research Service, *China Situation and Outlook Report* (Washington, D.C.: U.S. Government Printing Office, 1987). Calculation on wood used for housing is based on 50–70 cubic meters of timber being needed for each 1,000 square meters of new floorspace, according to Vaclav Smil, "Deforestation in China," *Ambio,* Vol. 12, No. 5, 1983; USDA, in *China Situation and Outlook Report,* says that between 1981 and 1985, 3.2 billion square meters of floor space were constructed; average annual growth of China's forests is 187 million cubic meters, according to *China in the Year 2000.*

58. 1985 planting statistics from USDA, *China Situation and Outlook Report;* planting goals from "State Bids to Increase Forests," *China Daily,* March 31, 1987.

59. Gandhi quote from national broadcast of January 5, 1985, as quoted in Government of India, "Strategies, Structures, Policies: National Wastelands Development Board," New Delhi, mimeographed, February 6, 1986. Funding rose from 6,925 million rupees in the Sixth Plan (1980–85) to 18,593 million rupees in the Seventh Plan, according to Glen Morgan, World Bank, Washington, D.C., private communication, October 26, 1987. Information about grant program from Sunita Narain, Centre for Science and Environment, New Delhi, private communication, October 7, 1987.

60. Francois Mergen et al., "Forestry Research: A Provisional Global Inventory," Center Discussion Paper No. 503, Economic Growth Center, Yale University, New Haven, Conn., May 1986.

Chapter 6. Avoiding a Mass Extinction of Species

1. For a comprehensive discussion of the causes and consequences of past extinctions, see Steven M. Stanley, *Extinction* (New York: Scientific American Library, 1987).

2. National Research Council (NRC), *Research Priorities in Tropical Biology* (Washington, D.C.: National Academy Press, 1980).

3. U.S. Congress, Office of Technology Assessment (OTA), *Technologies to Maintain Biological Diversity* (Washington, D.C.: U.S. Government Printing Office, 1987).

4. Estimate of area needed for comprehensive conservation is from Norman Myers, "Tackling Mass Extinction of Species: A Great Creative Challenge," 26th Horace M. Albright Lectureship in Conservation, University of California, College of Natural Resources, Berkeley, California, May 1, 1986.

5. R.H. MacArthur and E.O. Wilson, *The Theory of Island Biogeography* (Princeton, N.J.: Princeton University Press, 1967).

6. Daniel Simberloff, "Are We on the Verge of a Mass Extinction in Tropical Rain Forests?" in David K. Elliott, ed., *Dynamics of Extinction* (New York: John Wiley & Sons, Inc., 1986).

7. Estimates of forest clearing are from U.N. Food and Agriculture Organization (FAO), *Tropical Forest Resources,* Forestry Paper 30 (Rome: 1982).

8. William D. Newmark, "A Land-Bridge Island Perspective on Mammalian Extinctions in Western North American Parks," *Nature,* January 29, 1987; James Gleick, "Species Vanishing from Many Parks," *New York Times,* February 3, 1987.

9. Newmark, "A Land-Bridge Island Perspective."

10. Charles Darwin, *The Voyage of the Beagle* (New York: Doubleday & Co., Inc., 1962).

11. NRC, *Research Priorities in Tropical Biology*.

12. Julie Ann Miller, "Entomologist's Paradise," *Science News*, June 2, 1984; Edward O. Wilson, "The Current State of Biological Diversity," presented at the National Forum on Biodiversity, Smithsonian Institution and National Academy of Sciences, Washington, D.C., September 21, 1986.

13. Alwyn H. Gentry, "Endemism in Tropical versus Temperate Plant Communities," in Michael E. Soulé, ed., *Conservation Biology: The Science of Scarcity and Diversity* (Sunderland, Mass.: Sinauer Associates, Inc., 1986).

14. Richard Conniff, "Inventorying Life in a 'Biotic Frontier' Before it Disappears," *Smithsonian*, September 1986.

15. Miller, "Entomologist's Paradise."

16. Bill Knight and Chris Schofield, "Sulawesi: An Island Expedition," *New Scientist*, January 3, 1985; Dr. William Knight, British Museum of Natural History, private communication, January 14, 1987.

17. Knight and Schofield, "Sulawesi: An Island Expedition."

18. Otto T. Solbrig, review of *Foundations for a National Biological Survey*, in *Conservation Biology*, May 1987.

19. NRC, *Research Priorities in Tropical Biology*.

20. For overviews of conservation biology, see Michael E. Soulé and Bruce A. Wilcox, eds., *Conservation Biology: An Evolutionary-Ecological Perspective* (Sunderland, Mass.: Sinauer Associates, Inc., 1980); and Soulé, *Conservation Biology: The Science of Scarcity and Diversity*.

21. Roger Lewin, "Parks: How Big is Big Enough?" *Science*, August 10, 1984.

22. Ibid.

23. NRC, *Research Priorities in Tropical Biology*.

24. Edward O. Wilson, "The Biological Diversity Crisis: A Challenge to Science," *Issues in Science and Technology*, Fall 1985.

25. Otto T. Solbrig and Frank Golley, "A Decade of the Tropics," *Biology International* (Paris), Special Issue 2, 1983.

26. Peter Raven, Missouri Botanical Garden, St. Louis, Mo., private communication, March 13, 1987.

27. John Walsh, "Science Gets Short End in Foreign Aid Funding," *Science*, February 13, 1987.

28. Paul Ehrlich, *The Machinery of Nature* (New York: Simon and Schuster, Inc., 1986).

29. OTA, *Technologies to Maintain Biological Diversity*.

30. Brazilian forest figure from Norman Myers, "Tropical Deforestation and a Mega-Extinction Spasm," in Soulé, *Conservation Biology: The Science of Scarcity and Diversity*; tropical dry forest figure from Daniel H. Janzen, *Guanacaste National Park: Tropical Ecological and Cultural Restoration* (San José, Costa Rica: Editorial Universidad Estatal a Distancia, 1986); closed tropical forest data from World Commission on Environment and Development, *Our Common Future* (New York: Oxford University Press, 1987).

31. World Commission on Environment and Development, *Our Common Future*.

32. Susanna Hecht, Department of Architecture and Urban Planning, University of California-Los Angeles, private communication, March 31, 1987, based on estimates from the Brazilian National Institute of Space Studies.

33. Christopher Uhl, Department of Biology, Pennsylvania State University, University Park, private communication, February 3, 1987; William R. Jordan III, "Restoration

and the Reentry of Nature," *Orion Nature Quarterly*, Spring 1986.

34. Christopher Uhl et al., "Ecosystem Recovery in Amazon Caatinga Forest After Cutting, Cutting and Burning, and Bulldozer Clearing Treatments," *Oikos* (Copenhagen), Vol. 38, No. 3, 1982; Christopher Uhl, "You Can Keep A Good Forest Down," *Natural History*, April 1983.

35. Uhl, "Ecosystem Recovery in Amazon Caatinga Forest"; Uhl, "You Can Keep A Good Forest Down."

36. William R. Jordan III et al., "Restoration Ecology: Ecological Restoration as a Technique for Basic Research," in William R. Jordan, ed., *Restoration Ecology* (New York: Cambridge University Press, in press).

37. John J. Berger, "The Prairiemakers," *Sierra*, November/December 1985; Walter Truett Anderson, *To Govern Evolution* (New York: Harcourt Brace Jovanovich, Inc., 1987).

38. William R. Jordan III et al., "Ecological Restoration as a Strategy for Conserving Biological Diversity," background paper prepared for the Office of Technology Assessment, U.S. Congress, Washington, D.C., March 1986; Berger, "The Prairiemakers."

39. Gina Kolata, "Managing the Inland Sea," *Science*, May 18, 1984; Chris Madson, "America's Tallgrass Prairie: Sunlight and Shadow," *The Nature Conservancy News*, June/July 1986; Bryan G. Norton, "The Spiral of Life," *Wilderness*, Spring 1987.

40. For examples of wetland restoration, see John J. Berger, *Restoring the Earth* (New York: Alfred A. Knopf, 1985), William R. Jordan III, "Hint of Green," *Restoration and Management Notes*, Summer 1983, Signe Holtz, "Tropical Seagrass Restoration," *Restoration and Management Notes*, Summer 1986, and Signe Holtz, "Bringing Back a Beautiful Landscape—Wetland Restoration on the Des Plaines River, Illinois," *Restoration and Management Notes*, Winter 1986.

41. Based on data from FAO, *Tropical Forest Resources*.

42. Janzen, *Guanacaste National Park;* Constance Holden, "Regrowing a Dry Tropical Forest," *Science*, November 14, 1986.

43. Daniel H. Janzen, "How to Grow a National Park: Basic Philosophy for Guanacaste National Park, Northwestern Costa Rica," University of Pennsylvania, Philadelphia, October, 1986; Janzen, *Guanacaste National Park.*

44. "Bosques Colón—Ecological Restoration on Caribbean and Bahamanian Islands," Center for Restoration Ecology, University of Wisconsin, Madison, unpublished, 1986.

45. Arturo Gomez-Pompa et al., "The 'Pet Kot': A Man-Made Tropical Forest of the Maya," *Interciencia*, January/February 1987.

46. Mary Helena Allegretti and Stephen Schwartzman, "Extractive Reserves: A Sustainable Development Alternative for Amazonia," Report to World Wildlife Fund–U.S., Washington, D.C., 1987.

47. Government of India, "Strategies, Structures, Policies: National Wastelands Development Board," New Delhi, mimeographed, February 6, 1986.

48. Ibid.

49. Jim Riggle, Director of Field Operations, American Farmland Trust, Washington, D.C., private communication, November 10, 1987.

50. R. Michael Miller and Julie D. Jastrow, "Influence on Soil Structure Supports Agricultural Role for Prairies, Prairie Restoration," *Restoration and Management Notes*, Winter 1986.

51. Myers, "Tackling Mass Extinction."

52. OTA, *Technologies to Maintain Biological Diversity.*

53. Ibid.

54. Ibid.; amounts earmarked for biodiversity from Cary Bolognese, Subcommit-

tee on Human Rights and International Organizations, Committee on Foreign Affairs, U.S. House of Representatives, private communication, May 4, 1987.

55. Sarah Gates Fitzgerald, "World Bank Pledges to Protect Wildlands," *BioScience*, December 1986; Robert Goodland, "A Major New Opportunity to Finance Biodiversity Preservation," presented at the National Forum on Biodiversity, Smithsonian Institution and National Academy of Sciences, Washington, D.C., September 24, 1986; World Bank, *Wildlands: Their Protection and Management in Economic Development* (Washington, D.C.: 1986).

56. Goodland, "A Major New Opportunity."

57. Ibid.

58. Barber B. Conable, Address to the World Resources Institute, Washington, D.C., May 5, 1987; annual agricultural lending by development banks from Multilateral Development Banks Office, U.S. Department of the Treasury, Washington, D.C., private communication, May 4, 1987.

59. John Walsh, "Bolivia Swaps Debt for Conservation," *Science*, August 7, 1987.

60. Ibid.

61. World Wildlife Fund–U.S., "Linking Conservation and Development: The Program in 'Wildlands and Human Needs' of the World Wildlife Fund," Washington, D.C., December 1986.

62. International Union for the Conservation of Nature and Natural Resources, *World Conservation Strategy* (Gland, Switzerland: 1980); nations where strategies are currently under preparation from OTA, *Technologies to Maintain Biological Diversity.*

63. François Nectou and Nigel Dudley, *A Hard Wood Story* (London: Friends of the Earth Trust and Earth Resources Research Ltd., 1987).

64. David Swinbanks, "Japan Faces Both Ways on Timber Conservation in Tropical Forests," *Nature*, April 9, 1987.

65. Michael Soulé et al., "The Millennium Ark: How Long a Voyage, How Many Staterooms, How Many Passengers?" *Zoo Biology*, Vol. 5, 1986.

66. Nathan Flesness, Director of the ISIS Program, Minnesota Zoo, Apple Valley, Minn., private communication, March 4, 1987.

67. Conway cited in Roger Lewin, "Damage to Tropical Forests, or Why Were There So Many Kinds of Animals?" *Science*, October 10, 1986.

68. Kerry Walter, Senior Program Officer, Center for Plant Conservation, Jamaica Plain, Mass., private communication, April 16, 1987; OTA, *Technologies to Maintain Biological Diversity.*

Chapter 7. Controlling Toxic Chemicals

1. In this chapter, the terms hazardous, toxic, chemical, and industrial waste are used loosely and interchangeably, in part because of varying national definitions, to connote wastes containing substances potentially threatening to health. This usage does not conform to the official U.S. definition, under which toxic is a subset of hazardous waste, which also includes wastes that are explosive, flammable, or corrosive.

2. For a brief sketch of the organic chemicals industry, see David J. Sarokin et al., *Cutting Chemical Wastes* (New York: INFORM, Inc., 1985); James O. Schreck, *Organic Chemistry: Concepts and Applications* (Saint Louis, Mo.: The C.V. Mosby Company, 1975).

3. U.S. International Trade Commission, *Synthetic Organic Chemicals: United States Production and Sales 1985* (Washington, D.C.: U.S. Government Printing Office, 1986); number of chemicals in use from "The Quest for Chemical Safety," *International Register of Po-*

tentially Toxic Chemicals Bulletin, May 1985; number added annually from Michael Shodell, "Risky Business," *Science '85,* October 1985.

4. Michael J. Dover, *A Better Mousetrap: Improving Pest Management in Agriculture* (Washington, D.C.: World Resources Institute, 1985).

5. U.S. Environmental Protection Agency (EPA), "Pesticide Industry Sales and Usage: 1985 Market Estimates," Washington, D.C., September 1986; "Major Changes Coming in Pesticide Law," *Agricultural Outlook,* October 1986; 70 percent figure from Herman Delvo, agricultural economist, U.S. Department of Agriculture (USDA), Washington, D.C., private communication, August 6, 1987.

6. Winand D.E. Staring, *Pesticides: Data Collection Systems and Supply, Distribution and Use in Selected Countries of the Asia-Pacific Region* (Bangkok: United Nations Economic and Social Commission for Asia and the Pacific, 1984); Indian data from Y.P. Gupta, "Pesticide Misuse in India," *The Ecologist,* Vol. 16, No. 1, 1986.

7. See, for example, U.S. Congressional Budget Office, *Hazardous Waste Management: Recent Changes and Policy Alternatives* (Washington, D.C.: U.S. Government Printing Office, 1985).

8. H. Yakowitz, "Some Background Information Concerning Hazardous Waste Management in Non-OECD Countries," paper prepared for Organisation for Economic Cooperation and Development, Paris, 1985; H. Jeffrey Leonard, "Confronting Industrial Pollution in Rapidly Industrializing Countries: Myths, Pitfalls, and Opportunities," *Ecology Law Quarterly,* Vol. 12, No. 14, 1985; "China Plans Curbs on Solid Wastes," *China Daily,* May 1, 1985.

9. National Research Council (NRC), *Toxicity Testing: Strategies to Determine Needs and Priorities* (Washington, D.C.: National Academy Press, 1984); Charles Benbrook, Executive Director, Board on Agriculture, National Academy of Sciences, Washington, D.C., private communication, May 1986.

10. Foo Gaik Sim, *The Pesticide Poisoning Report* (Penang, Malaysia: International Organization of Consumers Unions, 1985); Dover, *A Better Mousetrap.*

11. Gupta, "Pesticide Misuse in India"; Centre for Science and Environment, *The State of India's Environment 1984–85* (New Delhi: 1985); Sean L. Swezey et al., "Nicaragua's Revolution in Pesticide Policy," *Environment,* January/February 1986.

12. David Weir and Mark Schapiro, *Circle of Poison: Pesticides and People in a Hungry World* (San Francisco: Institute for Food and Development Policy, 1981); NRC, *Regulating Pesticides in Food: The Delaney Paradox* (Washington, D.C.: National Academy Press, 1987).

13. A. Lees et al., "The Effects of Pesticides on Human Health," Minutes of Evidence presented to the Agriculture Committee, House of Commons, London, May 15, 1986.

14. Contamination figures from Office of Pesticide Programs, EPA, Washington, D.C., private communication, December 4, 1987; Office of Ground-Water Protection, "EPA Ground-Water Protection Strategy: FY 1985 Status Report," EPA, Washington, D.C., undated; George R. Hallberg, "From Hoes to Herbicides: Agriculture and Groundwater Quality," *Journal of Soil and Water Conservation,* November/December 1986; Charles M. Benbrook and Phyllis B. Moses, "Engineering Crops to Resist Herbicides," *Technology Review,* November/December 1986.

15. George W. Ware, *Fundamentals of Pesticides* (Fresno, Calif.: Thomson Publications, 1986); David Bull, *A Growing Problem: Pesticides and the Third World Poor* (Oxford: OXFAM, 1982); Perseu Fernando dos Santos, EMBRAPA, Jaguariúna, Brazil, private communication, April 9, 1987; Elizabeth G. Nielsen and Linda K. Lee, *The Magnitude and Costs of Groundwater Contamination from Agricultural*

Chemicals: A National Perspective (Washington, D.C.: USDA, 1987).

16. Robert L. Metcalf, "Changing Role of Insecticides in Crop Protection," *Annual Review of Entomology*, Vol. 25, 1980; Michael Dover, "Getting Off the Pesticide Treadmill," *Technology Review*, November/December 1985; W.C. Shaw, "Integrated Weed Management Systems Technology for Pest Management," *Weed Science*, Supplement to Vol. 30, 1982; Michael J. Dover and Brian A. Croft, "Pesticide Resistance and Public Policy," *BioScience*, February 1986.

17. George P. Georghiou, "The Magnitude of the Resistance Problem," in NRC, Board on Agriculture, *Pesticide Resistance: Strategies and Tactics for Management* (Washington, D.C.: National Academy Press, 1986).

18. Swezey et al., "Nicaragua's Revolution in Pesticide Policy."

19. Patrick W. Holden, *Pesticides and Groundwater Quality: Issues and Problems in Four States* (Washington, D.C.: National Academy Press, 1986); Dover and Croft, "Pesticide Resistance and Public Policy."

20. West German Ministry for Research and Technology, *The Japanese-German Panel for Research and Development on Environment Protection Technology* (Bonn: 1986); Kim Christiansen, Technological Institute of Copenhagen, Taastrup, Denmark, private communication, February 2, 1987. Exchange rates as of December 1, 1987.

21. RCRA/CERCLA Hotline, EPA, Washington, D.C., July 31, 1987; World Resources Institute/International Institute for Environment and Development, "Managing Hazardous Wastes: The Unmet Challenge," in *World Resources 1987* (New York: Basic Books, 1987); U.S. Congress, Office of Technology Assessment (OTA), *Superfund Strategy* (Washington D.C.: U.S. Government Printing Office, 1985).

22. Veronica I. Pye and Ruth Patrick, "Ground Water Contamination in the United States," *Science*, August 19, 1983; OTA, *Protecting the Nation's Groundwater from Contamination*, Vol. 1 (Washington, D.C.: U.S. Government Printing Office, 1984); "Congress Passes Bill for Renewal of Safe Drinking Water Act with Groundwater Protection Provisions," *The Groundwater Newsletter* (Plainview, N.Y.), May 30, 1986.

23. Eugeniusz Pudlis, "Poland: Heavy Metals Pose Serious Health Problems," *Ambio*, Vol. 11, 1982; Jean Pierre Lasota, "Darkness at Noon," *The Sciences*, July/August 1987.

24. NRC, *Toxicity Testing;* Stanford researcher cited in Dale Hattis and David Kennedy, "Assessing Risks from Health Hazards: An Imperfect Science," *Technology Review*, May/June 1986.

25. NRC, *Drinking Water and Health*, Vol. 6 (Washington D.C.: National Academy Press, 1986); Hattis and Kennedy, "Assessing Risks."

26. Aaron Blair et al., "Cancer and Pesticides Among Farmers," in The Freshwater Foundation, *Pesticides and Groundwater: A Health Concern for the Midwest* (Navarre, Minn.: 1987).

27. Charles M. Benbrook, Reactor Panel statement, in Freshwater Foundation, *Pesticides and Groundwater: Health Concern for Midwest*.

28. L. Brader, "Integrated Pest Control in the Developing World," *Annual Review of Entomology*, Vol. 24, 1979; Qu Geping, "Biological Control of Pests in China," *Mazingira*, Vol. 7, No. 2, 1983; Marcos Kogan, University of Illinois, Champaign-Urbana, Ill., private communication, May 20, 1987.

29. Michael Hansen, "Escape from the Pesticide Treadmill: Alternatives to Pesticides in Developing Countries," preliminary report, Institute for Consumer Policy Research, Consumers Union, Mount Vernon, N.Y., 1986; Décio L. Gazzoni and Edilson B. de Oliveira, "Soybean Insect Pest Manage-

ment in Brazil–II. Program Implementation," in P. Matteson, ed., *Proceedings of the International Workshop in Integrated Pest Control for Grain Legumes* (Brazília: EMBRAPA, 1984).

30. Virginia Cooperative Extension Service, Virginia Tech and Virginia State, and USDA Extension Service, *The National Evaluation of Extension's Integrated Pest Management (IPM) Programs* (Washington, D.C.: USDA, 1987).

31. R.E. Frisbie and P.L. Adkisson, "IPM: Definitions and Current Status in U.S. Agriculture," in Marjorie A. Hoy and Donald C. Herzog, eds., *Biological Control in Agricultural IPM Systems* (Orlando, Fla.: Academic Press, Inc., 1985).

32. Suzanne W.T. Batra, "Biological Control in Agroecosystems," *Science*, January 8, 1982.

33. International Institute of Tropical Agriculture (IITA), *Root and Tuber Improvement Program: Research Highlights 1981–1984* (Ibadan, Nigeria: 1985); Hansen, "Alternatives to Pesticides in Developing Countries."

34. IITA, *Research Highlights;* Hansen, "Alternatives to Pesticides in Developing Countries."

35. IITA, *Annual Report and Research Highlights 1985* (Ibadan, Nigeria: 1986); Hansen, "Alternatives to Pesticides in Developing Countries"; Jeffrey K. Waage, Research Director, Commonwealth Institute of Biological Control, Silwood Park, United Kingdom, private communication, January 20, 1987.

36. D.J. Greathead and J.K. Waage, *Opportunities for Biological Control of Agricultural Pests in Developing Countries* (Washington, D.C.: World Bank, 1983).

37. Sara S. Rosenthal et al., *Biological Methods of Weed Control* (Fresno, Calif.: Thomson Publications, 1984); P.C. Quimby, Jr., and H.L. Walker, "Pathogens as Mechanisms for Integrated Weed Management," *Weed Science*, Supplement to Vol. 30, 1982; Donald S. Kenney, "DeVine—The Way It Was Devel-

oped—An Industrialist's View," and R.C. Bowers, "Commercialization of Collego—An Industrialist's View," *Weed Science*, Vol. 34, Supplement 1, 1986.

38. R.J. Aldrich, *Weed-Crop Ecology: Principles in Weed Management* (North Scituate, Mass.: Breton Publishers, 1984); Alan R. Putnam et al., "Exploitation of Allelopathy for Weed Control in Annual and Perennial Cropping Systems," *Journal of Chemical Ecology*, May 1983.

39. Benbrook and Moses, "Engineering Crops to Resist Herbicides."

40. Ibid.

41. Author's meetings with various officials and hazardous waste specialists in several European countries, January-February 1987; see also Bruce Piasecki and Gary A. Davis, *America's Hazardous Waste Management Future: Lessons from Europe* (Westport, Conn.: Greenwood Press, in press).

42. Per Riemann, Kommunekemi a/s, Nyborg, Denmark, private communication, January 30, 1987; GSB, "Disposal of Special Refuse in Bavaria," Munich, West Germany, October 1983; Herr Ulrich Materne and Helga Retsch-Preuss, Gesellschaft zur Beseitigung von Sondermüll in Bayern MbH (GSB), Munich, West Germany, private communication, January 22, 1987.

43. Mark Crawford, "Hazardous Waste: Where to Put It?" *Science*, January 9, 1987; Steve R. Drew, Regional Community Relations Manager, Chemical Waste Management, Inc., Newark, Calif., private communication, May 4, 1987.

44. Piasecki and Davis, *Lessons from Europe;* Rochelle L. Stanfield, "Drowning in Waste," *National Journal*, May 10, 1986; Chemcontrol a/s, "3rd International Symposium on Operating European Hazardous Waste Management Facilities—Final Program," Odense, Denmark, September 16–19, 1986; George Garland, "Report on Consultancy to the Republic of Korea for the World Health Organi-

zation," April 16, 1987, provided by Garland, Office of Solid Waste, EPA, Washington, D.C.

45. EPA, *Report to Congress: Minimization of Hazardous Waste*, Vol. 1 (Washington, D.C.; 1986); Paul A. Chubb, "Managing Waste: Critical to Competitiveness," *Wasteline* (Du Pont Company), Spring 1986.

46. See OTA, *Serious Reduction of Hazardous Waste* (Washington D.C.: U.S. Government Printing Office, 1986); Sarokin et al., *Cutting Chemical Wastes*; Donald Huisingh et al., *Proven Profits from Pollution Prevention: Case Studies in Resource Conservation and Waste Reduction* (Washington, D.C.: Institute for Local Self-Reliance, 1986).

47. Kirsten U. Oldenburg and Joel S. Hirschhorn, "Waste Reduction: A New Strategy to Avoid Pollution," *Environment*, March 1987; Kenneth Geiser et al., *Foreign Practices in Hazardous Waste Minimization* (Medford, Mass.: Tufts University Center for Environmental Management, 1986); "How Sites Are Tackling Hazardous Waste," *Wasteline* (Du Pont Company), Spring 1986.

48. Donald Huisingh and John Aberth, "Hazardous Wastes: Some Simple Solutions," *Management Review*, June 1986.

49. Oldenburg and Hirschhorn, "Waste Reduction: A New Strategy"; Sarokin et al., *Cutting Chemical Wastes*; EPA, "Waste Minimization Findings and Activities," *Fact Sheet*, Washington, D.C., October 1986.

50. Geiser et al., *Foreign Practices in Hazardous Waste Minimization*; Walker Banning et al., "North American Waste Exchanges: A History of Change and Evolution," in Center for Environmental Studies, Arizona State University, *Proceedings of the Third National Conference on Waste Exchange* (Tempe, Ariz.: 1986).

51. Virginia Cooperative Extension Service, *National Evaluation of Extension's IPM Programs*; budget figures from C. David McNeal, Jr., IPM Program Leader, Extension Service, USDA, Washington, D.C., private communication, May 28, 1987.

52. Hansen, "Alternatives to Pesticides in Developing Countries"; G.W. Bird, "Alternative Futures of Agricultural Pest Management," paper presented at the IAA Symposium; federal research funding from estimates by Howard Waterworth, USDA Agricultural Research Service, Washington, D.C., and by Robert C. Riley, USDA Cooperative State Research Service, Washington, D.C., private communications, May 28, 1987.

53. Pesticide sales figure from EPA, "Pesticide Industry; 1985 Market Estimates."

54. Banpot Napompeth, "Biological Control and Integrated Pest Control in the Tropics—An Overview," paper presented at the symposium Towards a Second Green Revolution: From Chemicals to New Biological Technologies in Agriculture in the Tropics, Rome, September 1986; David Greathead, Director, Commonwealth Institute of Biological Control, Silwood Park, United Kingdom, private communication, January 20, 1987.

55. Robert Repetto, *Paying the Price: Pesticide Subsidies in Developing Countries* (Washington, D.C.: World Resources Institute, 1985); Dover, *A Better Mousetrap*.

56. The President of the Republic of Indonesia, Presidential Instruction No. 3, "Improvement of Control of Brown Planthopper (Wereng Coklat), An Insect Pest of Rice," Jakarta, Indonesia, November 5, 1986; "Against the Grain in Indonesia," *Asiaweek*, March 22, 1987; training figure from Michael Hansen, Institute for Consumer Policy Research, Consumers Union, Mount Vernon, N.Y., private communication, November 19, 1987.

57. Vibeke Bernson, National Chemicals Inspectorate, Solna, Sweden, private communication, February 5, 1987; Jesper Kjølholt, Centre for Terrestrial Ecology, National Agency of Environment Protection, Copenhagen, Denmark, private written communication, August 6, 1987.

58. Bernard Hoyer, Iowa Department of Natural Resources, Geological Survey Bureau, Iowa City, Iowa, private communication, June 10, 1987; Dave Jensen, Nebraska Department of Environmental Control, Lincoln, Nebr., private communication, May 27, 1987; Governor Madeline Kunin, "Pesticide Policy Statement," May 14, 1986 (made available by Vermont Public Interest Research Group, Montpelier, Vt.); Katherine Reichelderfer, Associate Director, Resources and Technology Division, Economic Research Service, USDA, Washington, D.C., private written communication, July 8, 1987.

59. Subtitle D, "Conservation Reserve," of the U.S. Food Security Act, *Congressional Record—House,* December 17, 1985; Michael R. Dicks and Katherine Reichelderfer, "Choices for Implementing the Conservation Reserve," Agriculture Information Bulletin No. 507, USDA Economic Research Service, Washington, D.C., March 1987; Michael Dicks, "More Benefits with Fewer Acres Please!" *Journal of Soil and Water Conservation,* May/June 1987; bill to amend the Food Security Act of 1985, introduced into the U.S. Senate, July 1987.

60. Florence Petillot, "The Policies and Methods Established for Promoting the Development of Clean Technologies in French Industry," *Industry and Environment,* October/November/December 1986. Exchange rate as of December 1, 1987.

61. Piasecki and Davis, *Lessons from Europe;* Klaus Müller, Ministry of the Environment, National Agency of Environmental Protection, Copenhagen, Denmark, private communication, February 2, 1987; Dr. Stolz, Ministry of the Interior, Bonn, West Germany, private communication, January 27, 1987.

62. OTA, *From Pollution to Prevention: A Progress Report on Waste Reduction* (Washington, D.C.: U.S. Government Printing Office, 1987).

63. Description of legislation from U.S. Representative Howard Wolpe, "The Hazardous Waste Reduction Act," *Congressional Record,* Washington, D.C., June 26, 1987.

64. OTA, *From Pollution to Prevention.*

65. U.N. Environment Programme, *International Symposium on Clean Technologies: Synopsis of the Country Reports* (Paris: 1986); Whitman Bassow, "Major Corporations to Train Indonesian Officials in Industrial Environmental Management," *Environmental Conservation,* Summer 1986.

66. See J. Clarence Davies, "Coping with Toxic Substances," *Issues in Science and Technology,* Winter 1985; Carl Pope, "An Immodest Proposal," *Sierra,* September/October 1985.

67. "Restrictions on Toxic Discharges into Drinking Water: Requirement of Notice of Persons' Exposure to Toxics," Proposition 65 description in literature distributed to California voters, 1986.

Chapter 8. Assessing SDI

1. U.S. Congress, Office of Technology Assessment (OTA), *The Effects of Nuclear War* (Washington, D.C.: U.S. Government Printing Office, 1979); Samuel Glasstone and Philip J. Dolan, *The Effects of Nuclear Weapons* (Washington, D.C.: U.S. Government Printing Office, 1977).

2. Reagan quote from "Weekly Compilation of Presidential Documents," Monday, March 28, 1983.

3. For a summary of the pro and con arguments, see American Physical Society (APS), *Science and Technology of Directed Energy Weapons* (New York: 1987).

4. Caspar Weinberger, Memorandum for the President on "Responding to Soviet Violations Policy (RSVP) Study," quoted in *Washington Post,* November 18, 1985.

5. A space-based chemical rocket interceptor system capable of destroying sub-

marine-launched missiles in boost-phase would cost two thirds of $1 trillion, or $66 billion per year over 10 years. By comparison, the United States recently has invested about $62 billion per year in manufacturing; see U.S. Department of Commerce, *Statistical Abstracts of the United States, 1987* (Washington, D.C.: U.S. Government Printing Office, 1987).

6. APS, *Science and Technology of Directed Energy Weapons.*

7. R.S. McNamara, *The Essence of Security* (New York: Harper & Row, 1968). Analysts assume that these numbers were picked mainly because they represented a set of targets that could be destroyed reasonably easily, and that inflicting greater damage would require a disproportionately greater effort. In other words, the level of damage was thought large enough to deter the Soviets from attacking, and that a larger retaliation would yield diminishing returns.

8. Robert S. McNamara, "Can Civilization Survive Defense in the Nuclear Age?" *Challenge,* March/April 1987; Harold A. Feiveson et al., "Reducing U.S. and Soviet Nuclear Arsenals," *Bulletin of the Atomic Scientists*, August 1985.

9. Richard Smoke, *National Security and the Nuclear Dilemma* (New York: Random House, 1984).

10. Ashton B. Carter, *Directed Energy Missile Defense in Space,* OTA Background Paper (Washington, D.C.: U.S. Government Printing Office, 1984).

11. Herbert Lin, "The Development of Software for Ballistic Missile Defense," *Scientific American,* December 1985.

12. OTA, *MX Missile Basing* (Washington, D.C.: U.S. Government Printing Office, 1982).

13. APS, *Science and Technology of Directed Energy Weapons.*

14. See Richard L. Garwin, "How Many Orbiting Lasers for Boost-phase Intercept?" *Nature,* May 23, 1985.

15. Written reply to question related to Abrahamson's testimony before the House Appropriations Committee, May 9, 1984.

16. The United States could launch a first strike that would leave the Soviets with fewer surviving silos containing hard-target-capable missiles than the United States would have after a Soviet first strike. But because the Soviet missiles carry 6 or 10 MIRVs, and the U.S. ICBMs carry an average of 2, the Soviets would retain a far larger force of warheads. Dietrich Schroeer, *Science, Technology, and the Arms Race* (New York: John Wiley & Sons, 1984).

17. Caspar Weinberger, "It's Time to Get SDI Off the Ground," *New York Times,* August 21, 1987; McNamara, *The Essence of Security.*

18. Two hundred silos times average of two reentry vehicles per silo times $0.335^{2/3}$ megatons equals 193 equivalent megatons.

19. Cost-exchange is defined here as the ratio of the marginal cost to the offense (to overcome an incremental defensive deployment) to the marginal cost to the defense (to make the deployment). For silo defense, it is the cost of an additional Soviet warhead deployed in response to the ballistic missile defense divided by U.S. cost to defend against one additional warhead. Cost-exchange for a space-based system can also be measured as the ratio of Soviet countermeasure costs—such as adding warheads or anti-satellite weapons—and U.S. interceptor costs.

20. Low-atmosphere interceptors could not successfully protect against airbursts above 8 kilometers, and an airburst at 10 kilometers could destroy unhardened interceptors or radar. For blast effects, see Glasstone and Dolan, *Effects of Nuclear Weapons.* See also OTA, *Strategic Defenses* (Princeton, N.J.: Princeton University Press, 1986).

21. OTA, *Strategic Defenses.*

22. The offense, however, because its missiles are not perfectly reliable, would probably send two warheads for every effective one they needed. They therefore would probably commit eight warheads per cluster if they needed to be sure four would reach U.S. airspace. If each cluster of interceptors contained more than eight HEDI, the United States would nevertheless face an unfavorable cost-exchange, unless HEDI were very cheap. Analysts commonly assume that clusters will contain a minimum of 10 interceptors.

23. William U. Chandler, "Early Deployment of Ballistic Missile Defenses," Worldwatch Institute, Washington, D.C., unpublished, August 28, 1987.

24. Weinberger, "It's Time to Get SDI Off the Ground"; Bruce G. Blair, *Strategic Command and Control: Redefining the Nuclear Threat* (Washington, D.C.: Brookings Institution, 1985).

25. Ashton B. Carter, "Assessing Command System Vulnerability," in Ashton B. Carter et al., eds., *Managing Nuclear Operations* (Washington, D.C.: Brookings Institution, 1987). All that is technically required to communicate a launch order to the submarine fleet is a short-wave communications system of the type that can be mounted on (perhaps large) vans.

26. Barry M. Blechman and Victor A. Utgoff, *Fiscal and Economic Implications of Strategic Defenses*, SAIS Papers in International Affairs No. 12 (Boulder, Colo.: Westview Press, 1986).

27. The maximum allowable cost of deploying a U.S. space-based interceptor system can be estimated and compared by assuming that the Soviets can add submarine-launched warheads at the same cost as the United States can add Trident C-4 warheads. Since the Trident submarine costs $2 billion and carries 192 warheads, the marginal cost of a Soviet submarine-launched warhead is assumed to be $10.5 million; see Schroeer, *Science, Technology, and the Arms Race*. The U.S. interceptors can cost no more than the cost per additional Soviet warhead divided by the number of extra interceptors needed because their orbit takes them out of range (i.e., the absentee ratio). A reasonable first cost might be $12 million. If economies of scale provided a cost reduction of 10 percent per doubling of production, and some 375,000 were produced, then the cost would be $1.7 million each; see Blechman and Utgoff, *Fiscal and Economic Implications*. For administration target for interceptor prices, see R. Jeffrey Smith, "Offensive Taken for Partial SDI Deployment," *Washington Post*, January 18, 1987. Moreover, analyst Richard Ruquist of the Massachusetts Institute of Technology has indicated that anti-satellite weapons would be available to the Soviets with a cost-exchange no worse than 1.5 in their favor, and perhaps as high as 30; Richard Ruquist, "Survivability and Cost-Effectiveness of the Early Deployment SDI System," *Arms Control Today*, July/August 1987.

28. Carter, *Directed Energy Missile Defense in Space*.

29. Comparison of U.S. and Brazilian foreign debt is as a percent of gross national product, from G.N. Hatsopoulos and P.R. Krugman, "U.S. Industrial Competitiveness: A Statement of the Problem," American Business Conference, Thermoelectron Corporation, mimeographed, December 1, 1986.

30. See William U. Chandler, "The U.S. Trade Deficit: Macroeconomic or Technological Solutions," prepared during course for mid-career Masters of Public Administration, John F. Kennedy School of Government, Harvard University, Cambridge, Mass., April 1987; U.S. Department of Commerce, *Statistical Abstracts of the United States, 1986* (Washington: U.S. Government Printing Office, 1986).

31. Japanese investment per worker from Hatsopoulos and Krugman, "U.S. Industrial Competitiveness." Labor productivity from "U.S. Technological Leadership is Slipping,

Erosion Also Exists in Manufacturing Technology, Brooks Says," National Academy of Engineering, Washington, D.C., press release, March 21, 1985. For discussions of relative U.S. and Japanese productivity changes and technology, see Robert U. Ayres, *The Next Industrial Revolution* (Cambridge, Mass.: Ballinger Publishing Co., 1984), and Ryuzo Sato and Gilbert S. Suzawa, *Research and Productivity: Endogenous Technical Change* (Boston, Mass.: Auburn Publishing Co., 1983).

32. Albert Carnesale, Harvard University, private communication, December 8, 1986.

33. National Science Foundation, *Science Indicators 1985* (Washington, D.C.: 1985).

34. Ibid.

35. John W. Kendrick, *Sources of Growth in Real Product and Production in Eight Countries, 1960–1978* (New York: New York Stock Exchange, 1981), as cited in Wendy Schacht, "Stevenson-Wydler Technology Innovation Act: A Federal Effort To Promote Industrial Innovation," Congressional Research Service, Washington, D.C., December 1, 1986. See also Erich Bloch, "Basic Research and Economic Health: The Coming Challenge," *Science*, May 2, 1986.

36. Sato and Suzawa, *Research and Productivity*.

37. Genevieve J. Knezo, "Science and Technology Policy and Funding: Reagan Administration," Congressional Research Service, Washington, D.C., mimeographed, December 1, 1987.

38. United Nations, *Monthly Bulletin of Statistics*, February 1986.

39. Organisation for Economic Co-operation and Development, *Science and Technology Indicators* (Paris: 1986).

40. National Research Council, *The Impact of Defense Spending on Nondefense Engineering Labor Markets* (Washington, D.C.: National Academy Press, 1986).

41. Albert Teich et al., "Congressional Action on Research and Development in the FY 1987 Budget," American Association for the Advancement of Science, Washington, D.C., December 1986.

42. See Daniel Deudney, "Realism's Eclipse of Geopolitics and the Loss of Strategic Bearings" (draft), Princeton University, Princeton, N.J., mimeographed, June 1987. See also Hilary F. French, "Of Nations and Nukes: The Failure of International Atomic Energy Control, 1944–1946," Honors Thesis, Dartmouth College, Hanover, N.H., May 26, 1986.

43. Article V section 1 reads "Each party undertakes not to develop, test, or deploy ABM systems or components which are sea-based, air-based, space-based, or mobile land-based"; *Treaty Between the United States of America and the Union of Soviet Socialist Republics on the Limitation of Anti-Ballistic Missile Systems*, Moscow, May 26, 1972. The definition of antiballistic missiles systems was agreed to include systems already existing or under development and "systems based on other physical principles . . . created in the future"; see *Agreed Statements*, appended to treaty.

Chapter 9. Planning the Global Family

1. Larry Rohter, "Central American Plight is People in Abundance," *New York Times*, September 6, 1987.

2. Population Crisis Committee, "Access to Birth Control: A World Assessment," Briefing Paper No. 19, Washington, D.C., October 1987.

3. Population Reference Bureau (PRB), *1987 World Population Data Sheet* (Washington, D.C.: 1987); World Bank, *World Development Report 1986* (New York: Oxford University Press, 1986).

4. PRB, *1987 World Population Data Sheet*.

5. Anrudh K. Jain, "The Impact of Development and Population Policies on Fertility

in India," *Studies in Family Planning,* July/August 1985; PRB, *1987 World Population Data Sheet;* Carl Haub, demographer, PRB, Washington, D.C., private communication, October 30, 1987.

6. PRB, *1987 World Population Data Sheet.*

7. Sheila Rule, "African Rift: Birth Control Vs. Tradition," *New York Times,* August 11, 1985.

8. U.N. Department of International Economic and Social Affairs, *Fertility Behavior in the Context of Development: Evidence from the World Fertility Survey* (New York: United Nations, 1987).

9. Indonesia's per capita income from PRB, *1987 World Population Data Sheet;* Kim Streatfield and Ann Larson, "The 1985 Intercensal Survey of Indonesia: Trends in Contraceptive Prevalence," Research Note from the International Population Dynamics Program, Department of Demography, Australian National University, Canberra, 1987.

10. Ronald Freedman, "The Contribution of Social Science Research to Population Policy and Family Planning Program Effectiveness," *Studies in Family Planning,* March/April 1987.

11. Samuel H. Preston, "Population Growth and Economic Development," *Environment,* March 1986.

12. Ruhul Amin et al., "Family Planning in Bangladesh, 1969 to 1983," *International Family Planning Perspectives,* March 1987.

13. "Nigeria: 95 Percent of Married Women Want More Children; Contraceptive Use Limited To Abstinence," *International Family Planning Perspectives,* September 1985; Ann A. Way et al., "Family Planning in Botswana, Kenya, and Zimbabwe," *International Family Planning Perspectives,* March 1987.

14. Esther Boohene and Thomas E. Dow, Jr., "Contraceptive Prevalence and Family Planning Effort in Zimbabwe," *International Family Planning Perspectives,* March 1987.

15. D.L. Nortman et al., "A Cost-Benefit Analysis of the Family Planning Program of the Mexican Social Security Administration," paper presented at the general conference of the International Union for the Scientific Study of Population, Florence, Italy, June 5–12, 1985. Exchange rate as of December 1, 1987.

16. WHO cited in Judith A. Fortney, "The Importance of Family Planning in Reducing Maternal Mortality," *Studies in Family Planning,* March/April 1987; J. Ties Boerma, "Levels of Maternal Mortality in Developing Countries," *Studies in Family Planning,* July/August 1987; Allan Rosenfield and Deborah Maine, "Maternal Mortality—A Neglected Tragedy: Where is the M in MCH?" *The Lancet,* July 13, 1985.

17. Beverly Winikoff and Maureen Sullivan, "Assessing the Role of Family Planning in Reducing Maternal Mortality," *Studies in Family Planning,* May/June 1987.

18. Christopher Tietze and Stanley K. Henshaw, *Induced Abortion: A World Review 1986* (New York: Alan Guttmacher Institute, 1986); Stanley K. Henshaw, Alan Guttmacher Institute, Washington, D.C., private communication, October 23, 1987; Dr. J. Joseph Speidel, Population Crisis Committee, Washington, D.C., private communications, October and November 1987.

19. Worldwatch Institute estimates based on Tietze and Henshaw, *Induced Abortion: A World View,* and on PRB, *1987 World Population Data Sheet.*

20. Winikoff and Sullivan, "Assessing the Role of Family Planning."

21. Fred T. Sai, "Family Planning and Maternal Health Care: A Common Goal," *World Health Forum,* Vol. 7, 1986; Fortney, "Importance of Family Planning"; Population Information Program, "Healthier Mothers and Children Through Family Planning," *Population Reports,* Series J, No. 27, Johns Hopkins University, Baltimore, Md., May/June 1984.

22. Winikoff and Sullivan, "Assessing the Role of Family Planning."

23. Ibid.

24. Ibid.; Rosenfield and Maine, "Maternal Mortality—A Neglected Tragedy."

25. Special Programme on AIDS, "AIDS and Poverty in the Developing World," Policy Focus No. 7, World Health Organization, Geneva, 1987; Lucy Callahan, Public Relations Officer, World Health Organization, Washington, D.C., private communication, December 4, 1987.

26. Population Crisis Committee, "Access to Birth Control."

27. Dr. Jeffrey Harris, U.S. Agency for International Development AIDS coordinator, private communication, October 29, 1987.

28. Population Information Program, "Hormonal Contraception: New Long-Acting Methods," Population Reports, Series K, No. 3, Johns Hopkins University, Baltimore, Md., March/April 1987.

29. Number of users of family planning from Speidel, private communication; discussion of natural family planning techniques can be found in Population Crisis Committee, *Natural Family Planning: Periodic Abstinence as a Method of Fertility Control* (Washington, D.C.: 1981).

30. Linda Atkinson et al., "Prospects for Improved Contraception," *Family Planning Perspectives,* July/August 1980.

31. Population Information Program, "Hormonal Contraception."

32. Atkinson et al., "Prospects for Improved Contraception."

33. Population Information Program, "Hormonal Contraception."

34. Linda Atkinson et al., "Worldwide Trends in Funding for Contraceptive Research and Evaluation," *Family Planning Perspectives,* September/October 1985.

35. Ibid.; Linda Atkinson et al., "The Next Contraceptive Revolution," *International Family Planning Perspectives,* December 1985.

36. Contraceptive prevalence needed to achieve population stabilization from Population Crisis Committee, "Access to Birth Control."

37. Nancy I. Heckel, "Population Laws and Policies In Sub-Saharan Africa: 1975–1985," *International Family Planning Perspectives,* December 1986; Kenyan official quoted in Rule, "African Rift."

38. Freedman, "Contribution of Social Science Research."

39. Population Information Program, "Population and Birth Planning in the People's Republic of China," Population Reports, Series J, No. 25, Johns Hopkins University, Baltimore, Md., January/February 1982. See also Chen Muhua, "Birth Planning in China," *International Family Planning Perspectives,* September 1979; Elisabeth J. Croll, "Production vs. Reproduction: A Threat to China's Development Strategy," *World Development,* Vol. 11, No. 6, 1983; Nathan Keyfitz, "The Population of China," *Scientific American,* February 1984; Arthur P. Wolf, "The Preeminent Role of Government Intervention in China's Family Revolution," *Population and Development Review,* March 1986.

40. Population Information Program, "Population Planning in the People's Republic."

41. Ibid.; Nicholas D. Kristof, "China's Birth Rate on Rise Again As Official Sanctions Are Ignored," *New York Times,* April 21, 1987; Daniel Southerland, "Despite Years of Controls, China Fears New Baby Boom," *Washington Post,* May 24, 1987.

42. Donald Weeden et al., "An Incentives Program to Increase Contraceptive Prevalence in Rural Thailand," *International Family Planning Perspectives,* March 1986.

43. Ibid.

44. William U. Chandler, *Investing in Children*, Worldwatch Paper 64 (Washington, D.C.: Worldwatch Institute, June 1985).

45. Odile Frank and Geoffrey McNicoll, "An Interpretation of Fertility and Population Policy in Kenya," Center for Policy Studies Working Papers, No. 131, The Population Council, New York, February 1987.

46. Ibid.

47. Speidel, private communication.

48. Ibid.

49. Ibid.

50. Ruth Leger Sivard, *World Military and Social Expenditures 1986* (Washington, D.C.: World Priorities, 1986).

51. Elizabeth Maguire, Chief of the Population Policy Division, U.S. Agency for International Development, Washington, D.C., private communication, October 29, 1987.

Chapter 10. Reclaiming the Future

1. International Co-operative Programme on Assessment and Monitoring of Air Pollution Effects on Forests, "Forest Damage and Air Pollution: Report on the 1986 Forest Damage Survey in Europe," Global Environment Monitoring System, United Nations Environment Programme, Nairobi, Kenya, mimeographed, 1987, with data on Belgium and East Germany from *Allegemeine Forst Zeitschrift,* Munich, West Germany, No. 46, 1985 and No. 41, 1986.

2. Michael Weisskopf, "Nations Sign Agreement to Guard Ozone Layer," *Washington Post,* September 17, 1987.

3. U.N. Food and Agriculture Organization (FAO), *Yearbook of Fishery Statistics* (Rome: various years); C.P. Idyll, "The Anchovy Crisis," *Scientific American,* June 1973.

4. U.S. conservation reserve program described in Norman A. Berg, "Making the Most of the New Soil Conservation Initiatives," *Journal of Soil and Water Conservation,* January/February 1987, and U.S. Department of Agriculture (USDA), Economic Research Service, *Agricultural Resources: Cropland, Water, and Conservation Situation and Outlook Report* (Washington, D.C.: 1987).

5. Data on African population from Population Reference Bureau, *World Population Data Sheet 1987* (Washington, D.C.: 1987); data on livestock populations from FAO, *Production Yearbook* (Rome: various years).

6. Roger Strohbehn, ed., *An Economic Analysis of USDA Erosion Control Programs: A New Perspective,* Agricultural Economic Report No. 560 (Washington, D.C.: USDA, 1986).

7. Berg, "New Soil Conservation Initiatives."

8. USDA, *Cropland, Water, and Conservation Report.*

9. Berg, "New Soil Conservation Initiatives."

10. Price support payments to farmers from *Economic Report of the President* (Washington, D.C.: U.S. Government Printing Office, 1987).

11. FAO, *Fuelwood Supplies in the Developing Countries,* Forestry Paper 42 (Rome: 1983).

12. Costs of establishing trees under different conditions discussed in John S. Spears, "Replenishing the World's Forests—Tropical Reforestation: An Achievable Goal?" *Commonwealth Forestry Review,* Vol. 62, No. 3, 1983.

13. Seedling costs discussed in Dennis Anderson and Robert Fishwick, *Fuelwood Consumption and Deforestation in African Countries,* Staff Working Paper No. 704 (Washington, D.C.: World Bank, 1984).

14. Estimate of family planning expenditures here are those of the World Bank, in *World Development Report 1984* (New York: Oxford University Press, 1984), which are slightly higher than those of the Population Crisis Committee cited in Chapter 9.

15. Based on data in World Bank, *World Development Report 1987* (New York: Oxford University Press, 1987).

16. For a study of the cost per student of providing primary education in low-income countries, see J.C. Eicher, *Educational Costing and Financing in Developing Countries: Focus on Sub-Saharan Africa,* Staff Working Paper 655 (Washington, D.C.: World Bank, 1984).

17. Based on William U. Chandler, *Investing in Children,* Worldwatch Paper 64 (Washington, D.C.: Worldwatch Institute, June 1985).

18. World Bank, *World Development Report 1984.*

19. Ibid.

20. Erik Eckholm, "Significant Rise in Sea Level Now Seems Certain," *New York Times,* February 18, 1986.

21. Agency for International Development, Office of U.S. Foreign Disaster Assistance, "Disaster History: Significant Data on Major Disasters Worldwide, 1900–Present," Washington, D.C., June 1987; size of stationary population is from World Bank, *World Development Report 1987.*

22. Tom Goemans and Tjebbe Visser, "The Delta Project: The Netherlands Experience with a Megaproject for Flood Protection," *Technology in Society,* Vol. 9, 1987.

23. Worldwatch Institute estimate of 1987 carbon emissions from fossil fuels is based on Ralph Rotty, University of New Orleans (formerly of Institute for Energy Analysis, Oak Ridge Associated Universities, Oak Ridge, Tenn.), private communication, June 16, 1987; estimate of carbon released by deforestation is from R.A. Houghton et al., "The Flux of Carbon from Terrestrial Ecosystems to the Atmosphere in 1980 Due to Changes in Land Use: Geographic Distribution of the Global Flux," *Tellus,* February/April 1987.

24. See William U. Chandler, "Designing Sustainable Economies," in Lester R. Brown et al., *State of the World 1987* (New York: W.W. Norton & Co., 1987).

25. World Energy Conference, *Survey of Energy Resources* (Munich: 1980).

26. Sam Rashkin, California Energy Commission, Sacramento, Calif., private communication, October 6, 1987; Judith Perera, "Indian Government Draws Up Plans to Exploit Renewable Energy," *Solar Energy Intelligence Report,* August 11, 1987.

27. D. Groves and I. Segal, *Solar Energy in Israel* (Jerusalem: Ministry of Energy and Infrastructure, 1984); International Energy Agency, *Renewable Sources of Energy* (Paris: Organisation for Economic Co-operation and Development, 1987).

28. Ministry of Energy and Mines, "Energy Self-Sufficiency: A Scenario Developed as an Extension of the Brazilian Energy Model," Government of Brazil, Brasília, 1984; Renewable Energy Institute, "The Philippines: Trade and Investment Laws Relating to Renewable Energy," Washington, D.C., March 1987.

29. Government of India, "Strategies, Structures, Policies: National Wastelands Development Board," New Delhi, mimeographed, February 6, 1986.

30. Motor Vehicle Manufacturers Association, *Motor Vehicle Facts and Figures '87* (Detroit, Mich.: 1987).

31. Houghton et al., "The Flux of Carbon"; Mary Helena Allegretti and Stephan Schwartzman, "Extractive Reserves: A Sustainable Development Alternative for Amazonia," report to the World Wildlife Fund— U.S., Washington, D.C., 1987.

32. "Action, Not Just Talk, on World Debt" (editorial), *New York Times,* September 26, 1987; Felix Rohatyn, "On the Brink," *New York Review of Books,* June 11, 1987.

33. Barber B. Conable, President, World Bank, address to the United Nations Conference on Trade and Development, Geneva, Switzerland, July 10, 1987.

34. Restructuring information from Barber B. Conable, President, World Bank, address to the World Resources Institute, Washington, D.C., May 5, 1987.

35. Canadian initiative described by Hon. Tom McMillan, "Canada's Perspective on Global Environment and Development," speech before the 42nd session of the U.N. General Assembly, New York, October 19, 1987.

36. Military expenditures level from Ruth Leger Sivard, *World Military and Social Expenditures 1986* (Washington, D.C.: World Priorities Inc., 1986); Clyde H. Farnsworth, "Soviet Economists See a New Order," *New York Times*, December 4, 1987.

37. Chinese military spending data from U.S. Arms Control and Disarmament Agency, *World Military Expenditures and Arms Transfers 1986* (Washington, D.C.: 1986); levels projected for 1986 are Worldwatch Institute estimates.

38. Paul Lewis, "Rare Unity Brings Smile to 'Toothless Tiger,' " *New York Times*, September 20, 1987.

Index